INTRODUCTION
TO THE
NEW TESTAMENT

BY

HENRY CLARENCE THIESSEN
B.D., Ph.D., D.D.
FORMERLY CHAIRMAN OF THE FACULTY
OF THE GRADUATE SCHOOL
WHEATON COLLEGE, WHEATON, ILLINOIS

Author of
INTRODUCTORY LECTURES IN SYSTEMATIC THEOLOGY

WM. B. EERDMANS PUBLISHING COMPANY
Grand Rapids   Michigan

INTRODUCTION TO THE NEW TESTAMENT
by HENRY CLARENCE THIESSEN, B.D., Ph.D., D.D.

Set up and printed, March, 1943
Tenth printing, July, 1958
Eleventh printing, July, 1960
Twelfth printing, April, 1962

PHOTOLITHOPRINTED BY CUSHING - MALLOY, INC.
ANN ARBOR, MICHIGAN, UNITED STATES OF AMERICA

PREFACE

For many years there have appeared few books on New Testament Introduction that were written from the strictly conservative standpoint. The older books that were written from this viewpoint are out of print and also somewhat out of date. Since the time that Godet, Salmon, and Zahn wrote, many archaeological and other discoveries have been made that have shed new light on the language in which the New Testament was written, on the character of the text in the first four centuries, and on the state of the canon in primitive Christianity. The conservative is gratified to note that in no case has his position been weakened by these discoveries, but rather sustained and strengthened.

The present volume is intended to set forth the conservative view of the New Testament in the light of these discoveries and to indicate what are the justifiable inferences that we may deduce therefrom. Historically it is an outgrowth of a series of class-room lectures that was first delivered in the Dallas Theological Seminary, Dallas, Texas, in the year 1934. Since then these lectures have been considerably expanded and repeatedly given at Wheaton College, Wheaton, Illinois. The author had hoped that J. Gresham Machen would give us a book on this subject, and he once suggested the idea to him; but Dr. Machen's death soon thereafter has cut short that hope. The urgent need for such a text in his large classes at Wheaton College has finally induced the writer to undertake the task himself.

The author makes no apology for his conservative position. Recent discoveries do not militate against the "traditional" view of the canon, but rather serve to strengthen it. The scrap of papyrus, known as John Rylands Papyrus 457, for instance, found in a provincial town in Egypt in 1920 and published in 1935, has done much to establish the traditional date of the

Fourth Gospel. Streeter and Lake have isolated the "Cæsarean" text within the old "Western" text and have introduced a valid reclassification of the families of texts. The acceptance of this classification by Sir Frederic Kenyon, formerly Director of the British Museum, who had continued the textual views of Westcott and Hort, would seem to have established it on a permanent basis. This new nomenclature has, therefore, been adopted throughout instead of that of Westcott and Hort. The author believes that the plenary inspiration of the autographs of the New Testament is the only logical view that can be held by those who accept the true deity as well as the perfect humanity of Christ. He has, therefore, approached his task with the reverence of one who accepts the Scriptures as the very Word of God.

In connection with the criticism of the Gospels, it would seem that the great differences among those who hold the Two-Document Theory of the Synoptics, and the tendency of *Formgeschichte* to destroy the validity of the whole Gospel record, demand a return to the original view of the supernatural origination of the Gospels. Literary criticism has assigned too much significance to the phenomena of style and vocabulary and not enough to the historical situations out of which the Gospels originated. Great weight has, therefore, been given to the latter in the discussion of Gospel origins. The author feels, further, that, while the testimony of the apostolic and church Fathers is not infallible, we should yet put more confidence in it than modern criticism is inclined to do.

With reference to the Pauline Epistles there is, happily, not so much difference of opinion today as there was a few decades ago. The Pastoral Epistles can be defended as genuine. There is good reason for believing that Paul was twice imprisoned and that he wrote 1 Timothy and Titus during the interim between the two imprisonments and 2 Timothy during the second imprisonment. Deissmann seems to have established the date of Gallio's proconsulship at Corinth on a firm basis, and we must, consequently, date all of Paul's Epistles, save the Pastorals, from one to two years earlier than we have been accustomed to do.

Finally, the author holds that the *Antilegomena* have rightly won their place in the canon and that inspiration was not absolutely confined to the Apostles. There is no valid reason for rejecting 2 Peter as a forgery; instead, its apostolic tone and autobiographical references favor the traditional view of its authorship. The linguistic peculiarities in that Epistle can be satisfactorily explained in harmony with the Petrine authorship of the book. So also can the same type of peculiarities in the five Johannine writings be reconciled with the Apostolic authorship of those books. Thus, in spite of the opposition to the conservative view in recent times, there is reason to regard our New Testament as an inspired account of the life and work of Jesus Christ, of the origin and early spread of the Christian movement, of the doctrines and practices of the apostolic Church, and of the purposes of God for the world.

The author makes no claims to originality beyond that of incorporating the new discoveries into the conservative position; others have labored, he has but entered into their labors. He is grateful to the publishers and authors for the benefits he has derived from the many works that he has read and consulted. Particular mention should be made of the writings of Henry Alford, George Salmon, B. F. Westcott, J. B. Lightfoot, Theodor Zahn, Alfred Plummer, R. J. Knowling, W. M. Ramsay, R. D. Shaw, Frederic Kenyon, and A. T. Robertson. His debt to these scholars is truly great!

In addition to this he would express his gratitude to several young scholars at Wheaton College who have aided him in one way or another in the preparation of this volume. In the first place mention should be made of Mr. Thomas P. Lindsay, M.A., an instructor in the department of Bible and Theology, who has, during the past semester, relieved the author of some of his teaching responsibility in order that he might the more speedily complete the work of composition; who has also made various helpful suggestions for the improvement of the book, and has rendered valuable assistance in the preparation of the Bibliography. Mention should also be made of Mr. Kenneth Hansen, B.A., a student in the graduate department of Theology, who has devoted much time and care to the preparation of the Index; of Mr. Paul L. Kaufman, B.A., a fellow in the department of Bible and Theology, who has assisted in many of the routine duties of the author; and of several other graduate students who have helped in the checking of references and the reading of the proof. To all these the author expresses his heartfelt gratitude.

It is with the prayer that God may use these pages for the instruction of those who seek light as to the origin of the New Testament, and for the establishing of those whose confidence in the inspiration and authority of the New Testament has been shaken, that this volume is sent forth.

HENRY C. THIESSEN

Wheaton, Ill.

CONTENTS

PART I

General Introduction

PART II

Special Introduction

CONTENTS—Continued

INTRODUCTION

THERE are four great fields of New Testament study, the critical, the historical, the exegetical, and the theological. The critical study inquires after the text and canon of the New Testament as a whole and after the authorship, occasion, date, design, destination, etc., of each separate book; the historical study traces the course of the life of Christ and the origin and growth of the Church in the New Testament; the exegetical study endeavors to ascertain the exact meaning of the statements of the writers in their contexts and so of the books that they have written; and the theological study formulates the teaching of the several books and of the authors of the New Testament into a doctrinal system.

But while we thus distinguish the four fields of study, we must not overlook the fact of the interrelation of the fields. We are constantly obliged to consider the contribution of all the fields if we want to do justice to the study of any one field. So then, although this book undertakes the critical study of the New Testament, it will, nevertheless, take note of various contributions made by the other fields in the accomplishment of its purpose. But before entering upon our main task, we wish to deal with two preliminary subjects: The Nature and Scope of New Testament Introduction and The History of New Testament Introduction.

I. *The Nature and Scope of New Testament Introduction*

The critical study of the New Testament is more commonly called *Introduction* or *Isagogics*. What we have just said about this type of study is, therefore, applicable to New Testament Introduction. But there has been a considerable change of opinion in recent years as to what should and what should not be included under this title. The term might well include all the preliminary studies useful to the understanding of the New Testament; and we actually have had Introductions that have dealt with grammar, philology, archaeology, geography, hermeneutics, dogma, the history of the translation and interpretation of the New Testament, and with its preservation in the Church and in literature.

An example of this conception of the term *Introduction* may be seen in Horne's *Introduction to the Critical Study and Knowledge of the Holy Scriptures,* first published in 1818, which was long a standard conservative work on the subject. In the eighth edition, for instance, he deals, in volume one, with the genuineness, authenticity, and inspiration of the Scriptures, the languages of Scripture and the history of the text, the ancient versions and the harmonies of Scripture, and with hermeneutics, or the laws of Biblical interpretation; in volume two, with the historical geography of the Holy Land, the political antiquities of the Jews, the sacred and domestic antiquities of the Jews and of the nations of Scripture, and with the analysis of the books of the Bible. There is a short discussion of the "sources" of the first three Gospels in the Appendix. It is to be regretted that in the tenth edition (1862) Samuel Davidson introduced a large element of German rationalism into this important work. Another example of this conception may be found in A. A. Hodge's *Outlines of Theology* (pp. 20, 21). He includes under the term *Introduction* the higher criticism, textual criticism, Biblical philology, Biblical archaeology, hermeneutics, apologetics, inspiration, history of interpretation, knowledge of dialect, authorship, occasion, design, and reception of each book.

But in recent times the conception of this term has been greatly narrowed down. It has been found that many of the themes formerly treated under this head should really be given separate and more extensive consideration than could be done under the old arrangement. Consequently the study of *Introduction* has now been almost completely limited to the problems of the literary, historical, and textual origination of the New Testament. In a broad way the subject has been divided into General and Special Introduction, the former dealing with the questions of the Canon and Text, the latter with those of the authorship, occasion, date, design, destination, etc., of each book of the New Testament. Some writers deal with both subjects in their treatises on *Introduction,* as Jülicher in his *Einleitung in das Neue Testament,* who first treats of Special Introduction, and then of General. Likewise McNeile in his *Introduction to the Study of the New Testament* deals with both aspects of the subject and in the same order as Jülicher. Generally, however, the term *Introduction* is today restricted to Special Introduction. It is thus used in the works of Dods, Peake, Moffatt, Zahn, Goodspeed, Lake and Lake, and Dibelius. General Introduction is today almost always treated as a separate subject, witness Gregory's *Canon and Text of the New Testament* and Souter's *Text and Canon of the New Testament.* Indeed, the subject is now generally divided into its two component parts, the Canon and the Text, and each part is treated separately, as Westcott and Goodspeed on the Canon, and Hort, Gregory, Warfield, Nestle, Souter, von Soden, La Grange, Kenyon, Robertson, Lake, and Streeter, on the Text. Bacon treats of the Canon and Special Introduction, and Salmon treats canonicity and Special Introduction together.

The present work treats of both General and Special Introduction, dealing with the Canon, the Text, and Inspiration under the former head, and with the usual problems of Special Introduction under the latter.

II. *The History of New Testament Introduction*

The believer in the divine inspiration of the Scriptures has often been accused of accepting blindly the traditions of the past. This criticism is unfair. We grant that the ordinary believer in the Bible has not personally examined the questions that belong to New Testament Introduction, but so neither has the ordinary unbeliever. Both have inherited or acquired their attitude toward the Scriptures on non-technical grounds. But it is not true that conservative scholars, whom the ordinary believer trusts and follows as the unbeliever trusts and follows the liberal, have not made a thorough-going investigation of the questions of the Canon, the Text, and of the authorship, date, design, destination, etc., of the several books. Orr says: 'There has never been a time when criticism of Scripture —

lower and higher—has been altogether absent."[1] The Jews employed a type of criticism to the Bible in the selection of the books they used and in the settlement of the text of these books. As proof of the former we may cite the debate that was carried on about the Song of Solomon, Ecclesiastes, and Esther, as reported in the Mishna (c. A. D. 200), and the objections to the book of Ezekiel, as reported in the Gemara (which dispute was not settled until A. D. 66. Not that the O. T. Canon was not closed until that time, but that there were still some discussions as to some of the books in the O. T., as there were some debates among the Reformers with regard to one or two of the books in the N. T. Canon. In proof of the latter we may refer to the marginal notes on the text in the Hebrew Scriptures, known as *Kere* and *Kethibh,* the former indicating that the reading given with it is to be substituted for that in the text, and the latter, that a reading of the Hebrew Bible is that of the text.

Sitterly says: "Abundant evidence exists and is constantly growing to show that critical opinion and methods were known at least from the very days of the formation of the New Testament Canon."[2] The Fathers of the early Church compared the manuscripts of the New Testament books, noting their differences and judging of the books themselves. The principle of selection was at work. The heretic Marcion accepted only ten of Paul's Epistles, after he had "purified" them, and the Gospel of Luke, with numerous omissions and variations from the received text; but the Church rejected his judgment as to both Canon and Text. *The Muratorian Canon* says some things about several of the books in the New Testament, relating to authorship, authority, etc., of the books in question. In connection with the critical work of the Fathers, we may ask, Why were 1 and 2 Clement, Ignatius, Barnabas, and the Apostolic Decrees excluded from the Canon? Why does Serapion, Bishop of Antioch in the reign of Commodus say: "We receive Peter and the other Apostles as Christ; but those writings falsely ascribed to him we decline to receive through our experience"?[3]

---

1. Art. "Criticism of the Bible," in *Inter. Stand. Bible Ency.*
2. Art. "Text and Manuscripts of the New Testament," in *Inter. Stand. Bible Ency.*
3. Eusebius, *H. E.*, VI. xii.

In this connection it is interesting to note also that the Fathers never placed the Gospels with the spurious books.

Neither was criticism entirely wanting in the third to the sixth centuries. Origen, we are told, concluded, "partly from internal evidence that St. Paul could scarcely have written the Epistle to the Hebrews, and his disciple Dionysius adduced linguistic ground for rejecting the Apocalypse as a work of St. John" (*Catholic Encyclopaedia,* art. "Criticism"). Bacon says : "The *Church History* of Eusebius (A. D. 324) served all the purposes of an Introduction to the New Testament for a millenium, and is still the great thesaurus of information."[4] Eusebius enumerates seven books in our New Testament that were not universally received in his day. He calls them *Antilegomena*. These disputed books were James, Jude, 2 Peter, 2 and 3 John, Hebrews, and the Revelation. But we shall see that further investigation finally led to the acceptance of all of them. Augustine held that Mark was an abridgment of Matthew and Luke. About 450 a certain Hadrian wrote perhaps the first *Introduction.* He called it, *An Introduction to the Holy Scriptures,* but it dealt primarily with methods of exegesis and was not strictly a book on Introduction. Moffatt mentions the work of Junilius of Constantinople, who during the first half of the sixth century produced the only work worthy of the name *Introduction,* prior to the 16th century.[5]

The Humanist movement gave no impulse to the study of this subject, beyond the fostering of interest in the study of the Scriptures in the original languages. But the Reformers, says Orr, "did not accept blindly the judgment of antiquity, but availed themselves of the best light which the new learning afforded."[6] There were also certain Dominican friars in the 16th century who wrote so-called *Introductions,* but they were dominated by the decisions of the Council of Trent upon the Canon and were not true *Introductions.*

Richard Simon, priest of the Oratory of Paris, who died in 1712, is commonly regarded as the originator of the literary and textual criticism of the New Testament. Simon was satis-

---

4. *An Intro. to the New Testament,* p. 3.
5. *An Intro. to the Lit. of the New Test.,* p. 5.
6. "Criticism of the Bible," in *Inter. Stand. Bible Ency.*

fied with the traditional view of the origin of the separate books of the New Testament and of the Canon as a whole, and devoted himself mainly to the history of the text. He gave, however, some impetus to the philological and historical study of the New Testament, which has developed into the modern liberal movement. In 1704 J. G. Pritius, a German pastor in Frankfort, published his Latin *Introductio* as a kind of protest against the trend of Simon's work. In it he defends the authenticity of everything in the New Testament. His work made its way to all parts of Germany in a number of editions. J. D. Michaelis of Göttingen published an *Introduction* in 1750 in the spirit of the newer criticism. He sought to defend the genuineness and credibility of the books of the New Testament rather than their divine inspiration, and declared that the Canon was not a mere divine fiat, but the outcome of a long process of human selection, although the selection was providentially directed. J. S. Semler of Halle (d. 1791) declared boldly that the New Testament Canon was the work of men, and that the judgment of these men as to the Apostolicity of any book ought not to debar us from independent investigation of the subject. After this F. Schleiermacher denied the genuineness of the Pastoral Epistles, and others questioned the authenticity of Hebrews, the Catholic Epistles, and the Revelation. F. G. Eichhorn and W. M. L. de Wette further strengthened the cause of liberal criticism; but the Catholic J. L. Hug of Freiburg upheld the cause of conservatism in opposition to the critical tendencies of the time. C. A. Credner began a work on *Introduction*, but did not live to carry it out. Ed. Reuss, however, undertook the task left unfinished by Credner and brought it to completion. His work first appeared in 1842, but it has since then appeared in many editions. Both these writers were of the liberal school of criticism.

F. C. Baur (1792-1860), founder of the Tübingen school of theology, inaugurated the most revolutionary change in the treatment of the history of the New Testament. He held that there were two great parties in the early Church, a Petrine party which taught circumcision and the Mosaic Law, and a Pauline party, which rejected both. He insisted that the true condition of the early Church is seen, not in the Book of Acts, a work of the 2nd century, written by a Paulinist of a mild type to minimize the differences between the original apostles and Paul, but in the four undoubted Epistles of Paul, Galatians, 1 and 2 Corinthians, Romans, and in the Book of Revelation. In these books he thought to see the Church represented as rent by divisions that threatened its very existence. Attempts were finally made at the reconciliation of the several factions, the stages of which may be seen in the Gospels, the Acts, and the other books of the New Testament.

Although Baur himself did not write an *Introduction,* his works on the apostolic age had, nevertheless, a powerful effect on later criticism. Many came to the support of Baur, among the older ones being Zeller, Schwegler, Köstlin, Hilgenfeld, and Volkmar, and among the younger, Holsten and Pfleiderer, although Hilgenfeld and Pfleiderer surrendered most of Baur's views as to the Pauline Epistles. David Strauss was not strict-ly a member of the Tübingen school. With his mythical the-ory of the New Testament story, he did not apply literary or documentary criticism to his sources; neither did his rival, Renan, in France. Strauss worked along Hegelian lines and subjected every part of the Gospel history to a destructive crit-icism in the interest of his mythical theory.

Baur's theory received its most serious blows, not at the hands of the conservative writers Thiersch, Lange, Ebrard, Guericke, Salmon, and von Hogmann, but at those of the lib-eral writers Ritschl, Hilgenfeld, Reuss, Holtzmann, and Har-nack. Peake says that Ritschl struck the most serious blow at the Tübingen school by the publication in 1857 of his second edition of *Die Entstehung der altkatholischen Kirche.*[7] Hil-genfeld's *Einleitung* also showed that the theory could not be worked out over the field of the literature of the New Testa-ment.[8] The same may be said about Harnack's *History of Dogma.* Bacon says, "Baur's Synoptic theory has not a living adherent, for Volkmar, and Pfleiderer follow the prevailing view. . . . Weizsäcker scarcely differs from the views of Holtz-mann, and even Hilgenfeld retains only the priority of a

---

7. *A Critical Intro. to the New Testament,* p. 4.
8. *Moffatt, Intro. to the Lit. of the New Test.,* p. 6.

proto-Matthew to Mark."[9] As a whole, then, the theory of Baur is dead and presents no problem to the student of the New Testament.

Since the time of Baur criticism has devoted itself more than ever to the literary and historical study of the books of the New Testament. It has paid much attention to the Synoptic Gospels and has developed and popularized the so-called Two-Document theory. During this time some definite contributions have been made to the conservative position. Harnack has written a powerful vindication of the Lucan authorship of the Third Gospel and the Book of Acts. Ramsay has likewise argued for the Lucan authorship of these books; he has also helped to establish the Pauline authorship of various Epistles. Sanday's *Criticism of the Fourth Gospel* is still a valuable argument for the Apostolic authorship of that Gospel. Recent criticism of the rest of the books of the New Testament has, in general, moved in a conservative direction. Practically all of the Pauline Epistles have been given back to the apostle, doubt being cast today only on the Pastoral Epistles and on one or two others. Second Peter and Jude are still questioned by many, and there are differences of opinion as to the authorship of the Apocalypse.

Special mention should here be made of the great work in this field by the late Theodor Zahn of Erlangen University, the virtual leader of the conservatives in New Testament criticism. He was an indefatigable writer, but among his many learned books and articles there is perhaps nothing that is more important than his monumental work, entitled, *An Introduction to the New Testament* (3 vols.). It was first published in German under the title, *Einleitung in das Neue Testament* (2 vols., 1897-1900), and it was translated under the direction and supervision of M. W. Jacobus, assisted by C. S. Thayer and a number of young scholars, all of Hartford Theological Seminary, in 1909. This work has had a very wide influence and is conspicuous not only for its conservative viewpoint, but also for its massive learning.

In most recent times a new form of criticism has been introduced. It is known as *Formgeschichte,* commonly translated

---

9. *An Intro. to the New Test.,* p. 17.

as *Form Criticism,* and was given to the public by Martin Dibelius of Heidelberg, in 1919. Dibelius defines *Formgeschichte* as, "The literary criticism of the forms in which ideas, thoughts, reports, descriptions, etc., are passed on orally or in writing."[10] According to him the Synoptic writers, for instance, were only to a small extent authors. They were chiefly collectors and editors. The requirements of public worship, missionary, edificatory, and apologetic aims had more significance for the writers than the desire to write artistically. Bultmann, Dodd, R. H. Lightfoot, Easton, and Riddle are outstanding believers in *Formgeschichte.* Dibelius' book, *Die Formgeschichte des Evangeliums,* appeared in 1919; the English translation, *From Tradition to Gospel,* in 1935. His *A Fresh Approach to the New Testament and Early Christian Literature* (1936) is an attempt to apply the theory to the whole New Testament. For a fuller discussion of *Formgeschichte* the reader is referred to the chapter on the *Synoptic Problem.*

The critics of recent times may be divided into three groups, as follows: (1) The Radical Group, of whom Bruno Bauer (1809-1882) was the forerunner. He cast doubt on the historicity of Jesus and Paul. Similar views were afterwards entertained by Pierson, Loman, van Manen, and Naber in Holland, and by Steck and Völter in Germany. These have been refuted by both liberal and conservative writers and can be practically ignored in New Testament study. (2) The Liberal Group, to which belong Holtzmann, Harnack, Jülicher, Moffatt, Bacon, Souter, Peake, Lake and Lake, Cadbury, McNeile, Goodspeed, and many other recent writers on *Introduction.* (3) The Conservative Group, to which belong Godet, Salmon, Zahn, M'Clymont, J. B. Lightfoot, Ellicott, Alford, Westcott, Knowling, Hayes, Robertson, and practically all the Roman Catholic writers. In speaking of this Group as *conservatives* we realize, however, that they do not all hold the same view of inspiration.

This brief historical sketch has shown us that there has never been a time when the critical study of the New Testament has been entirely wanting. It has also shown us that for the most

---

10. *From Tradition to Gospel,* p. xv.

part liberal scholarship has taken the lead in this field of investigation. The present writer feels the need for a careful examination of the current views and a restatement of the conservative position in the light of all the assured facts. He hopes that
his humble effort in this direction may prove that this position
is historically sound and logically necessary.

PART ONE

GENERAL INTRODUCTION

ever Paul went, as seen in the Book of Acts, he preached from the Old Testament. Even the Gentiles, when they accepted the Gospel, accepted the Old Testament as their first Bible. The Jewish Christians recognized both the Hebrew Old Testament and the Septuagint, as is evident from the many quotations in the New Testament from both; the Gentiles, who could neither read nor understand the Hebrew, accepted the Septuagint only. The Levitical system was regarded as a symbol and a type of the Christian economy, fulfilled in the life, death, resurrection, and present ministry of Christ (cf. Hebrews); and the predictions of the Messiah in the Old Testament were applied to Christ and His ministry.

Of course, that which drove the early Christians back to the Old Testament was the story of the life, death, resurrection, and ascension of Christ, brought to them by the messengers of the Gospel. Like the Bereans, they undertook to examine the Scriptures to see "whether these things were so" (Acts 17:11). It is this acceptance of the Old Testament by the Gentile converts that made the work of the Judaizers later so effective. The Gospel of the Grace of God was jeopardized, and Paul found it necessary to write his great Epistles to the Galatians and to the Romans to explain and defend the teaching of the Gospel.

As we have intimated, the Gospel was first proclaimed by word of mouth. Since the original apostles were the leaders in the Christian movement and they, no doubt, again and again repeated the story about Christ in much the same words, the Gospel early received a kind of stereotyped form. To the oral message there were soon added a number of short narratives, more or less complete and more or less accurate, of the life and ministry of Christ. When a community had received the oral message, the need for an authoritative written interpretation of the facts in the life of Christ, together with their application to life, became apparent. The Pauline and other Epistles were written to meet this need. About the same time and a little later the need for authentic accounts of the life of Christ itself became apparent. The Synoptic Gospels and the Gospel of John were written to supply this need. The Book of Acts was called for by the need for an authentic history of the

Apostolic period, and the Apocalypse was written to set forth God's revelation of the consummation of all things. Thus there appeared the inspired and authoritative literature, known to us as the Gospels, the Acts, the Epistles, and the Apocalypse, which the church used alongside of the Old Testament.

2. *The Formation of the Canon of the New Testament*

After a Gospel or an Epistle had been written, it would remain for some time the treasured possession of the individual or the church that had received it. In some cases the originals would be passed from church to church (as for example Colossians and perhaps Ephesians), but they would, no doubt, always find their way back to the original recipient of them. By and by the originals were more freely circulated and copied. Undoubtedly often individuals and churches would make copies of the document in their possession and send them to other individuals and churches, and sometimes individuals and churches may have sent scribes to make copies at the place where the originals were found. Thus gradually the churches all over the world would obtain a more or less complete set of the inspired writings of the new dispensation.

But the limits of the Canon were not at once established. A number of other writings than those in our present New Testament appeared early which were by some considered of equal authority with them. The so-called 1 *Clement,* a letter written by Clement of Rome in the name of his Church to the Church at Corinth (c. 96 A. D.) was highly and widely esteemed. It was read in the public service of the Church at Corinth about 170. Irenaeus of Gaul, and Clement and Origen of Alexandria, as well as various other writers in Egypt of the fourth and fifth centuries, testified to its value and used it. 1 *Clement* is found attached to Codex Alexandrinus (A), as is also 2 *Clement* (falsely ascribed to Clement). 2 *Clement* however, was not widely read, and only in the East; neither of the two Clements had canonical recognition in the West. The *Didache* (c. 120), also known as *The Teaching of the Twelve Apostles,* was regarded by Clement of Alexandria and by Origen as Holy Scripture; but although the work was widely circulated, only in Egypt does it seem to have attained to canonical recognition. The so-called *Epistle of Barnabas* (c. 130) is found in Codex Sinaiticus (Aleph), and had something like a canonical position in Egypt. Jerome regards it as an apocryphal book; but Clement of Alexandria and Origen treat it as canonical. After the fourth century it seems gradually to have been rejected. *The Shepherd of Hermas* (c. 140) also is found in Aleph. It was written by Hermas the brother of Pius, bishop of Rome. Irenaeus quotes Hermas as Scripture; but contrary to the opinion of Souter,[3] neither Tertullian nor Clement of Alexandria regard it as Scripture.[4] The Muratorian Canon speaks highly of it, but apparently does not regard it as equal to our canonical books.

Even less important books were sometimes highly regarded. The so-called *Apocalypse of Peter* (before A. D. 150) was extensively used in the East and was known in the West. The Muratorian Canon mentions it, but with disapproval; Clement of Alexandria commented on it; but Eusebius placed it among the spurious books. The fragment discovered at Akhmim (in 1885) contains two visions, one of heaven, the other of hell. The apocryphal *Acts of Paul* (c. A. D. 170), which originally included the Acts of *Paul and Thecla,* was probably composed by a presbyter in the province of Asia. Origen, and probably also Clement of Alexandria, cited it with respect. It was highlv respected in the ancient church. These books hovered on the border of the Canon in some sections of the country for a time, but were all rejected by and by. Many other later Gospels, Acts, Epistles, and Apocalypses appeared under the names of the Apostles which did not receive the serious consideration of the Church.[5]

Soon the books which we now consider canonical were gathered together. The process of collecting began almost immediately after the books had been written. Peter already speaks of the Pauline Epistles as well known (2 Pet. 3:15, 16). This statement may not include the Pastoral Epistles, for 1 Timothy and Titus had only just been written, and 2 Timothy was being written about the same time with 2 Peter. But

3. *The Text and Canon of the New Testament,* p. 180.
4. Gregory, *Canon and Text of the New Testament,* p. 242 f.
5. See *A Handbook of Patrology,* by J. Tixeront, for a description of them.

we know that the letters of Ignatius were being collected before his actual martyrdom,[6] and the inclusion of 1 Timothy and Titus in Peter's statement is not impossible, although highly improbable. The publication of the Book of Acts (c. A. D. 61) may well have aroused a general interest in all that Paul had written and have promoted the collecting and publishing of his writings. At any rate, the Pauline Epistles seem to have been the first to be gathered together and published. Ephesus became a great Christian center during the last half of the first century, and it may well be that these Epistles were first published as a body of Pauline literature in this city. We cannot, however, agree with Goodspeed that Ephesians was written in the last half of the first century as an introduction to this Pauline corpus.[7] The Synoptic Gospels were undoubtedly collected about the same time or only a little later, perhaps also at Ephesus, where the Gospel of John was published and added to the collection late in the first century. It is interesting to note that the Book of Revelation begins with a group of seven letters addressed to seven churches in Asia.

The process of collecting and publishing the recognized books continued into the second century. Kenyon says, the adoption of the codex form, i. e., our modern book form, by the Christians early in the second century, made possible the inclusion of a much larger quantity of material than was possible in a roll.[8] We now have, in the Chester Beatty papyri, a considerable portion of a codex containing the four Gospels and the Acts, and another of the Pauline Epistles, both written early in the third century.[9] By and by the remaining books of our present New Testament were collected, and the whole came now to be classified as the Gospels, the Pauline Epistles, Acts and the Catholic Epistles, and the Apocalypse. But the full recognition of some of these books was delayed for a time in certain quarters. Kenyon says the four Gospels were recognized as an authoritative group early in the second century, and so were the Pauline Epistles; but that was not true of 2 and 3 John, 2 Peter, Jude, Hebrews, and the Apocalypse.[10] But Westcott says: "From the close of the second century the history of the

6. Goodspeed, *The Formation of the New Testament*, p. 24.
7. *Op. cit.,* p. 28 f.
8. *Our Bible and the Ancient Manuscripts*, 4th ed., p. 12 f.
9. Kenyon, *Bible and Archaeology*, p. 213.
10. *Our Bible and the Ancient Manuscripts*, p. 99.

Canon is simple, and its proof clear. It is allowed even by those who have reduced the genuine Apostolic works to the narrowest limits, that from the time of Irenaeus the New Testament was composed essentially of the same books which we receive at the present, and that they were regarded with the same reverence as is now shown to them."[11] These facts must not be attributed to the "uncritical" judgment of the early church; for Westcott says again: "All the Fathers at the close of the second century agree in appealing to the testimony of antiquity as proving the authenticity of the books which they used as Christian Scriptures. And the appeal was made at a time when it was easy to try its worth."[12]

Several things very materially promoted the formation of the New Testament Canon. There was, first of all, the influence of the incomplete Canon of Marcion (c. 140), which was being widely accepted and threatened to destroy the authority of the other inspired books. This situation could not be tolerated. Both Irenaeus and Tertullian have much to say about how Marcion mutilated even the books which he received. It, therefore, became necessary to collect all the books that were recognized as inspired and to preserve them in their integrity. Then there was the recognition by many leaders, primarily in the East, of the *First Epistle of Clement,* the *Didache,* the *Epistle of Barnabas,* and the *Shepherd of Hermas,* as canonical or semi-canonical, that gave further impetus to the settling of the limits of the Canon. From time to time, also, there still appeared other apocryphal and pseudepigraphical books that purported to be inspired. Thus the church came to feel the need of excluding all the books that had no right to be in the Canon. And a little later, the edict of Diocletian (in 303) that all sacred books be destroyed by fire, gave further stimulus to the sorting and sifting of the books that were to be guarded against destruction. It is probably due to this persecution under Diocletian that we have so little of the New Testament from the first three centuries. These three primary factors led to the collecting and publishing of those books which the church came to regard as equally authoritative with the books of the Old Testament.

---

11. *On the Canon of the New Testament,* p. 6.
12. *Op. cit.,* p. 314.

There were four things which aided in the determination of which books should be accepted as canonical. The first was apostolicity: was the book written by an apostle, or, if not, did the author of the book sustain such a relation to an apostle as to raise his book to the level of the apostolic books? The latter question was especially used in determining the canonicity of the Gospel of Mark, the Gospel of Luke, the Book of Acts, and the Epistle to the Hebrews. The second was contents: were the contents of a given book of such a spiritual character as to entitle it to this rank? On the basis of this test most of the apocryphal and pseudepigraphical books were eliminated and the ones which we now have retained. The third was universality: was the book universally received in the church? It is this test that further aided in the elimination of the unworthy books; but it also perpetuated the debate about the canonicity of the so-called *antilegomena* for a long time. We shall consider this question in the next paragraph. The final test was inspiration: did the book give evidence of being divinely inspired? This was the ultimate test; everything finally had to give way to it. Angus-Green say: "The Holy Spirit, given to the Church, quickened holy instincts, aided discernment between the genuine and the spurious, and thus led to gradual, harmonious, and in the end unanimous conclusions. There was in the Church what a modern divine has happily termed an 'inspiration of selection'."[13]

But for a time the conclusions were not unanimous. Generally speaking, from the time of Irenaeus on the New Testament contained practically the same books as we receive today, and were regarded with the same reverence that we bestow on them today, as we have already learned from Westcott (see above); but there was a minority that continued to question the genuineness and authority of some of the books for a long time. It was not exactly the same books in each case, as we shall see later on, though in a general way that was the case. Origen distinguished between the *homologoumena,* the books universally recognized as Scripture, and the *antilegomena,* the books more or less opposed. In the former group he included the four Gospels, thirteen Epistles of Paul, 1 Peter, 1 John,

---

13. *The Cyclopedic Handbook to the Bible,* p. 36.

Acts, and the Revelation; in the latter he placed Hebrews, 2 Peter, 2 and 3 John, James, Jude, Barnabas, the Shepherd, the Didache, and the Gospel of the Hebrews. He himself, however, frequently cited Hebrews as though Pauline and canonical; in fact he cites as Scripture all but Jude and 2 and 3 John. Eusebius of Caesarea wrote his Church History somewhere between 300 and 325. Through his adopted father Pamphilus he inherited the library and the traditions of Origen. He, too, distinguishes between the *homologoumena* and the *antilegomena,* but divided the latter into those merely disputed and those actually spurious. Under the *homologoumena* he lists the four Gospels, Acts, the Epistles of Paul, 1 John, 1 Peter, and the Apocalypse; under those merely disputed he mentions James, Jude, 2 Peter, and 2 and 3 John; and under those actually spurious he lists the Acts of Paul, the Shepherd, the Apocalypse of Peter, Barnabas, the Didache, and perhaps the Apocalypse. Hebrews seems to have been omitted inadvertently; he, however, quotes it as by Paul and regards it as having been translated either by Luke or by Clement of Rome. He declares that the *antilegomena* are "known to the majority," and seems himself to accept them all; but he is far from certain as to the authorship, and therefore of the canonicity, of the Apocalypse. It is for this reason that he first includes it among the *homologoumena* and then again under the *spurious* books.

We ought not to wonder too much at this hesitancy of some leaders of the early Church to accept these seven books. It is clear that no one regarded them as written by James, Peter, John, and Jude and yet rejected them; the question was whether the books that bore these names were really written by these persons. Were not many pseudonymous books appearing still under the names of the Apostles? Had not Paul (2 Thess. 2:1, 2) and John (1 John 4:1) specifically warned their readers to be on their guard against spurious epistles and false prophets? Besides, the internal evidence for these books is peculiar. Hebrews does not give the author's name and differs in vocabulary and style from the recognized Epistles of Paul; 2 Peter differs from 1 Peter in the same way; in James and Jude the writers are represented as "servants" of Christ, not as apostles; and in 2 and 3 John the author calls himself a "presbyter," not an apostle. Jude was also questioned because it was thought to quote from an apocryphal book. Furthermore, these books were written either to Christians generally, or to private individuals, not to specific churches. No one was, therefore, from the human standpoint, immediately interested in preserving them. Perhaps that is the reason why the external evidence for them is more scanty. All these factors militated against the early reception of these books. Gradually, however, the so-called *antilegomena* came also to be universally accepted, as we shall see presently.

We shall get a better conception of the formation of the New Testament Canon if we now consider the evidence for the existence and recognition of the several books chronologically by countries. For this purpose we shall divide the early Christian world into three parts: Syria, Asia Minor, and Thrace; Egypt and Palestine; and Italy, Gaul, and North Africa. The several writers will be introduced according to the countries in which they wrote or are thought to have written on the subject under discussion, irrespective of their doctrinal viewpoint or the language in which they wrote. The various anonymous or pseudonymous documents, as also the early versions, will likewise be introduced according to their known or supposed provenance.[14]

Syria, Asia Minor, and Thrace

Ignatius, bishop of Antioch (martyred c. 116), clearly knows our New Testament in general. He knew the Epistles of Paul well, but the Gospels of Matthew and John appear to have been his favorites.

Polycarp, bishop of Smyrna (c. 69-155), uses much of the New Testament in his letter to the Philippians. He had the Gospel of Matthew, and probably also the other three Gospels; he had all of Paul's Epistles, 1 Peter, and 1 John; he had 1 Clement and probably also the Book of Acts.

Papias, bishop of Hierapolis (c. 80—c. 155), testifies that Mark wrote his Gospel according to what he had heard Peter

---

14. The author gratefully acknowledges his indebtedness to various writers on the Canon, especially to Westcott (*On the Canon of the New Testament*), Gregory (*The Canon and Text of the New Testament*), and Souter (*The Text and Canon of the New Testament*) for the historical facts in this section.

tell of the words and works of Christ, and that Matthew wrote his *Logia* in Aramaic. He knew John's Gospel, and Eusebius tells us that he quotes 1 John and 1 Peter.

The Didache, or Teaching of the Twelve Apostles (c. 120), has been assigned to Alexandria, Antioch, and Jerusalem, but more probably it is from Antioch. It uses Matthew a good deal and Luke some; Mark and John are not quoted. It knows most of our New Testament books.

Melito, bishop of Sardis (2d cent.), quotes from all the books of the New Testament except James, Jude, 2 John, and 3 John. He speaks of "the Old Books," "the Books of the Old Testament," which naturally implies a definite New Testament (so Westcott, Jülicher, Gregory, and Goodspeed).

Theophilus, bishop of Antioch (c. 115—c. 188), wrote a treatise to his pagan friend Autolycus. It seems clear that he had the bulk of our New Testament books and that he held them in equal esteem with the Old Testament. He first mentions the Gospel of John by name.

The Old Syriac Version (c. 200) appeared somewhat later than the *Diatessaron* of Tatian and was known as the *Evangelion da-Mepharreshe,* "the Gospel of the Separated Ones," i. e., in contrast with the combined text of Tatian. It may be that at first the version had only the Gospels, but it surely had most of the rest of the books also in time. The Assyrian Church had Paul's Epistles, 1 John, 1 Peter, and James, and Gregory thinks that the Old Syriac soon had all the books of our New Testament except Revelation, 2 and 3 John, 2 Peter, and Jude.[15]

Lucian of Antioch (martyred 312) revised the text of the Old and New Testaments. His version of the New Testament spread all the way to Constantinople and may well be the parent of the great majority of our present Greek manuscripts. It became known as the Antioch Canon and excluded the Apocalypse, 2 Peter, 2 and 3 John, and Jude.

Epiphanius, bishop of Salamis, in Cyprus (c. 315—403), was untiring in his hostility to Origen. In his invaluable work

15. *Op cit.,* p. 156.

Panarion (Drug Chest) he describes and teaches against eighty heresies. His list of the books of the New Testament is somewhat carelessly drawn up, but he undoubtedly accepts all the books we today have, even though he does not precisely mention the seven Catholic Epistles.

Basil the Great, bishop of Caesarea in Cappadocia (c. 329—379), recognized all the books in our present Canon, although he does not seem to quote from 2 and 3 John, and Jude. But we must beware against concluding that failure to quote from a book means that the writer does not know the book or does not accept it; there may not have been anything in the books not quoted that served the writer's purpose. **Gregory** of Nyssa (c. 335—395), brother of Basil, agreed with his brother in the reception of the books of the New Testament.

Gregory of Nazianzus (c. 330—c. 390), intimate friend of Basil, wrote against Julian, and produced many orations, essays, and poems. He was highly educated, having studied at Caesarea in Cappadocia, at Caesarea in Palestine, at Alexandria, and at Athens. He accepted all our books in the New Testament except the Revelation, although once he quotes it as by John. Being widely and favorably known, he, no doubt, had great influence in connection with the establishing of the limits of the Canon.

John of Antioch, later named **Chrysostom** (347-407), was the greatest preacher of ancient times. He ministered at Antioch for about sixteen years, first as deacon and then as presbyter, and for a little over six years (397-404) he served as archbishop of Constantinople. In an ecclesiastical sense Constantinople was a daughter of Antioch, and so it accepted the Canon of Antioch, namely twenty-two books, all but 2 Peter, 2 and 3 John, Jude, and the Apocalypse. In his *Synopsis* he names the twenty-two; and in his sermons he never quotes from the remaining five. **Theodoret** of Cyrrhus (386-458), also originally from Antioch, adopts the same Canon as Chrysostom.

Theodore, bishop of Mopsuestia in Cilicia (c. 350-428), was also born at Antioch and was one of the most learned men of the Antiochian school. He accepted the four Gospels, Acts, fourteen Epistles of Paul, but rejected all seven Catholic Epistles and the Apocalypse. He had great influence in the Nestorian Assyrian Church, and at least some in that Church followed his lead in rejecting all the Catholic Epistles.

The Peshitta (between 411-435) is a revision of the Old Syriac in accord with the Greek text of that day, made by order of Rabbula, bishop of Edessa. It will be seen that the Old Syriac was based on a text two centuries earlier than this, and that the Peshitta is based on a much later Greek text. Constantinople being now the center of the Church in the East, Rabbula adopted the Canon of Constantinople, i. e., he did not include 2 and 3 John, 2 Peter, Jude, and the Apocalypse. But about 508 **Philoxenus** had his Rural Bishop Polycarp make a new revision of the Syriac, which apparently included all the twenty-seven books of our present Canon. However the manuscripts that have come down to us have only the five books not found in the Peshitta.

In Syria, Asia Minor, and Thrace, then, we note various steps in the formation of the Canon. The silence of the earlier writers does not prove that they did not know or that they rejected the books which they did not quote. We have so little from these writers that the argument from silence is especially worthless in this case; besides, they may not have had occasion to use all the books in their writings. Melito in the second century seems to recognize the existence of a definite New Testament, although we do not know just which books he may have had in it. Theophilus of Antioch apparently had the bulk of our New Testament and held the books in the same high regard that we have for them. It is not until Lucian (martyred 312) that any books are known to have been definitely excluded. But shortly after this time we have Epiphanius of Salamis, Basil the Great of Caesarea in Cappadocia, and his brother Gregory of Nyssa, also of Cappadocia, who recognized the same twenty-seven books that we receive. Gregory of Nazianzus accepted all the books but the Apocalypse. Chrysostom was influenced by the newer Canon of Antioch and rejected five of the books; and Theodore of Mopsuestia was quite a reactionary in rejecting eight of the books. He was accused of too great intimacy with the Pelagians and the Nes-

torians.[16] McNeile calls attention to the fact that at the end of
the 4th century or the beginning of the 5th, Syria made an advance upon the Canon of Chrysostom and Theodoret. In the
Constitutions of the Holy Apostles, the last section is called
"Ecclesiastical Canons of the Same Holy Apostles," and in the
last part of this section we have a list of the canonical books of
Old and New Testaments. This list gives all our New Testament books but the Apocalypse, and adds 1 and 2 Clement.[17]
The omission of five of the books in the *Peshitta* was definitely
due to the influence of the Canon of Constantinople, which did
the same thing. The influence of this Canon was finally broken
when Philoxenus added these five books to the Syriac Version.
While, then, apparently, our present Canon was early widely
accepted in these lands, the controversy about some of the
antilegomena did not cease until the end of the fifth century.

Egypt and Palestine

Justin the Martyr (c. 100—165) was a Greek born in Samaria. He wrote a number of works; three of those which
have come down to us are unquestionably genuine: the two
Apologies and the *Dialogue with Trypho* the Jew. It is practically certain that he used Matthew, Luke, and John, and his
reference to the Memoirs of Peter probably means Mark's
Gospel. He knows Acts, 1 Peter, Romans, 1 Corinthians,
Galatians, Ephesians, Colossians, 2 Thessalonians, Hebrews,
the Apocalypse (which he regards as a work of the Apostle
John), and the *Didache.* Justin traveled widely and finally
settled in Rome, where he founded a school. His testimony is,
therefore, very important.

Hegesippus (c. 110-180), a Jewish Christian Church historian, is a witness against the Tübingen hypothesis.[18] He
gives us a lengthy account of the martyrdom of James, the
Lord's brother. Travelling a good deal, he finally came to
Rome. Eusebius tells us that on his way, "he found everywhere the same doctrine."[19] He embodied his findings in five

---

16. See Tixeront, *A Handbook of Patrology*, p. 198.
17. Cf. McNeile's *Intro. to the Study of the New Testament*, p. 360, and see the
Ante-Nicene Fathers, in loc.
18. Fisher, *Hist. of Chr. Doctrine*, p. 42.
19. *H. E.*, IV. xxii.

books, known as *Memoirs*. No doubt the bulk of our books in the New Testament were in use at Corinth and Rome at that time, and the absence of any note of surprise or of dissent in the writings of Hegesippus may be taken as a sign that he was accustomed to the recognition of the same books.

The Epistle of Barnabas (c. 130) is falsely ascribed to Paul's associate of that name on his first journey, but is yet a very early work. It was probably written at Alexandria and was especially valued and used there. It quotes Matthew twice, and there are echoes of Romans, 1 and 2 Corinthians, and Ephesians. The writer perhaps knew 1 Peter, and certain passages remind us of John. It was not as widely read as 1 Clement, but yet was treated as canonical by Clement of Alexandria and Origen. It is found in the manuscript *Aleph,* along with the *Shepherd of Hermas.*

The Gnostics, Basilides of Alexandria (fl. 130) and the more important **Valentinus** (taught at Alexandria c. 140 and at Rome afterward), knew and accepted in general the books which we have in our New Testament. Basilides quotes them precisely as he does the Old Testament books ("as it is written," "about which the Scripture saith," etc.). Valentinus used our four Gospels, and there is evidence that he knew Romans, 1 and 2 Corinthians, Galatians, Ephesians, Philippians, and Colossians, which practically means that he knew 2 Thessalonians and Philemon as well. Zahn, indeed, also finds traces of the Apocalypse, Acts, 1 and 2 Peter, and Hebrews in this writer. It appears, then, that their New Testament was just like that of the others.

Clement of Alexandria (c. 155—c. 215) has left us three great works, *The Exhortation to the Greeks, The Pedagogus,* or *Instructor,* and *The Stromata,* or *Miscellanies.* He was exceedingly well read. Clement accepted all the books in our present New Testament, not passing by the books that were disputed by some, as Jude and the rest of the Catholic Epistles. He held that Hebrews was written by Paul in Hebrew and that Luke had translated it. But he commented on only four of the Catholic Epistles, leaving out James, 2 Peter, and 3 John. He also recognized the Apocalypse.

Origen of Alexandria (c. 185—c. 253) knew Rome, Antioch, Arabia, Athens, and Cæsarea as well as Alexandria. His testimony has, therefore, unusual value. Besides, he was one of the greatest Biblical scholars of the Ante-Nicene period. He referred to Prov. 22:28 in the discussion of the Canon; but he held, nevertheless, that tradition was to be investigated. He distinguished between the *homologoumena*, the universally accepted books, and the *antilegomena*, the ones more or less disputed. To the former he assigned the four Gospels, thirteen Epistles of Paul, 1 Peter, 1 John, Acts, and the Apocalypse; to the latter, Hebrews, 2 Peter, 2 and 3 John, James, Jude, Barnabas, the Shepherd, the Didache, and the Gospel of the Hebrews. Yet he himself probably accepted nearly all of the disputed books. He frequently quotes Hebrews as Pauline and canonical; he also often cites 2 Peter and James as Scripture; but he does this also for the Shepherd and the Didache. He regards the Apocalypse as written by an inspired man, but not by the Apostle John. He appears to have valued Jude highly, though he seldom quotes it. This, then, would leave only 2 and 3 John unaccounted for, and Souter thinks it possible that he recognized them as genuine also.[20]

The Chester Beatty Papyri (of the 3d century or earlier) contain portions of three codices of the New Testament, which when complete would have covered all the New Testament, save the Pastoral and Catholic Epistles. Hebrews comes next after Romans, which goes to show that this Epistle was accepted as Pauline in Egypt as early as this. Kenyon thinks that the Pastoral Epistles were probably never included in these papyri, there being insufficient space for them.[21]

The Egyptian Versions which have come down to us are no great help in determining the extent of the early Canon. The earliest of the three that are best known, the Sahidic, has come down to us in about 750 fragments, which vary in date from the fourth to the fourteenth century. In these fragments we have practically the whole New Testament. The original seems to have appeared as early as A. D. 200. The Bashmuric

20. *Text and Canon of the New Testament*, p. 174 f.
21. *The Bible and Archaeology*, p. 224.

version probably appeared about the same time; but the part that has come down to us contains very little of the New Testament and has not yet been properly edited. Even less is known about the other two versions of Middle Egypt. The Bohairic version is from Northern Egypt and seems first to have appeared in A. D. 250. It contained all the New Testament from the first, save the Apocalypse, which was added later. All the manuscripts that we have contain the whole New Testament, but none is older than the twelfth century.

Dionysius of Alexandria (c. 200-265) was a pupil of Origen and a distinguished scholar in his own right. He became head of the Catechetical School of Alexandria about 231 and bishop for the last seventeen years of his life. Important fragments of his letters remain, and they contain numerous references to the New Testament. He makes use of Hebrews, calling it Paul's Epistle, of James, and of 2 and 3 John; he thinks the Apocalypse was written by a holy and inspired man, but not by the Apostle John. He says nothing about 2 Peter or Jude.

Eusebius of Caesarea, called also Eusebius of Pamphilus (c. 265-340), was an admirer of Origen and, like him, distinguished between the *homologoumena* and the *antilegomena*. He seems himself, however, to have accepted all the books, although he was uncertain as to the authorship of the Apocalypse. See above for details of his views. He had fifty manuscripts made of the Bible for the emperor Constantine. Gregory thinks that Codex Vaticanus and Codex Sinaiticus may be two of the fifty. Vaticanus ends at Heb. 9:13 and so has lost the rest of Hebrews, the Pastorals, Philemon and the Apocalypse; but Sinaiticus has all the twenty-seven books of our present New Testament, and also the *Epistle of Barnabas* and the *Shepherd of Hermas*.

Athanasius of Alexandria (298-373) is perhaps the first to apply the term "canonical" to the exact twenty-seven books that we now have in our New Testament; although, as we have seen, Origen had already spoken of the "canonized Scriptures." Goodspeed says that, in the East, due to the influence of Athanasius the New Testament took on a certain "fixity" of form

from this time on.[22] Henceforth not a single book remained
as a disputed book, at least not for Alexandria and those looking to this center for leadership.

Cyril of Jerusalem (315-386) in his Catechetical Lectures,
probably written about the year 346, lists as received all the
books of the New Testament which we receive, except the
Apocalypse. He warns against reading any of the books that
are not read in the churches. As bishop of Jerusalem (fr.
350-386) he expresses the opinion of that section of the church
at that time.

In Egypt and Palestine we again find that the early writers
are silent regarding some of the books in our present Canon.
They know and use a large number of them, as also some that
were later excluded from the Canon. The Gnostics Basilides
and Valentinus seem to have accepted the same New Testament as the leaders in the church. Not till Origen is there any
mention of the *antilegomena,* and we have seen that he himself
probably accepted all the books except 2 and 3 John and the
Apocalypse; indeed, he may have accepted these also. The
Beatty Papyri recognized the Epistle to the Hebrews as by
Paul, but seem not to recognize the Pastoral Epistles. Dionysius and Eusebius followed Origen in their doubts about the
Apocalypse, but they seem otherwise to have accepted all the
books that we have in our New Testament. Cyril of Jerusalem
rejected the Apocalypse but accepted all the other books.
Athanasius definitely declared his reception of all the twenty-
seven books. For a time, a number of extra-canonical books
were also recognized by some; but by and by they were all
rejected. In the the third century some questions arose about
Hebrews, 2 and 3 John, and the Apocalypse. The latter was
rejected by some from the time of Origen on. In these countries, then, there appears to have been very little opposition to
any of the books which we have in our present New Testament
until the third century, and even then the opposition appears
not to have been very definite nor very clear.

---

22. *Formation of the New Testament,* p. 141 f.

Italy, Gaul, and North Africa

Clement of Rome (c. 30-100) wrote a letter in the name of the Church at Rome to the Church at Corinth about A. D. 96, known as 1 *Clement,* which was regarded as canonical by some writers. He knew Matthew, Romans, 1 Corinthians, and is full of references to Hebrews. He may have been acquainted with James, 1 Peter, 1 Timothy, and Titus also, although this is not certain. There is nothing that does not fit in with the authenticity of the others also.

Marcion of Pontus and Rome (d. 165) in 140 presented to the world the first New Testament Canon of which we have any knowledge. He was a Gnostic and on doctrinal grounds accepted only the Gospel of Luke and ten of Paul's Epistles, after he had badly mutilated them. He rejected the Pastoral Epistles and arranged the remaining Epistles of Paul in the following order: Galatians, 1 and 2 Corinthians, Romans, 1 and 2 Thessalonians, Laodiceans (Ephesians), Colossians, Philippians, and Philemon (according to Tertullian, *Against Marcion,* V). His Canon, no doubt, had much to do with the Church's collection and approval of the present books in our Canon. Justin Martyr, Hippolytus, Irenæus, Epiphanius, and Tertullian all oppose him as a heretic.

Tatian of Syria and Rome (b.c. 120) studied Greek phillosophy in his youth. He finally came to Rome where he became a Christian and a disciple of Justin. After Justin's death he taught in his place; but a few years after Justin's death he broke with the Church. About 170 he produced in Rome a harmony of the four Gospels, interweaving the materials into a continuous story. For a long time it was thought that he wrote it in Syriac, but many recent scholars think that he originally wrote it in Greek and that later he or some one under his guidance translated it into Syriac, perhaps when he returned to Syria, about A. D. 170. Tatian, however, knew not only our four Gospels, but also pretty nearly all our New Testament books. He used many of Paul's Epistles, although he is said to have rejected 1 Timothy.

Hermas (brother of Pius, bishop of Rome from c. 141-157) is the reputed author of the *Shepherd* or *Pastor of Her-*

mas, which was regarded as inspired by Irenæus, Clement of Alexandria, and Origen. From the contents of this work it seems clear that the writer knew the Gospel of Matthew and Ephesians, and he may have known Hebrews and James. Of course he knew the Apocalypse very well. He may have known many of the other books in our present Canon also, but they are not alluded to in the *Shepherd.*

Irenaeus of Asia Minor and Gaul (c. 140-203) was probably born at Smyrna, although that is not certain. He saw Polycarp at Smyrna when but a boy and heard him tell of his intercourse with John and with others who had seen Christ. He also saw Florinus in the same city, who afterward became a heretic, taking up Valentinian Gnosticism. As bishop of Lyons he combined the traditions of Asia Minor, Rome and Gaul. He definitely used the four Gospels, the Book of Acts, 1 Peter, 1 John, all of Paul's Epistles except Philemon, and the Apocalypse. Souter thinks we should add 2 John to this list. But his silence regarding the others does not prove his ignorance or rejection of them.

The Muratorian Fragment of the Canon (c. 170 or a little later) derives it name from Muratori, an Italian, who discovered the fragment in the Ambrosian Library at Milan, in 1740. It may have been written at Rome, although that is not certain. Matthew and Mark were probably listed as recognized in the mutilated part of the Fragment at the beginning. That being true, we find all the books of our New Testament mentioned except 1 John, 1 Peter, James, 2 Peter, and Hebrews; but 1 John is quoted in another place in the Canon. Goodspeed, however, says, that the early writers sometimes thought of 1, 2, and 3 John as one letter (as Irenæus), and sometimes as two (Muratorian Canon). That being the case, all of John's Epistles would be included.

The Epistle of the Churches of Vienne and Lyons (177) to the Churches in Asia and Phrygia is full of Biblical language and thought. While it does not mention any book of the New Testament by name, the coincidences of language with Luke, John, Acts, Romans, Corinthians, Ephesians, Philippians, 1 Timothy, 1 Peter, 1 John, and the Apocalypse are unequivocal.

The importance of this evidence lies not in its recognition of all the books in our present Canon, but in its being the testimony of Churches which were not without connection with the Apostolic age.

The Old Latin Version (before 170) seems to have been in general use in Africa in the time of Tertullian. Westcott thinks it had the four Gospels, Acts, thirteen Epistles of Paul, the three Epistles of John, 1 Peter, Jude, and the Apocalypse. The Epistle to the Hebrews was added a little later, but before the time of Tertullian. There is no positive evidence that James and 2 Peter were also in the *Vetus Latina,* although there also is no evidence to the contrary.

Tertullian of Carthage (c. 150-222) was a lawyer of great influence, and a voluminous writer in Latin. He also wrote some in Greek. His writings laid the foundation for Latin theology. He accepts our four Gospels, thirteen Epistles of Paul (Souter raises a question about Philemon), Acts, 1 Peter, 1 John, Jude, and the Apocalypse. He holds that Barnabas wrote Hebrews, and does not accept the book as Scripture. He does not mention or quote from James, 2 Peter, and 2 and 3 John, which may or may not indicate the rejection of these books. In his case also 1 John may have been intended to mean 2 and 3 John as well.

Cyprian, bishop of Carthage (c. 200-258), was largely influenced by the writings of Tertullian. He was a teacher of rhetoric before he became a Christian. In 248 he was made bishop of Carthage; but under Valerian he was banished and finally was beheaded in his native city. He quotes all but Philemon, James, 2 Peter, 2 and 3 John, Jude, and Hebrews. But he probably followed Tertullian in regard to Hebrews and may have had no occasion to quote the remaining books. It is probable, however, that in the West as in the East there was a good deal of hesitancy regarding some of the Catholic Epistles.

Jerome of Pannonia, Rome, and Palestine (c. 340-420) traveled extensively, and made the Latin translation of the Scriptures known as the Vulgate late in his life, at the request of Damasus, bishop of Rome. His New Testament contained all the books which we today have in our New Testament. He explains how the various Catholic Epistles gradually came to be recognized. He accounts for the differences in vocabulary and style between 1 and 2 Peter on the ground that Peter had a different "interpreter" for them. Jerome pleads for the acceptance of Hebrews in writing to a friend in the West on the ground that the Epistle was received by the Churches in the East and by all Greek Church writers before his day, as by Paul, although he admits that some think it was written by Barnabas or Clement.

Augustine of Hippo (354-430) was perhaps the foremost of the Latin fathers. He was saved from a dissolute life under the preaching of Ambrose of Milan and then returned to his home in North Africa. He was bishop of Hippo from 395 to his death. He accepts all the seven books that had been questioned in some sections and, in fact, all the books we have in our present New Testament. Yet he seems to have recognized different degrees of value among the canonical books : not all books, in his opinion, were of equal authority. Furthermore, he seems to think that there were still some differences of opinion as to the exact extent of the Canon at that time.

In the West, then, as this brief survey indicates, the fortunes of the books in our New Testament were more like those in Syria, Asia Minor, and Thrace than like those in Egypt and Palestine. The earliest writers definitely recognized and used various books in our Canon, but do not mention the others. Marcion was the first to set a definite limit to the Canon. But since he selected the books that appear in his Canon on purely doctrinal grounds and not on the grounds of genuineness or authenticity, the character of his Canon does not indicate the opinion of the Church as such in his day. Many early writers oppose him as a heretic. There is no reason to think that Irenæus rejected the seven books which he does not clearly use in the works that have come down to us. The argument from silence is never very dependable. The Muratorian Canon recognizes all but four or five of the books, and, if Westcott's view is correct, the Old Latin had all but two or three of them. Tertullian mentions all but a few of them; Cyprian does not refer to six or seven of them. Jerome and Augustine, however, accept all twenty-seven books, although the latter seems to have had some mental reservation regarding Hebrews. It will be noticed that in the West Hebrews was long opposed, and in the East the Apocalypse. Both East and West delayed for a considerable time the full recognition of some of the Catholic Epistles.

It is a remarkable fact that no early Church Council selected the books that should constitute the New Testament Canon. The books that we now have crushed out all rivals, not by any adventitious authority, but by their own weight and worth. This is in itself a strong proof of the genuineness and authenticity of the books that have survived. It is not until the close of the fourth century that any Council even discussed the subject. Let us note briefly what action the Councils did take.

The Council of Nicaea (325) and **The Damasine Council,** held at Rome (382), have not left us any deliverances on the Canon of the New Testament. At the former both the followers of Arius and Athanasius drew on the Scriptures for their arguments. The seven disputed books were recognized as a definite collection, but only Hebrews seems to have been quoted. But the Scriptures themselves were never the subject of discussion. And the so-called Damasine Decree which listed exactly the same books that we now have in our New Testaments has been shown to be unauthentic by von Dobschütz. It can no longer be cited as issuing from the Damasine Council.

The Council of Laodicea (363) was more properly a Synod. There were, one account says, only thirty-two members present, and another reading says only twenty-four. It must have been merely a local gathering. The 59th Canon of this "Council" requested that only the "canonized" books of both Old and New Testaments be read in Church. The so-called 60th Canon gave a list of these books, twenty-six in number, all but the Apocalypse. But this Canon is omitted in various manuscripts and versions, and has now been quite definitely shown to be unauthentic. The 59th Canon most probably meant all the books in our present Canon, save possibly the Apocalypse, but we cannot cite the so-called 60th Canon as proof of this fact.

The Third Council of Carthage (397) gives us the first Conciliar decision on the Canon. Augustine was an influential member of this Council. One of the Canons of this gathering demands that nothing be read in the Church under the title of divine Scripture except the "canonical" books. Then it gives a list of the books that are canonical, which embraces exactly our twenty-seven books. The Epistle to the Hebrews is rather curiously introduced. After listing "thirteen Epistles of the Apostle Paul," the Canon goes on to say, "one Epistle of the same writer to the Hebrews." This was perhaps done in order to show that the ground on which Hebrews was recognized was because it was Pauline in origin.

The Council of Hippo (419) in its Canons gives the Carthaginian list of twenty-seven books. However, it says directly, "fourteen Epistles of Paul," instead of the odd way in which this is said in the list of Carthage.

In conclusion we may set down the following definite facts regarding the formation of the New Testament Canon. There was no early counciliar action that determined which books should be recognized and which not; the selection and acceptance of the books was a spontaneous process that went on throughout the Church. As we have seen, at the close of the second century the New Testament contained essentially the same books which we now receive and they were regarded with the same respect that Christians have for them today. During the third century the canonicity of the so-called *antilegomena* was debated. In the East there was especial opposition to the Apocalypse; in the West, to the Epistle to the Hebrews. By the end of that century practically all the extra-canonical books had been dropped from the list of authoritative books. During the fourth century the debate concerning the Canon was practically concluded in the West. Undoubtedly the influence of Athanasius in the East as well as that of Jerome and Augustine in the West had much to do with this result. The action of the Third Council of Carthage (397) stabilized the decision reached, and from that time on there was little further opposition to any of the books in the West. In the East the debate with regard to some of the books was prolonged for some time further. Finally the influence of

Athanasius and the great Cappadocian fathers, and the example of the West, swept away all opposition. With the Philoxenian addition of 2 and 3 John, 2 Peter, Jude, and the Apocalypse to the Peshitta, the question was virtually closed in the East also. Thus we may say that for the West the question was practically closed by the end of the fourth century; for the East, by the close of the fifth century.

3. *The History of the Canon of the New Testament*

Although many things that have been said in the preceding section regarding the fortunes of the books of the New Testament in the third, fourth, and fifth centuries are of a historical character, the real history of the Canon does not begin until we get to the latter part of these centuries. We therefore begin this brief survey at this point.

The first thing of interest to note is the debate that arose concerning the "Letter to the Laodiceans." Paul had spoken of an "epistle from Laodicea" (Col. 4:16), and in the fourth century someone composed a letter to meet this description. It is nothing but a cento of phrases taken from the Apostle's writings, especially from his letter to the Philippians. Although probably written in Greek, we have only Latin copies of it today. It is about the length of 3 John and is really quite harmless. By the close of the fourth century it was widely circulated both in the East and in the West. Between the sixth and the fifteenth centuries it frequently appears among the Pauline Epistles. The Second Council of Nicæa (787) warned the people against it. It was translated into Old English and German, and occurs after Galatians in all High German Bibles from 1466 to the appearance of Luther's Bible. Finally the revival of learning killed it. In Spain there arose another slight problem regarding the Canon. The Visigoths had brought the Gothic New Testament with them, which did not have the Apocalypse. The influence of this version called forth the denunciation of the fourth Council of Toledo (633), with the threat of excommunication if any one did not accept the Apocalypse.

Apart from a few such minor differences as to the Canon, the verdict of the first four centuries remained the verdict of the Church during all the Middle Ages. Since the Church soon attained supremacy, it imposed its view of the Canon upon all. During the reign of Charlemagne there was a great unifying in all things religious. As time went on the Latin Bible passed more and more into the hands of the clergy, and the clergy and the councils opposed the idea of translating it into the newer languages. Finally the laity were forbidden to have books of the Old and New Testaments. In 1441 Pope Eugene IV. re-affirmed the Canon of Augustine, which originated more than a thousand years before. We may say, then, that from the fifth century to the fifteenth century there was no marked change in the view of the Canon.

During this time for the Roman Catholic the Church had come to have supreme authority in all ecclesiastical matters. The Bible, the creeds, the councils, and the opinions of the Fathers were the sources of doctrine, but the Church was the selector and expounder of all these materials. Consequently one of the first things the Reformers undertook to do was to break this insistence on ecclesiastical authority. They did this by substituting an infallible Bible for an infallible Church as their final authority. With this change of view the question of the Canon came once more to the fore.

Erasmus (in his Greek Testament, 1516) denied the Pauline authorship of Hebrews, but insisted on its value no matter who wrote it. He accepted James as canonical, but thought the Epistle in some respects unworthy of this recognition. Erasmus was criticized by the doctors in the Sorbonne for his outspokenness, as a result of which he became more reserved in his statements. Luther (1483-1546) gave the first place, doctrinally, to John's Gospel and his First Epistle, to Paul's Epistles, especially Romans, Galatians, and Ephesians, and to 1 Peter. He excluded Hebrews, James, Jude, and the Apocalypse from the "true and capital books of the New Testament," and for this reason he put them at the end of his translation of the New Testament, where they still appear in modern editions of Luther's version. He spoke of James as "a right strawy Epistle," but added, "compared with them [i. e., the sixteen books listed above], for it has no character of the Gospel in it." He said that every one must form his own opinion of the Apocalypse, but he did not think it either apostolic or prophetic; he seems to have doubted whether it should be in the Canon. Yet he declares that the true Christian can use it for consolation and warning. Carlstadt, an early friend of Luther, was the first to assert clearly the supremacy of the Scriptures. He seems, however, to ascribe differences of dignity to the books of the New Testament: the four Gospels stand highest, the thirteen Epistles of Paul, 1 Peter, and 1 John come next, and the seven disputed books come last. He does not mention Acts, but Westcott thinks he may have considered it a continuation of Luke's Gospel and so not have felt the need of mentioning it specifically.

Zwingli of Zürich (1484-1531) recognized all the books in our New Testament as of equal value, although he believed that occasionally the Bible was in error in matters of fact and history. Calvin of Geneva (1509-1564) passed over 2 and 3 John and the Apocalypse without notice. He heartily accepts the Epistle to the Hebrews, but does not believe that Paul wrote it. 2 Peter is not by Peter himself, but by one of his disciples, and so a valuable work. He unhesitatingly accepts the Epistles of James and Jude. Grotius of Leyden (1583-1645) held that Luke wrote Hebrews and James the Lord's brother, James. He denied the authenticity of 2 Peter, 2 and 3 John, and Jude. But strangely enough he accepted the Apocalypse as by the Apostle John.

The Council of Trent (1546) made the contents of the Bible an absolute article of faith. It listed all the books in our Old and New Testaments and the Old Testament Apocrypha as sacred and canonical and pronounced a curse upon anyone who does not so regard them. The Thirty-nine Articles of the Church of England (1562, 1571) and the Westminster Confession (1643) list the twenty-seven books by name. The Nonconformist Churches of England have accepted the identical Canon as the Established Church. The Lutheran and Reformed Churches have likewise accepted the same books as canonical.

In recent times there has been little discussion of the question of the Canon of the New Testament. There are perhaps few that would favor the omission of any of the books that we have in our English New Testament today, although many would ascribe varying degrees of value to the several books. The tendency at present is to accept them all because of their traditional recognition, but to lower their dignity and to bring up some of the extra-canonical writings to a canonical level. Scholars try to show that the New Testament and the extra-canonical writings have much in common. In other words, the present-day interest in the New Testament is more intellectual than spiritual. This is the logical consequence of the abandonment of the doctrine of verbal inspiration. While this is the popular trend at the present time, we have also a number of young scholars and leaders in Christendom today who firmly believe that Divine Providence has over-ruled in the selection of the books that should constitute the Canon, and who are convinced from their own study of the twenty-seven books in our New Testament that they are supernaturally inspired and stand on an entirely different plane from all of the extra-canonical books.

Chapter II

THE TEXT OF THE NEW TESTAMENT
The Materials of Textual Criticism

IN OUR study of the Canon we came to the conclusion that we have in our present New Testament the very books which God intended the Church to have; can we say that we have also the very text in which they were originally written? In reply we are obliged to admit that none of the originals are known to exist and that what we have is but copies of copies of the originals. When we turn to these copies we find that there is much agreement among them, as also considerable disagreement. A careful examination of the various manuscripts leads us to the conclusion that no one of them is perfect. In view of this situation we seem doomed to lose a part of the argument for an authoritative account of what the evangelists and apostles wrote; for if we cannot produce the original text, what is the value in having the books which they wrote?

But, thanks to the science of textual criticism, we can say with some confidence that we have the text that was in the original writings. We shall see later how small a percentage is still in doubt. Textual criticism undertakes to examine all the materials that have any bearing on the nature of the original text, to apply sound principles of criticism to the various readings, and to reproduce the original text. This science was formerly known as "Lower Criticism," but this term is not frequently used today. Textual Criticism is distinguished from "Higher Criticism," which is the study that we now commonly call *Special Introduction*.

It should be emphasized that Textual Criticism is no longer content with anything less than what may be regarded as the original text. There was a time when for various reasons textual critics adopted a lower aim. Bentley (1662-1742)

31

planned a Greek Testament that would correspond to the text of the fourth century; and so did Lachmann (1793-1851). Tregelles (1813-1875) aimed not simply to produce the text of the oldest manuscripts in existence, as these two had done, but to reproduce the oldest text obtainable. Westcott (1825-1901) and Hort (1828-1892), however, set out to restore the original text, as far as possible. That is, they undertook to go back of the text of the oldest manuscripts to all the literature that in any way throws light on the character of the original text. The purpose of Westcott and Hort has been the purpose of all textual critics since their day.

Since, then, our present critical Greek text is not based upon any one manuscript, but is prepared on the basis of all the textual evidence ascertainable, it becomes important for the student of the New Testament to acquire some understanding of the way in which it has been prepared. He should know about the materials at our disposal on which the investigation is based; he should also know something of the methods employed in dealing with these materials. We shall therefore endeavor to set forth in a brief way the most important facts concerning the materials and methods of textual criticism.

The Materials of Textual Criticism

By materials we here mean the documents that are available to us for the determination of the original text. There are three kinds of materials: the Greek manuscripts, the early versions, and the apostolic and church fathers. We shall attempt a brief survey of the nature and importance of these materials; but before we do this we shall say something of the form in which these materials were prepared and have come down to us.

It is fairly certain that the books of the New Testament were originally written on papyrus. The papyrus sheet was made from a reed that grew chiefly along the River Nile in Egypt. It became very brittle with age and easily rotted when it became damp. Egypt alone offered the exceptional conditions above the Delta that made the preservation of these documents possible. Papyrus is known to have been used as writing material in Egypt as far back as the twenty-seventh century before

Christ; parchment was used for this purpose at least as far back as B. C. 2000. Since the Greeks mainly used papyrus for their books from the fifth century B. C. to the fourth century A. D., since parchment was too expensive for ordinary usage, and since actual papyrus fragments of the New Testament have come down to us from the second and third centuries, we have reason to believe that the autographs of the books of the New Testament were written on this material.

Parchment and papyrus were often used side by side with each other, although one or the other might be more popular at a given time. Pliny represents Varo as saying that Eumenes II of Pergamum (B. C. 197-158) restored the use of parchment as writing material, because the Ptolemy of Egypt had laid an embargo on the exportation of papyrus. The books of the Old Testament were probably written on parchment in the days of Jesus and the apostles.[1] Paul requests Timothy to bring with him the "parchments" when he comes to Rome (2 Tim. 4:13). The terms "parchment" and "vellum" are today used practically interchangeably, although, strictly speaking, vellum refers to materials derived from calves and antelopes, and parchment to those made from the skins of sheep and goats. In the first century the use of papyrus again came to the front. We may say that from the first century to the beginning of the fourth we have the papyrus period; from the fourth century to the ninth, the vellum period; and from the ninth century to the fifteenth, the vellum and paper (from the 14th century onwards) period. More basic than the materials used in these periods is the style of writing employed in them. In early times the writing was done in a rough flowing style or in large characters, separately formed, called *uncials,* and in later times in a flowing or *cursive* hand.

As we have already indicated, the autographs of the New Testament were probably written on papyrus. During the first four centuries many copies of these books were made on the same material. A number of papyrus fragments of the New Testament from these centuries have come down to us, as we shall presently show. With the adoption of parchment, the preservation of the text was made possible in all the world,

---

1. Josephus, *Ant.* XII. ii, 11.

whereas the writing on papyrus could be preserved only in very dry climates. Then, too, the manufacture of papyrus was confined to the Delta, while parchment could be made anywhere. Thus the introduction of parchment helped in the spreading and preservation of the Scriptures. Some of the parchments were purple and highly ornamented. The great Greek texts that have come down to us (*Aleph* A, B, C, D, W, etc.) are all written on parchment. In the 14th century parchment was superseded by paper as a writing material. Paper, like printing, seems originally to have come from China; it was brought to Western Europe by the Arabs. The paper manuscripts of the Greek New Testament are all late and of little consequence for the purpose of textual criticism. Since printing was introduced in the latter part of the 15th century, we have very few manuscripts from that time onwards.

The originals of the New Testament books were probably prepared in the form of rolls, similar to the roll that was handed Jesus in the synagogue in Nazareth (Luke 4:20). Until recently it was supposed that the roll form of book continued up to the fourth century, until the time when vellum took the place of papyrus; but we now know that in the case of Christian literature at least, codices appear as early as the first half of the second century. There was then a papyrus codex before the appearance of the great vellum codices. This early introduction of the codex form, as we have already pointed out in our study of the Canon, made possible the early bringing together of a much larger quantity of matter than could be contained in a roll. Some papyrus codices have come down to us from the third century or earlier containing considerable portions of the Scriptures, as we shall see a little later. All our great vellum manuscripts of the Greek New Testament are likewise in codex form.

We now turn to the direct study of the materials of textual criticism, and take them up in the order indicated above.

1. *The Greek Manuscripts*

These are our most important materials for textual criticism. The theory that various books in our New Testament were originally written in Aramaic and that the respective books in our Greek Testament are but translations from this original, as Matthew (Zahn), John (Burney, Montgomery), all the Gospels (Torrey), the first half of Acts (Torrey), James (Burkitt), etc., is not likely to gain general acceptance. Most of the writers on New Testament Introduction reject it. Goodspeed has written a good refutation of these theories,[2] and Colwell has written a book from the same view-point.[3] We admit, of course, that there is a good bit of Aramaic coloring in some portions of some books, as in the early chapters of the Third Gospel, in the Book of Acts, and the Apocalypse, but that is not true of any book as a whole. The discovery of the papyri has done much to undermine this theory. It has shown that practically every supposed mistranslation in the Gospels appears as a regular idiom in the Greek papyri of the period; and the latter certainly are not translations from the Aramaic. Special problems of this nature will be dealt with in our study of the books involved. Suffice it to say here that no single copy of an Aramaic Gospel or Epistle has survived and that those who hold the theory of an original Aramaic for any book, are first obliged to reproduce the Aramaic before they can explain the supposed mistranslations. We turn, then, to the Greek manuscripts that have come down to us as our most important materials for textual criticism. These manuscripts are of three kinds: papyri, uncials, and minuscules or cursives.

(1) **The Papyri.** The use of papyrus as writing material was, as we have seen, known long ago, and a few specimens of papyri have been in our possession for a long time. Forty or fifty such rolls were found by some Arabs in 1778, of which one was brought to Europe. No one regarded them as of importance. Minor discoveries were made during the following century. The first large scale discovery was made in 1877, but they were of a fragmentary character and all of late date, and so aroused little interest until long afterwards. In 1890 the famous work of Aristotle on the Constitution of Athens was discovered. But the discovery in 1897 by Grenfell and Hunt of literally tons of Greek papyri at Oxyrhynchus was epoch-making. Neither these two young scholars nor anyone else probably dreamed of the far-reaching effects on New

2. *New Chapters in New Testament Study,* ch. VI.
3 *The Greek of the Fourth Gospel.*

Testament study this discovery would have. Since that time many other such discoveries have been made, and New Testament scholarship is only just beginning to benefit by the new light the papyri are throwing on the text of the New Testament. Inasmuch as there are among these papyri a number that contain portions of the New Testament itself, some from 100-150 years earlier than our oldest uncial manuscript, the significance of these discoveries for New Testament study can scarcely be overestimated. So many of these have come to light within the past fifty years, that while Kenyon knew of only one papyrus book that contained a portion of the Scriptures when he published the first edition of his *Our Bible and the Ancient Manuscripts* (1895), he could say in the fourth edition of this work (1939, reprinted in 1941): "Fifty-three papyri are now included in the official lists."[4] But even this does not include them all. The same writer declares that if we add all the fragments, whether earlier or later than our vellum manuscripts, the total would run up to 170.[5] We turn, therefore, to a brief description of the most important among the fifty-three on the official lists.

The writing on these early papyri is chiefly in a kind of coarse, flowing style, and sometimes in uncials. Punctuation, accents, and breathings are almost entirely wanting in these documents. Textual critics have designated them by an antique 𝔓 and a raised number. The majority of them are rather small fragments and have little importance, but some of the more recent discoveries are of great significance for textual study.

P[1] contains eighteen verses of Matthew 1 (vss. 1-9, 12, 13, 14-20). It is of the third century and has the Alexandrian* type of text.

P[4] has parts of Luke 1 (vss. 74-80), 5 (vss. 3-8, 30-39), and 6 (1-4). It is of the fourth century and has a text like that of Codex Vaticanus.

---

4. *Op cit.*, p. 124.
5. *Op cit.*, p. 105.
* The terminology used throughout the book to designate the class of text is that employed by Kenyon in *Our Bible and the Ancient Manuscripts* (1941), rather than that of Hort. The Alexandrian type of text is roughly Hort's Neutral text. See below, ch. III, esp. pp. 71-74.

P⁵ has thirty-two verses of John: 1:23-31, 33-41; 20:11-17, 19-25. In date it is of the third century and its text is generally like that of Codex Sinaiticus.

P¹³ contains Hebrews 2:14-5:5; 10:8-22, 29-11:13, 28-12:17. It was written late in the third century or early in the fourth. Its text is much like that of Codex Vaticanus and it supplies much of Hebrews that is wanting in B.

P³⁸ contains Acts 18:27-19:6, 12-16. It is of the fourth century, if not earlier. It clearly has a Western text, agreeing frequently with Codex Bezæ. P⁴⁸ also has this type of text. These fragments show that the Western type of text was in use even in Egypt.

But the most important members of the class we are now discussing are the Chester Beatty Papyri. Mr. Beatty about 1930 purchased a group of papyrus leaves from a dealer in Egypt, which proved to be portions of codices of various books of the Old Testament and the New Testament. They range from the second to the fourth centuries. The collection contains portions of seven manuscripts of the Old Testament and of three of the New, besides some extra-canonical writings. Kenyon has edited all the Biblical texts,[6] and photographic facsimiles are being made available. The three codices of the New Testament, when complete, would have contained all of the New Testament, except the Pastoral and Catholic Epistles. They are all from the third century or even earlier. They, therefore, give us a text of from 125 to 150 years earlier than that of Codex Vaticanus.

P⁴⁵ Chester Beatty Papyrus I. Originally this codex contained all the Four Gospels and the Acts, but only about one-seventh of the whole has come down to us. Kenyon says: "The extant remains consist of portions of two leaves of Matthew, six of Mark, seven of Luke, two of John, and thirteen of Acts."[7] In Mark its text is more like the Cæsarean than like either the Alexandrian or the Western; in Luke and John it is intermediate between the Alexandrian and the Western. This may indicate that the Cæsarean text developed in Egypt before Origen brought it to Cæsarea.

6. *The Chester Beatty Biblical Papyri*, fasc. i-vii, 1933-37.
7. *Our Bible and the Ancient Manuscripts*, p. 125.

P⁴⁶ Chester Beatty Papyrus II. This consists of eighty-six nearly perfect leaves, out of a total of 104, of the Pauline Epistles. The Epistle to Philemon and the Pastoral Epistles are not represented, but Hebrews is included. Kenyon thinks the manuscript was probably written at the beginning of the third century.[8] The text is nearer the Alexandrian than the Western family.

P⁴⁷ Chester Beatty Papyrus III. This manuscript contains Rev. 9:10—17:2, except for the loss of one or more lines at the top of each page. It is probably from the third century. Its text is more like the Alexandrian type than like any other.

P⁵² Rylands Papyrus 457. This scrap contains five verses of John 18 (vss. 31-33, 37, 38). Grenfell brought it to the John Rylands Library at Manchester in 1920, but it was not noticed until some time later, when Mr. Roberts identified it as the oldest remains of the New Testament that have come down to us. Kenyon says it may be "confidently assigned to the first half of the second century."[9] The discovery of this bit of papyrus in Egypt has done much to confirm the traditional date of the Gospel of John.

(2) **The Uncials.** The great vellum manuscripts are commonly classified according to the kind of writing that characterizes them. On this basis they fall into two classes: the uncials and the minuscules, the latter being also called cursives. The uncial manuscripts are those which are written in a kind of half-capital character. The term *uncial* is derived from Jerome's preface to his Latin translation of the Book of Job, in which he uses the phrase, *uncialibus, ut vulgo aiunt, litteris,* in objecting to the style in which books were written in his day. It apparently means "inch-long" letters. These letters were not only large, but were also formed singly without connection with other letters; the cursive style has ligatures and binds the letters together. Uncial writing is comparable to our printing the letters with pen or pencil as contrasted with writing them.

The number of uncials known to date is 212. Of these the great majority are mere fragments. *Aleph* alone contains the whole New Testament, but a considerable number of the others

8. *Op. cit.,* p. 127.
9. *Op. cit.,* p. 128.

contain substantial parts of it, while a few originally contained the whole of it. Some have complete copies of the Gospels; others, of the Acts; others, of the Catholic Epistles; still others, of the Pauline Epistles; and a few of the Apocalypse. Of these two, B and *Aleph,* are from the fourth century; six, A, C, D, W, Q, and T, from the fifth century; and the rest later than that.

The present system of notation was introduced by J. J. Wetstein (1751-52). He denoted the uncials by capital letters and the cursives by Arabic numbers. Since, however, only a few manuscripts contain the whole New Testament, it was deemed wise to divide the books into four groups and to give to each group its own notation. For a century this system served its purpose fairly well, although it always had definite handicaps. For instance, Codex Vaticanus, designated B, does not contain the Apocalypse; hence, when another manuscript which does contain it was designated B also, the notation did not indicate that the two were different manuscripts. So Codex Bezae, designated D, contains only the Gospels and Acts. When then Codex Claromontanus, which contains the Pauline Epistles, was also called D, it again could not be known from the notation that the two were different documents.

Tischendorf and Scrivener revised this system and gave each group of books a separate notation. Codex Vaticanus was continued as B, but the manuscript containing the Apocalypse was changed to B_2; Codex Bezae was continued as D, but Codex Claromontanus was changed to D_2; Codex Basiliensis, containing most of the Four Gospels, was continued as E, while Codex Laudianus, containing Acts, was changed to E_2, and Codex Sangermanensis, containing the Pauline Epistles, was changed to E_3. Sometimes the designations of B^{apoc}, D^{paul}, etc., are used for safer identification.

When, however, more and more uncials came to light, the difficulty of this method of notation increased. Gregory, therefore, introduced a revision of the original system which is still predominant. He used an antique 𝔓 with a number for the papyrus fragments. He continued the use of the Roman letters for the uncials, but confined one letter to one uncial manuscript, except in the case of D E F G H K L P, for which he continued the suppressed numeral for the second or third use made of them. He also added the Greek letters which are different from the Roman letters, and retained Tischendorf's ℵ. The series formerly known as O T W were abandoned. In the present system twenty-five letters of the English alphabet are used (all but J), together with D_2 E_2 E_3 F_2 G_3 H_2 H_3 K_2 L_2 P_2; the one Hebrew letter, ℵ; and nine letters of the Greek alphabet, Γ Δ Λ Ξ Π Σ Φ Ψ Ω This makes a total of forty five. For the remaining uncials Gregory introduced the use of numbers in heavy type prefixed by a zero. Thus we have 046, 047, etc. For the minuscules he retained the Arabic numbers in ordinary type, but he abolished the four groups; i. e., each number is used but once, irrespective of the contents of the manuscript to which it is assigned. The lectionaries are also designated by Arabic number, whether written in the uncial or minuscule style; but they are designated by *Evl.* when they contain the Gospels, and by *Apost.* when they have Acts or the Epistles. Gregory wants 1 put before the Arabic numeral for Gospel lectionaries, 1^2 for Epistle lectionaries, and $1+^2$ for the combination of Gospel and Epistle lectionaries. The system of Gregory is not ideal, but it has been so generally accepted that there is little hope of any immediate departure therefrom.

H. F. von Soden (between 1902 and 1913) worked out an elaborate new system of manuscript notation. His object was to facilitate reference and to set up a system that would at once indicate the contents of the manuscript and the century in which it was written. To do this he divided all manuscripts into three classes without regard to the distinction between uncials and minuscules, and assigned the symbol δ (διαθήκη) to a manuscript and a number indicating the century to which it belonged when it contained the whole New Testament or all but the Apocalypse; the symbol ε (εὐαγγέλιον) and a number when it contained only the Gospels; and the symbol α (ἀπόστολος) and a number when it contained the Acts and and the Epistles, with or without the Apocalypse.

But stupendous as was the labor von Soden put into this work (the four volumes of his *Die Schriften des Neuen Testaments in ihrer ältesten erreichbaren Textgestalt* contain more than 3000 quarto pages), the information his notation affords is of little value and the system becomes very complicated. The dating of many of the minuscules is not yet established with certainty, and so his classification by centuries is too dogmatic. Furthermore, the manuscripts that are of most importance are those which come from the first nine centuries; but von Soden puts them all into one class. It is important, for instance, to know whether a manuscript belongs to the 4th, 5th, or 6th century as distinguished from the 8th or 9th; but his classification does not tell us this. Then also the adoption of the new notation would require the mastery of two systems, the old and the new, since all the scholarly works of the past have used the old notation, and the student would be obliged to interpret the old in terms of the new and vice versa. Finally, the system becomes after all very complicated. The student who arduously masters it would, no doubt, be able to use it with facility; but the one who merely uses it for occasional investigation finds it very complicated. It is not necessary to trouble the student further with von Soden's numeration, since the vast majority of experts have expressly declared their preference for Gregory's system.

We must now proceed to a brief description of the most important uncial manuscripts. Six of these, because of their importance, may be called primary uncials. These will be introduced in the order of their textual importance. Inasmuch as Gregory for the first forty-five uncials added Arabic numerals with a zero prefixed to the alphabetical designation, both systems of notation will be used in this description.

B. *Codex Vaticanus* (03). It is generally agreed that this is the most valuable of all the manuscripts of the Greek New Testament. The complete codex contains 759 leaves; of these 142 belong to the New Testament. The general opinion is that it originated in Egypt, although Hort thinks in Rome, and Rendel Harris in Caesarea. It is possible that it originated in Egypt and was transferred to Caesarea to the library founded by Pamphilus and Eusebius. It has been in the Vatican Library at Rome at least since 1481. Price says it was brought to Rome by Pope Nicholas V in 1448.[10] Though the document

---

10. *The Ancestry of Our English Bible*, p. 150.

was known to exist as early as this, the Vatican authorities allowed no one access to it. In 1669 Bartolocci made a collation of it, but his work remained unknown until 1819. Other imperfect collations were made later. Napoleon brought the manuscript to Paris, where the Catholic scholar Hug discovered its value. It was returned to Rome in 1815, where it was again secluded. Even Tischendorf in 1843 was allowed to study it for only six hours in two days, and later in 1866 he was allowed to examine it for but forty-two hours. Prior to that a friend supplied Erasmus with a few readings from this manuscript, but they came too late for use in his Greek Testament. In 1868-81, however, the Papal authorities themselves issued an edition of its text, and in 1889-90 a photographic facsimile of the whole manuscript appeared.

Codex Vaticanus is from the fourth century. Hug dated it in the middle of that century, and this is the opinion generally held today. In the New Testament it stops at Heb. 9:13 and so has lost all the rest of Hebrews, the Pastoral Epistles, Philemon, and the Apocalypse. It has three narrow columns to the page. Two correctors have written in various changes, the one being apparently nearly contemporary with the manuscript, the other, from the tenth or eleventh century. In the Gospels and the Acts this manuscript is the best representative of the Alexandrian class, but in the Pauline Epistles it has besides the Alexandrian also Western readings. Streeter thinks B represents the recension of Hesychius and that the later Alexandrian texts are degenerations from it.[11]

ℵ. *Codex Sinaiticus* (01). This is our second most important uncial. It was discovered by Tischendorf in 1844 in the monastery of St. Catherine on Mt. Sinai. On his visit there on that occasion he was able to rescue 43 leaves of the Old Testament from the waste basket of the monastery. These he brought to Leipzig and published soon thereafter. Tischendorf returned in 1853, but did not succeed in obtaining any additional manuscripts. But in 1859, when he again visited the monastery, he made the greatest discovery of all. It consisted of the entire remaining portions of the codex, namely of a great part of the Old Testament, all of the New Testament, the Epistle

---

11. *The Four Gospels,* p. 125.

of Barnabas, and the Shepherd of Hermas (incomplete). In all he now found 346½ leaves, which with the 43 leaves he had previously obtained, make a total of 389½ leaves that we have in our possession. Each page has four narrow columns, with 48 lines to the column. Tischendorf presented the manuscript to the Czar of Russia in November of the same year, but was permitted to take it with him to Leipzig for the preparation of his full edition of the codex. It was returned to the Imperial Library of St. Petersburg in 1869, where it remained until 1933, at which time it was sold by the U. S. S. R. to the British Museum for one-half million dollars. The Czar of Russia had paid the monks about $6,750.00 for it. It is now in the British Museum, except for Tischendorf's original discovery of 43 leaves, which is still at Leipzig. A photographic facsimile was produced in 1911 and is now available to scholars. This codex, too, probably originated in Egypt. Tischendorf thought it entirely possible that *Aleph* and B might be two of the fifty copies that Constantine, in 331, ordered Eusebius to prepare for the churches of Constantinople. He suggests that Justinian might have sent *Aleph* to the convent of Mt. Sinai, which he had founded.[12]

This codex, too, is from the fourth century, but apparently from the last part of the century, for it contains the Ammonian sections and the Eusebian canons in the Gospels, which Codex Vaticanus does not have. Gregory advances eleven reasons for assigning it to this century.[13] It has a total of seven correctors. Its text is mixed, now Alexandrian like B, now Western like D. The infiltration of the Western text into both *Aleph* and B is probably due to the close connection between Alexandria and Rome. Clement of Alexandria had lived many years in Southern Italy and came to Egypt rather late in life. He undoubtedly brought his copy of the Scriptures with him to Egypt, and from him and other Christians who came to Alexandria from Rome Western readings may easily have been introduced into the Alexandrian text. This is Streeter's view of the phenomenon[14] and it is very plausible, if we may believe that both these great manuscripts originated in Egypt. Tisch-

12. Price, *The Ancestry of Our English Bible*, p. 146 f.
13. *The Canon and Text of the New Testament*, p. 338.
14. *The Four Gospels*, p. 57 f.

endorf's 8th edition of the Greek Testament was based primarily on *Aleph* and B and is said to differ from his 7th edition in more than 3000 places.

A. *Codex Alexandrinus* (02). Cyril Lucar, Patriarch of Constantinople, offered this manuscript to King James I in 1624, but since James died before the gift arrived it was presented to his successor, Charles I, in 1627. It remained in the possession of the British rulers until the Royal Library was presented to the nation by George II, when it was placed in the British Museum. The story is that Lucar brought it from Alexandria when he transferred from that see to Constantinople in 1621. It was called "Alexandrinus" because, it was believed, it had come from Alexandria, and "A" because it was the first important uncial that was used by Biblical scholars. An Arabic note at the beginning of the manuscript says that it was given to the Patriarchal Library at Cairo by "Athanasius the humble," probably Athanasius III, who died about 1308; but a deacon of Cyril's declared that Cyril obtained it from Mt. Athos in 1616. If the latter be true, the manuscript has a connection with Constantinople rather than Alexandria, which would harmonize with the character of its text. Streeter thinks that it probably originated in some place like Caesarea or Beirut.[15]

This manuscript is from the first half of the fifth century. It now has 773 leaves of the original 822. The New Testament with the Epistles of Clement occupies 143 of these leaves. It has two columns to the page, whereas, as we have seen, Sinaiticus has four and Vaticanus three. In the New Testament it lacks Matthew 1:1-25:6; John 6:50-8:52; 2 Cor. 4:13-12:6. The manuscript appears to have been written by three different hands; there are also several correctors, but only one that is really important. In the Gospels it is the oldest and best example of the Byzantine text of the fourth century. But outside the Gospels its text is Alexandrian, ranking definitely with B and *Aleph*. Kenyon thinks that it is "perhaps an even better example of that class than they."[16] It is our best manuscript for the Apocalypse, unless it should be P[47] Streeter thinks

---

15. *The Four Gospels,* p. 120.
16. *Our Bible and the Ancient Manuscripts,* p. 138.

that this is the earliest Greek manuscript that gives us approximately the text of Lucian, but a small proportion of the readins seems to be earlier. He also thinks that the non-Byzantine element in A represents mainly, if not wholly, the *fam. Theta* text.[17]

C. *Codex Ephraemi Rescriptus* (04). This codex is now in the National Library of Paris. Early in the 16th century it was brought from the East to Italy, and then shortly thereafter by Catharine de Medici from Italy to Paris. This manuscript, as the epithet of its Latin title indicates, is a *palimpsest* (which means "rubbed off again"). The original was partly rubbed off, probably in the 12th century, and the sermons of Ephraem, a Syrian Father of the early 4th century, written over it. Near the end of the 17th century a student in the Royal Library discovered traces of a text underneath the sermons; but it was not until 1834 that any good progress was made in reading the underlying text. The original was brought to light by means of a specially prepared acid. Tischendorf was the first to read it successfully. This was in 1840-1841. Though it, too, once contained the whole Greek Bible, it now has only 64 leaves of the Old Testament and 145 leaves of the original 238 of the New Testament.

It is of the fifth century, perhaps a little later than Codex Alexandrinus. Two correctors have been at work upon it. It has but one column to a page, but the superimposed writing is in two columns. Parts of every book in the New Testament are represented, except 2 Thessalonians and 2 John. Its text is more mixed than that of any other manuscript; but Scrivener puts it about midway between A and B, inclining somewhat to the latter. Kenyon, however, thinks that it agrees perhaps oftenest with the Byzantine type of text.

D. *Codex Bezae* (05). There is no general agreement as to the place where this manuscript originated; Egypt, Rome, Italy, North Africa have all been suggested. Beza, the disciple and successor of Calvin in Geneva, procured it from the monastery of St. Irenaeus at Lyons in 1562, and presented it to the University of Cambridge in 1581, where it still is. The manuscript is bilingual, having the Greek text on the left-hand page,

---

17. *Op. cit.,* pp. 119, 579.

and the Latin text on the right-hand. It has 406 leaves, but must have had about 510 originally. It has one column to the page, like Codex Ephraemi Rescriptus. It is undoubtedly the most curious, though not the most trustworthy, manuscript known to us. The Greek and Latin texts may have arisen from independent authorities, but it seems clear that in this codex they have been in some measure assimilated to one another. Stephanus used some of the readings of this manuscript in the margin of his Greek Testament in 1550, and Beza also made some use of it in the later editions of his Greek Testament. Thos. Kipling published its text in full in 1793; Scrivener published a new edition of it in 1864; and in 1889 a photographic facsimile of it was published.

The presence of the Latin text in the manuscript is proof in itself that it was written in western Europe, where Latin was the common language. It contains the four Gospels, Acts, and the Latin text of 3 John 11-15. The Gospels are in the usual Western order: Matthew, John, Luke, and Mark. It is the best example of the Western type of text. On the whole it is nearer to the African than the European Latin. It has a number of additions and some omissions of words, sentences, and incidents. An interesting addition is found after Luke 6:4: "On the same day, seeing one working on the sabbath day, he said unto him, Man, if thou knowest what thou doest, blessed art thou; but if thou knowest not, thou are accursed and a transgressor of the law." In Acts 15:20, D omits "and from things strangled." In the account of Paul's travels this document and its allies have so many variations as to suggest, in the estimation of some, that they represent a separate edition of the Book of Acts or, if not that, that a scribe who lived in that country and was acquainted with local traditions added details to the original document. Streeter assigns it to the fifth century;[18] this is also the opinion of Kenyon and of scholars in general today,[19] although Gregory had put it into the sixth century.[20]

W. *Codex Washingtonianus* I (032). This manuscript was purchased by Mr. C. L. Freer of Detroit in Cairo, Egypt, in

---

18. *Op cit.*, p. 67.
19. *Our Bible and the Ancient Manuscripts*, p. 144.
20. *The Canon and Text of the New Testament*, p. 351.

1906. It has 187 leaves and contains only the four Gospels. They appear in the Western order. It is apparently from the late fourth or fifth century. In all of Matthew and from Luke 8:13 to the end, W has chiefly a Byzantine type of text. In the first seven chapters of Luke and in John 5:12 to the end its text is mainly of the Alexandrian type. In Mark 1:1-5:30 W agrees almost word for word with the old Latin version, and in Mark 5:31-16:8 Streeter says W is the oldest, though not quite the purest, authority for the Caesarean type of text.[21] It is now in the Freer Collection of the Library at Washington. In 1912 Prof. H. A. Sanders of the University of Michigan published a photographic facsimile of it.

We must content ourselves with a very brief word concerning some of the rest of the important uncials. Students can find a good description of a considerable number of them in Kenyon's revised edition of *Our Bible and the Ancient Manuscripts,* pp. 147-153.

D_2. *Codex Claromontanus* (06). It was found at Clermont, France, and at one time belonged to Beza. It was brought to Paris in 1656 where it still is. This codex has only the Pauline Epistles and, like D, is bilingual, containing both Greek and Latin texts. It is probably from the sixth century and is our leading Western authority for the text of the Epistles.

E. *Codex Basiliensis* (07). This is an eighth century copy of the Four Gospels with some lacunae. It has the Byzantine type of text. It is now in Basle, Switzerland.

E_2. *Codex Laudianus* (08). It contains only the Book of Acts. It is bilingual, but has the Latin text on the left and the Greek text on the right, the opposite of D and D_2. This codex has the Western type of text and is probably from the seventh century. It is in the Bodleian Library at Oxford.

E_3 *Codex Sangermanensis.* This manuscript has only the Pauline Epistles, and is merely a copy of D_2, made near the end of the ninth century. It has no independent value for textual criticism.

L. *Codex Regius* (019). This codex contains all the Gospels except for a few small lacunae. Though assigned to the eighth century by scholars, it seems to contain a very early

21. *The Four Gospels,* pp. 69, 599.

text, having many Alexandrian readings. It has not only the long ending of Mark 16 (i.e., vss. 9-20), but also an alternate short ending. It is now in the National Library at Paris.

T. *Codex Borgianus* (029). It contains 179 verses of Luke and John in both the Greek and Sahidic Languages. Its text is almost entirely Alexandrian; Hort ranked it next to B and *Aleph* in excellence. It is probably from the 5th century, and is now in Rome.

Theta. *Codex Koridethianus*. Formerly this letter was given to a number of uncial fragments, but it has now been assigned to a most important newly discovered manuscript. The document was discovered in a valley of the Caucasus, but belonged to a monastery at Koridethi at a much earlier date. Streeter hails the discovery as comparable in importance to that of *Aleph* and the Sinaitic Syriac, although for a different reason.[22] Beerman and Gregory published it in 1913, and that is the first time that its complete text became available to scholars, since the manuscript is now in the Library of Tiflis. It has only the Gospels and probably belongs to the eighth century. For the most part its text is the Byzantine type, but in Mark it is so nearly akin to two well-known groups of minuscules, namely, 1-118-131-209 and 13-69-124-346, that they have together come to be regarded as a single family, namely the Family *Theta*. Streeter has given the name of Caesarean text to this family, and most textual critics seem inclined to recognize the classification.

(3) **The Minuscules.** From the eighth century on codices begin to appear in the minuscule or cursive style of writing. In the tenth century, with the increasing demand for books, the cumbrous uncial style finally gave way to the flowing cursive style. Private documents had been written in this style for a long time, but now it came to be used for literary purposes also. Minuscule writing was developed from uncial writing. The word "minuscule" (fr. Latin, *minusculus,* rather small) is opposed to "majuscule" (somewhat greater or great). It means a small letter as distinguished from a capital or uncial. But the letters were not only smaller than the uncials, they were also, in some cases, different from them in form. Since the

---

22. *Op. cit.,* p. 79.

minuscule forms lend themselves readily to combination with other letters into a running hand, they are often referred to as "cursives."

The total number of extant minuscules runs up into the thousands. Kenyon says (1941) the number on the official list now is 2429,[23] but a good many have not yet been put on this list. They range in date from the ninth to the sixteenth century. Kenyon said in his *Textual Criticism of the New Testament* (1926 reprint), that "only forty-six complete minuscule copies of the New Testament are known" (p. 132), but this number has, no doubt, been augmented by this time. Minuscule manuscripts are designated by Arabic numerals. At first the four main divisions: the Gospels, Acts and the Catholic Epistles, the Pauline Epistles, and the Apocalypse, were numbered independently of each other; but Gregory revised this system also and brought about a more continuous notation, irrespective of the group that was meant. But a number of the older numbers were retained and the system is not fully satisfactory as yet.

Since the minuscules are later than the uncials, they are, as a class, of less importance than the uncials. But there are exceptions to this rule. The text of a cursive is not necessarily later than that of an uncial, and some late cursives must be treated like the older uncials.[24] Streeter regards several cursives as quite as important as the uncials A C W, and more important than any other uncial than B ℵ D L Θ A C W. [24a] H. von Soden's statement is even stronger, perhaps too strong. He says: "Minuscule codices afford not infrequently a much older and more interesting text than the uncials."[25]

Limitations of space do not permit of extended comment on the minuscules. Their value depends, like that of all the other manuscripts, upon the approximation of their text to that of the original. Some of these run in groups and show a kinship that can be traced back to the same uncial. We look first briefly at several of these groups, and then also at a few of the best individual documents.

---

23. *Op. cit.*, p. 153.
24. Streeter, *op. cit.*, p. 49 f.   24a. *Op. cit.*, p. 48.
25. *Die Schriften des Neuen Testaments*, I, 33. In German: "Minuskelcodices bieten nicht selten einen viel älteren und interessanteren Text als Mejuskelcodices."

Family 1 consists of minuscules 1 (tenth century), 118 (thirteenth century), 131 (eleventh century), and 209 (twelfth century). Kirsopp Lake investigated this group in 1902; and although it agrees frequently with ℵ B L, it now forms part of the Caesarean text. Erasmus used 1 in the second edition of his Greek Testament (1519), although in the main he used 2 in the Gospels, a poor minuscule of the twelfth century.

Family 13 consists of minuscules 13, 69, 124, 346, which are all of the twelfth century except 69, which is of the fourteenth or fifteenth. This group is also known as the Ferrar group, since W. H. Ferrar of Dublin first showed that they come from a common original. Minuscules 230, 543, 788, 826, 828, 983, 1689, and 1709 are now also included in the Ferrar group. As a family they have the Caesarean text. All in this group give the pericope about the adulterous woman (John 7:53-8:11) after Luke 21:38.

Minuscule 33 contains the Gospels, Acts, and the Epistles. It is of the ninth century and is now at Paris. Nestle calls it the "queen of the cursives,"[26] and Hort had the same high regard for it.

Minuscule 81 contains the Book of Acts. It was written in 1044, and is now in the British Museum. It ranks in quality with the best of the uncials, having in many cases the Alexandrian type of text.

Minuscule 157 has only the four Gospels. It is of the twelfth century and is now in the Vatican Library. Zahn claims that its text sometimes approaches that of Marcion; Hort said that it resembled the cursive 33; and Streeter classifies it as Caesarean in the type of its text.

Minuscule 565 contains the Gospels. It is of the ninth or tenth century, and is now in Leningrad. Streeter regards it as the most important ally of Θ in Mark.[27] In this Gospel it has a text akin to the Caesarean type.

Minuscule 1582 was recently discovered in the Vatopedi Monastery on Mt. Athos. Streeter regards it as of the tenth century and as the only one of the *fam.* 1 group of manuscripts that is equal in importance with 1.[28] It has the pericope of the

---

26. *Textual Criticism of the Greek New Testament*, p. 85.
27. *Op. cit.*, p. 49.
28. *Op. cit.*, p. 80.

adulterous woman (John 7:53-8:11) at the end of John, but
adds that it is not commented on by Chrysostom, Cyril of Alexandria, and Theodore of Mopsuestia. It also gives Mark
16:9-20 as a kind of appendix, but adds in the margin at vs.
19: "Irenaeus, who was near to the apostles, in the third book
against heresies quotes this saying as found in Mark."[29]

(4) **Lectionaries.** These are reading lessons that were used
in the public services of the church and do not have a continuous
text. They usually have an opening formula, such as, "On a
certain occasion," or, "The Lord said." There are also certain omissions from and alterations of the Biblical texts in the
lectionaries to adapt them for public reading. For this reason
they have been treated as of little value for textual criticism in
the past. But in recent years there has come a change of opinion. Gregory already perceived that the lectionaries are conservative in the type of text they use. He said they "avoid every new sentence, every new word, every new syllable, every
new tone."[30] Colwell and Riddle take the same view in the
series known as *Studies in the Lectionary Text of the New
Testament* now in process of publication. For this reason they
are valuable for textual criticism. More than 1600 of them are
known to exist. Those which have the Gospel lessons are called
Evangeliaria or *Evangelistaria* (*Evl.*); those which have the
Acts or Epistles, *Apostoli or Praxapostoli* (*Apost.*). They appear from the sixth century and onward. The majority of them
are written in the uncial hand. They are referred to by Arabic
numerals. The character of their text is not as yet well known,
although Robertson thinks that they "give some support to the
Western text, besides the Syrian."[31] We are anxious to know
whether they also have the Caesarean and the Alexandrian type
of text, and in what proportion.

2. *The Ancient Versions*

These are our second source of material for the reconstruction of the Greek text. The importance of the versions will be
evident when we observe that the Syriac and Latin translations

---

29. Quoted by Streeter, *op. cit.*, p. 124.
30. *Textkritik des Neuen Testaments*, S. 327.
31. *Textual Criticism of the New Testament*, p. 96.

of the New Testament were made about two hundreds years before Codex Vaticanus was written; the latter, as we have said, was written about A. D. 350, but the former were written about 150. The earliest Egyptian version was made about A. D. 200, 150 years before Vaticanus appeared. We are seeking for the original Greek text; and insofar as we can reproduce the original text of the Syriac or Latin translations, we can generally determine what kind of Greek text the translator used, i. e., the text that is about two hundred years older than that of our best uncial.

The versions appear first in the remoter parts of the countries to which the Gospel was early introduced. Three of these, because of their age and general character, are of special importance for textual study and may be called our *primary* versions. They are the Syriac, the Egyptian, and the Latin versions. We now proceed to a brief description of them.

(1) **The Syriac Versions.** Christianity was early introduced to Antioch (Acts 11:19), almost a second capital of the Roman world, a rival of Alexandria and Ephesus. Now while Greek was dominant in Antioch, Syriac was spoken in Syria, and Mesopotamia in general, and with some differences of dialect in Palestine, where it was known as Aramaic in the days of Christ and the Apostles. As long, then, as the Gospel was confined to Antioch, Greek was sufficient; but when it went inland to Damascus, Edessa, etc., the need arose for a Syriac translation. Several such translations were made and have come down to us, and we now turn to examine them briefly.

(a) *Tatian's Diatessaron.* As we have seen above, Tatian the Syrian, also called the Assyrian, about A. D. 170, prepared a harmony of the four Gospels by interweaving the materials in the Gospels into a continuous story. He did this either just before or immediately after leaving Rome. Some think that he wrote it originally in Syriac; others think that he first wrote it in Greek and on his return to Syria he or someone under his guidance translated it into Syriac. Gregory[32] and Kenyon[33] incline to the latter view. The recently discovered Dura fragment, from the upper Euphrates, containing fourteen im-

---

32. *The Canon and Text of the New Testament*, p. 399.
33. *Our Bible and the Ancient Manuscripts*, p. 156.

perfect lines of the *Diatessaron* in Greek, coming from the first half of the third century, supports the view that the original work was in Greek; however, this is not absolute proof, since Dura was a commercial town and military fortress, and there were, no doubt, many civilians as well as soldiers who could not speak Syriac.

But in whatever language it was originally written, it is the Syriac text of the harmony that principally circulated in Syria until the fourth century. Gregory thinks that Syriac translations of the separate Gospels appeared before the *Diatessaron* and influenced the text of the latter;[34] but Streeter points out that in Syria the "Separate Gospels" were very little used while the Diatessaron was known as "the Gospel."[35] We have it only in two manuscripts of an Arabic translation of the 11th century, edited by Ciasca in 1888 (except for the small Dura fragment). The text of the *Diatessaron* is Western in the true sense of the term, being closer to D and the European Latin than to the Old Syriac version. Robertson, however, says that it has some affinities also with the text of B and *Aleph*.[36]

(b) *The Old Syriac Version.* The very existence of this version is a discovery of the last century. It was formerly supposed that the Peshitta was from the second century and so the earliest translation of the New Testament into Syriac; but the discovery of a mass of documents in 1842 in Egypt and the examination of some eighty leaves among them of the Gospels in Syriac, have overthrown this opinion. Now we know that there was an Old Syriac version much older than the Peshitta, originating about the same time as the Diatessaron, or even a little earlier. Two manuscripts of this version have come down to us and we now turn to an examination of them.

The Sinaitic Syriac is somewhat the older of the two, although it was discovered later. Mrs. Lewis and Mrs. Gibson, of Cambridge, twin sisters, discovered it in the Monastery of St. Catherine on Mount Sinai, in 1892, where Tischendorf had discovered *Aleph* in 1844. It is a palimpsest and contains the greater part of the four Gospels. Burkitt and Bensly declared it to be a copy of the Old Syriac and to contain a second cen-

34. *Op. cit.*, p. 400.
35. *Op. cit.*, p. 10.
36. *Textual Criticism of the New Testament*, p. 108.

tury text. It differs considerably from the second manuscript, yet scholars believe that it represents the same version. It has, for instance, the remarkable reading in Matt. 1:16: "Jacob begat Joseph, and Joseph, to whom was betrothed Mary the Virgin, begat Jesus who is called Christ." The second manuscript has the more orthodox reading. Moffatt, in his *A New Translation of the New Testament,* has taken over this reading by way of von Soden's Greek text. The manuscript is still at Mt. Sinai, but it has been carefully copied and photographed, and in 1894 Mrs. Lewis published a translation of it into English. Kenyon[37] would classify it as the Syriac text, separating it from the Western family; but Streeter thinks it has affinities with the Caesarean text.[38] Further study needs to be made of this point.

The Curetonian Syriac is named after Wm. Cureton of the British Museum, who formally published it in 1858. It has only the Gospels and belongs to the fifth century. It represents a somewhat later form of the Old Syriac than the Sinaitic, having been to some extent revised on the basis of later Greek manuscripts. It was brought to the British Museum in 1842 from Egypt, along with many other Syriac manuscripts. Apparently to distinguish it from the combined text of Tatian's *Diatessaron,* this manuscript has at the beginning of Matthew the title, *Evangelion da-Mepharreshe,* which is usually understood to mean, "The Gospel of the Separated Ones." Its text is more Western than is that of the Sinaitic Syriac. As a whole, Streeter maintains that the Greek text from which the Old Syriac is translated is closer to that of *fam. Theta* than to that of any other Greek text known to exist.[39] Of the Old Syriac version of the rest of the New Testament we know practically nothing, except that the Older Assyrian Church had the Epistles of Paul, and three Catholic Epistles, 1 John, 1 Peter, and James. Ephraim in his commentary gives us a little help, but we have it only in an Armenian translation.

(c) *The Peshitta Syriac.* This was formerly regarded as the oldest of the Syrian versions; but Burkitt has shown that it is in reality a revision of the Old Syriac made by Rabbula, Bishop

37. *Our Bible and the Ancient Manuscripts,* p. 179.
38. *Op. cit.,* p. 74 f.
39. *Op. cit.,* p. 89.

of Edessa, about the year 425. This view is now held by nearly all Syriac scholars. Rabbula apparently used a manuscript
that had the Byzantine text. Since Constantinople was at this
time the center of the Church in the East, this text spread all
over that area. Consequently we find that the text of the great
bulk of the Greek manuscripts agrees with the Peshitta Syriac.
Gwilliam, Burgon, and Miller defended the older view that the
Peshitta originated in the second century, but they could not
substantiate their view. The text of the Peshitta is now identified as the Byzantine text, which almost certainly goes back
to the revision made by Lucian of Antioch about A. D. 300.
This text, as Streeter points out, follows alternately or, if possible, combines Alexandrian, Western, and Eastern texts; yet
it is nearer to the Alexandrian than to the Western type.[40]
Generally speaking, this is the text of the *Textus Receptus*
and of the Authorized Version of the Bible. The total number
of manuscripts that preserve more or less of the Peshitta is
243, of which almost one-half are in the British Museum. Two
of them are from the fifth century and a dozen others from
the sixth.

(d) *The Philoxenian* or *Harkleian Syriac*. In 508 Philoxenus, bishop of Mabug, in Eastern Syria, had the Peshitta revised by Polycarp. The manuscripts that are known to us contain only the books not in the Peshitta, viz., 2 and 3 John, 2
Peter, Jude, and the Apocalypse. The version is named after
the bishop and seems to have been made from a fairly pure
text, although it was the Byzantine type of text. In A. D. 616
Thomas of Harkel, later also bishop of Mabug, with the assistance of some Greek manuscripts, revised the Philoxenian version. The revision was extremely literal, whereas the Philoxenian version had been a free rendering, and was based on
Western manuscripts. About fifty manuscripts of this version
are known to exist, but all are in the Harkleian revision. Most
of them are in England.

(e) *The Palestinian Syriac* is known to us only in fragments
and in a dialect that is different from all the other versions. It
is thought to have originated in the sixth century and to have
been used exclusively in Palestine. It has a mixed text. It has

40. *Op. cit.,* pp. 113, 117.

the interesting reading in Matt. 27:17, "Jesus Barabbas," found in very few Greek manuscripts, but which Souter thinks is probably the right reading.[41] Fragments of this version are found in Rome, London, Leningrad, and at Mt. Sinai.

(2) **The Egyptian or Coptic Versions.** Many Jews lived in Egypt, especially in Alexandria, and Christianity early found its way into this country. Apollos was a Jew from Alexandria who knew the baptism of John (Acts 18:24, 25). In lower Egypt cultivated persons had spoken Greek at least as far back as the time of Alexander. The libraries of Alexandria contained practically all the literature of Greece. In this city also the Septuagint version was begun (c. B. C. 285) and Philo the Jew (c. B. C. 30—A. D. 50) did his great literary work. Egypt was under the special care of the Roman emperors and was guarded jealously. This gave it a kind of political isolation, which, together with its scholarly traditions, made it suitable for the better preservation of the text of the New Testament during the time when it was freely handled in the West. As is generally granted today, our most accurate documents come from Egypt. It is only when the Gospel penetrated to the degraded original Egyptians that a translation into the Egyptian dialects became imperative.[42] Manuscripts of three of these dialects have come down to us. We now turn to examine them briefly.

(a) *The Sahidic* or *Thebaic Version.* This version was current in upper Egypt, where one would naturally first expect a translation. It was unknown until near the end of the 18th century. J. Pierpont Morgan owns complete copies of Matthew, Mark, John, thirteen Epistles of Paul, Hebrews, 1 and 2 Peter. and the three Epistles of John; besides this we have numerous fragments of the version. Horner has prepared an almost complete Sahidic New Testament from these manuscripts and fragments. Some fragments go back to the fifth and even the fourth century. Its text is mainly like that of B and *Aleph,* although it also has some Western readings. It is probably the oldest of the Egyptian versions, going back to about A. D. 200.

---

41. *The Text and Canon of the New Testament,* p. 63.
42. *Souter,* op. cit., p. 65.

(b) *The Bohairic* or *Memphitic Version.* This version was current in lower (northern) Egypt and first became known near the end of the 17th century. More than a hundred manuscripts have come down to us, but none is very early. Bohairic was the most literary dialect of Egypt and ultimately superseded all the other dialects. The Bohairic version is the official version of the Coptic Church today. Horner produced a critical edition of it in 1898-1905. The text is mainly Alexandrian, having little mixture of Western readings and practically none of the Byzantine type. All but two copies have the last twelve verses of Mark. It is the best of the Egyptian versions and probably originated in the first half of the third century.

(c) *The Middle Egyptian Versions.* The remaining Egyptian versions have only recently been discovered and are still not well known. The *Fayumic* was current in the Fayum, and seems related to the Sahidic. The *Bashmuric,* or *Middle Egyptian* proper, comes from the region of Memphis and is also related to the Sahidic. The *Akhmimic* comes from the region of Akhmim, ancient Panopolis; this is thought to be the earliest dialect of the Egyptian language. We have only fragments of the New Testament in this dialect. Kenyon thinks our knowledge of the Egyptian versions will be greatly increased in the near future.[43]

(3) **The Latin Versions.** With the influx into Rome of many Greeks after the fall of Corinth in B. C. 146, Greek culture and the Greek language rapidly came to the fore in the imperial city. All people became bilingual, speaking both Greek and Latin. Paul wrote his Epistle to the Romans and Clement of Rome wrote to the Church at Corinth, in Greek. For nearly two centuries all the bishops of Rome had Greek names. Even Irenæus and Hippolytus wrote in Greek. It was only when Christianity reached the lower strata of society and the very remote sections that a translation was called for. With the setting up of the eastern empire, however, early in the fourth century, there came a change. Henceforth in the West a knowledge of Greek became confined to the educated class, and a translation was needed. Only in the province called "Africa," annexed to Rome in B. C. 146, was it different.

---

43. *Op. cit.,* p. 168.

Here Latin was the language of state and society. It is probable that the Gospel came to this province from Rome, but we do not really know. Here a translation was early called for. We now turn to examine briefly the Latin translations of the New Testament of which we know.

(a) *The Old Latin Versions.* It seems as if there were but two Old Latin versions, the African and the European. Augustine deplored the fact that so many had undertaken to translate the New Testament into Latin, and recommended that the *Itala* version be given the preference. Wordsworth and White, Westcott and Hort, Gregory, and Kenyon either hold or incline to the view that this refers to a third Old Latin version; but Burkitt and Zahn argue that Augustine had reference to Jerome's Vulgate. This view is supported by the fact that in his extended quotations in the latter part of his life Augustine certainly used the Vulgate. Perhaps absolute certainty cannot as yet be attained on this point; but we adopt the view that there were two Old Latin versions and grant that there may have been a third. All Latin versions are represented by small italic letters, irrespective of their supposed genealogical descent.

The African Latin. Since Latin was the language of state and society in North Africa, the need for a Latin translation of the New Testament first arose in this area. Tertullian often translated the Greek text for himself, but he also definitely quotes Latin translations of Luke, John, Galatians, 1 Corinthians, Romans, and Ephesians, and there is no reason for doubting that he had a copy of the African Latin version. It is perhaps safe to say that as early as A. D. 150 this version was made. Certainly Cyprian had a practically complete Latin New Testament, for he quotes it frequently.

The African Latin manuscripts are not very numerous. As a rule, they support the Western type of text. *k* and *e* are the chief texts for the Gospels. The former (*Codex Bobiensis*) is at Turin. It is from the 4th or the 5th century. Its text is Western and Alexandrian, but the manuscript is quite inaccurate. The latter (*Codex Palatinus*) is now at Vienna. It is from the 5th century, and is probably a revision of *k*. Isolated African Latin readings in the Gospels can be found also in *c,* of the twelfth century. *d* designates the Latin part of Codex Beza. The manuscript *h* (the *Fleury Palimpsest*) has parts of Acts, the Catholic Epistles, and the Apocalypse. It is now at Paris. The manuscript *r* has parts of Paul's Epistles. It is of the fifth century and is now at Munich.

The European Latin. We do not yet know whether this version had a separate origin or whether it grew out of the African Latin. H. von Soden holds the former view; Burkitt the latter. However that may be, we know that Novatian (c. 250) used a text like that of *a,* as did also Jerome himself in Luke. The Latin translation of Irenæus' writings also has the European Latin text. This version must, therefore, have originated in the third century. Kenyon says that the European manuscripts, seeing they deviate less from the ordinary text, may have been affected by a comparison with Greek manuscripts.[44]

The bulk of the Old Latin manuscripts are of this type. *a* (*Codex Vercellensis*), at Vercelli, Italy, is next to *k* the most important Old Latin manuscript of the Gospels. Souter says: "As a sacred relic, it has suffered much from the kisses of worshippers throughout the centuries."[45] It agrees with the African version more than any other European manuscript. It is from the 4th century. *b* (*Codex Veronensis*), at Verona, Italy, is of the 5th or the 6th century. It has only the Gospels. Burkitt considers this the type which Jerome used in the Vulgate. *d* is the Latin of D (*Codex Bezae*), as *e* is of E, and *g* of G. *ff* (*Codex Corbeiensis*), now at Paris, is of the 5th century and contains most of the Gospels. *q* (*Codex latinus Monacensis*) has the Gospels and is from the 7th century. It has a text modified by a Greek manuscript with an up-to-date text. *p* is a small manuscript of the New Testament, now at Paris, from early in the 13th century. It has the Vulgate text throughout, except in about one-half of Acts and in the Catholic Epistles, which have the Old Latin text. *gig* (for *gigas*, from its great size) is of the 13th century and is now at Stockholm. It represents a fourth century text of Acts and the Apocalypse.

(b) *The Latin Vulgate.* Owing to the innumerable conflicting copies in the Old Latin manuscripts, both African and

---

44. *Op. cit.,* p. 173.
45. *Op. cit.,* p. 40 f.

European, Damasus, bishop of Rome, in 382 asked Eusebius Hieronymus, now known as Jerome, to prepare an authoritative revision of the Latin Bible which should take the place of all the others. Jerome was well prepared for his task. The Gospels appeared in 384 and the rest of the New Testament somewhat later. In the Gospels he made only such changes from the Old Latin as were absolutely necessary to bring out the sense of the Greek; in the rest of the New Testament he used even greater caution in introducing new renderings. There is a manuscript known as *f,* which is ninety per cent like the Vulgate, and some think that it represents the type of text used by Jerome. But it seems more probable that this manuscript is a revision to the Vulgate than that the latter is based on it. Jerome must have used manuscripts of the Alexandrian rather than the Western type, for the Vulgate is much more Alexandrian than the Old Latin. Important as was the work of Jerome, his translation only gradually overcame the opposition that was raised against it. It was not until the ninth century that it gained anything like an assured supremacy, and it is not until the Council of Trent (1546) that it became the standard version of the Roman Catholic Church as a whole.

During all this time the original text of the Vulgate became greatly corrupted. Again and again it was "revised" back to the favorite renderings of the Old Latin text; but again and again also serious attempts were made to purge from it the corruptions. In 1455 the first complete book was issued from the newly invented printing press; it was the Vulgate, in two volumes, by Gutenberg and Fust (known as the Mazarin Bible). When the Council of Trent made this version the authoritative Scripture in all "public reading, controversy, preaching, and exposition," and declared that no one should dare to reject it on any ground whatever, it became necessary to designate or prepare an authorized edition. The critical edition of Stephanus (1528, 1532, etc.) was then in circulation, and Hententius, of the University of Louvain, issued a private edition in 1547, which was often reprinted.

But in 1590 Pope Sixtus V brought out an edition that he declared the official version of the Church. It was practically based on Stephanus' edition. But the Sixtine version did not meet with universal favor, and so in 1592 Pope Clement VIII brought out a new edition in which appeared some 3000 variations from the 1590 publication. He inserted the name of Sixtus V on the title page, thus issuing it as a new Sixtine edition. This Clementine Vulgate is the standard version of the Roman Catholic Church today. Only slight variations occur in the editions that have been issued since 1592. Wordsworth and White were at work, singly or jointly, from 1877 to 1934 on a critical edition of Jerome's Vulgate, and completed and published the major part of the version. F. D. Sparks, editor, in 1937 brought out Philippians, Colossians, and Thessalonians. It was hoped that the rest might soon follow. Within the last generation or so the Roman Catholic Church itself has undertaken to revise the Vulgate. It has entrusted the task to the English Cardinal Gasquet, who has already issued a part of his revision.

We have numerous copies of the Vulgate, some holding that there are more than 8000 in Europe alone. The majority of these have never been fully examined. They are designated by the first syllable of the name they bear, except *f*, which is now regarded as a manuscript of the Vulgate. Although the manuscripts are so numerous, only a few deserve our attention here. We shall gather together the most important facts concerning these in one paragraph.

Codex Amiatinus, from the eighth century, was written in Northern England. It is now at Florence. Wordsworth and White held it to be the first and most important authority for the Vulgate text. It contains the whole Bible and is in excellent shape. *Codex Cavensis,* at La Cava, Italy, from the ninth century, was written in Spain and is a good representative of the Spanish type of text. It, too, has the entire Bible. *Codex Dublinensis,* in Dublin, is from the eighth or ninth century. It has the whole New Testament, including the apocryphal Epistle to the Laodiceans. It has apparently been corrected by Greek manuscripts that are akin to the Ferrar group. *Codex Fuldensis,* at Fulda, Germany, was written in A. D. 546. It contains the entire New Testament, as also the Epistle to the Laodiceans. The Gospels are woven into a continuous text, similar to that in Tatian's Diatessaron. It has a very good text, being akin to that of the uncial A. *Codex Lindisfarnensis,* of the late seventh or early eighth century, contains the Gospels and has a text akin to that of the uncial A. And *Codex Stony-hurstensis,* of the seventh century, has The Gospel of John and an excellent text.

The secondary versions must be dismissed with a passing word. *The Armenian Version* probably originated in the third or fourth century. It was originally based on the Old Syriac, but was later revised by means of the Byzantine type of Greek text. A manuscript of the Gospels, written in 989, contains the last twelve verses of Mark, but says in the heading that they are from "the elder Aristion." But there is no confirmation of this statement. *The Gothic Version* was made by Bishop Ulfilas in the fourth century. The New Testament was trans-lated from the Byzantine type of Greek text. This version represents the oldest Teutonic literary remains, but we know it only in fragments, the longest of which is in Upsala, Sweden. *The Ethiopic (Abyssinian) Version* was probably made about A. D. 600, but we know it only in late manuscripts. The orig-inal seems to have been based on the Old Syriac, but little is really known about the character of its text. *The Georgian Version* may have originated in the sixth or seventh century, but it may also be earlier. Conybeare and Burkitt hold that it was originally made from the Old Syriac, from a text almost identical with the Armenian text, but that it was later revised from the Greek text. *The Arabic Versions* come partly direct from the Greek, partly through the Syriac, and partly through the Coptic versions. The oldest manuscript is from the eighth century. The *Slavonic* and *Persian Versions* are late and of no importance for textual criticism.

3. *The Patristic Writings*

The writings of the so-called Apostolic and Church Fathers are our third source for the reconstruction of the text of the Greek Testament. The value of these writings consists in this that we know pretty closely when and where the authors lived when they wrote; we cannot be equally sure of the exact time and place at which the Greek manuscripts were produced. The patristic writings, then, have definite value in determining the type of text in use in a given locality at a given time. They may also indicate whether or not certain disputed passages (such as Mark 16:9-20; John 7:53-8:11) were in the New Testament which the writers used.

The patristic writings have, however, certain definite disadvantages. The first is that the Fathers often quote loosely, from memory, either not having the particular manuscript with them or finding it too tedious to turn up the passage in a cumbersome roll. Then again sometimes they quote the same verse in several different ways in their several writings or in different parts of the same work. These are disadvantages. Then, also, since we do not have the original documents that the Fathers wrote but only copies of them, we cannot always be sure that we have the exact wording that they employed. A good deal has been done in recent years to edit the most important of the patristic writings according to the accepted canons of textual criticism, as by Lightfoot, Lake, etc., but the task is still far from finished. Until we have critical editions of these writings we must content ourselves with such as we have.

But even with these disadvantages there is much that has value for textual criticism in the Fathers, for they often quote formally and indicate that they quote. In that case the writings definitely indicate what type of text they had, especially if they say they quote from a Greek manuscript. Then also in their commentaries we may assume that they quote accurately, especially when they use a Greek manuscript. All in all, then, we see that the patristic writings have considerable value in the determination of what was the original text of the several books of the New Testament.

We can only devote a very little space to these writings and shall introduce them according to the language employed by their authors, rather than according to the century or the country they come from. The most important witnesses to the text are the Greek, Syrian, and Latin writers, and to the outstanding ones among them we now turn.

(1) **The Greek Writers**. These always use Greek manuscripts and therefore are the most important for our purpose.

We regret, however, that although the writings of the Greek Apostolic Fathers are valuable in the study of the canon, they are of little significance in the study of the text. In 1905 the Oxford Society of Historical Theology published a volume entitled *The New Testament in the Apostolic Fathers.* It deals with the quotations from or allusions to the New Testament in the *Epistle of Barnabas,* the *Didache, First* and *Second Clement,* Ignatius, Polycarp, and the *Shepherd of Hermas;* but it has little value for textual criticism. It is not until after the middle of the second century that the writings of the Fathers begin to help in this respect. Generally speaking, the evidence points to the use of the Western type of text in the earlier years. But let us note the type employed by several individual writers.

Marcion of Pontus and Rome (d. 165) used the Western type of text in Luke, sometimes one like that of the Old Syriac. In the ten Pauline Epistles which he received he seems to have used a text like that of the Old Syriac. *Justin Martyr* (c. 100-165) quotes very loosely, but appears to have used a Western text, like that of D, the *Diatessaron,* the Old Latin, and the Old Syriac. *Tatian* of Syria and Rome (b. c. 120) used the geographically Western type of text as distinguished from that of the Old Syriac. H. von Soden assigned an unduly important place to Tatian's *Diatessaron* in the history of the text. *Irenaeus* of Asia Minor and Gaul (c. 140-c. 203) probably used a purer and earlier form of the Greek text of Codex Bezae in the Gospels (Souter), and this is probably true also of the rest of the New Testament. *Clement* of Alexandria (c. 155-c. 215) does not quote very carefully, but used a text like that of Codex Bezae in the Gospels. In the Acts and Epistles his text seems to have some relationship to that of *Aleph* and B All these wrote in the second century.

In the third century the evidence for the text becomes still fuller. *Hippolytus* of Rome and Sardinia (177-236) was a pupil of Irenæus and wrote much, although only a little has survived of his work in Greek. He appears to have used the Western type of text in the Gospels and Pauline Epistles, but the Alexandrian type in the Apocalypse. *Origen* of Alexandria (c. 185-c. 253) was the best textual critic among the ancient writers. He seems to have been acquainted with every form of text in existence in his day. His text in the Gospels was formerly considered of the D type, with some admixture of the Alexandrian, but Streeter strongly argues for the Cæsarean instead of the Western type, especially in the Gospel of Mark.[46] In the Pauline Epistles he appears to have used an Alexandrian type of text, especially in Romans. A re-study is being made at the present time of the whole textual problem in Origen. *Pamphilus* of Cæsarea (d. 309) was educated at Alexandria and established a theological library at Cæsarea. His own literary labors are not very important, but his library played a great part in the textual history of the New Testament.

Only a few of the writers of the fourth century can here be mentioned. *Eusebius* of Cæsarea (c. 265-340) was a pupil of Pamphilus and made good use of his library. It was to him that Constantine applied for fifty copies of the Bible for the churches of Constantinople. He rarely quotes a long passage, but when he does he agrees with Origen in the type of text in the Gospels. *Athanasius* of Alexandria (298-373) used chiefly the Alexandrian type of text. *Basil* of Cæsarea (c. 329-379), *Gregory* of Nazianzus (c. 330-c. 390), and *Gregory* of Nyssa (c. 335-395) commonly called the three great Cappadocians, chiefly used the Byzantian type of text, although there are also more ancient elements in the quotations. *Chrysostom* of Antioch and Constantinople (347-407) first made full use of the Byzantine type of text, although there are indications in his writings that he was also acquainted with the Western type. Later Greek writers used substantially the text of Chrysostom.

(2) **The Latin Writers.** The writings of the Latin Fathers are in a much better textual condition than those of the Greek and Syrian, and some of them go back almost as far as the originals themselves. Unfortunately, however, many of them have remained practically unused in the libraries of Europe. The printed editions, with few exceptions, have been made from one or two manuscripts and so are not entirely trustworthy. We confine ourselves to a brief word concerning those of which something definite is known.

---

46. *Op. cit.*, pp. 91-102.

Only about three of the Latin writers of the second and third centuries have importance for textual criticism. *Tertullian* of Carthage (c. 150-222), as we have seen under the Canon, wrote both in Latin and in Greek. His text is distinctly Western, like D. Souter says that his chief Greek allies are Clement and Origen.[47] *Cyprian* of Carthage (c. 200-258) quotes frequently and accurately from the New Testament. In the Gospels his text is like that of the Old Latin *k*, which is Western and Alexandrian; in Acts and the Apocalypse it is like *h*.[48] *Novatian* of Rome (flourished 250), leader of the stricter party in regard to the treatment of the "lapsed," used the European Latin type of text.

Five Latin writers of the fourth century may be mentioned. *Priscillian* of Spain (d. 385) seems to have had a text like that of the African Latin for the Catholic Epistles and one like that of the European Latin for the Apocalypse. *"Ambrosiaster"* of Rome and Spain (fl. 375-385) is now generally thought to have been *Isaac,* a converted Jew, who opposed Bishop Damasus. He used the European Latin type of text. *Ambrose* of Milan (340-397) appears to have used the European Latin text; in the Pauline Epistles it seems to be the same text as that used by "Ambrosiaster." *Jerome* of Rome and Palestine (c. 340-420) was, like Origen, a textual scholar by profession. He used the Western and Alexandrian type of text in the Vulgate, and sometimes the Byzantine. *Augustine* of Hippo (354-430) began by quoting the Old Latin. But after 400 he used the Vulgate for long quotations, while still using the Old Latin for quotations from memory.

(3) **The Syriac Writers.** Only a very few of these are important enough to mention. The apocryphal *Acts of Judas Thomas,* probably written near the end of the second century by an unknown author, is the clearest witness for the Old Syriac. *Aphraates,* bishop in a monastery near ancient Nineveh, wrote homilies, a good many of which are extant, in Syriac. From these we learn that he used the Old Syriac version, not the Peshitta. The homilies were prepared between the years 336-345. *Ephraem Syrus* (d. 373) wrote sermons,

---

47. *The Text and Canon of the New Testament,* p. 87.
48. Souter, *op. cit.,* p. 87.

theological treatises, and commentaries. He used some form of the Old Syriac as his text. Souter declares that Burkitt's discovery that Ephraem had no knowledge of the Peshitta, as was formerly held, has "cleared the way for the correct dating of the Peshitta."[49] Though, as we see, the Syrian writers that have value for textual criticism are few, they are very important for the proper rating of the Syriac texts.

49. *Op. cit.*, p. 93.

Chapter III

THE TEXT OF THE NEW TESTAMENT

Methods of Textual Criticism

OUR study thus far has shown that we are not embarrassed by the paucity of important materials for textual criticism, but by the quantity and quality of the documents that have come down to us. Streeter says in his recent book that we have more than 1400 Greek manuscripts of the Gospels, of which about forty are more than a thousand years old; over 1300 lectionaries; fifteen versions in ancient languages; and multitudinous quotations in the early Fathers.[1] When we put beside this the fact that, with a very few exceptions, we have less than half a dozen manuscripts of a very large number of the famous classical works and that, except for fragments, we have no manuscripts of the Greek classics earlier than the ninth and very few older than the twelfth century, we can see how great and important is the task of the textual critic.

Our problem now is how to use this bewildering amount of material in the restoration of the original text. Shall we simply list all the readings in the various documents by authorities and decide according to our best judgment in each case? Much has been and can be done by this method. If we give due weight to the leading uncials and do not allow the mere numerical preponderance of late cursives to overbalance the uncials, we shall probably find the true reading. But sometimes the leading uncials do not agree and sometimes a reading in a cursive is manifestly better than that in an old uncial. What shall we do then?

In order to answer this question we wish to say that there are but two kinds of evidence to which we can appeal: external

---

1. *The Four Gospels*, p. 33.

and internal. External evidence inquires after the testimony of single documents, groups of documents, and families of documents; internal evidence, after the probability of a reading from the standpoint of the author and the scribe. Let us look at the two types of evidence more carefully.

1. *The External Evidence*

Since external evidence is the evidence of documents as such, it is more objective than internal evidence. It should, therefore, first be appealed to and usually be given the preference. Yet external evidence is to some extent based on internal evidence. For, be it remembered, it is not the mere quantity of manuscripts that have a reading that is determinative, nor the mere age of a manuscript. The great majority of our manuscripts are late and the result of many copyings, and the oldest manuscripts do not always have a pure text. Textual critics have, therefore, by laborious processes ascertained the age of the readings in the manuscripts by comparison with the early versions and quotations in the Fathers, and have assigned value to the manuscripts on this ground; they have also determined the purity of the texts in these manuscripts by means of internal evidence, both transcriptional and intrinsic. When, then, the oldest text is manifestly also the purest text, we may be pretty sure that we have the true text.

But in some instances not all the manuscripts that have the oldest text have also the purest. This is due to the fact that all the manuscripts which have come down to us have suffered corruption in the copying, some more and some less. When, then, not all the oldest manuscripts range themselves also on the side of the purest text, what shall we do? Sometimes we can find the true text by an appeal to the evidence of groups of documents. Hort combined various manuscripts into groups and applied the criteria of age and purity to them. By this method he ascertained the value of certain groups of manuscripts. When, in an instance, not all the oldest manuscripts had what seemed to be the purest reading, he appealed to the evidence of the group of manuscripts that was know to be good in general. By this method he often reached a decision, and by it we, too, may often find the true text. It should be understood, however, that the evidence of groups requires every member of the group to have the reading in question; if even one member of the group fails to have the reading we no longer have the evidence of the original group. Each group of manuscripts has to be evaluated as a group and used as a group or its value as evidence is destroyed.

However safely in some instances we may determine what is the true text by the methods thus far set forth, we still feel the need, in most cases, of appealing to all the evidence that we have. To do this we need a classification of all the materials of criticism according to the age and purity of the text. Our study of the groups forces on us "the self-evident principle that community in readings argues community of origin."[2] The basis of our classification must therefore be that of genealogical connection. Westcott and Hort's greatest contribution to textual criticism is their establishment of the theory of families of documents.

These Cambridge scholars held that there are only four types of text: the Syrian, the Neutral, the Alexandrian, and the Western. These names in each case were held to represent actual genealogical relations as shown in the manuscripts themselves. The Syrian class is the latest. It consists of those readings which are supported only by late Fathers. As a class it also shows signs of having been derived from a combination of non-Syrian readings. Hort found this class in the late uncials, such as E F G H K, and in A in the Gospels, the mass of the minuscules, the late versions, and the late Fathers. There is no purely Syrian reading that is earlier than the late third or early fourth century. So when the Syrian text stands alone we must reject it as not being the original. The Neutral class these scholars regarded as most nearly the original text of the New Testament. It appeared mainly at Alexandria, but was found also in places far removed from that center. It is free from the corruptions found in the other classes. They found it in *Aleph*, B, L, a few minuscules such as 33 and 81, the Bohairic and Sahidic versions, often in Origen and Athanasius. The Alexandrian class they did not find so much in any manu-

---

2. Warfield, *Textual Criticism of the New Testament*, p. 141f.

script or version, as in certain readings in the manuscripts
which otherwise belong to one of the other groups. They
regarded this text as a scholarly revision of the form and
syntax in certain readings of the other classes of texts. They
found it chiefly in C, L, Origen and a few other documents.
And the Western class they considered an early corruption of
the original text. Verses and sometimes longer passages are
found in this class that are entirely absent from all the other
copies; and sometimes there are omissions. Westcott and Hort
held that this text developed during the non-critical second
and third centuries, when the books of the New Testament
were copied for immediate edification rather than for the
preservation of the original text. They found this text in D,
the Old Latin, the Old Syriac, Cyprian, Irenæus, and Tertullian. Although they did not declare the Neutral text to be
always right, in practice they virtually treated it in that way.

There has, however, been some strong opposition to the
theory of Westcott and Hort. Burgon and Scrivener opposed
it on the ground of the almost complete domination of the
Syrian type of text in the later Middle Ages and of the great
numerical preponderance of the manuscripts that have that
kind of text. But we have already pointed out that the bulk
of our manuscripts are of late date and almost always have
an inferior type of text. This opposition has gradually dis-
appeared, and for the past fifty years the theory of Westcott
and Hort has held the field. In recent times, however, as
instances of pre-Syrian readings that are yet not Neutral have
multiplied, there has arisen a new problem. It has been customary to assign all such pre-Syrian non-Neutral readings to
the Western class. The result is that the Western text came
to be less and less Western in the geographical sense of the
term. It has therefore become necessary to establish new limits
for the Western type of text.

B. H. Streeter and Kirsopp Lake have had the leading part
in isolating a new class of readings. They have shown that
the so-called Western text is composed of two distinct types,
an Eastern and a Western type in the geographical sense of
these terms. Streeter holds, indeed, that the Eastern can be
further subdivided into an Alexandrian, Cæsarean, and Anti-

ochian, and the Western into an Italian and a Carthaginian.[3]
He also has shown that though Hort's Alexandrian text exhib-
ited certain stylistic improvements, it is in reality "a partially
degenerate form of the B text."[4] And since we know of no
manuscript that preserved this text in its entirety, nor of any
manuscript that had these so-called Alexandrian readings that
did not also have many Western readings, we may classify
the readings that have this character in some other way and
discontinue the use of the term Alexandrian in the sense in
which Westcott and Hort used it.

Kenyon, formerly a strong supporter of the theory of Westcott and Hort, has adopted the new view, and so have textual
critics generally. We must, therefore, understand the new
classification of documents and know something of their rela-
tive importance for textual criticism. It is not necessary here
to give the full classification of documents, nor is it possible
at this stage of the study to do so, for the character of the
Cæsarean text has thus far been established only in the Gospel
of Mark. For the following facts as for much of the information concerning the text, we are deeply obligated to Kenyon[5]
and Streeter.[6]

(1) The Byzantine Family was called Syrian by Westcott
and Hort, but that term led to much confusion with the Syriac
versions. It has also been called Antiochian and Constantino-
politan, but these terms too are inadequate. We follow Streeter
and Kenyon in calling it the Byzantine family. To this family
belong the great majority of the later manuscripts. It first
appears in the quotations of Chrysostom; by the eighth century
it was practically everywhere in use in the Greek world. It is
a smooth and easily understood text. Warfield says, it "appears
to have been an effort to replace by a purer and smoother text
the corrupt Western type."[7] The Byzantine type of readings
appear first in A and C in the Gospels, in W except in Mark,
in N O *Sigma,* and *Phi,* in the great mass of the later uncials
and minuscules, and in the later versions and Fathers. It is
substantially correct and was used as the basis of the so-called

3. *The Four Gospels,* p. 32.
4. *Op. cit.,* p. 60.
5. *Our Bible and the Ancient Manuscripts.*
6. *The Four Gospels.*
7. *Op. cit.,* p. 160.

Textus Receptus, but is now set aside when it conflicts with the earlier families.

(2) The Alexandrian Family is practically identical with Westcott and Hort's Neutral class. Though of greater excellence than any of the other classes, the Alexandrian text, too, is not always right. It apparently originated in Alexandria and so deserves the name Alexandrian. To some extent the former "Alexandrian" text has now been included in the newer Alexandrian type, and to some extent it has been assigned to one of the other classes. To this new Alexandrian Family belong as of the first rank, B and *Aleph,* which are often supported by L R T Z, A and C (except in the Gospels), minuscules 33, 81, and 157, the Sahidic and Bohairic versions, and the quotations of Origen in the earlier books of his lectures.

(3) The Cæsarean Family has only recently been discovered, as we have shown above. Kenyon regards this text as being "between the Alexandrian and Western."[8] And Streeter says that the Greek text behind the Old Syriac is "more closely related to that of Family *Theta* than to any extant Greek manuscript."[9] The Cæsarean text is to be found in W from Mark 6 on to the end of that Gospel, in *Theta* in Mark, in Family 1 of the minuscules (1-118-131-209), in Family 13 (13-69-124-346), in certain other minuscules (28-565-700 and others), in the Chester Beatty Papyri P^{45}, P^{46}, and P^{47}, in the Armenian and Georgian versions, in the later works of Origen and in Eusebius. We await with interest the establishment of the more exact critical value of this family.

(4) The Western Family has now been narrowed down to the text that is definitely Western in the geographical sense of the word. The recent application of the term "Western" to all non-Alexandrian pre-Syrian readings had robbed the term of all true significance. It is, therefore, a relief to confine the term to that which is a truly Western text. This type of text is found in the Græco-Latin uncials, first of all in D, and then also in D_2 E_3 F_2 G_3, the African Old Latin, especially in *k* and *e,* and in the quotations of Cyprian, Priscillian, Tyconius,

8. *Our Bible and the Ancient Manuscripts,* p. 118.
9. *Op. cit.,* p. 89.

and Primasius.[10] It has a good many variations from the other families, as we have already pointed out, especially in the Gospels and the Book of Acts. Because it is an early text it has great value for textual criticism, in spite of its many peculiarities.

(5) The Syriac Family embraces the Old Syriac version and the quotations that are in harmony with this text. This version was formerly included in the Western Family, but Kenyon holds that it is nearer akin to the Alexandrian type than to the Western. It is possible that such Western readings as are found in it may have been introduced from Tatian's Diatessaron. Kenyon further suggests that this text was "eventually revised under Byzantine influences by Rabbula into the form of the Peshitta, which became the authorized Bible of the Syrian Church."[11]

Mention should here perhaps be made of H. F. von Soden's classification of the textual authorities; but since no one (save Erwin Nestle in his *Novum Testamentum Graece*) seems inclined to adopt it, we may dismiss it with a mere word. He divides all textual authorities into three classes and designates them by the letters K, H, and I. His K (for *Koine*) is Westcott and Hort's Syrian text; his H (for Hesychius, whom he regards as the author of it), their Neutral, and his I (for Jerusalem) includes their Western and some others. But the latter is too large and unwieldy to be helpful as a classification, and the isolation of the Cæsarean text within this class has discredited it. There are also other heterogeneous elements in his I-text that make the classification unsatisfactory. Students who use Erwin Nestle's Greek Testament will, however, need to familiarize themselves with this classification in order to profit from Nestle's critical apparatus.

It is too bad that students are still obliged to use Tischendorf's Eighth Edition (*octava critica maior*) for practice in textual criticism, since the work is written in Latin and is now quite out of date. C. R. Gregory was about to publish a revision of Tischendorf, but lost his life in the first World War and the task remains unfinished. In 1935 the Oxford

---

10. Kenyon, *op. cit.*, p. 178 f.
11. *Op. cit.*, p. 179.

University Press, under the editorship of S. C. E. Legg, published the first volume of what is to be a new critical edition of the evidence of manuscripts, versions, and Fathers. This was the Gospel of Mark; the Gospel of Matthew has since then appeared. It is to be regretted that the work is marred by a good many errors. The textual student today is, therefore, obliged to use Tischendorf and to supplement him with von Soden and other collations of texts.

2. *The Internal Evidence*

In our search for internal evidence we look at the problem from the standpoint of the scribe and the author. Being more subjective than external evidence, we should not appeal to it until we have first ascertained the evidence of the documents. Usually the internal evidence supports the external evidence, and if so, the case is closed. But there are times when there is something in the context that makes it impossible to accept the external evidence (e. g., the reading *eis Ierousalēm* of *Aleph* and B at Acts 12:25). Then we have to appeal to internal evidence to solve the problem. Now internal evidence is of two kinds: transcriptional and intrinsic. Looked at from the standpoint of the scribe it is called transcriptional evidence; looked at from the standpoint of the author it is called intrinsic evidence. Let us now proceed to consider these more fully.

(1) Transcriptional Evidence. The scribes who prepared the extant documents were not infallible; they made both unintentional and intentional changes in the text. The textual critic must reckon with these facts when studying a reading if he would find the original text. A few typical ones of both kinds may now be mentioned.

There were several kinds of unintentional corruption. There were errors of the eye due to the similarity of some of the Greek letters, the variety of abbreviations employed, and the running of words together without a break between them; for the same reason words or clauses were sometimes omitted that are alike or identical and sometimes words were written twice. There were errors of the ear when a manuscript was written from dictation, as is seen in the great variety of itacistic spellings in the manuscripts. Then there were errors of memory, as the use of a synonym or of a different word order than that which appeared in the sources. Sometimes there were errors of judgment, as when the scribe introduced marginal glosses into the text. And finally there were errors of speech, i. e., errors that were due to the scribe's habits of speech, which he tended to reproduce in spite of what he had in his sources.

There were also several kinds of intentional corruptions. Now it should be realized that most of the conscious changes by the copyists were made from the best of motives, from sincere conviction that they were correcting an error in their sources. Such were the linguistic and grammatical changes that were made to bring a document into line with better usage; the changes made to clear up difficulties and supposed inaccuracies; the harmonistic corruptions, especially in the Gospels; the doctrinal corruptions, to support the views of the owner or scribe; and the liturgical adaptations which appear so frequently in the lectionaries. Of these the doctrinal corruptions are the most serious. J. Rendel Harris says: "To Dr. Hort the scribes were all angels, as far as theology was concerned,"[12] and Warfield says: "It is doubtful if any doctrinal corruptions can be pointed to with complete confidence."[13] But "Irenæus, Clement of Alexandria, and Tertullian accused the heretics of tampering with the text,"[14] and we must not entirely ignore this possibility in our study of the text.

In the quest for transcriptional evidence textual critics fairly agree in the use of five canons: First, prefer the reading which best explains the origin of the others; secondly, accept as a rule the more difficult reading (scribes tended to simplify rather than to complicate a reading); thirdly, decide in general for the shorter reading (scribes tended to add rather than omit words and phrases); fourthly, adopt the reading most characteristic of the author, if that can be determined; and fifthly, discount the value of the readings that are manifestly peculiar to a scribe (they may have no other authority than the scribe's). Like most other things in life, these must be used wisely if the results are to be trustworthy.

---

12. *Sidelights on New Testament Research*, p. 34.
13. *Textual Criticism of the New Testament*, p. 96.
14. Robertson, *Intro. to the Textual Criticism of the New Testament*, p. 159.

(2) Intrinsic Evidence. This is looking at the problem from the standpoint of the author. It seeks to determine which reading makes the best sense in the context and is most in harmony with the author's known style and habits of speech and thought. One must make a comprehensive and sympathetic study of the writer and exercise a high type of mental honesty to attain the results we want. There is constant danger here of wanting to make an author say what we prefer that he should say, rather than to let him say what he wants to say. When carefully and conscientiously carried out, the study of intrinsic evidence will generally lead to conclusions that support the best attested readings.

It is sometimes asked, to what extent we may trust the present critical text to be the true text. From the reading of these pages on textual criticism the student may easily get an exaggerated impression of the proportion of the text that is still in doubt. It should be emphasized, therefore, that concerning the great bulk of the words in the New Testament there is complete agreement among textual critics. Witness the great similarity of the texts of Tischendorf (8th ed.), Westcott and Hort, and B. Weiss. Eberhard Nestle prepared his text on the basis of these three recensions and said: "The readings adopted in the text are those in which at least two of these editions agree. An exception to this rule has been made in St. Mark 1:1; St. John 5:3, 4, and 7:53-8:11. These passages have been retained in the text, but they are placed within special marks."[15] Concerning the differences among textual critics Westcott and Hort say: "If comparative trivialities, such as changes of order, the insertion or omission of the article with proper names, and the like, are set aside, the words in our opinion still subject to doubt can hardly amount to more than a thousandth part of the whole New Testament."[16] This would be a total of a little more than a half page of the Greek Testament from which this statement is taken. Truly, this is not very much!

---

15. *Advertisement* to the 1904 edition of the British and Foreign Bible Society.
16. *Greek New Testament*, p. 564 f.

Chapter IV

THE INSPIRATION OF THE NEW TESTAMENT

WE HAVE seen how the twenty-seven books which we have in our New Testament have won their way into the Canon and have maintained themselves in it from century to century; we have also seen how the study of the text has progressed to the point where we feel that we have substantially the text of the autographs. The question arises, why is it that these books have attained to this place of pre-eminence; why is it that so much labor has been bestowed upon the text of this one book? Various explanations have been put forward, but most of them seem to us to be inadequate. We believe that this is due to their divine inspiration.

It is evident, of course, that one's view of this phenomenon has a definite bearing on one's approach to the study of the New Testament. Unfortunately, few people have come to their views on inspiration by an intelligent first-hand investigation of the whole question. The great majority have accepted the views of their teachers without ever trying to understand just what is meant by the term "inspiration" and without considering the question of the possibility and probability of the inspiration of the Scriptures. We must, therefore, briefly discuss the subject in this connection. We shall omit the discussion of the views that appear to us inadequate and deal only with what seems to us to be the true view.

The author fully realizes that modern scholarship generally takes a different view from the one which he accepts, but he also knows that there is a great Christian public and a growing number of young scholars who feel that this is the only logical and true view. May we invite our readers to give patient consideration to this viewpoint? We shall first define the term "inspiration," then offer some proofs of inspiration, and finally reply to various objections to the doctrine of inspiration.

1. *The Definition of Inspiration*

In our judgment, L. Gaussen, Professor of Systematic Theology, Oratoire, Geneva, has given us one of the most satisfactory definitions of inspiration. According to him it is "that inexplicable power which the divine Spirit put forth of old on the authors of Holy Scripture, in order to their guidance even in the employment of the words they used, and to preserve them alike from all error and from all omission."[1] Let us examine the definition more closely and see just what it says and what it does not say.

It declares at the outset that inspiration is really "inexplicable." It is power put forth by the Holy Spirit, but we cannot tell exactly how that power operated. We do well, therefore, not to give such names to our theories of inspiration as recognize but one of the ways in which the Holy Spirit worked. Then, it limits inspiration to the authors of Holy Scripture; there has been no other inspiration in this sense, neither before nor since the Scriptures were written. This sets aside all other so-called "sacred" books as uninspired; it also rejects all the claims of Churches, Church Councils, Creeds, and Ecclesiastics to an authority in religious matters that equals or exceeds that of the Bible. The definition next represents this operation of the Spirit as "guidance." This we understand, on the one hand, to mean the Spirit's superintendence in the selection of the materials that should be used, whether they came from personal observation, oral information, written sources, or direct revelation to the individual; and to mean, on the other hand, His superintendence in the choice of the words to employ. The definition finally insists that the authors were kept, not only from all error, but also from all omission. That is, the original documents were not only accurate, but were also complete, in the sense that they contained all that God wanted us to have as Scripture.

Let us observe several further facts about this definition. First of all, it does not teach any mode of inspiration. The Holy Spirit wrought in the hearts and minds of the authors, but we cannot say exactly what He did, except that He guided them in the production of their works. The Spirit's revelation

---
1. *Theopneustia,* p. 34.

to the heart and His illumination of the mind to understand truth were, no doubt, often starting points for the Spirit's guidance in the writing of the books. At times the Spirit probably dictated the very words that were to be used; but that can scarcely have been His usual method, for the various authors of Scripture display distinct grammatical and stylistic differences, which could hardly have been the case if all had been directly dictated by the Spirit. It is best, we believe, to leave the question of the mode of inspiration unsettled and to insist merely that the Holy Spirit guided the authors of Holy Scripture in the writing of the Word of God.

But this is not all; the definition indicates, in the second place, the extent of inspiration. It declares that inspiration is verbal. Now a good many hold that verbal inspiration means dictation. But that is to confuse the result of inspiration with the mode of inspiration. Others think that God merely gave men the thoughts or concepts and left it to them to write them down as best they could. In opposition to these positions we hold that, by whatever method the Holy Spirit may have employed, He guided the writers to choose such words to express His message as were normal to their style and vocabulary and yet were the very words in which He wanted it expressed.

And thirdly, the definition ascribes inspiration only to the autographs of Holy Scripture. It does not, as some ignorantly suppose, affirm inspiration of any of the existing versions, either modern or ancient. Nor does it affirm this of our present critical Greek texts in the fullest sense of the term; for there is still a measure of doubt concerning a small number of words occurring in them. It does, however, assert that the original documents, and they alone, were verbally inspired. But at once the question arises, What is the value of such a theory of inspiration since all the autographs are lost? Why insist on verbal inspiration when no one can produce the documents that are to be regarded as thus inspired? The reason is twofold: First, if the theory is true, then we would dishonor God if we held any other. Surely, we would not want to do that! Secondly, we have shown under *The Text of the New Testament* (above) that such competent textual critics as Westcott and Hort hold that, aside from comparative trivialities, the words in the New Testament that are still in doubt amount to no more than a thousandth part of the whole. Milligan says: "We may take it that in all substantial particulars the words of the autographs have been recovered."[2] It can be said that no doctrine of Scripture is endangered by this small number of words still in doubt. To the extent, then, to which we have in our present critical texts the original text, to that extent we have in our hands today the verbally inspired New Testament.

A word should here be added on the distinction between inspiration and authority. Usually the two are identical, so that what is inspired is also authoritative for life and conduct; but occasionally that is not the case. For example, Satan's words to Jesus (Matt. 4:5, 6), Peter's advice to Christ (Matt. 16:22, 23), and Gamaliel's opinion (Acts 5:38) are recorded by inspiration, but they are not divinely authoritative, because they are not divinely sanctioned. The same thing can be said about some statements when they are taken out of their contexts: the words of the statements have been recorded by divine inspiration, but they do not convey the intended meaning when separated from their contexts. So then we regard every statement as both inspired and authoritative, unless there is some hint in the context that the latter is not the case in a given instance.

2. *The Proofs of Inspiration*

This is a very high view of the Scriptures: Can we prove that it is the true view? Many say that it is impossible to do this, that the view is but a survival from Mediaeval times, a *petitio principii*, etc. But it certainly was the view of the Christian Church generally for the earliest centuries. Gaussen says, that "with the single exception of Theodore of Mopsuestia," whose writings were condemned at the Fifth Ecumenical Council (at Constantinople, 553), "it has been found impossible to produce, in the long course of the eight first centuries of Christianity, a single doctor who has disowned the plenary inspiration of the Scriptures, unless it be in the bosom of the most violent heresies that have tormented the Christian Church; that is to say, among the Gnostics, the Manicheans, the Anomeans,

---

2. Quoted by Cobern, in *New Archaeological Discoveries*, p. 105.

and the Mahometans."[3] Gaussen uses the terms *verbal* and *plenary* (from the Latin *plenus, full*) interchangeably, and we think rightly so.

In modern times, however, the majority deny the verbal inspiration of the Scriptures. We would, therefore, give our reasons for differing from the opinion of the majority of scholars and for accepting the view of the earliest centuries. Although some would argue this question on the ground of miracles, fulfilled prophecy, archaeological discoveries, etc., we hold that none of these is fundamental enough to support this view. A given miracle may be accepted as true, a specific prophecy as fulfilled, and a certain geographical or historical statement as credible and yet the Scriptures as a whole not be accepted as verbally inspired. We, accordingly, do not argue the question on these or similar grounds. It appears to us that there are two fundamental things that support the theory of verbal inspiration: (1) our conception of the character of God and (2) the nature and claims of the Scriptures, particularly of the New Testament. Let us consider these more carefully.

(1) *The Character of God.* A high view of God seems to require a correspondingly high view of inspiration. We believe that God is a person, omnipotent, omniscient, omnipresent, perfect in holiness, righteousness, and love; and that He is the Creator, Preserver, and Governor of the universe. It is not possible here to defend this conception of God; we must assume that our readers agree with us in this respect. If we accept this view of God, then we have already laid the foundations for the belief in a supernatural revelation and inspiration. If God is a person, then He has intelligence, sensibilities, and will, and fellowship with Him becomes possible; if He is omnipotent, then He is able to create, preserve, and govern this universe; if He is omniscient, then He knows all about the needs of His creatures; if He is omnipresent, then He is able to reveal Himself to man; if He is perfect in holiness and righteousness, then there is an absolute standard of morality in the universe; if He is perfect in love, then He may seek to save the undeserving.

3. *Op. cit.,* p. 139 f.

These are not mere theories, for God has displayed these qualities in the universe. He is its Creator, Preserver, and Governor. The heavens declare the glory of God and the firmament shows forth His handiwork. From the very beginning, says Paul, the invisible things of God have been clearly seen, being perceived through the things that are made, even His eternal power and divinity; and is he not expressing a universal conviction? God keeps the planets in their orbits and orders the stars in their courses. He preserves man and beast. He rules in the army of heaven and among the children of men. This conviction cheers the heart in the darkest hour of social and political upheaval. It sustains man in the times when heaven seems to be indifferent to the cruelest kinds of injustice; for he cannot abandon himself to the view that this universe is without a moral governor. Man more or less fully knows these things.

More particularly man knows that He is dependent upon God for life and breath and all things. He knows that all creatures wait on Him for their daily sustenance; that what He gives they gather; that when He hides His face they are troubled; that He takes away their breath and they return to their dust. He knows also that he is accountable to God for his character and conduct. He sees the wrath of God revealed from heaven against all unrighteousness of men and also in his own conscience. Kant argued for the existence of God, freedom, and immortality on the basis of conscience; for to him nothing was more certain than conscience. And man also knows that he is a sinner; he has the sense of condemnation resting upon him. He knows that his condemnation is just and suffers the tortures of an accusing conscience. He wonders what to do about his sins. Even if he could live a sinless life in the future, that would not atone for the sins of the past. He cannot undo the past, for what has been done has been done. He cannot forget his sins nor ignore them. If he seeks to drown out the voice of an accusing conscience for the moment by sinful indulgence, this voice cries out all the louder when the indulgence is over. Is there no solution to the sin-question? Is there no balm in Gilead? Is there no physician there?

Nature and conscience do not give him an answer. They merely say that man is dependent upon God and accountable to Him. God is holy and righteous, but is He also loving? True, there are indications in nature of His love; for He has given us rains from heaven and fruitful seasons; He has filled our mouths with food and our hearts with gladness. But how can He be both righteous and loving? Human governments exact the penalty from the criminal and do not excuse his crime, even though he confesses and repents of it. Can God forgive sin without first exacting the penalty for sin? Has God done anything about it, and if so, what? And if He has, how can I, the sinner, enter into the benefits of God's provision? Man naturally asks, since God has supplied so abundantly for man's temporal wants, will He not also provide for his greatest needs, his spiritual wants? And if He does provide for this greatest need, will He not inform man as to the fact of such a provision, as to the nature of it, and as to the conditions on which man may enter into the benefits of it? It seems that from so high a view of God we may conclude that He will do all that.

We naturally turn to the so-called "sacred" books of the world for an answer to our problems. But we cannot find any logical and adequate solution of the sin-question in the five Classics of Confucianism, the Vedas of the Hindus, the Zend Avesta of Zoroastrianism, or the Koran of Mohammedanism. When Joseph Cook, many years ago at the Parliament of Religions in Chicago, challenged the priests of the ancient religions to answer Lady Macbeth's question: "How cleanse this red right hand?" all the priests were dumb. They had no answer to this question. But when we turn to the Bible, particularly to the New Testament, we get an answer that satisfies both the mind and the heart. In substance it is this: Christ "bare our sins in his body upon the tree, that we, having died unto sins, might live unto righteousness; by whose stripes ye were healed" (1 Pet. 2:24). God has found a way by means of which He can remain just and yet justify the sinner that believes in Jesus (Rom. 3:26).

But suppose that it is granted that the Bible presents the only satisfactory solution of the sin-question, does that require a belief in the verbal inspiration of the record? It is apparent on the surface that it would be an advantage to have such a record, for it would reduce the possibilities of uncertainty to a minimum. A presumption in favor of such a view may be found in the fact that God is perfect in all His works. If He is the Author of the Bible, we seem warranted to expect that His Book, too, will be perfect. But we must turn to the second topic for an answer to this question.

(2) *The Nature and Claims of the Scriptures, particularly of the New Testament.* We cannot go far into the problems connected with the Old Testament; but since we believe with Augustine that "the New is in the Old concealed, the Old is in the New revealed," we hold that there is an organic connection between the two and that they stand and fall together. We shall, therefore, say a few things about the nature of the Bible as a whole and about the claims of the Old Testament to full inspiration before turning more directly to the subject of the New Testament.

The Bible is primarily a religious book and as such it is unique in the world of literature. How could uninspired man write a book that commands all duty, forbids all sin, including the sin of hypocrisy and lying, denounces all human merit as insufficient for salvation, holds out as man's only hope faith in the atoning death, physical resurrection, and present intercession of Christ, and condemns to hell for all eternity all who reject this one way of salvation and persist in sin? How could about forty different men over a period of approximately 1500 years write sixty-six books that are in reality one book? These books have one doctrinal viewpoint, one moral standard, one plan of salvation, one program of the ages, one world-view. Kings were no more allowed to practice polygamy than ordinary people (Deut. 17:17); divorce was permitted on certain conditions, but never really sanctioned by God (Deut. 24:1-4; Matt. 19:8). The peculiarities of the Mosaic system can be interpreted in the light of a progressive revelation. Law and grace and the doctrine of the Holy Spirit find their reconciliation in the distinctive purpose of God for the several ages. The combination of the political and the religious in the Jewish polity was divinely purposed for the old economy, but is not intended for the new order.

There are no other "sacred" books that anywhere nearly come up to the Scriptures in the character of their contents and the unity of their plan. Speaking of the Mohammedan, Zoroastrian, and Buddhist Scriptures, James Orr says, they are "destitute of beginning, middle or end. They are, for the most part, collections of heterogeneous materials, loosely placed together. How different everyone must acknowledge it to be with the Bible! From Genesis to Revelation we feel that this book is in a real sense a unity. It is not a collection of fragments, but has, as we say, an organic character. . . . There is nothing exactly resembling it, or even approaching it, in all literature."[4]

When we come to the claims of the Old Testament for itself we are first of all confronted with the question whether it is proper to argue for the inspiration of the Scriptures from the claims of the Scriptures. To this we reply in the affirmative on the ground that if they are truthful when speaking about other things they may be expected to be truthful also when speaking of themselves. That they are truthful in speaking about other things is assumed here. Objections to this position will be taken up in the following section. We turn, then, very briefly to the claims of the Old Testament for itself.

More than 3,800 times[5] the writers of the Old Testament introduce their messages with such statements as these: "The Lord spake," "the Lord said," "the word of the Lord came." Will you stop to figure out how often this is on the average per page in your Bible? Repeatedly the writers of the Old Testament tell us that God commanded them to write and that they did write what He told them to write (Ex. 17:14; 24:4; 34:27; Num. 33:2; Deut. 31:24; Jer. 30:1, 2; 36:1, 2, 4, 27-32; Hab. 2:2). Some writers claim absolute perfection and authority for "the law and the testimony" (Deut. 28:58, 59; Ps. 19:7; 119:142; Isa. 8:20). One book recognizes another book as speaking with absolute authority (Josh. 1:8; 8:31, 32; Ezra 3:2; Neh. 8:1; Dan. 9:1, 2, 11, 13; Zech. 7:12; Mal. 4:4).

To this we may add the fact that Jesus and the Apostles recognized the Old Testament as fully inspired. Jesus said He

---

4. *The Problem of the Old Testament*, pp. 31, 32.
5. According to Evans, *Great Doctrines of the Bible*, p. 203.

came not to destroy either "the law or the prophets" (Matt. 5:17). This expression is often used for the entire Old Testament (*e.g.,* Matt. 7:12; 11:13; 22:40; Luke 16:16; John 1:45; Acts 13:15; 24:14; 28:23; Rom. 3:21). Jesus further said: "Till heaven and earth pass away, one jot or one tittle shall in no wise pass away from the law, till all be accomplished" (Matt. 5:18; cf. Luke 16:17). Since He had just declared the equal permanence of the law and the prophets, He seems now to indicate by the expression: "Till all be accomplished" the inclusion of the prophets with the law in His statement concerning verbal reliability. In Luke 24:44 He uses the terms "the law of Moses, and the prophets, and the psalms" for the whole Old Testament. Sometimes "the law" denotes the whole (*e.g.,* John 10:34; 12:34; 15:25; Rom. 3:19; 1 Cor. 14:21). Inasmuch as our Lord speaks of the Old Testament as "your law" in John (10:34), it seems probable that He does this in Matt. 5:18 also. In other words, Jesus taught that the Old Testament was verbally inspired. Broadus says: "And we know from Josephus and early Christian writers, that all Jews of our Lord's time would understand 'the Scriptures' or 'the law and the prophets' as meaning a well-known and well-defined collection of sacred books, the same as our Old Testament."[6]

Two of the Apostles also testify definitely to the full inspiration of the Old Testament, although all, no doubt, took the same view of the matter. Paul says: "All scripture is given by inspiration of God, and is profitable for doctrine, for reproof, for correction, for instruction in righteousness" (2 Tim. 3:16). The translation, "Every scripture inspired of God is also profitable," etc., is open to several criticisms: its rendering of *pasa graphe* and of *kai,* and its disposition of the verbal adjective *theopneustos.* Robertson says, with abstract substantives, proper names, and single objects *pasa* is tantamount to "all"; and "since *graphe* is sometimes regarded as definite *pasa graphe* (2 Tim. 3:16) can be 'all Scripture' or 'every Scripture'."[7] Lock so translates it.[8] Other considerations make this the preferable rendering. There is no copula in the Greek text, but we have to insert one in the translation.

---

6. *Comm. on the Gospel of Matthew*, p. 99.
7. *New Short Grammar of the Greek New Test.,* p. 281.
8. *Comm. on the Pastoral Epistles,* p. 110.

The rendering we are criticizing treats *theopneustos* as an attributive and so inserts the copula after "God." This requires that the particle *kai* be rendered as "also," an adjunctive particle. Now "also" implies that we are adding one co-ordinate idea to another; but the words "is also profitable" are not an addition to anything that goes before. It is better, therefore, to treat *theopneustos* as a predicate and to insert the copula after "Scripture." The statement will then read as it is in the Authorized Version: "All Scripture is inspired of God and is profitable," etc. In other words, the correct rendering of this verse makes Paul teach the full inspiration of the entire Old Testament.

Peter says: "Knowing this first, that no prophecy of scripture is of private interpretation. For no prophecy ever came by the will of man: but men spake from God, being moved by the Holy Spirit" (2 Pet. 1:20, 21). The "prophecy of Scripture" refers primarily, if not exclusively, to the prophecies of the Old Testament. Peter has encouraged the study of prophecy (v. 19); but he adds that no one must interpret it just as he likes, for prophecy was not given by the will of man, and so it cannot be interpreted by the will of man. God gives both the prophecy and the interpretation of prophecy. It "came" or "was brought" (the same Greek word as in v. 18, where it is rendered "borne" out of heaven), and "men spake from God," *i. e.,* as mouth-pieces of God, not by their own will, but as they were "borne along by the Holy Spirit." If Peter thus teaches the full inspiration of the prophetic Scriptures of the Old Testament, he would surely teach the same regarding all the rest of the Old Testament.

We need to say but a very few things about the nature of the New Testament, since we have already included it in our discussion of the nature of the Bible as such. Written by eight or nine different authors within half a century the New Testament, if anything, excels the Old in its intellectual depth, doctrinal unity, spiritual tone, and practical value. Much of what is presented in the Old Testament in the forms of types and symbols is in the New set forth in literal terms; many of the prophecies in the Old Testament are in the New applied to Christ and His mission. But the New Testament goes beyond this. It not only fills in the outlines of God's plan of redemption revealed in the Old Testament, but it also sets forth the nature and mission of the Church as these were not known in other ages (Eph. 3:2-12). In all this there is no clash of opinion among the writers of the New Testament; all is seen to be perfect harmony when we grasp the idea that God progressively reveals His purposes and works them out in the history of the ages.

We must, however, discuss more fully the question of the inspiration of the New Testament. In the first place, note the claims of the writers concerning the oral message that was being proclaimed. Peter says that the word of the Lord is being preached to his readers in the Gospel (1 Pet. 1:25); indeed, he puts "the commandment of the Lord and Savior through your apostles" on the same plane with "the words which were spoken before by the holy prophets" (2 Pet. 3:2). Jude reminds his readers of "the words which have been spoken before by the apostles of our Lord Jesus Christ" as absolutely dependable (Jude 17). Paul declares to the Thessalonians that he had preached "the word of God" to them when he was with them and rejoices in the fact that they had "accepted it not as the word of men, but, as it is in truth, the word of God" (1 Thess. 2:13). Indeed, he pronounces an "anathema" upon any man or angel as well as himself, if he should preach any other Gospel than that which the Galatians had received (Gal. 1:8, 9). He had neither received it from man nor been taught it. but had obtained it by revelation from Christ (Gal. 1:11, 12). He that teaches any other doctrine is puffed up, ignorant, and given to strife (1 Tim. 6:3). This is surely ascribing a divine origin and authority to the preaching of the apostles, which suggests naturally the divine inspiration of their writings also.

In the second place, note the more specific claims of the authors concerning their writings. Peter puts the Epistles of Paul on the same plane with "the other scriptures" (2 Pet. 3:15, 16). The word "Scriptures" was so fixed at that time that it can only mean the Old Testament. Bigg favors this view. He says: "There can be little doubt that the apostles were regarded, and regarded themselves, as *hupo Pneumatos hagiou pheromenoi.*"[9]

---

9. *Comm. on the Epistles of St. Peter and St. Jude*, p. 302.

Paul writes to the Thessalonians about the coming of Christ, "by the word of the Lord" (1 Thess. 4:15). He declares that what he has written to the Corinthians is "the commandment of the Lord" (1 Cor. 14:37). He charges Timothy in the sight of God to "keep the commandment, without spot, without reproach, until the appearing of the Lord Jesus Christ" (1 Tim. 6:13, 14); he even asks him to "hold the pattern of sound words" which he had heard from him (2 Tim. 1:13). In his First Epistle to the Corinthians he speaks still more strongly. He says that he proclaims the wisdom of God, "not in the words which man's wisdom teacheth, but which the Spirit teacheth" (1 Cor. 2:13). In this statement he declares that inspiration had something to do with the *words* of the message. Several times John quotes the Lord as saying: "These words are faithful and true" (Rev. 21:5; 22:6). The same Apostle warns against adding to the words of his book and against taking from them (Rev. 22:18, 19). This, then, is the claim of the writers of the New Testament to inspiration.

In the third place, note the teaching of Jesus concerning the coming and ministry of the Holy Spirit insofar as that has to do with inspiration. As early as the time when He sent out the Twelve He encouraged them not to be anxious when they were hailed before the authorities, adding, "for it is not ye that speak, but the Spirit of your Father that speaketh in you" (Matt. 10:19, 20). Later on He said that the Holy Spirit would come and make them competent teachers of the truth. This He would do by teaching them all things, by bringing to their remembrance all that He had said unto them, by guiding them into all the truth, and by showing them things to come (John 14:26; 16:12, 13). These promises broadly embrace the events of Christ's earthly life, the lessons taught by the experiences of the early disciples, the doctrines of the Epistles, and the predictions of the Apocalypse. The apostles claim to have received this Spirit (Acts 2:4a; 9:17; 1 Cor. 2:10, 12; James 4:5; Jude 19) and to speak under His influence and with divine authority, as we have already seen (see also Acts 2:4b; 4:8, 31: 13:9; 1 Cor. 2:13; Gal. 1:1, 12; 1 Thess. 4:2, 8; 1 Pet. 1:12; 1 John 5:10, 11).

The promise of Jesus in John 16:12, 13 is understood in a very different way by the Roman Catholic Church. Roman Catholicism holds that this promise implies that the Holy Spirit will lead the Church progressively into all the truth and that therefore it is authorized to add to the inspired teaching of the New Testament. This has resulted in the development of a body of tradition that has in some cases superseded the true Word of God and in other cases has made it void. John Calvin properly holds that this promise was in a peculiar sense limited to the Apostles. He asks: "If they were guided by the Spirit of truth unto all truth when they published their writings, what prevented them from embracing a full knowledge of the Gospel, and consigning it therein?"[10]

3. *The Objections to the Doctrine of Inspiration*

It seems to us that in the light of the above facts we ought to be slow to question the full inspiration of the Scriptures. If the Bible is to be recognized as the foundation for our faith in any real way, is it not more reasonable to have such a high view of it than to speak of it as our foundation without such a view?

But there are problems connected with this view and we must look at some of the more important ones that have been brought forward. And at the very outset we are told that Paul denies his inspiration two times (Acts 23:5; 1 Cor. 7:10, 12, 25). Acts 23:5 may be dismissed at once as confusing limitation of knowledge with inspiration. Paul did not know that Ananias was the high priest because he was not omniscient, but Luke's record of Paul's statement is fully inspired. And when Paul says, "But to the rest say I, not the Lord" (1 Cor. 7:12), he does not disclaim inspiration, as is evident from his assertion that he has "obtained mercy of the Lord to be trustworthy" (v. 25) and that he also has "the Spirit of God" (v. 40). Meyer says: "Paul knew from the living voice of tradition what commands Christ had given concerning divorce (Matt. 5:31 f.; 19:3-9; Mark 10:2-12; Luke 16:18. . . .) He distinguishes, therefore, here and in vss. 12, 25, not between his own and in-

---

10. *Institutes of the Christian Religion,* II, 399.

spired commands, but between those which proceeded from his own (God-inspired) subjectivity and those which Christ Himself supplied by His objective word"[11]

However, some real problems involving this view of inspiration have been brought forward. We grant that if the Bible is thus fully inspired, then there can be no errors in the original documents and practically none in our present critical texts. But various apparent errors are pointed out by those who take a lower view of the Scriptures. Let us consider the principal ones of these. Again we feel that because of the organic union of the Old and New Testaments we ought to touch briefly on the supposed errors in the Old Testament before dealing with those of the New.

(1) *In Science and History.* Though the Bible is not a textbook on either science or history, it must speak truthfully on these subjects whenever it touches on them, if it is verbally inspired. Some so-called errors in science are simply truths presented in popular language. With our scientists today, the Bible may be allowed to speak of the rising and setting of the sun, of the four corners of the earth, etc. The Genesis story of creation may be harmonized with the assured facts of geology, either by the theory of restitution or by the day-age theory. In recent times scientists have admitted that light is earlier than the sun. There is too much difference of opinion concerning the age of man among geologists and anthropologists to warrant the assertion that the representations of Scripture on this point are untrue.

Archaeological discoveries have done much to confirm the historical accuracy of the Scriptures. Hammurabi, Sargon II, the Hittites, and Belshazzar are no longer problems to the historian. Garstang has now established the date of the Exodus on solid ground,[12] which makes it possible to work out a consistent chronology from Abraham to Solomon. The large sums of money of which we sometimes read can be partly explained as required by the recurring changes in the value of money and partly as transcriptional errors. This latter suggestion applies also to the large armies of which we sometimes read. Robt. Dick Wilson shows that forty-some kings of Scripture have

11. *Comm. on* I *Corinthians, in loc.*
12. *The Foundations of Bible History,* p. 65.

been found in archaeological research.[13] Geo. L. Robinson, formerly of the Presbyterian Theological Seminary, Chicago, says: "No explicit contradiction of Scripture of any moment whatever has ever been found. More and more, scholars are coming to recognize the substantial verity of the Bible. And less and less do archaeologists endorse the evolutionary hypothesis of Higher Criticism to explain the growth of Law and religion in Israel."[14]

Similar solutions may be adopted for the problems that are brought forward from the New Testament. The differences in Num. 25:9 and 1 Cor. 10:8 vanish on a careful reading of the two texts. The "level place" in Luke 6:17 was probably on the same mountain as is mentioned in Matt. 5:1, and so the "Sermon" in the two Gospels is the same sermon. There was an old Jericho and a new Jericho, and the blind man was probably healed between the two Jerichos (Matt 20:29; Mark 10:46; Luke 18:35). The fact that Matthew speaks of two men and Mark and Luke only of one may be explained on the ground of the particular interest of the writers. This is also true of the account of two (Matt. 8:28) or one (Mark 5:2; Luke 8:27) demon-possessed men in Decapolis. The so-called mistakes of Stephen (Acts 7) have been harmonized satisfactorily.[15]

Archaeological discoveries also confirm the truthfulness of the New Testament. Quirinius (Luke 2:2) was apparently twice governor of Syria (B. C. 16-12 and 6-4), the latter being the time referred to by Luke. "Lysanias the tetrarch" is mentioned in an inscription on the site of Abilene at the time to which Luke refers. An inscription at Lystra, by the native Lycaonians, records the dedication of a statue to Zeus (Jupiter) and Hermes (Mercury), which shows that these gods were classed together in the local cult, as implied in Acts 14:12. Ramsay found that when Paul went from Iconium to Lystra he crossed from Phrygia into Lycaonia (Acts 14:6); but before this discovery every authoritative geographer taught that Acts was wrong.[16] Luke calls the officials of Philippi "prae-

13. *A Scientific Investigation of the Bible*, pp. 72-83.
14. *The Bearing of Archaeology on the Old Testament*, 1941, p. 12.
15. See Hackett's *Comm. on Acts* and Knowling's notes in *The Expositor's Greek Testament*.
16. *St. Paul the Traveler*, p. 110 f.

tors," which is not technically correct, but Ramsay declares that the inscriptions indicate that the term was "frequently employed as a courtesy title for the supreme magistrates of a Roman colony."[17] An inscription from Paphos refers to the "proconsul Paulus," who has been identified as the Sergius Paulus of Acts 13:7.

(2) *In Miracle and Prophecy*. We cannot go into the proof of the possibility and credibility of miracles, but, as we have already said, to one who believes in a personal God in the Christian sense of the term, they really present no problem. In nature lower laws are constantly overcome by higher; man overcomes the lower laws, sometimes without means, at other times with means. The miracles of Jesus are so organically connected with the record of the rest of the Life of Christ that it is impossible to excise the former without virtually destroying the latter. To one who believes in the physical resurrection of Jesus there is no insuperable hindrance to the acceptance of all the other well attested miracles. Scripture miracles are well attested.

In the light of the fulfillments of various predictions concerning the great world empires of Babylon, Medo-Persia, Greece, and Rome, concerning Israel and the Iraelitish polity, and concerning the character of the present age, we ought not to be biased against the possibility of predictive prophecy. What are regarded as errors in prophecy are usually but misinterpretations of prophecy. Parts of Dan. 2, 7, 9, 11, 12 and of Zech. 12-14 are still future. The preterist view of the Apocalypse holds that the last book of the Bible has already been fulfilled; but that is manifestly a misinterpretation of the book. Paul did not teach that Christ *would* come within his life-time (2 Cor. 5:4; 1 Thess. 4:15-17), but merely that He might come at any time. In later life he definitely believed that his death was impending (Phil. 1:20-25; 2 Tim. 4:8). The Scriptures which seem to teach that the Lord will come at once (James 5:9; Phil. 4:5) must be read alongside of such as 2 Pet. 3:4, 9.

(3) *In Quoting and Interpreting the Old Testament*. In reply to the objections to the inspiration of the Scriptures that have

17. *Op. cit.*, p. 218.

been based on these grounds we offer the following explanations: (1) Sometimes the New Testament writers merely select certain familiar words from an Old Testament passage to describe the righteousness which is by faith, and do not pretend to expound the Old Testament reference in which the words occur (Rom. 10:6-8; cf. Deut. 30:12-14); (2) sometimes they recognize a typical element in a passage and point out its fulfillment (Matt. 2:15; cf. Hos. 11:1); (3) sometimes they seem to give the credit to an earlier prophecy when in reality they are quoting from a later form of it (Matt. 27:9; cf. Zech. 11:13); (4) sometimes they seem to quote an apparently false translation in the Septuagint on the ground that the mistranslation conveys at least a part of the fulness of meaning found in the original Hebrew text (Eph. 4:26; cf. Ps. 4:4 in the LXX); and (5) sometimes they combine two quotations into one and assign the whole to the more prominent author (Mark 1:2, 3, A. S. V.; the A. V. is incorrect here).

Furthermore, if we believe in the possibility of a supernatural work of the Holy Spirit in the heart of man, then we ought not to find it difficult to believe also in the possibility of a supernatural operation of the Spirit in the production of the Scriptures. And if we recognize Him as the real Author of the Scriptures, then we cannot deny to Him the right to use an earlier inspired statement in a new way, if He sees fit. He may, then, guide the human authors of the Bible to employ any one of the methods cited in the preceding paragraph without doing violence to His own Word. Only then could the writers of Holy Scripture be accused of misusing the Old Testament if they said they were quoting formally and then interpreted the quotation in a manner that was out of harmony with the context of the Old Testament. It does not seem that they ever do this.

(4) *In Morals and Religion.* Practically all the so-called errors in morals and religion are found in the Old Testament; but since the two Testaments are so intimately bound together, the objections to the former affects also the latter. There can, however, be no difficulty at this point if we note the following facts:

(1) The sinful acts of men may be recorded, but they are never sanctioned, as Noah's drunkenness (Gen. 9:20-27), Lot's incest (Gen. 19:30-38), Jacob's falsehood (Gen. 27:19-24), David's adultery (2 Sam. 11:1-4), Solomon's polygamy (1 Kings 11:1-3; cf. Deut. 17:17), Esther's severity (Esth. 9:12-14), and Peter's denials (Matt. 26:69-75); (2) some evil acts appear to be sanctioned, but it is really the good intention or accompanying virtue that is recognized and not the evil act itself, as Rahab's faith, not her duplicity (Josh. 2:1-24; Heb. 11:31; James 2:25), Jael's patriotism, not her treachery (Judges 4:17-22; cf. 5:24), and Samson's faith, not his vagabondage (Judges 14-16; Heb. 11:32); (3) some things were permitted in pre-Christian times as relatively, not absolutely, right, as divorce (Deut. 24:1; Matt. 5:31, 32; 19:7-9) and retaliation (Ex. 21:24, 25; cf. Matt. 5:38, 39); (4) some prayers and divine commands express but the purpose of a sovereign God Who frequently uses men to carry out His designs (Ps. 35, 69, 109, 137; Deut. 7:1-5, 16; 20:16-18). Strong says, the imprecatory Psalms are "not the ebullition of personal anger, but the expression of judicial indignation against the enemies of God," and, "an exterminating war was only the benevolent surgery that amputated the putrid limb, and so saved the religious life of the Hebrew nation of the after-world."[18]

It is not required of us that we refute every objection to the doctrine of inspiration that has ever been brought forward, nor that we carry the refutation in every case to the point of demonstration. All that can be expected of us is that we present a plausible argument for every point that we advance. To some minds we probably have not done this; to them certain of the above replies may seem evasions of the problem. But to the believer in an authoritative revelation from God they constitute a strong support for the doctrine of inspiration. The fragmentary nature of many narratives and the elliptical character of many arguments make it difficult to reproduce all the factors that are needed to interpret such a passage. But since we have already had so many confirmations of the Scriptures from

18. *Systematic Theology,* p. 231.

recent archaeological, historical, anthropological, and literary investigations, we ought to give the benefit of the doubt to the Scriptures in those cases where as yet we have had no outside confirmation, and not to some naturalistic explanation that robs us of an authoritative Bible. Let us, then, recognize both Old and New Testaments as the verbally inspired Word of God!

PART TWO

SPECIAL INTRODUCTION

Chapter V

THE SYNOPTIC PROBLEM

THE term "synoptic" comes from the Greek word *sunopti-kos* and means "seeing the whole together, taking a comprehensive view." But as applied to the Gospels the word has come to mean *affording, presenting,* or *taking the same or a common view.* We call the first three Gospels in our English versions the "Synoptic Gospels," because they present the same general view of the life, death, resurrection, and teaching of our Lord. The Fourth Gospel does not contradict the Synoptic Gospels; it merely surveys the life and work of Christ from a different standpoint. The contents and arrangements of the Synoptic Gospels raise various questions, and we therefore turn to the discussion of the Synoptic Problem.

1. *The Problem Stated*

Every reader of these Gospels knows that they contain marked resemblances along with equally marked differences. This is true not only of the subject-matter and the vocabulary, but also of the order in which the materials are introduced. Many attempts have been made to tabulate the agreements and the differences. That of Archbishop Thomson may serve as an example. He says: "If the history be harmonized and then divided into 89 sections, it will be found that in 42 of these [nearly a half] all the narratives coincide, that 12 more are given by Matthew and Mark only, that 5 are common to Mark and Luke only, and that 14 are found in Matthew and Luke. To these should be added 5 peculiar to Matthew, 2 to Mark, and 9 to Luke, and the number is complete."[1] Different students divide the materials differently. Eichhorn said that there were 44 sections that coincided in the Synoptics. Bishop Westcott

---

1. *Bible Commentary,* N. T., I, viii.

reduced the materials to a percentage basis. According to his system Mark has 7 peculiarities and 93 concordances; Matthew has 42 peculiarities and 58 concordances; Luke has 59 peculiarities and 41 concordances; and John has 92 peculiarities and 8 concordances.[2]

We are not now concerned about exact statistics, but rather about the obvious fact that these Gospels have much material in common, as also a considerable amount of material that is common to only two of them and some that is peculiar to each of the three. This is a most interesting situation. It raises the question of the literary origin of these Gospels. How is it that they have so much in common and yet so much that is different?

2. *Proposed Solutions Examined*

From the earliest times attempts have been made to harmonize the materials in the four Gospels. Tatian's *Diatessaron* c. A.D. 170 was the first effort of this kind. Tatian took the materials that are found in the four Gospels and wove them into one continuous account, without repeating any part that is common to two or more of them. About A.D. 220 Ammonius of Alexandria introduced a novel method of harmonizing the Gospels. He took Matthew as his standard and divided it into 335 sections; Mark he divided into 236 sections; Luke into 342; and John into 232. The same sections in any two, three, or all four were designated by Greek letters that indicated in which Gospels the sections occurred, while the sections that were peculiar to any one Gospel received other letters. Eusebius modified Ammonius' system in a measure some time before A.D. 340.

But there seems to have been no early attempt to deal with the literary problems presented by the Synoptics. Augustine is probably the first that expressed an opinion in this respect. He suggested that the similarities of language in the Gospels indicated literary dependence among them. In his opinion Mark was a condensation of Matthew. There seems to have been no further discussion of the problem either in the Middle Ages or during the time of the Reformation. About the middle of the

---

2. *Intro. to the Study of the Gospels*, p. 201.

eighteenth century the problem was really brought forward. Lachmann first gave definite expression to that which we now call the *Synoptic Problem.* Since his day many solutions of the problem have been proposed. The history of Synoptic Criticism may be briefly surveyed under the following six heads.

(1) *The Urevangelium Theory*

The German critic and dramatist, G. E. Lessing, and the theologian, J. G. Eichhorn, held that there was an original Gospel from which all three Synoptic writers drew their materials. Lessing held that Matthew wrote the Aramaic *Gospel of the Nazarenes,* the germs of which originated in the time immediately following the death of Christ; that before he left Palestine to preach among the Hellenists he made an abstract of this Gospel in Greek for his new hearers; and that this Greek Gospel is our canonical Matthew. He also held that Mark and Luke were nothing but excerpts from this Aramaic Gospel, made from their own points of view and for their own purposes. Papias' statement that every one interpreted Matthew's Logia as best he could, was the basis for Lessing's theory. Eichhorn, however, asserted that only the sections which the three have in common came directly from this Aramaic original, which had been written by a disciple of one of the Apostles about the year 35. He held that during the decades following this original Gospel was frequently recast, enlarged, and abbreviated, first in Aramaic and then also in Greek; and that from these many Gospels which thus came into existence between A.D. 35 and 60, the rest of the materials in our canonical Gospels were produced. His theory was so artificial and the "sources" so many that it has never commended itself to many scholars.[3]

The theory of an Urevangelium has no historical support and is improbable to a high degree. If our Gospels are but excerpts from this "source," why was not the source itself preserved? The theory cannot account for the omissions in the several Gospels of materials that were pertinent to their evident purpose. If the writers had all these materials before

---

[3] Zahn's *Intro. to the New Testament,* II, 403 f.

them, why then did they not include all in their source that furthered their objectives?

(2) *The Interdependence Theory*

This theory holds that one of the three wrote first, largely on the basis of oral tradition; that the one who wrote next used this first Gospel; and that the third used both the earlier Gospels. The second and third also added some materials of their own. Every possible permutation of the order of the Synoptics has had advocates. Grotius (1583-1645), Dutch jurist, seems to have been the first to suggest this theory. The following are the permutations that have been suggested and the men who have held them: Matthew, Mark, Luke: Grotius, Mill, Wetstein, Hug, Greswell; Matthew, Luke, Mark: Griesbach, Fritzsche, Meyer, De Wette, Baur; Mark, Matthew, Luke: Storr, Weisse, Wilke; Mark, Luke, Matthew: Hitzig, Bruno Bauer, Volkmar; Luke, Matthew, Mark: Evanson; Luke, Mark, Matthew: Vögel.

This theory is not now held by any important scholar. It was impossible to work out such an interdependence in a scientific way, as is evident from the disagreements among the advocates of this view. Alford gives one of the best refutations of it.[4] Westcott says the theory "offers no explanation of the peculiar distribution of the coincidences, or of the differences between the several narratives." He also says the theory "appears to be inconsistent with the results of a careful analysis of the language and of the contents of the Gospels. Every attempt to show on this hypothesis why a later Evangelist has omitted details which are noted by an earlier one; why he adopted his language up to a certain point, and then suddenly abandoned it; why he retained in some sentences nothing more than a remarkable word, and in others the fulness of an entire answer, has always failed."[5] The combination Mark, Matthew, Luke was the last of the permutations held. From it there was developed the current "two-source" theory, which will be discussed presently.

4. *Greek Testament*, I, 3-6.
5. *Op. cit.*, p. 206 f.

(3) *The Fragmentary Theory*

Schleiermacher (1768-1834) held that the basis of all Gospel literature was neither an oral nor a written Gospel, but a large number of short written narratives. Although from time to time this theory has been revived, it has never had general acceptance. Recently, however, *Formgeschichte* has taken it over and has done much to establish it. Schleiermacher's view of the origination of our canonical Matthew and Mark has had more general acceptance. In his view Papias knew nothing of our Matthew or Mark. He knew only Matthew's collection of the sayings of Jesus in Hebrew and a much less complete and orderly Mark than our Mark. Our Greek Matthew, according to him, is one of the many recensions of this collection of Sayings, and our Mark is a much worked-over edition of the Mark of which Papias speaks. In other words, Schleiermacher became the "discoverer" of an original Matthew and Mark from which our Matthew and Mark were later prepared. This "discovery" opened the way for new attempts to solve the synoptic problem. All who accept the testimony of Luke 1:1,2 agree that there were many written accounts prior to our canonical Gospels, and to this extent Schleiermacher was on the right track. But the claim that there were both an *Ur-Matthäus* and an *Ur-Markus* is challenged today. We shall deal with this problem in connection with our study of the Two-Document Theory.

(4) *The Oral Tradition Theory*

Barton, editor of Dom John Chapman's book, calls this "a Protestant theory" and declares that it "remains essentially Protestant";[6] but the Catholics Schegg, Kaulen Fouard, Fillion, Knabenbauer, and Cornely also have held it. The first one to suggest it was Giesler (in 1818). Westcott, Ebrard, Nösgen, Alford, Godet, Pressense, Guericke, Thiersch, Norton, Wetzel, and Veit are Protestants who have held it. With modifications it is advocated by A. Wright in his *Synopsis of the Gospels in Greek* (2d. ed., 1908).

---

6. *Matthew, Mark, and Luke,* p. xvii.

According to Giesler the common basis of the Synoptics was entirely oral. Due to the instruction of the Apostles during their prolonged stay at Jerusalem (Acts 1:1-8:4), this material came to be repeated in much the same way by all. Giesler offered the following proof for this theory: The N. T. writings and the post-apostolic literature are silent regarding the use of written Gospels; the way in which the words and deeds of Jesus are introduced in this literature supports the oral tradition; the fact that comparatively little writing was done in the apostolic age also favors this theory; and the simple character of the culture of the early Christians in Palestine makes it impossible to suppose that records of the Gospels should have been made thus early.[7] Westcott argues for this view as follows: (1) The language of Luke's preface points clearly to an oral tradition as the source of his own Gospel. and by implication of the corresponding parts in the other Gospels; (2) the oral hypothesis is most consistent with the general habit of the Jews and the peculiar position of the Apostles; (3) it is supported by the earliest direct testimony, and in some degree is implied in the Apostolic writings; and (4) an oral source is pointed to by the internal character of the Gospels.[8]

We believe that this theory is true so far as it goes, but it does not go far enough. Surely, the facts concerning the life and teachings of Christ were first given to the world by word of mouth and not in the form of written documents. Luke's reference to the testimony of eye-witnesses as sources for those who had taken in hand to draw up narratives of the life of Christ is proof of this fact (Luke 1:2). So is also Papias' statement that Mark's Gospel embodies the preaching of Peter. Thus we have here an oral base for Mark's Gospel. But the oral theory is inadequate to account for all the phenomena. It may account for the sections common to all three Synoptics; but how about those which are found in two of them or only in one? If all the materials in these Gospels are directly traceable to the Apostles, then why did not all three include all of them? Peake sees a difficulty here. He thinks it hard to explain on what principles the oral tradition was formed and to account

---

7. As summarized by Zahn, *op. cit.*, II, 409 f.
8. *Op cit.*, p. 212.

for the fixity which was reached by the tradition.[9] There is some problem here, it is true, and we shall deal with it in setting forth our own view; but it is not nearly as difficult as Peake thinks it is. For further discussion of this point see under *A Proposed Solution* below.

(5) *The Two-Document Theory*

Although the documentary theory had its origin with Eichhorn (1794), B. Weiss and Holtzmann are usually recognized as the originators of the Two-Document hypothesis. In the language of Iverach this view holds: "(1) One source is a Gospel like, if not identical with, the canonical Gospel of Mark. As regards this 2d Gospel there is a consensus of opinion that it is prior to the other two, and the view that the 1st and 3d used it as a source is described as the one solid result of literary criticism. . . . (2) The other source (now commonly named Q) is found first by an examination of the matter not contained in the 2d Gospel, which is common to Matthew and Luke. While there are differences as to the extent and character of the 2d source, there is something like general agreement as to its existence. It is not agreed as to whether this source contained narratives of events, as well as sayings, or whether it was a book of sayings alone (the former is thought to be the more probable view), nor is it agreed as to whether it contained an account of the Passion week; but while disagreement exists as to these and other points, the tendency, as said, is to accept a 'two-source' theory in some form as the only sufficient account of the phenomena of the Gospels."[10] It must be added that besides these two main sources, there are thought to have been also some secondary sources, as for the birth narratives in Matthew and Luke, and for the so-called Perean section in the Third Gospel.

There is some difference of opinion, as has just been said, as to the nature of the first source, some holding, as Schleiermacher had already suggested, that there was an original Mark, known today as *Ur-Markus,* from which we get not only our Mark, but from which Matthew and Luke also borrowed;

---

9. *A Critical Intro. to the New Testament,* pp. 106-109.
10. Art. "Syn. Gospels," in *Inter. Stand. Bible Ency.*

while the majority hold that our canonical Mark is the only Mark that ever existed. Reuss holds that there was an *Ur-Markus*. Recently Cadoux has written a book entitled, *The Sources of the Second Gospel*, in which he maintains that Mark used three sources: The Palestinian Gospel, the Gospel of the Dispersion, and the Gentile Gospel. He goes so far as to arrange the materials in our Mark according to these three supposed "sources." But the theory is too arbitrary and fanciful to deserve serious consideration. Very few will follow Cadoux in this view.

The whole theory of an *Ur-Markus* has fallen into disrepute. Holtzmann at first held it, but later on gave it up. Lake and Lake say: "There is no valid reason for thinking that there ever was an earlier form of Mark (the Ur-Markus theory) of which the present text is an abbreviation. All the evidence, such as it is, points the other way."[11] Streeter says: "Renounce once and for all the chase of the phantom *Ur-Markus,* and the study of the minor agreements becomes the highway to the purest text of the Gospels."[12] In another place he says: "I have also, I hope — by a new use of the Ms. evidence available — finally disposed of the troublesome phantom of an '*Ur-Markus*' (or earlier version of Mark) which has for too long haunted the minds of scholars."[13] This should mean the disposal of Cadoux' new theory likewise.

Many hold that the second source was an *Ur-Matthäus,* meaning the reputed Logia of Matthew of which Papias speaks. B. Weiss held this view. He said that the original Gospel was much like our Matthew, except that it did not have the Passion story. Declaring that the account of the Passion in the three Synoptists differs radically from that contained in the Fourth Gospel, he held that the account in Matthew could not have originated with an apostle. Zahn held that Matthew wrote an Aramaic Gospel, which was used in the composition of Mark and our Greek Matthew. Some hold that the Aramaic Matthew contained only the Sayings of Jesus. But while many still hold that Matthew first wrote an Aramaic Gospel to which our Greek Matthew is somehow related, they are becoming

---

11. *Intro. to the New Testament,* p. 17.
12. *The Four Gospels,* p. 331.
13. *Op. cit.,* p. xxix.

more and more uncertain as to the exact relation that it sustains to our canonical Gospels.

The usual way in which the Two-Document Theory is held today is that the first source of Matthew and Luke was our canonical Mark, and the second, Q, whatever the character of that source may have been. Schweitzer says Weisse, in 1838, came to the conclusion that Mark's Gospel was the earliest of the four. He came to this position when he observed that "the graphic details of Mark, which had hitherto been regarded as due to an attempt to embellish an epitomizing narrative, were too insignificant to have been inserted with this purpose." It therefore seemed clear to him that only one other possibility remained, viz., that their absence in Matthew and Luke was due to omission. Yet Weisse did not base the priority of Mark solely on these incidentals. His more weighty argument for this view is the composition and arrangement of the whole Gospel material.[14] Wilke's book on *The Earliest Gospel,* appeared in the same year as Weisse's, and it did much to confirm Weisse's theory of the priority of Mark in the minds of New Testament critics.

As for the second source, Q, there is today much disagreement as to the exact nature of it. Weisse had suggested that the Logia of Matthew supplied the sections common to Matthew and Luke. B. Weiss and Holtzmann fully developed this idea. For the special material in Luke Holtzmann saw only oral tradition, while Weiss thought he saw a written source for this material which he called L. Easton says, subsequent research has added little to the findings of Weiss and Holtzmann.[15] While today some would make Q identical with Papias' *Logia of Matthew,*[16] many are doubtful of the identification.[17]

It may, perhaps, be said that the Two-Document theory as a whole is disintegrating. The advocates of *Formgeschichte* still profess to accept it, but they lay the major stress upon the many short documents that preceded the writing of any of the

---

14. Schweitzer, *The Quest of the Historical Jesus,* p. 122.
15. *The Gospel Before the Gospels,* p. 5.
16. Hawkins, "Probabilities as to the So-Called Double Tradition of St. Matthew and St. Luke, in *Oxford Studies in the Synoptic Problem,* p. 105.
17. Goodspeed, *Intro. to the New Testament,* p. 174; Bacon, *Intro. to the New Testament,* p. 196 f.

Gospels. Ropes is skeptical with regard to the very existence of Q. He bewails the fact that within the past hundred years and more of incessant labor nothing more has been achieved than the fact that Matthew and Luke both drew on Mark, in substantially its present form, for the greater part of their narratives of events and incidents. With regard to the origin of the great mass of sayings of Jesus common to Matthew and Luke, but not found in Mark, he says, "Agreement among scholars is less than it was forty years ago. The widespread idea of a common source, now lost, for these two gospels — the theory of the 'Logia' or 'Q' — has tended to be modified, refined, and complicated to such a degree as, for that reason if for no other, to arouse doubts of its validity."[18]

Goodspeed is very emphatic on this point. He says: "This supposed Aramaic document mentioned by Papias used to be reckoned the second source of Matthew and Luke, from which they obtained their greater richness in Jesus' teaching. But their common discourse material shows so much identity of Greek language that this view has been given up. The non-Marcan materials of Matthew and Luke came to them from Greek sources; there can be no possible doubt of that, as an hour's examination of the non-Marcan parallels in Matthew and Luke will show."[19]

Orr, too, feels that the Two-Document Theory is inadequate. He says: "A theory which commands the assent of so many scholars has necessarily great weight. It cannot, however, be regarded as finally established. Many grave difficulties remain; there is, besides, a *prima facie* improbability in a Gospel like Mark's being treated in the manner supposed or included among the 'attempts' which Luke's own Gospel was designed to supersede."[20] Even Bacon declares that it "lacks much of meeting all the requirements of the case."[21]

In the estimation of the writer the Two-Document Theory is open to the following criticisms:

(1) It is based upon an unproved theory of development. For a long time now Biblical criticism has been strongly influenced by the theory of evolution. The idea that all things pro-

---

18. *The Synoptic Gospels*, p. 93.
19. *Intro. to the New Testament*, p. 174.
20. *Criticism of the Bible*, in *Inter. Stand. Bible Ency.*
21. *An Intro. to the New Testament*, p. 177.

ceed from the simple to the complex has so gotten hold of the minds of scholars that, it seems, they can believe nothing else. Any one that raises a question as to the validity of this basic assumption is by these writers considered hopelessly benighted. Yet there are indications that the simple does not always precede the complex, indeed, that in many instances there is a tendency toward simplification. The engineering feat displayed in the erection of the great pyramids of Egypt is still the wonder of the world. We still turn to the Greek writers as the masters of the intellect. The Sanskrit language, the oldest member of the Indo-European family, with its eight cases and other structural complexities, challenges the keenest powers of linguists even today. Even the Anglo-Saxon language was more complicated with its six case-forms and for some words eight, than our present two nominal and three pronominal forms. Many a mechanical invention is far more complex originally than it comes to be in time. In itself it is equally possible that Mark may have extracted material from Matthew that served his purpose or that Matthew may have borrowed from Mark. Perhaps neither used the other Gospel. At any rate, the simple does not always precede the complex nor does the simple always develop into the complex.

But the Two-Document Theory avowedly rests upon this sort of theory of development. R. H. Lightfoot exults over the discovery of these "laws of development." He says: "We have been granted, during the lifetime of many who are still with us, a new and very remarkable revelation with regard to the laws of development and growth; we are allowed, if we will, to understand much that was necessarily hidden from those who went before us."[22] He denominates the time of certain earlier critics as "the cloudy and dark day of the new discoveries."[23] But in the absence of any external proofs to that effect, the view that the laws of development operated in the production of our Gospels in any such way as these scholars insist, is at best a mere assumption, if it is not unscientific. It is a *petitio principii* for which no solid evidence is furnished, but merely the inference of the writers.

---

22. *History and Interpretation in the Gospels*, p. 216.
23. *Op. cit.*, p. 217.

(2) It is *prima facie* improbable that a Gospel like Mark's would be treated in the manner supposed. Applying the above assumption of literary development to the Gospels, these scholars insist that similarity of content, arrangement, and phraseology proves the derivation of the longer Gospels from Mark and some other primitive documents. Allen, for example, attempts to account for the material in Matthew's Gospel sentence by sentence, phrase by phrase, almost word by word, "proving that much of it came from Mark's Gospel"[24] Sir John C. Hawkins' *Horae Synopticae* is the most thorough-going study of this kind. Streeter tries to justify the variations between Matthew and Mark on the one hand and between Luke and Mark on the other on the following grounds: Emendation of Mark's awkward and ungrammatical sentences; substitution of the usual Greek word for Mark's Latinisms; elimination of Mark's eight Aramaic words; agglomoration and conflation.[25]

Mark's Gospel being the shortest, it is also by nearly all present-day critics considered the simplest, and therefore the earliest. But so far as we can go back, that is to the 3d century, we never find Mark in the first place among the Gospels. Matthew or John stand first in all our documents, Mark and Luke never. An early tradition is preserved by Origen that Matthew was written first, then Mark, then Luke, and finally John. This order is found in the large majority of the manuscripts and versions.[26] Indeed, in the early days Mark was less esteemed than the other Gospels. Robertson says: "Victor of Antioch (fifth or sixth century A.D.), the earliest known commentator on Mark, complains that while St. Matthew and St. John had received the attention of a number of expositors, and St. Luke also had attracted a few, his utmost efforts had failed to detect a single commentary upon St Mark."[27]

Luke represents certain "eye-witnesses and ministers of the word" as his principal informants (Luke 1:2); but whether their information was oral or written or both, whether it was in Aramaic or in Greek he does not tell us. Westcott, as we have already noted, held that Luke's statement points to an

---

24. *Vide his Critical and Exegetical Commentary on the Gospel according to St. Matthew.*
25. *The Four Gospels*, pp. 164-166, 192.
26. Moffatt, *Intro. to the Lit. of the New Testament*, p. 15.
27. *Studies in Mark's Gospel*, p 21 f.

oral tradition as the source of his own Gospel.[28] But Luke also speaks of the many narratives that had been drawn up of the life of Christ. We thus have historical proof of the early existence of many written accounts of the life, work, and passion of Christ before Luke wrote. In all probability he used some of these in making his own investigations. Plummer thinks that he had written sources for the first two chapters and for the genealogy in ch. 3; but he doubts whether he used Mark. He thinks we cannot account for Luke's omission of the whole of Mark 6:45-8:9 on the view of his depending on the Second Gospel, for this material "would have been full of interest to Luke's Gentile readers."[29] Streeter suggests that Luke used "a mutilated copy of Mark" for this section;[30] but though this is an ingenious way out of the difficulty, it savors too much of wishful thinking. Dom John Chapman once held the Two-Document view, but was converted to the idea of the priority of Matthew. He says: "The arguments which are usually given to demonstrate the dependency of Matthew on Mark are perfectly compatible with the dependence of Mark on Matthew."[31]

What Kerr says in rejecting the interdependence theory applies equally well to the Two-Document Theory, except that in the latter case the wrong is done to Mark only. He says: "This theory degrades one or two Synoptists to the position of slavish and yet arbitrary compilers, not to say plagiarists; it assumes a strange mixture of dependence and affected originality; it weakens the independent value of their history; and it does not account for the omissions of most important matter, and for many differences in common matter."[32]

Alford also rejects the theory of the use of one of our Synoptic Gospels by the others. He says: "It is inconceivable that one writer borrowing from another matter confessedly of the very first importance, in good faith and with approval, should alter the diction so singularly and capriciously as, on this hypothesis, we find the text of the parallel sections of our Gospels changed Let the question be answered by ordinary considerations of

28. *Op. cit.*, p. 212.
29. *Critical and Exegetical Commentary on the Gospel of St. Luke*, p. xxiii f.
30. *Op. cit.*, p. 175.
31. *Op. cit.*, p. 4.
32. *Intro. to New Testament Study*, p. 11.

probability, and let any passage common to the three Evangelists be put to the test. The phenomena presented will be much as follows: first, perhaps, we shall have three, five, or more words identical; then as many wholly distinct; then two clauses or more, expressed in the same words but differing order; then a clause contained in one or two, and not in the third; then several words identical; then a clause not only wholly distinct, but apparently inconsistent; and so forth, with recurrences of the same arbitrary and anomalous alterations, coincidences, and transpositions. Nor does this description apply to verbal and sentential arrangement only; but also, with slight modification, to that of the larger portions of the narratives. Equally capricious would be the disposition of the subject-matter. . . . Can an instance be anywhere cited of undoubted borrowing and adaptation from another, presenting similar phenomena?"[33]

In the light of these facts we conclude that it is improbable that either Matthew or Luke so treated Mark.

(3) The very existence and nature of the so-called "Q" is uncertain. Salmon contends that Papias is the only sure witness to the Aramaic Logia of Matthew. He regards Irenæus's statement (*Against Heresies,* III. i. 1) as not certainly an independent testimony, since he knew the work of Papias and may have drawn from it. He also shows that Epiphanius' reference is to an Ebionite Gospel and not to the genuine Matthew, and that Jerome's quotation is not from our canonical Matthew, but from an Apocryphal Gospel.[34] Ropes says, "This theory of a second written source, devised to explain the resemblances of Matthew and Luke, seems first to have occurred to the mind of man, or at least to have been published to the world, just one hundred years ago. In the present state of knowledge, whether such a document ever existed must be regarded as uncertain."[35] Dom John Chapman speaks of "the impossibility of Q," devoting a whole chapter to proving its non-existence.[36] His arguments may be summarized as follows: There is no agreement in Matthew and Luke as to the order of the sections in Q; sometimes Matthew and Luke in the sections common to

---

33. *Greek Testament,* I, 5, 6.
34. *Intro. to the New Testament,* pp. 173-180.
35. *Op. cit.,* p. 68.
36. *Op. cit.,* ch. 9.

them use identical language and sometimes they have no Greek words in common; though Q is supposed to be Palestinian in origin, it has none of the Matthean points which would especially interest Palestinian Jews; finally, Q would have overlapped Matthew, Mark, and Luke and might be the source of all three Synoptics, i.e., it would have no characteristics of style or matter of its own.[37]

Streeter, however, regards the existence of Q as certain. He attempts to "reconstruct" it, but does not definitely identify it with the Logia of Matthew referred to by Papias.[38] He deplores the fact that scholars have spoken of the "Two-Document Hypothesis," since it conceals the assumption that the evangelists either used no other sources, or that the other sources did not have anything like the same value as the "Big Two." He advocates a Four-Document hypothesis, saying that this hypothesis "not only offers an extremely simple explanation of all the difficulties which the Two-Document Hypothesis cannot satisfactorily meet, but also reflects far better the historical situation in the primitive Church."[39] These four sources for Matthew and Luke are: Mark and Q, which both used; then Matthew also used a Jerusalem source which Streeter calls M; and Luke a Cæsarean source which he denominates L. Besides this Matthew had an Antiochene tradition, and Luke some other source, for the birth narrative.[40] But Streeter's theory is too much bound up with his conception of "local texts." He has made a real contribution in separating the "Cæsarean" from the so-called "Western" text; but we do not think that he has any ground for believing that his "Four-Document Hypothesis" is either a true or worthy solution of the problem.

In view of this uncertainty among scholars concerning the nature and existence of the supposed Q, we think it precarious to build dogmatic theories on this foundation.

(4) There is no reason for supposing that Matthew and Luke cannot have written independently. Lawson says: "After all, St. Matthew held an important position in the Roman Civil Service, a position demanding some education and ability.

---

37. *Op. cit.*, pp. 95-99.
38. *The Four Gospels*, ch. 10.
39. *Op. cit.*, pp. 227, 269.
40. *Op cit.*, ch. 9.

St. Luke, too, was a man of the educated class, being of the medical profession. . . . It might, therefore, be allowed that their Gospels may be entirely independent, if it were not for the assumption that they must have copied St. Mark, since both together have absorbed almost his whole contents. The independence of each writer of the Gospels may be assumed as the most probable solution of the difficulties presented."[41] To one who believes that the Apostle Matthew is the author of our first Gospel, it certainly seems strange that he should be supposed to derive even the account of his own conversion from Mark! Since he was an apostle, and since all that is in his Gospel, save chs. 1-4, the story of the cleansing of the Leper (8:1-4), the account of the healing of Peter's mother-in-law (8:14-17), and the incident of the Paralytic borne of four (9:1-8), occurred *after* his conversion and call, we think it strange to suppose that he should have to resort to "sources" for the information that he had received first hand.

Luke tells us something of the way in which he had prepared his own materials. He says that he had traced all things accurately from the beginning regarding the life of Christ, even before deciding to reduce his discoveries to writing; for the Greek word (*parēkolouthēkoti*) used in 1:3, is in the perfect tense. He speaks of many who had taken in hand "to draw up a narrative concerning those matters which have been fulfilled among us, even as they delivered them unto us, who from the beginning were eyewitnesses and ministers of the word"; but he does not seem to include our canonical Mark in these earlier narratives. This is implied in his statement that he attempts to present an *accurate* account of the events of the life of Christ. It does not seem possible that Luke would imply that Mark's account was inaccurate.

Our Lord was fully aware of the insufficiency of His disciples to prepare an accurate and adequate report of His earthly life and ministry. He therefore said: "The Comforter, even the Holy Spirit, whom the Father will send in my name, he shall teach you all things, and bring to your remembrance all that I said unto you" (John 14:26). Accordingly Matthew was not entirely dependent upon his own memory, but was

---

41. "The Dates and Origins of the Gospels," in *The Evangelical Quarterly*, July 15, 1938, p. 278.

reminded of the things which he had seen and heard by the Holy Spirit. There are indications that the disciples did not understand our Lord's conduct on many occasions until after they had received the Holy Spirit. John says: "These things understood not the disciples at the first: but when Jesus was glorified they remembered that these things were written of him and that they had done these things unto him" (John 12:16). This is in conformity with Christ's other promise: "Howbeit when he, the Spirit of truth, is come, he shall guide you into all the truth: for he shall not speak from himself; but what things soever he shall hear, these shall he speak; and he shall declare unto you the things that are to come. He shall glorify me: for he shall take of mine, and shall declare it unto you" (John 16:13,14).

We hold therefore that Matthew and Luke are independent authors of the facts they record.

(5) The priority of Mark was "discovered" just at the time when the Bible was losing its age-long position and prestige as the infallible Word of God. R. H. Lightfoot says: "So long as this view of inspiration prevailed, the four gospels could only be regarded as of equal value, historically and otherwise. It chanced, however, that just as this belief began to crumble, the discovery was made that among the four gospels one was quite definitely on a superior historical level . . . and the discovery that there were good grounds for finding in St. Mark a chief authority for the gospel of St. Matthew and St. Luke gave birth to the hope that in St. Mark's Gospel above all we might hope to discover the Jesus of history."[42]

It is this degradation of the Gospels of Matthew and Luke by the exponents of the Two-Document theory that constitutes the chief reason for the rejection of the theory by those who believe in the equal inspiration of all the Gospels. We feel that Matthew and Luke are not mere human adaptations of the materials in Mark, together with some more or less reliable supplementary materials derived from other sources; but that they are equally inspired with Mark, divinely originated to give specific pictures of the wonderful life and work of our Lord. Some exponents of the Two-Document theory still hold to the

---

42. *History and Interpretation in the Gospels*, pp. 10, 12.

inspiration of all the Synoptics; but, really, if Matthew and Luke derive 42 sections from Mark, Matthew 12 additional sections, and Luke 5 additional sections, then in 59 sections out of a total of 89 Mark would seem to be more original than either Matthew or Luke. On the basis of such an assumption of dependence it is easy to elevate Mark above the other two Synoptics in these sections, as those who do not believe in the full inspiration of the Scriptures do.

In the absence of all historical proof that Matthew and Luke were thus dependent upon Mark; in view of the possibility of explaining this phenomenon of agreements in the Synoptics in another way (see under *A Proposed Solution,* below); in the light of Lightfoot's declaration as to the doctrinal sacrifice necessary to the development of the theory; and because of our firm belief in the full and equal inspiration of all the Gospels, we are obliged to reject the Two-Document theory.

(6) *Formgeschichte*

In 1919 Martin Dibelius of the University of Heidelberg approached the study of Gospel origins from the standpoint of the literary forms now contained in the Synoptics. He regarded the composers as little more than "collectors, vehicles of tradition, editors."[44] According to Dibelius we have in the Synoptics the following types of literature: (1) The Passion story, (2) Paradigms (stories of the deeds of Jesus that were introduced as *examples* in support of the message), (3) Tales (descriptions of the illness and healing of the sick, and other miraculous events, together with the proof of the success of the miracle, told for the pleasure of the narrative itself), (4) Legends (narratives of saintly men in whose work and fate an interest is taken, — definitely edifying), (5) Sayings of Jesus (His words put together to form "speeches" with a single theme, and the parables, edited in the interest of exhortation), and (6) the interpretation of the short narratives and striking sayings, ending in the mythological element that takes charge of the entire material of evangelical history (the ascription of the qualities of deity to Christ, His virgin birth, resurrection.

---

44. *From Tradition to Gospel,* p. 3.

and ascension). These unliterary materials were collected, revised, arranged, and published in the form of our Synoptic Gospels.

Dibelius says that the "Paradigms" are only relatively trustworthy;[45] that the historical reliability of the "Tales" is not guaranteed;[46] and that Luke gives the sufferings of Jesus the character of a martyrdom, which he does because of "the need of speaking about Jesus in the manner elsewhere employed in speaking of the heroes of Legends."[47] Bultmann holds that the Synoptics have taken over the essential content of the Aramaic tradition of the oldest Palestinian community, but that there are different layers in this material. By means of critical analysis an oldest layer is determined; but "we have no absolute assurance that the exact words of this oldest layer were really spoken by Jesus. There is a possibility that the contents of this oldest layer are also the result of a complicated historical process which we can no longer trace."[48]

R. H. Lightfoot regards William Wrede (d. 1907) and Julius Wellhausen (d. 1918) as the forerunners of the present *Formgeschichte*.[49] Wrede was one of the first to undermine the historical dependability of even Mark's Gospel.[50] Lightfoot represents Sanday as saying that Wrede's work is "not only very wrong, but distinctly wrong-headed."[51] Wellhausen added to this that Mark's Gospel is largely made up of little narratives or sections which at first had a separate existence; that they were subjected to revision, or revisions, before they reached their present form; and that the contents represent not only the life of Jesus Christ, but to some extent also the beliefs of the early church at the time when they were written.[52] The teaching of Wrede and Wellhausen has been developed into the present *Formgeschichte*. The chief exponents of this view today are Dibelius of Heidelberg, Rudolph Bultmann of Marburg, C. H. Dodd of Mansfield College, Oxford, R. H. Lightfoot of New College, Oxford, B. S. Easton of The General

45. *Op. cit.*, p. 62.
46. *Op. cit.*, p. 292.
47. *Op. cit.*, p. 300.
48. *Jesus and the Word*, p. 13.
49. *History and Interpretation in the Gospels*, pp. 16-25.
50. *Ibid*, p. 18-21.
51. *Ibid.*, p. 17.
52. *Ibid.*, p. 23.

Theological Seminary, New York City, and D. W. Riddle of Chicago University.

Streeter thinks there is truth in the claim of *Formgeschichte* that "Mark is a collection of vignettes — scenes from the life of the master"; but he adds that in his opinion "the pendulum of German scholarship has by now . . . swung too far — in the direction towards which I was myself at that time looking" [he refers to something he wrote in *Oxford Studies* in 1910].[53] Other writers not entirely unsympathetic with *Formgeschichte* have yet sensed the dangers involved in it. Thus Ernest F. Scott of Union Theological Seminary has written a book entitled *The Validity of the Gospel Record,* and E. Basil Redlich, Canon Theologian of Leicester, has written one entitled *Form Criticism: Its Value and Limitations;* in both of these the authors endeavor to maintain the substantial truthfulness of the Synoptic Gospels.

We do not deny or even question the existence of an oral tradition, nor of short written accounts of the life of our Lord which were used as bases for the Synoptic Gospels; but we seriously object to any theory that shrouds the whole life of Christ in mystery and uncertainty. Advocates of *Formgeschichte* deny, as we have seen, that we can be certain that the tradition which was incorporated in our canonical Gospels is true, and some go so far as to say that we cannot be sure of even a single word that Jesus spoke. This is asking the true believer in Christ to make a renunciation that he can no sooner make than deny the Lord Himself. Such a conception of the production and preservation of the Synoptic Gospels cannot be harmonized with the idea of the providential care of a loving heavenly Father for the truth concerning His own Son. Albright says: "Only modern scholars who lack both historical method and perspective can spin such a web of speculation as that with which form-critics have surrounded the Gospel tradition. The sureness with which early Christian leaders distinguished between the normative and aberrant sayings of Jesus becomes very clear when we analyze the so-called *agrapha,* or apocryphal *logia,* collected from extant and from recently excavated documents. The *agrapha* generally express gnostic

---

53. *Op. cit.,* p. xiv.

or antinomian ideas which are foreign to the Gospels."[54] Albright also says: "From the standpoint of the objective historian data cannot be disproved by criticism of the accidental literary framework in which they occur, unless there are solid independent reasons for rejecting the historicity of an appreciable number of other data found in the same framework."[55]

The disagreements among the sponsors of *Formgeschichte* are further evidence of the fact that the theory is far from scientific. Albright says: "As E. Fascher has pointed out, the leading exponents of the school disagree completely in their theories as to the relation of the principal categories of form-criticism to the life of the early Church, and vicious circles are evident throughout their work."[56] In spite of the fact, therefore, that this view has gained tremendous popularity within the short time of its existence, we believe that the mere disagreements among the leading expounders of the theory are ample proof of the inadequacy of its assumptions.

3. *A Proposed Solution*

We have pointed out the errors and inadequacies of the preceding views; it now remains to set forth our own view. Intimations of that view have, indeed, been given at various points, but no complete statement of it has as yet been attempted. This we must now do. As contrasted with these other views, the true view gives primary consideration to the divine aspect in the composition of the Synoptics. It grants that the authors may have used "sources" for some of the materials in the Gospels but holds that they used them under the guidance and control of the Holy Spirit. This means that sometimes they used materials that had come to them from the immediate apostles of our Lord, and in the case of Matthew, materials that had come from his own observation and experience; that at other times they probably adopted parts of the oral tradition concerning the life and work of Christ that had come to their notice; that at still other times they appropriated a part or all of an account that was already in circulation in writing; but

54. *From the Stone Age to Christianity*, p. 298.
55. *Op. cit.*, p. 293f.
56. *Op. cit.*, p. 293.

that over and above all the Holy Spirit quickened their memories as to the things which they had heard and seen and guided them in the selections they made and in the editing and arranging of the materials. It is in this way that each one of the three produced in a most natural way an independent and verbally inspired account of the life of Christ. But let us look at these things more in detail.

1. *Direct Knowledge.* The questions of authorship and date will be dealt with when we consider each of the Synoptics separately, but we would here anticipate our conclusion that the first Gospel was written by the Apostle Matthew. On the basis of such an assumption, it would be strange if we should make him dependent upon "sources" for much of his materials. We have shown above (under 5 (4)) how little of the first Gospel did not come under the direct knowledge of the Apostle. Matthew could record from his personal observation and memory all but a very small portion of the life of Christ as contained in that Gospel. We do not deny the possibility that he may have consulted some of the other apostles and eye-witnesses before he wrote, with reference to some particular incident or saying of Christ: he may well have done that. But we believe that he must have drawn primarily on his own observation and experience as a follower of Jesus. The parts that deal with facts, incidents, and teachings of Christ which antedate his conversion he probably had heard others relate or had learned by inquiry. If we believe in addition that he wrote by the inspiration of the Holy Spirit, we have all the elements needed to make the first Gospel an original and authoritative account.

Mark and Luke were not apostles, and so they did not have this same direct knowledge of the earthly life of our Lord. Papias says, in a fragment preserved by Eusebius,[57] that Mark "neither heard the Lord nor accompanied Him." But since he later, at any rate, lived at Jerusalem (Acts 12:12,25) and was associated with the Apostle Peter for some time, he probably learned many things about Christ in a somewhat more direct way than Luke. But in the case of all three, we do not argue for the reliability of their Gospels primarily on the ground of the directness of their information, but on the ground of their

---

57. *History Eccl.* III. xxxix.

inspiration by the Holy Spirit. Mark and Luke are, therefore, equally authoritative with Matthew and John, who had been followers of Jesus, although Mark and Luke received their information, humanly speaking, more indirectly than the former two.

2. *The Oral Teaching of the Time.* Many scholars today admit that the original basis for our canonical Gospels was oral. Salmon, Jülicher, Zahn, Peake, Dibelius, and Albright may be mentioned as doing this. It may well be, as has often been argued, that, due to the instruction of the Apostles during their long stay at Jerusalem (Acts 1:1-8:4), the facts concerning the life, teaching, death, resurrection, and ascension of Christ came to be repeated in much the same way by all. The missionaries who went out from Jerusalem to preach to Jews, Samaritans, and Gentiles in other parts of the world proclaimed their message in much the same words as it was done in Jerusalem. Thus there developed a body of statements that formed the nucleus of the preaching of the earliest disciples everywhere, which the authors of the Synoptic Gospels used in their narratives of the facts concerning Christ.

There are various reasons for believing that such an oral tradition grew up. Papias tells us that when anyone who had attended on the elders came, "I asked minutely after their sayings, — what Andrew or Peter said, or what was said by Philip, or by Thomas, or by James, or by John, or by Matthew, or by any other of the Lord's disciples: which things Aristion and the presbyter John, the disciples of the Lord, say. For I imagined that what was to be got from books was not so profitable to me as what came from the living and abiding voice."[58] Zahn maintains that there was at first an unwritten gospel. He says that the term "gospel" is not used "to designate written records of the gospel history" until after the beginning of the second century.[59] He holds that even the opening words of Mark refer to the Gospel that originated with Jesus (subjective genitive). He shows that Paul makes various references to the oral teaching of Christ, as follows: (1) The saying, "It is more blessed to give than to receive" (Acts 20:35); (2) the

---

58. *Hist. Eccl.* III. xxxix.
59. *Op. cit.*, II, 373.

Lord's charge to the married (1 Cor. 7:10); (3) the Lord's appointment that laborers in the Gospel should live of the Gospel (1 Cor. 9:14); (4) the words of Jesus in the institution of the Lord's Supper (1 Cor. 11:23-25); (5) and the Lord's promise of His return (1 Thess. 4:15). And again, since only with Ignatius, Barnabas, and Justin, in the 2d century, it gradually became customary to quote from the Gospel with *gegraptai,* Paul cannot have referred to written Gospels.[60] Albright holds that J. Jeremias has correctly concluded that Matthew and Luke show by their use of "mnemotechnic devices" that they have drawn on oral tradition in many instances.[61]

Peake thinks it hard to explain on what principles the oral tradition was formed and to account for the fixity which was reached by the tradition.[62] But on the theory that the oral teachings originated with the Apostles themselves, the difficulty largely disappears. Their disciples merely repeated what they had heard from the Apostles. Some have questioned the theory on the ground that the people of that day could not have memorized such quantities of material. We do not agree with C. C. Torrey in his view that our four Gospels were originally written in Aramaic, but we agree with him that they originated in some measure in an oral tradition. He says: "Such verbal or material variation, often very noticeable in the Synoptic parallels, is not to be charged to copyists, nor is it due to any process of redaction; it is merely the usual result of oral transmission." Again: "The *accuracy* of such memory, wherever this quality was felt to be important, is also to be emphasized. Any one of a multitude of readers could retain exactly the work in which he was deeply interested, its text being already fixed; as Dante knew the Aeneid by heart. . . . Very many Jewish scholars have known the Talmud throughout by page and line. . . . Both Old Testament and New Testament scriptures have been memorized entire by numerous saints of church or synagogue. The Mohammedan traditionists surpassed even these feats of memory, able, as some of them were, to recite any portion of the mass of material, without the alteration of a word. When the Grimm brothers collected the

---

60. *Op. cit.,* II, 381-383.
61. *Op. cit.,* p. 297.
62. *A Critical Introduction to the New Testament,* pp. 106-109.

German folk-tales, they were surprised to see the extent to which they had been preserved in unvarying verbal form."[63]

We hold, then, that the writers of the Synoptic Gospels probably availed themselves to some extent of the oral tradition current in their day and that this fact accounts for the linguistic similarities and dissimilarities of the several Gospels.

3. *Short Written Accounts.* As we have seen, the theory that there were at an early time short written accounts of the life of Christ has recently been revived. Lake thinks it "almost certain" that "the Matthean quotations from the Old Testament, proving the fulfillment of prophecy, were taken from an early collection of *Testimonia* or proof-texts from the Old Testament."[64] Souter differs with Zahn as to the source of Paul's sayings of Christ. He says: "The conviction deepens on the present writer that Paul had a written compendium of Jesus' teaching, of which traces appear in his writings." He mentions Acts 20:35; 1 Thess. 5:4 and 1 Cor. 13:2 as proof.[65] Dibelius thinks there are probable traces of the collections of Jesus' words in 1 Clem. 13:2; 46:8; cf. Polycarp 2:3.[66] Alford admits that along with oral tradition there is "the probability of a very early collection of portions of such oral teaching into documents, some of which two or even three Evangelists may have used."[67] He states his view thus: "That the Synoptic Gospels contain the substance of the Apostles' testimony, collected principally from their oral teaching: that there is however no reason from their internal structure to believe, but every reason to disbelieve, that any one of the three Evangelists had access to either of the other two Gospels in its present form."[68]

As we have seen, the author of our third Gospel, Luke, testifies to the existence of both oral and written accounts of the life of Christ in his day. These are his exact words: "Many have taken in hand to draw up a narrative concerning those matters which have been fulfilled among us, even as they delivered them unto us, who from the beginning were eyewitnesses and ministers of the word" (Luke 1:1,2). It is to

63. *The Four Gospels*, p. 259f.
64. *Op. cit.*, p. 16.
65. *Op. cit.*, p. 151 f.
66. *From Tradition to Gospel*, p. 242.
67. *Greek Testament*, "Prolegomena," p. 11.
68. *Op. cit.*, I, 11, 12.

be noted that he traces the origin of these "narratives," including his own Gospel, to those "who from the beginning were eyewitnesses and ministers." These "eyewitnesses and ministers" were not two classes but one; the use of the one article for the two words makes that clear. The apostles most naturally qualify for this identification. That the meaning is limited to the apostles is made still more probable by the explanation that they were such "from the beginning," that is, from the beginning of the ministry of Jesus (cf. Acts 1:21,22). If it be asked whether the identification *has* to be limited to the Apostles, we would emphasize the word "eyewitnesses," which translates a Greek word that means "seeing with one's own eyes." The priority of oral teaching is also seen in the words, "wherein thou wast instructed," which are a translation of a Greek word that means oral instruction. Bruce says the probable meaning here is "formally and systematically instructed."[69]

When the testimony of these "eyewitnesses and ministers of the word" was set down in writing, it was done "just as" it had been delivered to the writers. The words "even as" are really "just as," and Plummer thinks this should be marked in the translation. This would indicate, then, that Luke assigned a very large degree of accuracy to these early written narratives. Furthermore, the infinitive "to draw up a narrative" (*anataxasthai*) means "to set forth in order a narrative; the expression points to a connected series of narratives arranged in some order (*taxis*), topical or chronological, rather than to isolated narratives."[70] Plummer says, this "implies more than mere notes or anecdotes."[71] Luke does not commit himself as to whether he used any of these earlier narratives, although that is probably to be inferred from the statement, mentioned above, that he "traced the course of all things accurately from the first," even before deciding to write. He probably used some of these documents in so far as he regarded them as reliable. But we do have his definite assertion that he had heard the testimony of the "eyewitnesses and ministers of the word." So he had the oral reports and knew of the written accounts, some of which he may have used. Although Matthew and

69. *Expositor's Greek Testament*, I, 460.
70. Bruce, *op. cit.*, I, 458.
71. *Commentary on Luke*, p. 2.

Mark do not say anything about "sources," we may yet suppose that, to some extent, they too used them. They may even have been influenced under the guidance of the Holy Spirit, in their decision as to what to reproduce in their own Gospels, by some things which they found in these earlier accounts.

4. *The Inspiration of the Holy Spirit.* We have seen above (under 5 (5)) that R. H. Lightfoot admits that so long as the age-long view of inspiration prevailed, "the four gospels could only be regarded as of equal value, historically and otherwise."[72] That is, he holds that one must either abandon the belief in the verbal inspiration of the Gospels or the newer critical theories. He, with the majority of critics, prefers to do the former. Some conservatives question whether that applies to the Two-Document Hypothesis as well as to the other theories. They ask whether the Holy Spirit might not have caused Mark to produce an inerrant account and then have led Matthew and Luke to use Mark and Q (and possibly some other source or sources) in the production of their Gospels. To this we reply, that theoretically this may be possible, but we do not deem it probable. That theory degrades the evangelists Matthew and Luke to the position of slavish and yet arbitrary compilers, not to say plagiarists. Particularly, as we have said before, it is *prima facie* improbable that a Gospel like Mark's would be treated in this manner. It may still be asked whether there is any clear indication anywhere that any one else ever composed historical narratives in any such manner as this.

Furthermore, it seems to the writer that the very differences of opinion among the students of the Synoptic Problem indicate the weakness of their position. The whole approach in recent years has been too naturalistic. The Two-Document Hypothesis, as we have repeatedly intimated, is disintegrating; Streeter's Four-Document Hypothesis, along with several minor sources, is not giving promise of becoming generally accepted. *Formgeschichte,* with its destruction of the values of the Gospels as sources for the authentic teaching of

---

72. *History and Interpretation in the Gospels,* pp. 10, 12.

Christ, is likely to die of its own extravagances. Why not return to the belief in a verbally inspired record? The writer finds that many of the supposed difficulties in the harmonization of the accounts in the Synoptics are purely subjective. Critics start from the false assumption that each writer undertook to relate all that had taken place or been said. As a result they conclude that the variations in the same accounts in the several Gospels are contradictions. But this is to take an unfair attitude toward the authors; for no writer can be assumed to be exhaustive unless he expressly says that he gives a complete account. If he makes no such assertion and intimates no such intentions, we ought to assume that he reports only such things as are pertinent to his purpose and view the several accounts as supplementary to each other. We certainly have no right to speak of contradictions until we have first exhausted every possibility of harmonizing them. Some give up too easily trying to harmonize difficulties.

The superscription over the cross of Christ may be cited as an example of this kind. All four writers of the Gospels refer to it, but no one of them definitely claims to state it in its entirety. Matthew says, "This is Jesus the king of the Jews" (27:37); Mark, "the king of the Jews" (15:26); Luke, "this is the king of the Jews" (23:38); and John, "Jesus of Nazareth, the king of the Jews" (19:19). The full superscription no doubt was as follows: "This is Jesus of Nazareth, the king of the Jews." To some, this will not seem like a solution to the problem, but to the writer it does seem to be the solution. With a tendency on the part of many critics today to destroy the authority of the Gospels, we deem it imperative to defend the verbal inspiration of the autographs of the evangelists.

*   *   *   *

We believe that modern Synoptic criticism has too largely ignored the historical situations out of which our Gospels grew. The Book of Acts indicates that the Church was at first Jewish and that persecutions caused the Christians to scatter to various parts of Palestine and other countries. It indicates that the Gospel was then carried to the Greeks at Antioch; after that through Asia Minor and Macedonia, and on to Greece. It indicates further that the Gospel was taken to Rome and to the uttermost parts of the earth. At each of these new steps in the progress of Christianity a written Gospel seems historically necessary. That is, the historical situations gave rise to our four Gospels. We shall deal with each of these steps when we take up the Gospels separately in the next chapter.

Chapter VI

THE HISTORICAL BOOKS
The Synoptic Gospels

WE HAVE dealt with the Synoptic Problem in the preceding chapter; in the next two chapters we shall deal with each of the Historical Books separately. There are five of these in the New Testament: Matthew, Mark, Luke, John, and Acts. In any study of the Synoptic Problem as such and of the separate Gospels a certain amount of repetition is unavoidable. In order to deal comprehensively with the former we were obliged to anticipate and take into account a number of our conclusions concerning the individual Gospels; and now, in dealing with each of the Gospels separately, we must present the grounds for the conclusions there accepted. So while the author apologizes for these repetitions, he yet deems them necessary to a complete treatment of the subject. With this explanation we turn to the study of the Historical Books.

---

1. THE GOSPEL OF MATTHEW

Because of its position among the canonical Gospels, Matthew has been most widely read and has exerted a most powerful influence in the world. Nestle gives five lists of the four Gospels in the early manuscripts, versions, and writings which put Matthew first, and three which put John first.[1] Origen[2] preserves an early tradition which arranges the Gospels in the order in which we have them in our New Testament today. Matthew was given first place because it was considered to be the earliest Gospel, and also because the author was an apostle.

1. **Attestation and Authorship.** The external evidence abundantly testifies to the early existence and use of Matthew. The

1. *Textual Criticism of the New Testament*, pp. 161,162.
2. Eus. *H. E.* VI.xxv.3.

Didache first clearly indicates this. The Gospel of Matthew is more frequently used in it than any other Gospel, especially chapters 5-7 and chapter 24. The *Epistle of Barnabas* first uses the authoritative formula, "It is written," in its quotation of Matt. 20:16; 22:14. There is a possible allusion to Matt. 3:15 in Ignatius' *Epistle to the Smyrneans* (ch. i). Hermas seems to paraphrase Matt. 13:5-8, 31, 32; 18:3 in *Similitudes*.[3] Justin Martyr quotes Matt. 17:12. That Justin here quotes from a written document is clear from his reference to v. 13 immediately after that in the following language: "And it is written, 'Then the disciples understood that He spake to them about John the Baptist'."[4] Justin also makes a number of references to Matthew 2 and quotes Matthew 7:15 and 24:5.[5] Eusebius says Pantaneus found the Hebrew "Gospel According to Matthew" in India, near the end of the second century;[6] but some question the accuracy of this statement. Dionysius of Corinth alludes to Matthew 13:24 ff. in one of the fragments that have been preserved by Eusebius.[7] Hegesippus, the early Jewish Church Historian, uses expressions corresponding to Matt. 26:64.[8] Theophilus of Antioch quotes Matt. 5:28 as "the voice of the Gospel."[9] Athenagoras the Athenian quotes loosely Matt. 5:44, 45.[10] Use seems also to have been made of Matthew by Cerinthus, Basilides, and Valentinus. And we know that Matthew was incorporated in Tatian's *Diatessaron*, the Old Latin, and the Old Syriac Versions.

The early Church unanimously ascribed this Gospel to the Apostle Matthew. Note again what Papias says: "Matthew composed the Logia in the Hebrew tongue; and each one interpreted them as he was able." Irenaeus says: "Matthew also issued a written Gospel among the Hebrews in their own dialect."[11] Irenaeus claims that he knew Polycarp in his early youth, and that Polycarp always taught the things he had learned from the apostles.[12] His testimony is therefore espe-

---

3. IX.xix-xxi; VIII.iii; IX.xxix.
4. *Dialogue with Trypho*, ch. xlix.
5. *Ibid.*, chs. xxxv, lxxviii, cii.
6. *H. E.*, V.x.
7. *H. E.*, IV.xxiv.

8. Euseb. *H. E.* II.xxiii.
9. *To Autolycus*, III. xiii.
10. *A Plea for the Christians*, XI.
11. *Against Heresies*, III. i. 1.
12. *Ibid.*, III. iii. 4.

cially important. Origen also assigned this Gospel to Matthew.[13] After that there are many others who refer our first Gospel to Matthew. Schodde maintains that the testimony of Papias, Irenaeus, and Origen, "may be accepted as representing a uniform second century tradition."[14]

In considering the internal evidence we note first that some, as Clement of Alexandria and Origen, distinguished between Levi (Mark 2:14-17; Luke 5:27-32) and Matthew (Matt. 9:9-13). But inasmuch as the accounts of the call of "Levi" and of "Matthew" are given in almost exactly the same words, it is more than probable that the two were one and the same. Simon was also called Peter; Lebbaeus was surnamed Thaddaeus; Thomas was called Didymus; Joses was called Barnabas; John was surnamed Mark; Simon was called Niger; Judas was surnamed Barsabas; and Saul was also called Paul. It is therefore more than probable that Matthew also had two names. Mark calls him "the son of Alphaeus" (Mark 2:14); but this cannot have been the Alphaeus who was the father of James the Less, for we would doubtless have been told that the two were brothers, if they had had the same father, as is the case with Peter and Andrew, James and John.

Matthew was not conspicuous among the apostles, and it would be strange for tradition to assign the Gospel to him if he did not write it. But we can see his fitness for the task. As a tax-collector, probably under Herod Antipas, he had the standing of a civil servant and would need to know not only his native Aramaic, but also the Greek spoken in Galilee. His ready acceptance of Jesus' invitation shows that he must have cherished the Jewish expectation of the Messiah. Tradition declares that for fifteen years he preached in Palestine, and that after that he went to foreign nations,—the Ethiopians, Macedonians, Syrians, Persians, Parthians, and Medes being mentioned. If we note that he quotes or alludes to the Old Testament more frequently than any other of the evangelists; that he quotes from both the Hebrew and the Septuagint; that he makes use of Hebrew parallelism; that his thought and outlook are Hebraistic; that he speaks much of the "kingdom of

---

13. *Eusebius*, H. E., VI. xxv. 4.
14. Art. "The Gospel of Matthew," in the *Inter. Stand. Bible Ency.*, p. 2010.

heaven," perhaps in allusion to the prophecies in Daniel; we feel impressed that this Gospel was written by a patriotic Christian Jew. Zahn suggests that the freedom in the arrangement of great discourses is much more conceivable in the case of an apostle who is not called upon to write history but to publish the commandments of Jesus, who felt confidence on account of his own recollections of the events and sayings in the life of Christ, than in a younger contemporary who depended upon others for information.[15]

2. **Dependence and Language.** Is our present Greek Gospel the original Gospel of Matthew? We have noted repeatedly Papias' statement that Matthew composed the Logia in Hebrew (Aramaic). Some maintain that "Logia" here must be interpreted strictly as "Sayings." They hold that Papias refers to a work of Matthew that contained only the Discourses of Jesus. But in all the four places in which the term "logia" occurs in the New Testament (Acts 7:38; Rom. 3:2; Heb. 5:12; I Pet. 4:11) it always means "oracles" rather than "sayings." That is, it refers to God's message to man, whether in the form of narratives, discourses, or other inspired utterances. There is nothing to indicate that Papias used the word in any other than the New Testament sense.

But how shall we interpret Papias' statement? Four views have been entertained: (1) Papias referred to a work of Matthew that contained the Discourses of Christ, and someone later used these "Logia" and Mark and some other sources, and composed our Greek Matthew. This is the Two-Document Theory, which we have already evaluated. (2) Papias taught that our Matthew was originally written in Aramaic, and someone else later translated it into Greek. This is Zahn's view. But the quality of the Greek in this Gospel makes it doubtful whether it is a translation. (3) Papias was right only in the sense that Matthew wrote the "Logia," meaning our first Gospel; he was wrong as to the language in which he wrote it, for he really wrote it in Greek. This is Salmon's view, and was that of most of the conservatives until the time of Schleiermacher. But we do not have sufficient ground to question the knowledge and accuracy of Papias as to the language used, es-

---

15. *Introduction to the New Testament,* II, 584 f.

pecially since there are other ancient witnesses to the Aramaic Logia. Take the statement of Eusebius as an example.[16] (4) Papias was right as to an Aramaic original, but Matthew also wrote our Greek Matthew. This hypothesis, though comparatively recent in origin, is very plausible, for it reconciles the declarations of the Fathers concerning an original Hebrew (Aramaic) Matthew with the evidence that our present Matthew was written in Greek. Gloag mentions Bengel, Olshausen, Thiersch, Schaff, Townson, Horne, Lee, and Ellicott as holding this view.[17] It is evident that when the Greek Matthew had once become current in the Church, the Aramaic edition of it dropped out. Josephus wrote his *Wars of the Jews* in Aramaic and secured the help of Greek writers in freely reproducing and improving it in the Greek language. The Greek edition alone has come down to us. We believe that in the same manner, though perhaps without the assistance of Greek writers, Matthew reproduced his Gospel in Greek.

If, then, our Greek Matthew is not dependent upon the Aramaic "Logia" spoken of by Papias in any such manner as some have supposed, we should be clear also that it is not dependent upon two other documents on which some have endeavored to make it dependent. The first is the *Gospel of the Ebionites,* also called the *Gospel of the Twelve Apostles,* though the Ebionites gave the name of *Gospel of the Hebrews* to it. Epiphanius' description of it indicates that it was very different from our canonical Matthew. It was a Greek book, probably compiled by the Ebionite sect known as the Elkesaites, purporting to be a translation of the Hebrew Gospel; but in reality it was a forgery put forth by this sect. It expresses definite hostility to the offering of sacrifices and the eating of flesh, which was characteristic of the Elkesaites. Nor, in the second place, is it dependent upon the more respectable *Gospel According to the Hebrews,* or the *Nazarene Gospel,* of which Jerome speaks, and which he proceeded to translate into Greek and Latin; for it contains things in it that could not have been omitted by Matthew. One such is the report of our Lord's appearance to James (cf. 1 Cor. 15:7), in which interesting details are added

---

16. *H. E.* III. xxiv.
17. *Introduction to the Synoptic Gospels,* p. 118.

that would surely have appeared in our Matthew, if it were a translation of this "Gospel." Origen also quotes from the *Nazarene Gospel;* but although he believed that the original Matthew was in Hebrew,[18] he seems never to identify his quotations from the Hebrew Matthew with the *Nazarene Gospel.* Nor does any other Church writer do this who quotes the *Gospel According to the Hebrews.* In other words, the Hebrew Gospel of Matthew is never identified with this *Gospel According to the Hebrews.* One quotation from the latter in Origen further strengthens the view that the two are not identical. He quotes our Lord as saying in the *Nazarene Gospel*: "My mother the Holy Ghost lately took me by one of my hairs and carried me to the great mountain Tabor."[19] We may thus dismiss the idea that our Matthew is descended from or related to either of these "Gospels."

3. **Occasion and Date.** Insufficient consideration has been given by modern criticism to the circumstances and occasions that called forth our canonical Gospels. In postulating the priority of Mark, "a short Gospel for Gentiles," as Chapman points out, "containing only one sermon and short fragments of teaching, was set up as the origin of a Gospel addressed to Jews." He goes on to say: "This topsy-turvy theory seems to suggest that the Gospel was first preached to the Gentiles and later carried to the Jews, first propagated at Rome and then in Palestine."[20] This criticism is true, and it reminds us that we must go back to the historical development of the Church and its growing needs for the origin of the Gospels. Lawson says: "It is this one element which most writers, who regard the Gospels as merely human compositions, ignore, and yet it is that which lifts the Gospels up to the higher plane of the divine, and guarantees their accuracy apart from copyists' errors."[21] We emphasize, then, that each writer was confronted with a definite need; that he formed a definite purpose for his Gospel; and that he selected his materials, under the guidance of the Holy Spirit, with that object in view.

18. Euseb., *H. E.,* VI., xxv. 4.
19. *In Johan.,* tom. ii, 6; *Hom. in Jerem.,* xv, 4.
20. *Matthew, Mark,* and *Luke,* p. 183.
21. "The Dates and Origins of The Gospels," in *The Evangelical Quarterly,* July, 1938, p. 279.

The disciples were to begin witnessing in Jerusalem, to go on to Judæa and Samaria, and finally to the ends of the earth (Acts 1:8). The Book of Acts shows how they carried out this command. The Church was born in Jerusalem on the Day of Pentecost, with 3,000 converts. Shortly thereafter this church had increased to where it had 5,000 men (Greek, *andres*) alone (4:4); a little later we read that multitudes, both of men and women, were added to the Lord (5:14), and once again that the number of the disciples was multiplying (6:1). Lawson asks: "Would it be too much to say that there were twenty thousand Jews in Jerusalem who believed that Jesus Christ was the promised Messiah, King, Priest, and Prophet?"[22]

Acts tells us that the believers kept frequenting the temple and worshipping in its sacred precincts, although they also had their own private meetings (4:23-31). It was inevitable that great opposition should develop on the part of those who adhered to the Jewish faith. This opposition resulted in the arrest of Peter and John, of all the apostles, and finally of the fiery Stephen. Having spoken out boldly for the faith and against Jewish formalism, Stephen was cast out of Jerusalem and stoned. Saul, afterwards Paul, came on the scene at this time (7:58), and a great persecution broke out against the believers under his leadership, so that all were scattered throughout Judæa and Samaria, except the apostles (8:1,2). Apparently most of these later returned to Jerusalem (cf. Acts 11 and 15); but the continued opposition to the Christians finally made it necessary for them to leave Jerusalem permanently. Lawson says: "Do not these circumstances suggest the need of a life of Christ which would encourage and confirm these persecuted believers in their faith, and at the same time confute their opponents and prove to both that the Gospel was not a break with, or contradiction to the teachings of the Old Testament, but a fulfillment of the promises made to Abraham and his seed?"[23] As Peter's sermons in the first part of Acts indicate, the Gospel moved in the sphere of the Law, the Prophets, and the Psalms during this time, since as yet almost all the believers were Jews.

---

22. *Op. cit.,* p. 282.
23. *Op. cit.,* p. 282.

Matthew is just such a Gospel, as we shall see in the next section. Perhaps the tradition (above mentioned) that after fifteen years of preaching in Palestine, Matthew left for foreign nations, but left behind his Hebrew (Aramaic) Gospel as a kind of compensation for his absence, is not far wrong after all. This would roughly give a date of A.D. 45 for the Aramaic Gospel of Matthew. It is the Aramaic Gospel that Papias refers to. When he said that "each one interpreted them [the oracles] as he was able," it is obvious that he was referring to a time when no translation was available, when each one who used the Gospel with Greek-speaking people was obliged to make an oral translation of it to the best of his ability. Papias wrote about A.D. 130 and used the past tense; he was not referring to his own time, for the Greek Matthew was well known by that time. Since none of the Synoptics, not even the Greek Matthew, report the fall of Jerusalem and the temple, but speak of these events as still future, they must have been written before this tragedy or long after it. Few writers would put them long after it; so they must have been written before A. D. 70. Furthermore, since Acts also is silent with regard to these catastrophes, it, too, must have been written before A. D. 70. And since Luke's Gospel is earlier than the Book of Acts, and Matthew undoubtedly is earlier than Luke, we believe that Matthew must have prepared his Greek Gospel shortly after he wrote the Aramaic. We, therefore, date the Greek Matthew about A. D. 50.

4. **Purpose and Plan.** As has already been intimated, Matthew wrote to encourage and confirm the persecuted Jewish Christians in their faith, to confute their opponents, and to prove to both that the Gospel was not a contradiction of the teachings of the Old Testament, but rather a fulfillment of the promises made to Abraham and to David. The Epistle to the Hebrews also shows how the Old Testament is fulfilled in the New, but from a different standpoint. It is evident that under the circumstances the Jewish Christians needed a clear proof of the nature of Christ's person and mission, and a refutation of the objections of unbelieving Jews. Matthew undertakes to do this in his well arranged Gospel.

How does he set out to achieve this purpose? By submitting proof that Jesus in His person is the foretold divine-human Messiah; that His words and works are those predicted of the Messiah; that the nation through its leaders slew Him; that His death was yet a ransom for many; that He has rejected the nation for the time being; that the "kingdom" will assume a new form during the time of the nation's rejection; that He will build His Church during this time; that His followers are commissioned to carry the Gospel to all nations; and that Christ will return to reward His followers and set up His kingdom. Are not all these ideas important to his purpose? We may represent his plan in a tabulated form as follows:

(1) The Birth and Qualifications of the Messiah, ch. 1.

(2) The Recognition of the Messiah, ch. 2.

(3) The Preparation of the Messiah for His Ministry, 3:1-4:11.

(4) The Presentation of the Messiah to Israel, 4:12-16:20.

(5) The Words and Works of the Messiah in Face of the Cross, 16:21-20:34.

(6) The Rejection of Israel by the Messiah, chs. 21-23.

(7) The Messiah's Predictions to His Disciples, chs. 24,25.

(8) The Passion, Triumph, and Commission of the Messiah, chs. 26-28.

5. **Points and Peculiarities.** Various points and peculiarities appear in Matthew that accord with the general purpose of the writer.

(1) Matthew is the Jewish Gospel, dealing with the King and the Kingdom. In Greek, the term "kingdom of heaven" occurs thirty-three times, and the term "kingdom of God," four times. Jesus is called "Son of David" nine times (three times in Mark, three times in Luke, and never in John). Matthew quotes from or alludes to the Old Testament about sixty-five times, sometimes using the Hebrew Old Testament and sometimes the Greek Septuagint.

(2) The first four chapters of Matthew are chronological; chs. 5-13 are topical; and chs. 14-28 are again chronological, with the exception of 21:18, 19.

(3) The words "righteous" and "righteousness" occur more often in Matthew than in all the other three Gospels combined.

(4) The Greek word *tote* ("then") occurs 90 times (six times in Mark, fourteen times in Luke, ten times in John). It is probable that the frequency of its occurrence in this Gospel is due to Matthew's thinking in Aramaic.

(5) Matthew is the only Gospel in which the word "church" occurs. It appears three times, 16:18 and 18:17 (twice).

(6) Matthew has six great addresses: The Sermon on the Mount (chapters 5-7), the address to the Twelve (chapter 10), the seven great parables of the kingdom (chapter 13), the discourse on humility, stumbling-blocks, and forgiveness (chapter 18), the denunciation of the scribes and the Pharisees (chapter 23), and the Olivet discourse (chapters 24, 25).

(7) There are fifteen parables and twenty miracles in Matthew. Of these, ten parables and three miracles are peculiar to this Gospel.

(8) Matthew's interest in the Gentiles is shown in his mentioning two Gentile women in Christ's genealogy (1:5); in his story of the wise men (2:1-12); in his reproduction of the saying that many from the east and the west will sit down in the kingdom of heaven, while the sons of the kingdom will be cast out (8:11, 12); and in his quoting the prophecy that Messiah would proclaim judgment to the Gentiles and that the Gentiles would hope in Him (12:18, 21).

(9) Matthew alone tells of Judas' "repentance" (27:5-10); of the Jews' request that Christ's blood be upon them and upon their children (27:25); of the sealing of the stone, the setting of the guard, and the fabrication of the story that the disciples came and stole the body while the guard slept (27:62-66; 28:11-15); and of the rising of many of the saints after Christ's resurrection (27:51, 52).

——————

2. THE GOSPEL OF MARK

As we have seen, recent criticism has assigned to Mark not only priority in point of time, but also primacy in point of importance. But in the Greek manuscripts, catalogues, and Fath-

ers this Gospel appears in the second, third, and fourth places,—
never in the first. Until Lachmann's "discovery" of the priority of Mark, in 1835, there was no special interest in this
Gospel. We refer again to Robertson's statement concerning
this point: "Victor of Antioch (fifth or sixth century A.D.),
the earliest known commentator on Mark, 'complains that,
while St. Matthew and St. John had received the attention of
a number of expositors, and St. Luke also had attracted a few,
his utmost efforts had failed to detect a single commentary
upon St. Mark."[24] When we recall also that Lachmann's "discovery" was made "just at the time when the Bible was losing its age-long position and prestige as the infallible book,"
we cannot suppress the feeling that there is a definite connection between the two things. We must, therefore, inquire dili-
gently as to the origin, authorship, date, etc., of this Gospel.

1. **Attestation and Authorship.** Since Mark has so little
material that is peculiar to him, we find it difficult to prove that
the early writers quoted from Mark. We confine ourselves,
therefore, to the testimonies that ascribe the Gospel to Mark
for proof. Papias is again the first to bear witness. He refers
to the "Elder," who is apparently the Apostle John, and says:
"And the Elder said this also: Mark having become the interpreter of Peter, wrote down accurately everything that he remembered without however recording in order what was either
said or done by Christ. . . . So then Mark made no mistake,
while he thus wrote down some things as he remembered them;
for he made it his own care not to omit anything that he had
heard, or to set down any false statement therein."[25] Papias
does not mean that Mark interpreted Peter's sermons on his
preaching tours; for Peter needed only the Aramaic and the
Greek languages, both of which he knew, in order to preach in
all the places to which ancient tradition represents him as having gone. He means instead that Mark reproduced Peter's
preaching in his book, and that he was the Apostle's interpreter
in that sense. Justin Martyr a little later refers to this Gospel
as the "memoirs of him," i. e , Peter.[26] That the pronoun refers to Peter is evident from the fact that in the same sentence

---

24. *Studies in Mark's Gospel,* p. 21 f.
25. Lightfoot's translation of this fragment from Eusebius *H. E.,* III. xxxix.
26. *Dialogue with Tryho,* ch. cvi.

Justin represents the change of names of one of the apostles to Peter, and of the two sons of Zebedee to Boanerges, as reported in these "memoirs." These two things are found together only in Mark (3:16, 17), which means that he called this Gospel Peter's "memoirs." Justin may possibly quote Mark 16:19, in his *On the Resurrection* (ch. ix), although this statement may have been taken from Acts 1:9.

The Muratorian Fragment is mutilated at the beginning. It commences with the last words of a sentence which Westcott thinks refer to the Gospel of Mark.[27] Mark is also found in Tatian's *Diatessaron* and the Old Latin and the Old Syriac Versions. Irenaeus represents Peter and Paul as going to Rome and as preaching in the Imperial City; and then he adds: "After their departure (*exodon*), Mark, the disciple and interpreter of Peter, did also hand down to us in writing what had been preached by Peter."[28] Clement of Alexandria,[29] Tertullian,[30] Origen,[31] Eusebius,[32] all ascribe the second Gospel to Mark. Likewise the title *Kata Markon*, found in the earliest manuscripts, indicates the author, not the person from whom the writer obtained his information; otherwise it would have to be *Kata Petron*. Thus the evidence for the Markan authorship is early and unanimous. There seems to be no reason why tradition should assign this Gospel to a minor character like Mark rather than Peter, if he did not write it.

The internal evidence is not very abundant, but such as it is harmonizes with the external. The incident about the youth that fled in the Garden (Mark 14:51, 52), is peculiar among Gospel incidents, and gains significance if it was Mark; he might want to indicate his personal contact with Jesus, even if only in this rather dishonorable way. The guest room in which Jesus ate the last Supper may have been his mother's home. Notice the detailed description in Mark 14:12-16, and contrast this with Matthew 26:17-19; John 13:1 ff. Farmer thinks the word "ready" in Mark 14:15 is the echo of a housewife. Cf. Acts 12:12-17.

---

27. *The Canon of the New Testament*, p. 193.
28. *Against Heresies* III. i. 1.
29. *Hypotyposes*, quoted in Eusebius *H. E.* VI. xiv.
30. *Against Marcion* IV. v.
31. Quoted by Eusebius, *H. E.* VI. xxv, from *his Commentary on Matthew*.
32. *Dem. Evang.* III. v.

Assuming then that Mark wrote this Gospel, we note next a few biographical facts concerning him. His first name was John; Mark was his surname (Acts 12:12, 25; 15:37). His mother's name was Mary and, by A. D. 45 at least, she lived in Jerusalem. Her house was used for a meeting place for the Christians (Acts 12:12-17). Mark was a cousin of Barnabas (Col. 4:10. A. S. V.; the A. V. is wrong here). As we have intimated, Mark was in all probability the young man in the Garden who fled on the night of the betrayal (Mark 14:51, 52). He is first definitely mentioned as accompanying Barnabas and Paul from Jerusalem to Antioch (Acts 12:25). After that we find him with these two on their first missionary tour from Antioch to Perga in Pamphylia, from which place he returned to Jerusalem (Acts 13:5, 13). Paul was greatly displeased with this move and considered Mark a slacker.

When Paul proposed to Barnabas that they set out on the second journey, Barnabas suggested that they take Mark with them again. But Paul strongly objected, and as a result Paul and Barnabas separated (Acts 15:36-39a). Barnabas took Mark with him and went to Cyprus (15:39b), but Paul took Silas in place of Barnabas and left for Syria and Cilicia (15:40, 41). Mark drops out of the picture at this point for about ten years. We next find him with Paul in Rome, sending greetings to Colosse (Col. 4:10; Philemon 24). So Paul and Mark must have made up their differences. It appears that Mark was really Peter's convert (1 Pet. 5:13). At any rate, Peter was well acquainted with Mark's mother and went to her home when he was miraculously released from prison (Acts 12:12). Probably Mark assisted Peter during the time that he was not with Paul. In his last Epistle Paul requests Timothy to come to him at Rome and bring Mark, adding "for he is useful to me for ministering" (2 Timothy 4:11). His early history and later associations with the apostles eminently fitted him to write a Gospel.

2. **Dependence and Language.** We have already refuted the *Ur-Markus* theory as also Cadoux' theory of three sources for Mark. But there is a true sense in which Mark is dependent,—not on any canonical Gospel, but on Peter the Apostle. We have seen (under 1 above) that Papias represents Mark

as reproducing Peter's teaching in his Gospel, and that Irenaeus does the same thing. Clement of Alexandria's full statement is as follows: "After Peter had publicly preached the word in Rome and declared the Gospel by the Spirit, many who were present entreated Mark, as one who had followed him for a long time and remembered what he said, to write down what he had spoken, and Mark after composing the Gospel, presented it to his petitioners. When Peter became aware of it, he neither eagerly hindered nor promoted it."[33] In another fragment from Clement of Alexandria preserved by Eusebius, the former is made to say that the Romans persuaded Mark to write "the Scripture called the Gospel by Mark," and that Peter "sanctioned the composition for reading in the churches."[34] Tertullian says of this Gospel: "Whilst that which Mark published may be affirmed to be Peter's whose interpreter Mark was."[35] Likewise Origen says of it: "The second is that according to Mark who composed it, under the guidance of Peter, who therefore, in his Catholic Epistle acknowledged the evangelist as his son."[36] Eusebius himself, Epiphanius, and Jerome make similar statements about the relation of Mark's Gospel to Peter. The external evidence, then, uniformly represents Mark as dependent upon Peter for his materials.

There is, further, the very great possibility that Peter himself had in mind the publication of the memoirs of the life of Christ. He says in his Second Epistle: "And I think it right, as long as I am in this tabernacle, to stir you up by putting you in remembrance; knowing that the putting off of my tabernacle cometh swiftly, even as our Lord Jesus Christ signified unto me. Yea, I will give diligence that at every time ye may be able after my decease to call these things to remembrance" (2 Pet. 1:13-15). To what does the expression "these things," refer? Evidently, to the things he has in mind at vs. 12, viz., to the importance of practising the Christian graces mentioned in vss. 5-11, and, back of that, to the knowledge of God and of Jesus Christ our Lord (vvs. 2-4). Strachan says: "The larger reference must be to some systematic body of instruction. This

---

33. *Hypotyposes*, in Eusebius H. E., VI. xiv.
34. *H. E.*, II. xv.
35. *Against Marcion* IV. v.
36. Quoted from his *Commentary on Matthew*, in Eusebius H. E., VI. xxv.

might easily take the form of reminiscences of the example of Jesus Himself, and the allusion may be to the Petrine reminiscenses contained in the Gospel of St. Mark."[37] Mayor says: "He had already referred to Christ (vs. 3), as having called them to his own glory and virtue; surely nothing could be more appropriate, more helpful to a godly life, than that Peter should leave behind the picture of this glory and virtue drawn from his own recollection. And the following words, 'for we did not follow cunningly devised fables' (vs. 16) seem to imply a statement of facts."[38]

The internal evidence is in harmony with the external. The many graphic details in Mark point to an eyewitness as the ultimate source of the writer's information.[39] The scope of Mark's Gospel (rather than that of Matthew's, Luke's, or John's) corresponds to that of Peter's address at Caesarea (Acts 10:34-43). The narrative abounds in details of time, place, and circumstances, and the feelings and manner of Jesus and of others are mentioned,[40] all indicating that the writer either was himself an eyewitness or received his information from an eyewitness. Since tradition ascribes the Gospel to Mark and not to Peter, the writer must have received his information from an eyewitness, i. e., from Peter.

Blass contended that Mark was originally written in Aramaic; but generally speaking, except for those who hold that all our Gospels were at first written in Aramaic, all today believe that Mark was written in Greek. Its language is neither technical nor slangy. Farmer says: "It is the clean, vigorous, direct speech of the sturdy middle class. . . . The style is very simple. . . . The stately periods of the classics are wholly absent. The narrative is commonly terse and concise. . . . The descriptions are wonderfully vivid."[41] There are 151 historical presents in Mark in Westcott and Hort's Greek Testament, and only 78 in Matthew and 4 in Luke. Mark is fond of diminutives; there is frequent superfluous fulness of expression from the modern viewpoint. He gives us a very realistic conception of the life of Christ.

37. *Expositor's Greek Testament*, V, 129.
38. *Commentary*, p. cxliii.
39. E. g., 7:33; 9:36; 10:16; 5:32; 6:41; 7:34; 3:34; 10:21; 11:11.
40. E. g., 1:13, 20, 41; 3:5, 9, 19-21; 4:35-41; 5:3-5 etc.
41. "The Gospel of Mark," in the *Inter. Stand. Bible Enc*, e

3. **Occasion and Date.** In our study of Matthew we traced the spread of the Gospel to the dispersion that followed the stoning of Stephen. From Judaea the Good News spread to Samaria. At Caesarea the Roman Centurion Cornelius became a Christian. The Book of Acts records the onward march of Christianity through Syria, Asia Minor, Macedonia, Greece, and to Italy. No doubt a good many of the Gentiles who were saved during this time were Romans. Acts shows in various ways how the Roman officials were friendly to Paul. Finally the time came when a Gospel was needed that was designed especially for the Romans. Plummer says: "In the Gospel itself there are a few features which harmonize with the tradition that it was written in Rome, primarily for Roman readers, and there is nothing which militates against this. What are called the 'Latinisms of Mark' are a slight confirmation of this; but they are not numerous, and they are such as were being adopted in various parts of the Roman Empire by such as spoke and wrote Greek. The mention of Rufus may be a more substantial confirmation."[42] The immediate occasion for this Gospel, if we may believe the tradition preserved by Clement of Alexandria and quoted in Eusebius H. E., VI. xiv,[43] was the request of many Romans that Mark reduce to writing the preaching of Peter.

Accepting the tradition that Mark was written at Rome and under the influence of Peter's preaching in that city, we get some clues as to the time when the Gospel was written. When Paul, in A. D. 56, wrote the Romans, no apostle had as yet visited that city. It is improbable that Peter got to Rome before the Neronian persecution in A.D. 64; he probably did not get to that city until about 65. The internal evidence indicates that the Gospel was written before the destruction of Jerusalem, i. e., before A.D. 70. Much depends upon the interpretation we put upon Irenaeus' statement, when he says: "Matthew also issued a written Gospel among the Hebrews in their own dialect, while Peter and Paul were preaching in Rome, and laying the foundations of the Church. After their departure, Mark, the disciple and interpreter of Peter, did also hand down

---

42. *Comm. on Mark*, p. xxxi.
43. See above under *Dependence and Language.*

to us in writing what had been preached by Peter."[44] Irenaeus'
term is *exodus,* which may mean "departure." but it may also
mean "death." Farmer argues that Irenaeus means after the
departure of Peter and Paul from Palestine or Syria, and that
the place of writing may be Caesarea or Antioch.[45] He, accordingly, dates Mark "in the fifties." This important Greek word
occurs only three times in the New Testament: in Luke 9:51;
Heb. 11:22; 2 Pet. 1:15. In Hebrews it clearly means "departure"; in Luke it means "death"; and in 2 Peter the meaning is
uncertain. Jerome, Epiphanius, Origen, and Clement of Alexandria, take it to mean departure from a region, and therefore
date Mark within Peter's lifetime. More commonly, however,
the word is taken to mean "death."[46] This view seems to accord
best with the Scriptures and with tradition, and we therefore
believe that Mark was published in A. D. 67 or 68, or immediately after Peter's death.

4. **Purpose and Plan.** Matthew depicts the Messiah as
King; Mark, as the Servant of Jehovah. The Greeks were con-
templative; the Romans, active. In his association with Paul,
Barnabas, and Peter, Mark had often observed how certain incidents and sayings went home to the hearts of the listeners.
They were facts that represented Christ as the Servant of Jehovah. Farmer says: "It is not strange that this Servant-con-
ception—this remarkable blend of strength and submission,
achieving victory through apparent defeat—should appeal to
Peter. He was himself an ardent, whole-souled man who knew
both defeat and victory. Moreover, he himself had hired servants (Mark 1:20), and now for years had been a servant of
Christ (cf. Acts 4:29). That it did appeal to him and became
familiar to the early Christians can be seen from Acts 3:13
and 4:30. . . . Temperamentally Mark seems to have been
like Peter. And his experience in a wealthy home where servants were kept (Acts 12:13), and as himself *hupēretēs* of
apostles in Christian service, fitted him both to appreciate and
record the character and doings of the perfect servant — the

---

44. *Against Heresies.* III. i. 1.
45. "The Gospel of Mark," in the *Inter. Stand. Bible Ency.*, p. 1992.
46. E.g., Westcott, *Intro. to Study of Gospels*, p. 192; Plummer. *op. cit.*, p. xxxi.

Servant of Jehovah. For Roman Christians that heroic figure would have a peculiar fascination."[47]

If this was his purpose, how does he set out to achieve it? By filling in, consciously or unconsciously, the outline of Peter's sermon in Acts 10:34-43. Mark, like Peter, introduces John the Baptist as the predicted forerunner of Christ, and thus, like him, supports his whole narrative with the authority of the Old Testament. Mark, like Peter, represents the baptism and temptation of Christ as the preparation of the Servant for His task (Acts 10:37, 38a), and His ministries in Galilee and on the way to Jerusalem as His going about, "doing good, and healing all that were oppressed of the devil; for God was with him" (vss. 38b, 39a). Mark, like Peter, sets forth in detail the Servant's defeat and final triumph in the crucifixion and resurrection of Christ (vss. 39b, 40a), and like him declares that He had manifested Himself to the disciples after His resurrection and charged them to preach the Gospel to all the people (vss. 40b-43). We may represent the plan of this Gospel in tabulated form as follows:

(1) The Preparation of the Servant, 1:1-13.

(2) The Ministry of the Servant in Galilee, 1:14-7:23.

(3) The Ministry of the Servant North and East of Galilee, 7:24-9:50.

(4) The Ministry of the Servant on the Way to Jerusalem, ch. 10.

(5) The Ministry of the Servant in Jerusalem, chs. 11-13.

(6) The Submission of the Servant to Death, chs. 14,15.

(7) The Triumph of the Servant in the Resurrection and Ascension, ch. 16.

5. **Points and Peculiarities.** This Gospel, too, has its points and peculiarities, in harmony with the purpose of the writer. We note some of the more significant of them.

(1) Mark represents Jesus as the Servant of Jehovah. Isaiah represents the Messiah as King and as Servant. In Isa. 40-53 there is much said about the Servant of Jehovah, more especially is this true of chs. 40-45. Matthew depicts Christ as

---

47. "The Gospel of Mark," in the *Inter. Stand. Bible Ency.*, p. 1994.

King, but also refers to Him as Servant (Matt. 12:18-21); Mark represents Him as Servant, but also refers to Him as King (Mark 11:10; 14:62; 15:2).

(2) Mark is a Gospel of deeds. Jesus is a strenuous worker hastening from one task to another. The servant's word *euthus* occurs 41 times in Westcott and Hort's Greek Testament. Matthew uses this word only 7 times and Luke only once. This word means "straightway," "forthwith," "immediately." In Mark's Gospel 14 of these are used of the personal activity of Jesus, as compared with two in Matthew and none in Luke.

(3) The Second Gospel has no genealogy, no account of the Virgin Birth, no history of the childhood years of Jesus. These things were of no importance to Mark's purpose, which was to present Jesus as the Servant of Jehovah.

(4) Though Mark stresses the Servant aspect of Christ's ministry, he is by no means silent about Jesus as a teacher. Indeed, teaching is part of His work. We have a number of discourses in this Gospel, as the four parables in ch. 4, the discussion concerning defilement in 7:1-23, concerning humility, sectarianism, and offences in 9:33-50, concerning divorce, little children, riches, rewards, and worldly ambition in ch. 10, and concerning the great questions that were asked Jesus in ch. 12. But it is to be noted that His discourses grow out of His works, not His works out of His discourses, in all but the first of these instances.

(5) It is significant that Peter is mentioned by name in various connections in this Gospel, while his name is omitted by the other evangelists; as in 1:36; 11:21; 13:3. Perhaps a sense of modesty has led to the omission of his name in 6:50, 51; 7:17; 14:13.

(6) Although Mark is the shortest Gospel, the writer yet often has greater fulness in the common incidents related. Note this in 6:14-29; 7:1-23; 9:14-29; 12:28-34. Maclear calls attention to a number of details that are peculiar to Mark's Gospel.[48]

---

48. *Gospel According to Mark*, pp. xxii-xxiv.

(7) Mark himself quotes the Old Testament only once (1:2, 3). This quotation is a combination of Mal. 3:1 and Isa. 40:3. But he represents Jesus as quoting it frequently. In all, Mark has 19 formal quotations; three of which are peculiar to him (9:48; 10:19; 12:32).

(8) Mark records 19 miracles of Jesus and 5 parables. Two of the miracles and two of the parables are peculiar to him.

(9) Mark's Gospel traces the order of events chronologically. Papias' statement that Mark "wrote accurately, though not in order," cannot refer to the chronological order. Matthew and Luke, whenever they deal with the same incidents or narratives, follow the chronology, or at least one of them does. Plummer suggests that Papias is comparing Matthew with John in the above statement.[49]

(10) Two endings for Mark have come down to us: a shorter one of one verse and a longer one, the one we have in our English translations. The shorter one occurs in minuscule 274 (in the margin to vs. 7) and in the Old Latin *k*. It also occurs, along with the longer ending, in four uncials (L, Psi, 099, 0112); but merely as an alternative, not as a substitute, for the longer reading. *Aleph* and B stop at vs. 8. The shorter ending can be dismissed at once as not genuine. The longer ending presents somewhat of a problem.

Burgon, Miller, Scrivener, Salmon, and a few others, accept it as genuine. But the majority of New Testament scholars reject it, including such conservatives as Tregelles, Warfield, Zahn, and A. T. Robertson. Yet few, if any, scholars hold that Mark originally ended at vs. 8; instead, all hold that there was another section after that verse, but that it was lost at an early date. Irenaeus plainly quotes vs. 19 as being found "towards the conclusion" of Mark's Gospel.[50] It should be added, however, that many who regard the longer ending as not a part of the original Mark, yet regard it as a truthful passage. But in spite of the weakness of both the external and the internal evidence, the conservative still asks, If these verses are not genuine, why did God in His providence so long allow them to pass for genuine? Interpolations of a few words or phrases do not present the same problem as does a long section like this.

---

49. *Commentary on Mark*, pp. xxiii-iv.
50. *Against Heresies*, III. x. 5.

3. THE GOSPEL OF LUKE

The Gospel of Luke is found in the second place in the so-called Ambrosiaster (ca. A. D. 380), in a Catalogue of the Sixty Canonical Books, in the Old Latin codex *k,* and in the cursives 90 and 399. The order in our English versions is found in nearly all the Greek and Syrian manuscripts and was popularized by Eusebius and Jerome. Origen knew this order, though he frequently cites the Gospels in the order Matthew, Luke, and Mark. Clement of Alexandria before him had argued for this order, claiming that he had received information on this point from the elders before him. The Bohairic version and some of the Catalogues put Luke in the fourth place. It never appears in the first place. Renan called this "the most literary of the Gospels."[51] Luke's Prologue (1:1-4) is the most classic piece of Greek in the New Testament. The author has more literary ambition than any of the other evangelists and possesses the art of composition in a marked degree.

1. **Attestation and Authorship.** The external evidence abundantly testifies to the early existence and use of Luke. Justin Martyr used it, for he quotes Luke 22:44[52] and 23:46[53]. Eusebius[54] represents Hegesippus as quoting Luke 23:34 verbally. The Muratorian Fragment calls the third Gospel "Luke." Theophilus of Antioch quotes Luke 18:27 verbally (Matthew 19:26 is different).[55] Tatian had this Gospel, for he used it in his *Diatessaron.* Celsus referred to the Gospel that traced the descent of Jesus to Adam.[56] The Clementine Homilies contain various statements that are probably allusions to Luke's Gospel.[57] Marcion accepted only the Gospel of Luke into his Canon, but he omitted a good deal of it as inconsistent with his view. Plummer says Irenaeus, who represents the traditions of Asia Minor, Rome, and Gaul, quotes from nearly every chapter in the Gospel of Luke, especially from those which are peculiar to this Gospel, as chs. 1, 2, 9-19, 24.[58] Luke is also found in the Curetonian Syriac, the Sinaitic Syriac, the Afri-

---

51. *Les Evangiles,* ch. xiii.
52. *Dialogue with Trypho,* ch. ciii.
53. *Ibid.,* ch. cv.
54. *H. E.,* II. xxiii.
55. *To Autolycus,* II. xiii.
56. Origen, *Contra Celsus.* II. xxxii.
57. E.g., III. lxiii—Luke 19:5; XI. xx—Luke 23:34, etc.
58. *Commen. on Luke,* p. xvi.

can Latin, all of which date to the 2d century. Clement of Alexandria quotes the Gospel very frequently, and Tertullian uses chs. 4-24 in his treatise against Marcion. Robertson says: "Surely the general use and acceptance of the Third Gospel in the early 2d century is beyond reasonable doubt. It is not easy to decide when the actual use began, because we have so little data from the 1st century."[59]

Nor has there been any difference of opinion as to the authorship of this Gospel until recent times. Plummer says: "It is manifest that in all parts of the Christian world the Third Gospel had been recognized as authoritative before the middle of the second century, and that it was universally believed to be the work of St. Luke. No one speaks doubtfully on this point. The possibility of questioning its value is mentioned; but not of questioning its authorship. In the literature of that period it would not be easy to find a stronger case."[60] Likewise Jülicher admits that "the ancients universally agreed that the writer was that Luke, disciple of Paul, who is mentioned in Philemon 24; 2 Tim. 4:11, and called 'the physician' in Col. 4:14: presumably a native of Antioch,"[61] although he himself rejects this view.[62] The first document definitely to ascribe the Gospel to Luke is the Muratorian Fragment. It says that Luke, the physician whom Paul had taken with him on his journey, composed the Third Gospel in his own name. Irenaeus says: "Luke also, the companion of Paul, recorded in a book the Gospel preached by him."[63] Tertullian says: "For even Luke's form of the Gospel men usually ascribe to Paul."[64] Clement of Alexandria also definitely ascribes the Gospel to Luke.[65] While Hilgenfeld, Holtzmann, Jülicher, Pfleiderer, von Soden, J. Weiss, and Weizsäcker reject the Lucan authorship of this Gospel, men like Blass, Harnack, Hawkins, Hobart, Plummer, Ramsay, and Zahn accept it. We think the latter have the better of the argument.

The internal evidence supports this conclusion. It is difficult, if not impossible, to establish the Lucan authorship of the Gos-

---

59. Art. "Luke," *in Int. Stand. Bib. Ency.*
60. *Comm. on Luke,* p. xvi.
61. *Intro. to the New Testament,* p. 330.
62. *Ibid.,* Section 32. 3, 5.
63. *Against Heresies,* III. i. 1.
64. *Against Marcion,* IV. v.
65. *Strom.* I. xxi.

pel apart from a survey of the evidence presented by the Book
of Acts. We may summarize the arguments thus: (1) The
"we" sections in Acts (16:10-17; 20:5-21:18; 27:1-28:16) indicate that the author was one of Paul's companions on his
journeys. Now Timothy, Sopater, Aristarchus, Secundus,
Gaius, Tychicus, and Trophimus are all excluded by Acts 20:4.
Silas cannot be easily fitted into the "we" sections; Titus can
be, but there is neither internal nor external evidence for him,
while there is both for Luke. (2) The rest of the Book of Acts
is by the same writer as the "we" sections. Harnack has argued with great skill that the same linguistic peculiarities occur
in all parts of Acts as we have in the "we" sections.[66] (3) The
same characteristics of vocabulary and style and the same dedication in both Luke and Acts indicate that the Gospel was
written by the same man who wrote Acts. Hawkins has shown
the likeness and variations in style in these two books.[67] Harnack, Ramsay, and Zahn likewise have shown that the two books
come from the same writer.[68] (4) The medical language in both
the Gospel and the Acts and the writer's interest in sickness and
the sick, as pointed out long ago by Hobart[69] and emphasized
more recently by Harnack,[70] suggest that the author was a
physician. Inasmuch as Luke is called the "beloved physician"
(Col. 4:14) and inasmuch as he accompanied Paul for a considerable time, we naturally conclude that he is the author of
the Third Gospel. Cadbury thinks he has shown that there is
no more medical language in Acts than in the writings of any
other educated man at any period;[71] but he has done nothing
more than weaken the evidence. Taken together with the writer's interest in disease and the sick, his vocabulary is significant.
Note the physician's interest in the sick as compared with the
same narratives in Mark: Luke 4:38, with Mark 1:30; Luke
5:12, with Mark 1:40; Luke 6:6, with Mark 3:1; Luke 8:43,
44, with Mark 5:26, 29; Luke 8:55, with Mark 5:42; Luke
9:38 ff., with Mark 9:17 ff.; Luke 22:50, 51, with Mark 14:

66. *Acts of the Apostles.*
67. Cf. his *Horae Synopticae*, 15-25, 174-189.
68. Harnack, *Luke the Physician*, Ramsay, *Luke the Physician*, Zahn, *Intro. to the New Testament*, III, 142-165.
69. *Medical Language of St. Luke.*
70. *Luke the Physician*, p. 14, 175-198.
71. "Style and Literary Method of Luke," in *Harvard Theological Studies*, VI, 39 ff.

47. We do not feel that Cadbury has succeeded in "completely wrecking Hobart's proof," as Cartledge holds,[72] although he has taught us to treat this factor more cautiously. On the basis of the external and internal evidence, therefore, we conclude that Luke wrote the Third Gospel.

We note a few facts about the writer. The term "Luke" is apparently an abbreviation for *Loukanos*; in the inscriptions the form *Loukios* is also found as a synonym of *Loukas* or *Luke*. But this name must not be confused with Lucius in Acts 13:1 and Rom. 16:21. Luke's name occurs only in Paul's Epistles (Col. 4:14; 2 Tim. 4:11; Philemon 24), never in either the Gospel or the Acts. In Col. 4:14 he is distinguished from those "of the circumcision" (viz., from Aristarchus, Mark, and Jesus Justus). He, together with Epaphras and Demas, are Gentiles. He may or may not have been a Jewish proselyte,—the indications are not clear,—but he was a Gentile. An early tradition made him a native of Antioch in Syria, and this is probably true, although Ramsay regards him as a Philippian.[73] He displays a peculiar interest in Antioch (Acts 6:5; 11:19-27; 13:1-3; 14:26-28; 15:1, 2, 22, 30-40; 18:22, 23), although he lived in Philippi for some time (Acts 16:11-17, 40-20:5). It is probable, therefore, that he was a native of Syrian Antioch.

Luke joined Paul at Troas on the second journey, but remained at Philippi until Paul came to that city on his return trip on the third journey. From that time on he seems to have been with Paul almost continually—on the return to Jerusalem, at Caesarea, on the voyage to Rome, and in Rome (Acts 20:3-28:31). Luke was a physician (Col. 4:14) and probably served Paul as medical adviser. Many suppose, on the basis of 2 Cor. 8:18, that Titus was a brother of Luke. If that is true, then we can understand why Titus' name is omitted in Acts. The late claim that Luke was one of the Seventy sent out by Jesus,[74] the story that he was one of the Greeks who came to Philip to see Jesus (John 12:20 f.), and the tradition that he was the companion of Cleopas on the way to Emmaus (Luke 24:13, 18) are all pure fiction. He was with Paul when

72. *A Conservative Introduction to the New Test.*, p. 82.
73. *St. Paul the Traveler*, pp. 201-203.
74. Epiphanius, *Haer.*, II. li.

Colossians and Philemon were written (Col. 4:14; Philemon 24), but apparently not when Philippians was written (Phil. 2:20). He only was with Paul during the second Roman imprisonment (2 Tim. 4:11). There is an ancient legend that makes Luke a painter, even declaring that he painted a portrait of the Virgin Mary; but it is not very reliable. He had a good education, both literary and medical, and certainly was a word-painter. In a Latin work it is asserted that he never married and that he died at the age of 74 in Bœotia (some Mss. say Bithynia); but another tradition says that he died at Constantinople and that his sarcophagus is now found in the Church of Santa Giustina, at Padua.

2. **Dependence and Language.** We reject the view that Luke was dependent on Josephus' *Antiquities* (written A. D. 93-95) for his reference to Quirinius (Luke 2:2), for Ramsay shows that the inscription at Tibur proved that this man twice governed Syria under Augustus, and that Josephus referred to the one and Luke to the other.[75] We reject also Streeter's theory of a *Proto-Luke,* which he holds was a combination of Q and the bulk of the material peculiar to our Third Gospel, made by Luke himself.[76] Streeter holds further that Luke took his *Proto-Luke* some time later, expanded it by prefixing the Infancy stories and inserting extracts from Mark, and making minor alterations and additions in the original work (*ibid*). We have tried to show that none of the Gospels is dependent on another canonical Gospel, in our treatment of the *Synoptic Problem,* and refer the reader to that chapter for our views on this point.

We sum up briefly our view of the matter. Luke used "sources,"—oral at least, perhaps also written,—but he used them under the direction of the Holy Spirit. Surely, in his associations with Paul, Luke met with some of the original apostles, with many other disciples of Christ, and with Christ's Mother and brethren. From them he would get much information about Christ. During Paul's imprisonment at Caesarea Luke would make investigations of various kinds; and because he was a physician he would no doubt get information

---

75. *Was Christ Born in Bethlehem?* p. 277 ff.
76. *The Four Gospels,* p. 217f. Sparks refutes Streeter's theory in the *Journal of Theological Studies,* July-October, 1943, pp. 129-138.

that would be kept from the ordinary inquirer. As we have seen before, Irenaeus says that Luke "recorded in a book the Gospel preached" by Paul. Tertullian calls Paul "the enlightener of St. Luke."[77] But of course Paul could impart to Luke only that which he had himself received (1 Cor. 15:3). From Paul he got the ideas of the universality of salvation and the boundlessness of God's grace; his materials he obtained from eye-witnesses.

Perhaps it may not be invidious to repeat the substance of what was said in our discussion of the *Synoptic Problem* (III.3) on this point. Luke shows that there were many narratives of the Life of Christ in existence in his day; that the writers of these narratives had received their information from those "who from the beginning were eyewitnesses and ministers of the word," and that he, too, had received his information from them; that these "eyewitnesses and ministers" were not two classes but one, the use of the one article for both terms making this clear; that Luke ascribes a large measure of accuracy to these earlier narratives; that he himself undertakes to set forth a narrative "in order," either topical or chronological,— not to write mere notes or isolated narratives; and that he traced the course of all things accurately from the beginning, before he even decided to write. He does not tell us whether he used any of these earlier written documents, although he probably did; but we know that he had the oral reports, which probably came chiefly from the other apostles and early friends of Christ, and he knew of the written accounts. Thus Luke may be regarded as having used oral information and probably earlier written accounts. It is not likely, as we have shown above (under the *Synoptic Problem*), that he used Mark or any other canonical Gospel. We repeat that Luke made his investigations and did his writing under the guidance and inspiration of the Holy Spirit.

We have already said that Luke is the most literary of the four Gospels. It has a classical preface like Herodotus and Thucydides. Whether or not Luke was a painter, he surely had the ability to paint word pictures! His Gospel comes nearest of the four to being a biography of Jesus. He writes history

---

77. *Against Marcion*, IV. ii

and connects the events in the life of Christ with the history of Syria and Rome. Luke writes as a man of culture and is cosmopolitan in outlook and tone. He has a rich vocabulary (about 312 words are peculiar to him in the Gospel) and a good command of *Koinē* Greek. He writes in the spirit of Paul and the style of Hebrews. We do not know whether he knew Hebrew, but he seems to have used Aramaic sources for the first two chapters of his Gospel.

3. **Occasion and Date.** Luke was first of all moved by the desire to confirm Theophilus in the faith of Christianity (1:3, 4). He addresses him as the "most excellent Theophilus." "The epithet *kratistos,* often given to persons of rank (Acts 23:26; 24:3; 26:25), is strongly in favor of the view that Theophilus was a real person. The name Theophilus was common both among Jews and among Gentiles."[78] Since in the above passages the title is given to persons of bad character, we must conclude that it is a purely official epithet. Zahn thinks Theophilus was a man of worldly distinction and not a Christian when Luke wrote his Gospel, but that he had probably ceased to be the former and had become a Christian when he wrote the Acts.[79] Notice the omission of the term "most excellent" in Acts (1:1). Generally, however, Theophilus is regarded as already a Christian and as merely needing further instruction and confirmation in the faith. It is possible that Theophilus may have played the part of *"patronus libri,* and paid the expenses of" the production of the Gospel, as Bruce suggests.[80] All agree that the Gospel was intended for the public, especially the Greek public, and Bruce's theory explains how this purpose was realized. His theory may, therefore, be the correct one.

But we must also look at the question of what occasioned this Gospel from another standpoint. With the missionary journeys of Paul, the Gospel was introduced to the whole Greek-speaking world. While many of those who heard the Apostle were bilingual, speaking their native tongue as well as Greek, many others were pure Greeks. Thus already at Antioch the Gospel was brought to pure Greeks (Acts 11:20, 21, so the correct

78. Plummer, *Comm. on Luke,* p. 5.
79. *Intro. to the New Testament,* III, 42 f.
80. *Exp. Greek Test.,* I, 460.

text). We are told that on his first journey, at Iconium, "a great multitude both of Jews and of Greeks believed" (14:1). On his second journey he circumcised Timothy, because although his mother was a Jewess, his father was a Greek (16:1, 3). It is evident that on this journey, as also on the third which took him through Macedonia and Greece proper, he encountered and brought to Christ many Greeks (Acts 17:4; 18:4; 19:10, 17; 20:21). Soon the demand for a Gospel especially suited to the Greek mind became evident. Such a Gospel would need to have a world-outlook. It would have to be in excellent form. All this we have in Luke's Gospel. It emphasizes the humanity of Christ, taking Zechariah's theme: "Behold, the man, whose name is the Branch" (Zech. 6:12). Luke traces the genealogy of Christ back to Adam (3:38). His is the cosmopolitan Gospel; he speaks of the "good tidings of great joy which shall be to all the people" (2:10). He represents Simeon as saying of Christ that He is, "A light to lighten the Gentiles" (2:32). The widow of Zarephath and Naaman the Syrian are mentioned only by Luke (4:25-27). He alone relates the parable of the Good Samaritan (10:25-37); he alone tells of the Samaritan who returned to praise God (17:16); he alone speaks of the "times of the Gentiles" (21:24). He makes the Great Commission more specific than any of the others (24:47). His cosmopolitanism is also seen in his frequent mention of the publicans and sinners (e. g., 3:12, 13; 5:27-32; 7:37-50, etc., etc.) as well as of the more respectable people (7:36; 11:37; 14:1); in his mention of the poor (1:53; 2:7, 8; 4:18, etc.) as well as of the rich (19:2; 23:50). He alone quotes Isa. 40:5: "All flesh shall see the salvation of God" (Luke 3:6).

Coming to the question of the date, we would suggest that this Gospel is earlier than Mark's. We have shown reasons why Mark's Gospel was written about 67 or 68; and we hope to show that Acts was written about 61. Since we believe that Luke wrote both the Gospel and the Book of Acts, and he himself tells us that the Gospel was written first (Acts 1:1), we must conclude that the Gospel was written before 61. Since, as we have already shown, Luke was in Cæsarea while Paul was imprisoned in that city (Acts 27:1), he would have opportunity during that time to make the kind of investigations that he mentions in Luke 1:1-4. It is probable that he wrote the Gospel during this period, say about A. D. 58. Those who hold that Luke was dependent upon the *Antiquities* of Josephus for some of his information, place the Gospel after A. D. 95; but this is a bad mistake.

Objection may be made to this view on the ground that it conflicts with the traditional order of the Gospels. We have shown, however, that while the present order of the books is very ancient, it is not the uniform order. Let us recall the fact that Origen frequently cites the Gospels in the order Matthew, Luke, and Mark, and that Clement of Alexandria before him puts the Gospels that contain the genealogies first, on the basis of the tradition which he received from "the elders before him."[81] We have also seen that Luke stood in the second place in Ambrosiaster, in the Catalogue of the Sixty Canonical Books, in the Old African Latin codex *k,* and in the cursives 90 and 399. Since the tendency was so strong to put the Gospels written by apostles in the first two places, it is remarkable that Luke ever received the second place. Clement's explanation may, therefore, preserve the true tradition. At any rate, Luke's Gospel must have been written before 61, and Mark's cannot have been written until after Peter's death. We, therefore, date the Third Gospel at about A. D. 58, holding that this is in harmony with the demands of the time and the growth of Christianity, and that the view is not unsupported by external evidence.

4. **Purpose and Plan.** We have said that Luke's Gospel was occasioned by the author's desire to confirm Theophilus in the Christian faith and through or by him to do the same for all who might read the Gospel. Here we would notice the real purpose of the writer and the method by which he seeks to realize his purpose. Moorehead has some discerning remarks on this subject. He says Luke's design is "mainly to set forth the perfections of the Son of man as the Friend and Redeemer of men, the Savior of all that believe and receive Him. . . . In a very special sense Messiah was to be the Redeemer of His people. He was to discharge in full the awful debt they had

---

81. Accord. to Eusebius, *H. E.,* VI. xiv.

incurred, and to secure their complete deliverance. . . .
Luke's object is mainly to reveal the redemption wrought out
by our glorious Kinsman-Redeemer, the Lord Jesus Christ.
Here for the first time in the New Testament do we meet with
the word redemption (1:68, R. V.)"[82]

Thus Anna "spoke of him to all that looked for redemption
in Jerusalem" (2:38); thus the two on the way to Emmaus
said: "We trusted that it had been he who should have
redeemed Israel" (24:21); and thus Christ encouraged His
followers to look up, for the "redemption" draweth nigh
(21:28). Lev. 25:23-55 gives the law concerning the Redeemer. He must be a kinsman; no one else can take his place.
He redeems the inheritance (vs. 25) and the persons (47-50),
and he executes judgment on his enemies (Num. 35:19-21;
Deut. 19:12). The book of Ruth gives us a striking picture
of the work of the Kinsman-Redeemer (2:1; 3:12); compare
also the work of Jeremiah in redeeming a field (Jer. 32:6-8).
In other words, Luke is occupied with Christ as one of kin to
us in the work of redemption.

Let us notice the story of how he carries out his purpose
in tabular form.

The Introduction, 1:1-4.

(1) The Birth of the Redeemer's Forerunner, 1:5-80.

(2) The Birth and Childhood of the Redeemer, ch. 2.

(3) The External and Internal Preparation of the Redeemer, 3:1-4:13.

(4) The Redeemer's Early Ministry in Galilee, 4:17-7:50.

(5) The Redeemer's Later Ministry in Galilee, 8:1-9:6.

(6) The Redeemer's Withdrawal Northward, 9:7-50.

(7) The Redeemer's Later Judean and Perean Ministry,
9:51-19:28.

(8) The Redeemer's Closing Ministry in Jerusalem, 19:
29-21:37.

(9) The Redeemer's Betrayal, Trial, and Death, 22,23.

82. *Studies in the Four Gospels,* pp. 142-145.

(10) The Redeemer's Resurrection and Appearance to His Disciples, 24:1-49.

(11) The Redeemer's Ascension, 24:50-52.

4. **Points and Peculiarities.** The Third Gospel also has a number of distinct characteristics. We note the principal ones briefly.

(1) This is the Gospel of the perfect humanity of Christ. Our Lord is seen as having the development, feelings, sympathies, and powers of a man. Luke gives us the fullest account of the birth, childhood, growth, domestic and social life of Jesus. As a child He grew, waxed strong in spirit, was filled with wisdom, and the grace of God was upon Him (2:40,52). He was subject to Joseph and Mary (2:51). He "rejoiced in the Holy Spirit" (10:21); He "wept over the city" (19:41); He "prayed more earnestly; and his sweat became as it were great drops of blood falling down upon the ground" (22:44); He cried, "Father, into thy hands I commend my spirit" (23:46). He had a meal with Simon (7:36-50), with Martha and Mary (10:38-42), with another Pharisee (11:37-52), with a ruler of the Pharisees (14:1-24); He went to lodge with Zacchæus (19:1-10); He ate a piece of broiled fish before the disciples after His resurrection (24:41-43).

(2) Luke makes much of *Prayer*. Christ is represented as praying 15 times in the four Gospels, 11 of which are found in Luke's Gospel, 3 in Matthew's, and 4 in both Mark and John. Luke also has a good deal of teaching on prayer not found in the other Gospels (e. g., 11:5-13; 18:1-8; 21:36; cf. 18:11-13).

(3) The Third Gospel also makes much of *Praise and Thanksgiving.* "It begins and ends with worship in the temple (1:9; 24:52)."[83] Luke alone gives us the words of the great hymns which have since been set to music: The Ave Maria (1:28), the Magnificat (1:46-56), the Benedictus (1:68-79), the Gloria in Excelsis (2:14), and the Nunc Dimitis (2:29-32). Often it is said that men "glorified God" (2:20; 5:25,

---

83. Plummer, *op. cit.,* p. xlvi.

26; 7:16; 13:13; 17:15; 18:43); and the expressions "praising God" and "blessing God" are almost limited to Luke.

(4) Women and children are prominent in this Gospel. Luke tells us most about Elizabeth and Mary. Anna, the widow of Nain, the woman bound by Satan, the women who ministered to Him of their substance, the woman who was a sinner, and the widow who appealed to the unrighteous judge, are all mentioned only in Luke; Martha and Mary are mentioned in both Luke and John. Children are referred to more affectionately than in the other Gospels. Certain children brought to Him are called "infants" (18:15); Jairus' daughter was "an only daughter" (8:41,42); and the widow of Nain's son was "the only son of his mother" (7:12).

(5) The Gospel of Luke is the most literary and beautiful of the Gospels. It has a classic introduction, as we have noted above, like Herodotus and Thucydides. Both vocabulary and diction indicate that the author was an educated man.

(6) Luke uses many medical terms and shows special interest in sickness and in the sick.[84] Cadbury has somewhat weakened the evidence for this point, but has by no means destroyed it.

(7) Luke records 20 miracles of Christ, of which 6 are peculiar to him, and 23 parables, of which 18 are peculiar to him. He omits only 11 of the total number of parables in the Gospels, 10 of which are peculiar to Matthew and 1 to Mark.

(8) The long passage, 9:51-18:14 and the shorter passage, 19:1-28, are peculiar to Luke. Together they contain 16 of the parables of Luke and many of the most interesting events in the life of Christ. There are only 4 miracles in these passages.

---

84. See Hobart's *Medical Language of St. Luke,* and Harnack's *Luke the Physician,* pp. 175-198

Chapter VII

THE HISTORICAL BOOKS
John and The Book of Acts

1. THE GOSPEL OF JOHN

THE Gospel of John appears in all four possible positions. In the third and fourth centuries it was sometimes put first, as in the Bohairic version, in Chrysostom, in the Latin codex *k*, in the Vocabularies of the Egyptian versions, in Tertullian, and in codex 19. D and the other Western documents generally follow the order Matthew, John, Luke, Mark, assigning first place to the apostles. As we have seen, the present order was established by an early tradition. John was put last because it was regarded to have been written last. Inasmuch as most writers hold today that in John we have the result of the reflection of the Church on the facts contained in the Synoptics at the beginning of the second century, we do well to investigate afresh the true status of the Fourth Gospel. Has conclusive evidence been produced for the present popular view, or can one still honestly hold the so-called "traditional" view? Let us look at the facts.

1. **Attestation and Authorship.** The external evidence for the early date and Apostolic authorship of the Fourth Gospel is as great as that for any book in the New Testament. When we recall that all writers hold that this Gospel was published long after the other three, we are surprised that it was received from the first. The *Epistle of Barnabas* seems to allude to John 1:14 in the words: "Because He was to be manifested in flesh, and to sojourn among us" (ch. vi). The *Epistle* also uses the story of the uplifted serpent, but it is not certain whether the reference is to John 3:14-18 or to the account in Numbers (ch. xii). Some think Ignatius is silent in this respect, but is not his statement in the *Epistle to the Ephesians,* when he speaks

of the believers as "drawn up on high by the instrument of Jesus Christ, which is the cross,"[1] an allusion to John 12:32? Lightfoot thinks that Ignatius makes reference to John 4:10, 11, in the *Epistle to the Romans* (ch. vii) and to John 3:8 in the *Epistle to the Philippians* (ch. vii.) There are probably other allusions to John in the writings of Ignatius. Polycarp alludes to 1 John 4:2,3 thus: "For whosoever does not confess that Jesus Christ has come in the flesh, is antichrist" (ch. vii); and it is generally admitted that to recognize 1 John is to recognize the Gospel also. Westcott says: "Papias appears to have been acquainted with the Gospel of St. John."[2] It is uncertain whether Justin Martyr refers to this Gospel, though there may be reminiscences of it in his *Discourse to the Greeks* and in his *Hortatory Address to the Greeks*. In his *First Apology* (ch. lxi) he seems, however, clearly to refer to John 3:5. Sanday says: "That Justin also used it I think we may take as at the present time generally admitted."[3] Furthermore, Justin's doctrine of the Logos "presupposes a knowledge of the Fourth Gospel," for it contains marked differences from Philo's doctrine in the direction of John's.[4] Tatian not only used the Fourth Gospel in his *Diatessaron,* but quotes John 1:3[5] and John 1:5.[6] Theophilus of Antioch writes thus: "John says, 'In the beginning was the Word, and the Word was with God.'"[7] Westcott finds tacit references to John's Gospel also in Athenagoras.[8] The Muratorian Canon says: "John, one of the disciples, wrote a fourth book of the Gospels." The heretics Basilides and Valentinus refer to this Gospel: Basilides to John 1:9 and 2:4; Valentinus to 10:8 and 6:35. The *Epistle of the Churches of Vienne and Lyons* to the brethren in Asia and Phrygia has clear references to John.

From Irenæus on the evidence becomes clear and full. He himself frequently quotes the Gospel of John, and he does it in such a way as to show that it had long been known and used in the Church. His testimony is perhaps the most important

---

1. *Shorter Epistle,* ch. ix.
2. *On the Canon of the New Testament,* p. 67.
3. *Criticism of the Fourth Gospel,* p. 246.
4. E. g., *Apology* I. xxxii, lxvi; *Dialogue with Trypho* xlv, *xxxiv, lxxxvii, c;* Hovey, *Comm. on John,* p. 10.
5. *Address to the Greeks,* ch. xix.
6. *Ibid.,* ch. xiii.
7. *To Autolycus,* II. xxii.
8. *Op. cit.,* p. 208.

of all the testimonies, for he was a pupil of Polycarp, and Polycarp was a friend of the Apostle John. Irenæus also had fellowship with Pothinus, his predecessor at Lyons, who was a very old man when he was martyred. Through him he had access to the traditions of the earliest times. We do not consider it necessary to prove that Clement of Alexandria and Tertullian of Carthage frequently quote from the Fourth Gospel, the evidence is so patent. The only exception to the immediate and universal acceptance of this Gospel as by the Apostle is found in the obscure sect of the Alogoi. This word may mean either *without the doctrine* of the Logos or *without reason.* Cerinthus had taught that Christ was a mere man upon whom the Logos or Christ descended at baptism, and for this reason the word *Logos* in John may have led this sect to suspect the Gospel. Apart from this sect there was no opposition to this Gospel until the early part of the 19th century. Recently a new bit of evidence for the early date of this Gospel has been brought to light. In 1920 Grenfell acquired some papyri for the John Rylands Library of Manchester, among which C. H. Roberts later discovered a scrap of five verses of John 18, "which," according to Kenyon, "can be confidently assigned to the first half of the second century." Kenyon argues that by that time the Gospel had not only been written, but had "spread to a provincial town in Egypt . . . which goes far towards confirming the traditional date of composition, in the last years of the first century."[9]

If now this is the evidence for the early existence of the Fourth Gospel, what are the facts concerning its authorship? Theophilus of Antioch (c. 170) is the earliest writer to name John as the author. He says: "And hence the holy writings teach us, and all the spirit-bearing (inspired) men, one of whom, John, says, 'In the beginning was the Word, and the Word was with God.' "[10] There can be little doubt that he means the Apostle John. Irenæus says : "Afterwards, John, the disciple of the Lord, who also leaned upon His breast, did himself publish a Gospel during his residence at Ephesus in Asia."[11] Eusebius has preserved a part of a letter of Irenæus

---

9. *Our Bible and the Ancient Manuscripts,* p. 128.
10. *To Autolycus,* II. xxii.
11. *Against Heresies,* III. i.

to Florinus, in which the writer tells of his vivid recollection of the account that Polycarp gave of his intercourse with John who had seen the Lord.[12] He has also preserved a statement from a letter of Irenæus to Victor the Bishop of Rome, to the effect that "Anicetus could not persuade Polycarp not to observe what he had always observed with John the disciple of our Lord and the other Apostles with whom he had associated."[13] It is thus evident that Polycarp was a disciple of John the Apostle and that Irenæus had heard Polycarp tell of his intercourse with him. The testimony of Irenæus may, therefore, be taken as the testimony of Polycarp, and of the Apostle himself. Eusebius preserves also a statement from Clement of Alexandria, to the effect that "John, the last of all, seeing that what was corporal was set forth in the Gospels, on the entreaty of his intimate friends and inspired by the Spirit, composed a spiritual Gospel."[14] Clement's great respect for Pantænus, his predecessor in the catechetical school at Alexandria, leads us to the conclusion that he merely continued the tradition from him. Tertullian undoubtedly assumes the genuineness of the Gospel. He calls the four Gospels *Evangelicum Instrumentum*, i. e., a valid document finally declaring the mind of the Church. In addition to all this is the well-known fact that the Gospel of John is found in the Old Syriac and the Old Latin versions.

But recent criticism has been greatly impressed with the "discovery" of Eusebius that there were two Johns at Ephesus in Papias' day, one, John the Apostle, and the other, John the Presbyter. So generally, indeed, has it adopted this view that nearly all modern writers hold that John the Presbyter, not John the Apostle, wrote the Fourth Gospel. Salmon says: "A whole school of critics speak of him [John the Presbyter] with as assured confidence as if he were a person concerning whose acts we had as much information as concerning those of Julius Cæsar; but in truth his very existence seems to have been first discovered by Eusebius, and it is still a disputed matter whether the discovery be a real one."[15] Since this is

12. *H. E.*, V. xx.
13. *H. E.*, V. xxiv.
14. *H. E.*, VI. xiv.
15. *Intro. to the New Testament*, p. 279.

the case, it is necessary to note exactly what Papias says,[16] and to examine his statements first hand. These are the words of Papias, together with the comments of Eusebius:

"But I shall not hesitate also to put down for you along with my interpretations whatsoever things I have at any time learned carefully from the elders and carefully remembered, guaranteeing their truth. For I do not, like the multitude, take pleasure in those that speak much, but in those that teach the truth; not in those that relate strange commandments, but in those that deliver the commandments given by the Lord to faith, and springing from the truth itself. If, then, any one came, who had been a follower of the elders, I questioned him in regard to the words of the elders, — what Andrew or what Peter said, or what was said by Philip, or by Thomas, or by James, or by John, or by Matthew, or by any other of the disciples of the Lord, and what things Aristion and the presbyter John, the disciple of the Lord, say. For I do not think that what was gotten from the books would profit me as much as what came from the living and abiding voice." Eusebius comments on this quotation as follows: "It is worth while observing here that the name John is twice enumerated by him. The first one he mentions in connection with Peter and James and Matthew and the rest of the apostles, clearly meaning the evangelist; but the other John he mentions after an interval, and places him among others outside of the number of the apostles, putting Aristion before him, and he distinctly calls him a presbyter. This shows that the statement of those is true, who say that there were two persons in Asia that have the same name, and that there were two tombs in Ephesus, each of which, even to the present day, is called John's."

The fallacy of Eusebius' reasoning is evident. He ignores the fact that in the first instance John, along with the other persons mentioned, all of which are manifestly apostles, is called both a "presbyter" and a "disciple" of the Lord, not an "apostle." Why could he not then call him "presbyter" in the second instance without denying that he was also an "apostle"? For those who believe that 2 John and 3 John were written by the same man as 1 John and the Gospel, there is proof of the

---

16. As he is quoted by Eusebius, *H. E.*, III. xxxix. 1-7.

fact that John himself calls himself an "elder" rather than an "apostle." The question has been asked, Why mention the same person twice in this context? Because, presumably, although he had heard from all persons in this list in the past, they were all dead at the time to which he refers, save the Apostle John, and he no longer received information from them; but Aristion and the Apostle John were still living and he still heard from them on occasion. That is why he changes from the past tense, "had said," to the present tense, "say." Does Papias not rather take pains to identify the John of the second statement with the John of the first statement by designating him both "presbyter" and "disciple" in both statements? It is an awkward way of making himself clear, to be sure, but it seems that this is what he means to say. Zahn has refuted the theory of two Johns at Ephesus[17] and Dom John Chapman has proved almost conclusively that the Elder John in Papias' statement is John the Apostle.[18] The Apostolic authorship of the Fourth Gospel is also defended by Sanday[19] and Drummond.[20]

The internal evidence supports the external. The statement in 21:24 clearly points to "the disciple whom Jesus loved, who also leaned back on his breast at the supper," in 21:20, as the author of the Gospel. But since there is much debate as to who this is, we present the following internal evidence to show that it is the Apostle John. We note that the writer is, —

(1) A Jew. This is seen in his attitude toward the Old Testament, which he thrice quotes from the Hebrew (12:40; 13:18; 19:37). Compare also his opening words with Gen. 1:1, and 3:13 with Deut. 30:12, and his regard for the Old Testament in 10:35. Note also his application of the prophecies of the Old Testament to persons and events (13:18; 17:12; 19:24,28,36,37). It is seen in his acquaintance with the Jewish feasts. Note the three Passovers (2:13,23; 6:4; 13:1; 18:28, with a possible additional one in 5:1), the feast of Tabernacles (7:37), and the feast of Dedication (10:22). It is also seen in his acquaintance with Jewish customs and

---

17. *Op. cit.,* II, 435-438, 451-453.
18. *John the Presbyter and the Fourth Gospel.*
19. *Criticism of the Fourth Gospel.*
20 *Character and Authorship of the Fourth Gospel.*

habits of thought. He gives us a picture of a Jewish marriage feast and knows about the prescribed way of arranging the waterpots (2:1-10). He knows about the questions of purifying (3:25; 11:55), the burial customs of the Jews (11:38,44; 19:40), the Jewish estimate of women (4:27), the disparagement of the Dispersion (7:35), the law against leaving bodies on the cross over the Sabbath (19:31), the feeling between the Jews and the Samaritans (4:9). It has been objected to this view that the writer cannot be a Jew because he so often represents "the Jews" in a bad light; but the reply to this is that at the time when John wrote the Jews had developed from what they were in Jesus' day into the bitterest adversaries of the Gospel.[21]

(2) A Palestinian Jew. Many of the preceding statements already point to a Palestinian home. He knows that Jacob's well is deep (4:11), that there is a descent from Cana to the Sea of Galilee (2:12). Bethsaida and Bethany are the homes of friends (1:44; 12:21; 11:1); Bethany is distinguished from Bethany (1:28; 11:18). He knows about the city of Ephraim (11:54) and of Aenon (3:23), and about Mt. Gerizim (4:20). In Jerusalem he knows about Kidron (18:1), Bethesda and Siloam (5:2; 9:7), the details about the Temple (10:22 f.; 2:20; 8:20), the sale of oxen, sheep, and doves in the temple (2:14-16), and about Golgotha as the place of a skull (19:17).

(3) A Contemporary of the Persons and the Events Narrated. The deputation sent to John deals with a still living question (1:19 ff). He speaks of the chief priests and Pharisees, not the Sadducees and Pharisees, knowing that the Sadducees held the office of chief priest in that day (e. g., 11:47-53). He knows the opposition of the Pharisees (7:45-52; 11:46) and that the chief priests and the Pharisees had given orders to arrest Christ (11:57). The writer was known to the high priest and went into the high priest's palace with Jesus (18:15); he alone tells us that it was the high priest's servant Malchus whose ear Peter cut off (18:10). The controversies with which he deals are not those of the second century, when

---

21. Cf. 1 Thess. 2:14-16.

the Gnostic and Ebionite heresies were active, but those which characterized the Jews before Jerusalem was destroyed, when they still looked for a Deliverer from Rome (6:15; 11:47-50; 19:12). The violation of the Sabbath law was not important in the second century (5:9-11; 9:14-16).

(4) He was John the Apostle. We conclude this from the above facts and from his claims to have been an eyewitness of the Lord Jesus (1:14; 19:35; 21:24; cf. 1 John 1:1). Of course, even this might only mean that he was one of the Twelve, but we shall see that only John qualifies for the distinction. He tells of the emotions and motives of Christ (2:24; 4:1-3; 6:15; 11:33; 13:1,21; 18:4); he expresses the opinions or reflections of the disciples (2:11,17,22; 12:16); he reports the discourses in Solomon's porch (10:23) and in the Treasury (8:20); he indicates the hours when things happened (1:39; 4:6, 52; 19:14); he reports the things said by Philip (6:7; 14:8), Andrew (6:9), Thomas (11:16; 14:5), and Judas (14:22). He was the disciple who leaned on Jesus' breast at the Last Supper (13:23-25), and so one of the three: Peter, James, and John. But Peter is distinguished from the writer by name (e. g., 1:41,42; 13:6,8, etc.), and James had been killed long before this time (Acts 12:2). It is to be noted that the writer never mentions either James or the Sons of Zebedee in the Gospel. Notice how he introduces himself (13:23; 19:26; 20:2; 21:7,20). We have already shown that 21:24 identifies this one with the writer. From all these facts we draw the conclusion that John the Apostle wrote the Fourth Gospel.

A few details about the author's life will add to our understanding of the Gospel. To begin with, there are five Johns in the New Testament: (1) John the Baptist, the only John mentioned by name in the Gospel; (2) John the Father of Peter (John 1:42; 21:15-17, A. S. V.), who is also called Jonah (Matt. 16:17); (3) John Mark (Acts 12:12,25); (4) the John who sat in the Sanhedrin (Acts 4:5,6); and (5) John the Apostle. The latter was a son of Zebedee; James was his brother, and probably the older of the two; Salome seems to have been his mother, and she was probably a sister of the mother of Jesus. Zebedee was a fisherman, and both James and John assisted him in this business. John is apparently the unnamed disciple who early left the Baptist to follow Jesus (1:35-40). But he seems to have returned to his business for a while (Luke 5:10), until Jesus called both him and James to follow Him (Matt. 4:21,22; Mark 1:19,20). Later on they were both appointed as apostles (Matt. 10:2). Jesus surnamed them Boanerges, sons of thunder (Mark 3:17), apparently because of their vehemence, zeal, and intensity (cf. Luke 9:54). Both went with their mother to ask for places of honor by the side of Jesus (Matt. 20:20-24; Mark 10:35-41).

John was one of the three in the inner circle (Mark 5:37; 9:2; 14:33) and leaned on Jesus' bosom at the Supper (John 13:23). He followed the Master into the high priest's palace (18:15) and to the place of crucifixion. Jesus committed His mother to John (19:26,27). John ran to the tomb with Peter on the resurrection morning and in the evening saw the risen Lord (20:1-23). After Pentecost he was a companion of Peter on several occasions (Acts 3:1; 4:19; 8:14). He was in Jerusalem when Paul visited the city after his first missionary journey (Acts 15:6; Gal. 2:9). Tradition almost without exception represents John as spending his last years at Ephesus. He must not have come to Ephesus, however, until after Paul's last visit to the city in A. D. 65 or 66. Domitian banished John to Patmos, but with the accession of Nerva he was freed and returned to Ephesus. Irenæus says that he remained at Ephesus until his death, which was in the reign of Trajan. The statement ascribed to Papias that John was killed early by the Jews, was probably developed from Christ's word to James and John about drinking the same cup that He drank (Mark 10:39; Matt. 20:23). Moffatt defends the statement as genuine; but it is not found in any early authority and certainly not in any of great critical value.[22] These brothers drank the "cup" — James as an early martyr (Acts 12:1 f.), John as an exile to Patmos. Jesus' final word concerning John supports this view (21:20-23).

2. **Dependence and Language.** Not much need be said on these subjects. If John the Apostle wrote the Fourth Gospel, then the writer is primarily dependent upon his own knowledge

---

22. Robertson, *Word Pictures,* V. xii.

of the facts. We have shown that he repeatedly represents himself as an eyewitness. Recall the character of the reminiscences and the details of the stories and incidents. Moffatt maintains that in spite of the differences between him and Philo, John shows familiarity with the Philonic methods and materials and used them for higher ends. He thinks these similarities are not only found in the Logos-doctrine, but in numerous other places in the Gospel as well.[23] To this we reply, that at Ephesus John no doubt became acquainted with certain forms of thought that were largely unknown in Palestine, and that there he may have come to know a good deal about Philo's teaching. But certainly there is nothing to show that he was trained in the Hellenistic philosophy of Alexandria.[24] We may even grant that he uses some of the forms of expression that are found in Philo; but he always filled them with a Christian content, for he differs widely from Philo. Others hold that John uses some of the phraseology of the Synoptics and that he is dependent upon them. Some hold that he was indebted to the Synoptics for almost all the facts in his Gospel. However, apart from the two miracles in 6:4-21 and the passion story, all is different in the Fourth Gospel. There are intimations of Jesus' Galilean ministry, but no full accounts of it (2:1-12; 4:43-54; 6:1-7:9). John, instead of directly borrowing from the Synoptic accounts, supplements them with the history of the early Judæan ministry, which they omit. The Fourth Gospel assumes the existence of the Synoptics and does not repeat much that is found in them. It has its own plan and purpose and selects its own materials to attain that purpose. This is not denying that John used some of the same phrases that occur in the first three Gospels; but this is no positive proof that he borrowed them from the Synoptics, — he may just as well have taken them from his own recollections.

The Gospel is written in the *Koinē* Greek of the time, although the author's thought and tone, and sometimes his forms of expression also, are thoroughly Hebrew. It is a simple and smooth Greek, but characterized rather frequently

---

23. *Intro. to the Literature of the New Testament*, pp. 523-525.
24. Cf. Sanday, *Criticism of the Fourth Gospel*, Lect. VI.

by Hebrew parallelism. Burney's theory that John's Gospel is the earliest and that it was originally written in Aramaic,[25] has not received general recognition. Robertson says: "Some of the examples cited are plausible and some quite fanciful.[26] Montgomery also argues for an Aramaic original,[27] and Torrey has given us a "translation" of the Four Gospels from his reconstructed Aramaic original.[28] But Colwell has written a good refutation of the theory that John was originally written in Aramaic.[29]

3. Occasion and Date. The Muratorian Canon says that John wrote at the entreaties of his fellow-disciples and bishops. According to this his fellow-disciples in Asia Minor were the external reason for the Gospel. We have seen (above) that Clement of Alexandria represents John as, moved by "the entreaty of his intimate friends and inspired by the Spirit," proceeding to compose "a spiritual Gospel." Eusebius argues that John wrote to supply the deficiences of the Synoptic writers.[30] Some of these assertions may contain elements of truth; but John certainly does not "supply the deficiences" of the other three Gospels, — he, instead, supplements their accounts. Primarily John had the leading and enabling of the Holy Spirit in the writing of his Gospel; his intimate friends and fellow-disciples in Asia Minor may, however, also have had a part in encouraging him to write it. There was, no doubt, also the felt need that the Church should have a fuller commentary on the work and teachings of Jesus than had hitherto been produced. At any rate, this Gospel is just such an intermingling of interpretation with narrative materials. There must have been the feeling that certain incidents and addresses that are omitted by the Synoptists ought to be added. It would seem, then, that a combination of all these factors led to the writing of the Fourth Gospel.

There is very general agreement that John's Gospel was written after the other three Gospels and rather late in the first century. We have seen that Irenæus placed it after Matthew,

---

25. *The Aramaic Origin of the Fourth Gospel.*
26. *Word Pictures,* V, xx.
27. *The Origin of the Gospel According to St. John.*
28. *The Four Gospels: A New Translation.*
29. *The Greek of the Fourth Gospel.*
30. *H. E.,* III. xxiv.

Mark, and Luke[31] and that Clement of Alexandria says John wrote "last of all."[32] Jerome uses language to the same effect. The manner in which the Gospel refers to "the Jews" accords best with the view that it was written after the nation had become the confirmed enemies of the Church and many years after the author had been absent from Palestine. The absence of any reference to the destruction of Jerusalem seems to require that we either put the Gospel some time before that event, or sufficiently far after it to make reference to it a matter of indifference, i. e., into a period when interest in the calamity had largely subsided. Westcott puts it late in the first century. The best evidence points to Ephesus as the place of writing. Irenæus definitely declares that John wrote it from that city. He says: "Afterwards, John, the disciple of the Lord, who also leaned upon His breast, did himself publish a Gospel during his residence at Ephesus in Asia."[33] The same writer also testifies that John lived until the time of Trajan, who began to reign in A. D. 98.[34] Polycrates, bishop of Ephesus, testifies that the John who leaned on Jesus' breast, lies buried at Ephesus.[35] If the Gospel was written at Ephesus, we must date it after A. D. 70; for John did not get to that city until 69 or 70. Furthermore, the destruction of Jerusalem must have ocurred a good many years before he wrote, say 15 or 20 years before. Therefore, in the light of all these facts we conclude that the Fourth Gospel was written by the Apostle John at Ephesus, about A. D. 85-90.

4. **Purpose and Plan.** Many views have been held as to the purpose of the writer of the Fourth Gospel. Some have held that he endeavors to supplement and correct the synoptics, so as to meet the needs at the opening of the second century; others have held that his aim is polemical, seeking to oppose early Gnosticism; still others have held that he wrote to support the developing sacramentarianism of the early second century; and yet others have held that he tried to make the Gospel more acceptable to the Gentiles.

---

31. *Against Heresies*, III. i. 1.
32. *H. E.*, VI. xiv.
33. *Against Heresies*, III. i. 1.
34. *Ibid.*, III. iii. 4.
35. *H. E.*, III. xx.

To this we reply that although John manifestly supplements the Synoptics in a good many ways, he never corrects them. Even the date of the Passover can be harmonized with that of the Synoptics. Again, although the Fourth Gospel uses some of the terms characteristic of Gnosticism, it uses them in a distinctively Christian sense; and although the Gospel furnishes many suitable refutations of Gnostic speculation, there is no conspicuous polemic object in the Gospel, as there is in the First Epistle. Further, although John reports our Lord's great discourse on the Bread that has come down from heaven, and emphasizes the importance of eating Christ's body and drinking His blood, he distinctly points out that the spirit is life, the flesh profits nothing (6:32-65). Certainly, John is not supporting sacramentarianism in this Gospel. And finally, although John criticizes the Jews for their attitudes toward Christ, he really does not tone down his message to accomodate the Gentiles. He is really cosmopolitan in his outlook and appeal.

While we, then, recognize some elements of truth in some of these positions, we yet hold that they are entirely inadequate representations of John's real design. His real aim is directly spiritual. He says: "Many other signs therefore did Jesus in the presence of the disciples, which are not written in this book: but these are written, that ye may believe that Jesus is the Christ, the Son of God; and that believing ye may have life in his name" (20:30,31). That is, he had a directly spiritual purpose: he wanted to lead men to faith in Christ, and so to eternal life. This he sought to do by proving the deity of Christ; and he proves the deity of Christ by the "signs" that he represents Jesus as having done. But a study of the Gospel shows that he also tries in various other ways to prove the same thing, as in representation of the person and work of the Lord (e.g., 1:1-5,9-18; 2:23-25; 3:31-36; 5:30-47; 6:66-69; 8:46-59; 9:35-41; 10:22-39, etc.), and by the various figures applied to Christ (e. g., Bread, Light, Shepherd, Truth, Life, Vine, etc.). This, then, is his real purpose; let us note how the plan of the Gospel works this out. John deals with:

(1) The Essential Glory of the Son of God, 1:1-5.

(2) The Incarnation and General Reception of the Son of God, 1:6-18.

(3) The Revelation of the Son of God to Israel, 1:19-12:50.

(4) The Revelation of the Son of God to the Disciples, chs. 13-17.

(5) The Glorification of the Son of God in His Passion, chs. 18,19.

(6) The Manifestation of the Son of God in Resurrection Power and Glory, 20,21.

5. **Points and Peculiarities.** There are so many of these that only the most outstanding can be listed.

(1) This Gospel has an announced purpose (John 20:30, 31; cf. Luke 1:1-4). "Signs," figures, and discourses are chosen with a view to attaining this purpose.

(2) It omits the account of the birth of John the Baptist, and of Jesus' birth, genealogy, youth, baptism, temptation, transfiguration, and ascension. Christ is preeminently deity, and for deity these things have no significance.

(3) John is the only one who reports the early Judæan ministry. Without the Fourth Gospel Christ's ministry would seem to have lasted for but one and one-third year; but by means of the four Passovers mentioned in the Gospel (2:13; 5:1, possibly; 6:4; 13:1; 18:28) we know that it lasted for somewhat more than three years. (Aleph and C and the Syrian MSS. have *hē heortē* in John 5:1; A B D G K and Origen omit the article.)

(4) The Greek particles *oun* and *hina* occur with unusual frequency, the former occurring about 210 times and the latter 130 times. The former is weakened in many cases to *then, next in sequence;* the latter, to that of *result.*

(5) There are no parables in John. The word *paroimia* in 10:6 should be rendered "proverb," or "allegory," not "parable."

(6) There are eight miracles in John, all but two, the feeding of the 5000 and the walking on the sea (6:4-21), being peculiar to John.

(7) John has at the utmost an account of but 20 days of our Lord's ministry. Chapters 13-19, 237 verses out of 879, or nearly one-third of the whole Gospel, cover but one day in the life of Christ.

(8) Some of the characteristic words in John are: "Believe" and cognates, about 100 times (strangely enough, "belief" and "faith" never occur in this Gospel); God as "Father," 122 times; "glory" and cognates, 33 times; "love" and cognates, 57 times; "verily, verily," 25 times.

(9) Christ appears under many different titles, as, the Word, the Only Begotten, the Lamb of God, the Son of God, the True Bread, the Light, the Shepherd, the Door, the Way, the Truth, the Life, the Resurrection, the Vine. Many of these are introduced by the formula, "I am." All these imply deity; but there are also many other ways in which the deity of Christ is intimated.

(10) The section about the adulteress (7:53-8-11) is, no doubt, a true story from the life of Jesus; but it is poorly supported by documentary evidence. It is not found in *Aleph* A B C L T W X *Delta* and at least seventy cursives and numerous *Evangelistaria* (Gospel Lectionaries). It is also wanting in the Old Syriac, the Peshitta, the Harklean, in some copies of the Old Latin, and in several of the minor versions. Really, it appears in no Greek manuscript earlier than the eighth century, save in Codex Beza (5th cent.), which has many textual peculiarities. It is not quoted as by John until late in the fourth century; at which time Augustine says that some have removed it from their copies, fearing, he supposes, that its presence might give their wives undue license. Jerome says that in his day it was contained "in many Greek and Latin MSS."[36] Plummer reminds us, however, that "most of the worst corruptions of the text were already in existence in Jerome's time."[37] Practically all scholars today accept it as a true incident in the life of Jesus, but not as a genuine part of John's Gospel. This includes such conservative scholars as Warfield and A. T. Robertson. Yet there we have the statements of Jerome and Augustine!

---

36. *Against Pelagius,* II. xvii.
37. *Comm. on the Gospel of St. John,* p. 182.

2. THE BOOK OF ACTS

The Four Gospels relate the things which "Jesus began both to do and to teach, until the day in which he was received up." They deal with Christ's birth, ministry, death, resurrection, and ascension. The Book of Acts begins with Christ's post-resurrection ministry and ascension, and continues with the account of what "Jesus began both to do and to teach" through the instrumentality of the Holy Spirit after He had returned to heaven. The importance of "Acts," as *Aleph* calls it in the inscription, or of "The Acts of the Apostles," as *Aleph, B,* and D call it in the subscription, appears from the fact that without this book, except for some fragmentary allusions in the Epistles, we would have no authentic record of Apostolic history.

We have, of course, the apocryphal "Acts" (such as the Acts of Paul, the Acts of Peter, the Acts of John, the Acts of Andrew, the Acts of Thomas); but as sources of information for the life and work of the Apostles they are altogether worthless. Although the Book of Acts says very little about any of the apostles except Peter, John, and Paul, it came early to be recognized as "The Acts of the Apostles." Clement of Alexandria, Origen, Dionysius of Alexandria, Cyril of Jerusalem and Chrysostom call it by that name. Although the view of the Tübingen School that in this book a Paulinist of a mild type seeks to minimize the differences between Peter and Paul has been almost entirely abandoned in our day, the Lucan authorship of the book is still disputed by many of those who maintain a naturalistic view of the origin of Christianity. We need, therefore, still to inquire after the true status of the book.

1. **Attestation and Authorship.** The evidence for the use of Acts does not appear as early or as frequently as that for the Gospels and Pauline Epistles, but yet it is ample to show that it was early recognized as an authoritative book. Ignatius seems to be silent regarding Acts in his Shorter Epistles, although Holtzmann[38] holds that he used the book. Polycarp seems to allude to Acts 2:24 in his *Epistle to the Philippians* (ch. i) and possibly to Acts 5:41 (*ibid.,* ch. viii). In the

---

38. *Einleitung,* p. 406.

Epistle to Diognetus (ch. iii) there seems to be an allusion to Acts 17:24,25; and in the *Didache* (ch. iv) to Acts 4:32. Justin Martyr clearly alludes to Acts 1:9, in *On the Resurrection* (ch. ix) and possibly to Acts 7:22, in *Hortatory Address to the Greeks* (ch. x). There is also a possible allusion to Paul's speech at Athens in Tatian's *Address to the Greeks* (ch. iv). The Muratorian Canon says: "But the Acts of all the Apostles were written in one volume. Luke compiled for 'most excellent Theophilus' what things were done in detail in his presence, as he plainly shows by omitting both the death of Peter and also the departure of Paul from the city, when he departed for Spain." The *Epistle of the Church of Vienne* uses language similar to that of Acts 7:59 ff.[39] Acts is found in the Old Latin, the Bohairic, and the Sahidic versions, as also in the Peshitta. Kirsopp Lake thinks there probably was also "an Old Syriac version of Acts";[40] but no copy of this has come down to us. Irenæus frequently quotes from or alludes to Acts, e. g., 22:8; 26:15, in *Against Heresies* (III.xv.1), 2:30-37, in the same work (III.xii.2), 3:6, also in the same work (III.xii.3), etc. Tertullian also frequently quotes from or alludes to Acts, e. g., 2:9, 10, in *An Answer to the Jews* (ch. vii), 8:9, in *A Treatise on the Soul* (ch. lvii), and 15:1-31, in *On Idolatry* (ch. xxiv). The same is true of Clement of Alexandria, as 2:41, in *Stromata* (I.xviii), 5:1, in the same work (I.xxiii), ch. 17, also in the same work (VI.xviii), and 9:10-15, in the *Instructor* (II.i). After this the evidence for the book is abundant.

Tradition ascribes the book to Luke. We have already noted the statement of the Muratorian Fragment (above). It is certainly very definite. Clement of Alexandria says: "As Luke in the Acts of the Apostles relates that Paul said, 'Men of Athens, I perceive that in all things ye are too superstitious," in *Stromata* (V.xii). Tertullian says: "In the self-same commentary of Luke the *third* hour is demonstrated as an hour of prayer, about which hour it was that they who received the initiatory gift of the Holy Spirit were held for drunkards," in *On Fasting* (ch. x). Irenæus says: "Simon the Samaritan was

---

39. Eusebius, *H. E.*, V. ii. 5.
40. *Dict. of Apost. Church*, s. v., "Acts of the Apostles."

that magician of whom Luke, the disciple and follower of the apostles, says," etc., in *Against Heresies* (I.xxiii), and again : "Luke also recorded that Stephen who was the first elected into the diaconate by the apostles, and who was the first slain for the testimony of Christ, spoke regarding Moses as follows," in the same work (IV. xv. 1). Thus Irenaeus and the Muratorian Canon testify to the Lucan authorship of Acts in the Western Church, Tertullian, in the African Church, and Clement of Alexandria, in the Egyptian Church. Robertson says : "By the time of Eusebius the book is generally acknowledged as part of the canon."[41]

The internal evidence has already been largely stated in our study of the Gospel of Luke. Briefly we may repeat the argument so far as the Book of Acts itself is concerned : (1) The "we" sections in Acts (16:10-17; 20:5-21 :18; 27 :1-28 :16) indicate that the author was one of Paul's companions on his journeys. (2) The rest of Acts is by the same writer as the "we" sections, as is evident from the similarity of style and language in all of the book. It would be absurd to suppose that the author assimilated the "we" sections to the rest of the book and at the same time was so stupid as to leave the plural "we" stand as in his sources. (3) The medical language in the Acts and the writer's interest in sickness and the sick suggest that the author was a physician. Knowling points out that the medical phraseology of Acts was fully recognized before Hobart wrote his notable book, *The Medical Language of St. Luke* (in 1882), e. g., in Belcher's, *Our Lord's Miracles of Healing*[42] and in the *Gentleman's Magazine,* June, 1841. The latter is often referred to as a starting-point for this inquiry, although Wetstein and Bengel, even before this, fully recognized the hand of a medical writer in Luke and the Acts. Knowling points to the writer's *tendency* to employ medical language more frequently than the other evangelists and to introduce miracles of his own of healing; to the way in which he abstains from using in a medical sense words which medical writers abstain from so using, although they are thus employed in the other Gospels; and to the frequency with which he uses medi-

---

41. "Acts of the Apostles," in the *Int. Stand. Bible Ency.*
42. 1st ed., 1871, 2d ed., 1890.

cal language in a secondary sense.[43] Cadbury has not "completely wrecked Hobart's proof," but has merely taught us to examine each word and phrase more carefully before we cite it as an example of the author's use of medical terminology.

In the light of these facts it is not surprising to find that such recent scholars as Harnack, Ramsay, Knowling, Rackam, Robertson, Hayes, and Machen accept and defend the Lucan authorship of the Acts. The writers who still reject the Lucan authorship do so chiefly on the ground (1) of the supposed late date for the Third Gospel (after A. D. 70), making Acts too late to be written by Luke; (2) of the assumed dependence of Acts upon Josephus for some of its material; and (3) of the type of miracles recorded in the book. We have already shown that Luke's Gospel was written before A. D. 70, and so there is no difficulty here about the lateness of Acts; in the next section we shall show that Acts is not dependent upon Josephus; and the believer in the plenary inspiration of the Scriptures has no difficulty with the miracles in Acts. We may, therefore, heartily embrace the view of the early Church that Luke the physician wrote the Book of Acts.

The biographical data concerning Luke have already been set forth in connection with our treatment of the Third Gospel, and the reader is referred to that discussion for the facts concerning the life and work of the author.

2. **Dependence and Language.** Harnack has shown that in no part of the Acts can the use of sources be proved on the basis of linguistic investigation.[44] He holds, however, that Luke has used sources for the first fifteen chapters of the book, but has worked them over so completely that the language is all that of Luke and not of any of the sources. On the ground of the scenes and the persons with which the narrative is concerned he postulates three main sources for the first part of the book: (1) A Jerusalem-Caesarean or Petro-Philippine source, 3:1-5:16; 8:5-40; 9:31-11:18; 12:1-23. This he regards as the first recension and as a good written source. (2) A Jerusalem or Palestinian source, ch. 2; 5:17-42, and possibly 1:15-26 (1:1-14 he regards a legend which Luke inserted, coming ap-

---

43. *Exp. Greek Test.*, II, 5-10.
44. *The Acts of the Apostles*, p. 163.

parently from Jerusalem also). This he regards as a second recension of what is found in the first and as far inferior to the first. (3) A Jerusalem-Antiochean source, 6:1-8:4; 11:19-30; 12:24-15:35. He assigns high historical value to this source, although he thinks up to 13:4 it is open to some criticism in its details. The conversion of Paul, 9:1-30, he regards as interpolated from some other source, and the Apostolic Decree in 15:22-29 he treats as unhistorical as it appears in its Eastern form and that of most of the Uncials (and in our English versions), because he regards it as inconsistent with Gal. 2:1-10 and with the corresponding passages in 1 Corinthians. He thinks, however, that in the form in which it was held by the Western Fathers, including Irenaeus, and as it appears in Codex D, it can be accepted as historical. For chs. 16:6-28:31 he thinks Luke was an eyewitness of the events or had received his information from eyewitnesses, and the section is generally speaking reliable.

It is to be regretted that after Harnack has done so much to establish the Lucan authorship of Acts on linguistic grounds he should so degrade the book as to make it largely worthless for authentic information in the first fifteen chapters! The believer in the verbal inspiration of the Scriptures does not necessarily reject the idea that for some of the materials Luke may have used written "sources," but he rejects the idea that he employed mere human insight in the choice and adaptation of the materials. How much better is Knowling's conception of Luke's procedure in the preparation of this book. He says: "It is plain from the narrative that a man in St. Luke's position would be brought into contact with many persons from whom he could have obtained rich and varied information, and in many cases the details of his narrative point unmistakably to the origin of the information. A good example may be seen in ch. 12, in which the vivid and circumstantial details of St. Peter's escape from prison are best accounted for on the supposition that the narrative comes from John Mark."[45] He points out that Luke could have learned from Barnabas, the cousin of Mark, about the origin of the Christian community (4:36; 11:28); from the men of Cyprus and Cyrene, who fled

---

45. *Exp. Greek Test.*, II, 16 f.

from Judea to Antioch (11:19), about the work in Antioch; from Mnason of Cyprus, an early disciple (21:16), as Humphrey thinks, from the first Pentecost (cf. 11:15), about many of the events in the early Church; from Philip the Evangelist, with whom he stayed for several days (21:8-12), about the events in 8:4-40, as also those in 6:1-8:3; 10:1-11:18; from James, whom he met in Jerusalem (21:18), about the events in Jerusalem and Palestine; and from Silas, whom he must have met at Philippi (16:19 ff.), the events on Paul's journeys when he was not in the party. Luke also knew the foster-brother of Herod Antipas, Manaen (Acts 13:1; cf. Luke 8:3), a teacher in the Church at Antioch, and he may well have gotten the two incidents connected with Herod which he alone records (Luke 13:31-33; 23:6-12, 15; cf. Acts 4:27) directly from Manaen. Luke may have had written documents of Peter's and Stephen's speeches, it is true; but really he did not need any other sources for the writing of Acts, or at least for much of it, than his own recollections of what he had seen and heard and of what Paul had told him; as for 6:8-8:3; 9:1-30; 13-28. If it be said that in the first 12 chapters the style is more Hebraistic than in the rest of the book, we may explain that in these chapters Luke would often obtain his information regarding the earlier events of Christianity from Jewish Christians in Palestine, and that he may have purposely retained the Hebraistic coloring in his use of the materials. This explanation is equally plausible whether we think of his "sources" as written or oral or both.

Some writers insist that Luke was dependent upon Josephus for some of his materials (as Schmiedel, Keim, and apparently McGiffert). Certain words that are common to the two are cited as proof of this fact. But as Robertson points out, they are "in the main untechnical words of common use,"[46] such as might be used by most any writer. But the mention of Theudas and Judas the Galilean, in Acts 5:36, 37, and in *Ant.* XX. v. 1, 2, is held to be a more definite proof of the dependence of Luke upon the Jewish historian. Peake thinks Luke had a cursory acquaintance with this section of the *Antiquities,* but holds that although this would make Luke a rather old man at the

---

46. "Acts of the Apostles," *Int. Stand. Bible Ency.*

time, he is yet the author of Acts.[47] But von Dobschütz says: "The theory would impute to St. Luke an almost incredible misunderstanding, which would indeed presuppose his having used Josephus in a manner so superficial as to lead one to say that, if he had ever read the work of Josephus at all, he must have forgotten it entirely. The two authors, in point of fact, are obviously quite independent of each other."[48] Furthermore, the Theudas of whom Josephus speaks appeared in the reign of Claudius, some ten years after the speech of Gamaliel. The Theudas of whom Gamaliel speaks must, therefore, be another man of the same name. The name was not an uncommon one, and there may well have been more than one person of the same name who led in an insurrection. The name Judas was even more common; but it appears that Luke and Josephus refer to the same Judas, who was defeated before Gamaliel spoke (ca. 34 or 35 A. D.), but whose followers again gathered and formed a kind of party about ten years later. In any event Luke and Josephus appear to have narrated the facts concerning Judas independently of each other.[49]

The language of Acts is even better Greek than that of the Third Gospel. At the same time there is a distinct Aramaic coloring in the first twelve chapters of the book. The author makes use of a large number of medical terms. His command of nautical language is abundantly attested by chs. 27, 28. In his speech on Mars Hill (ch. 17) Paul is represented as making choice use of words and idioms. Codex Bezae (D) has an unusually large number of variations from the received text in Acts, Borneman even holding that this was the original text. Blass has shown that in Luke and Acts, esp. in Acts, the Western text has its most marked characteristics. Robertson thinks "these readings deserve careful consideration, and some of them may be correct, whatever view one holds of the D text."[50] Ramsay also attaches more importance to the Western text than some do although he regards the most vivid additions to this text in Acts as for the most part nothing but a second-cen-

---

47. *A Critical Intro. to the New Test.*, p. 135.
48. *Dict. of the Apost. Church*, art. "Josephus."
49. See Hackett, *A Commentary on the Acts of the Apostles*, and Knowling, in the *Expositor's Greek Testament*, for a defense of the independence of Luke.
50. "Acts," in *Int. Stand Bible Ency.*

tury commentary.[51] Zahn, Belser, Zöckler, Nestle, Knowling, and Salmon, all express their interest in these readings in Acts. It may be that here and there a Western reading will ultimately be accepted as correct.

3. **Occasion and Date.** The Book of Acts, like the Four Gospels, grew out of some very definite situations in the early Church. There was, first of all, the definite need for authoritative information concerning the activity of the leading apostles, Peter, John, and Paul, esp. concerning Peter and Paul, and the influential brother of Jesus, James. How were they related to each other in the spread of Christianity? Then there was the need for showing that the Christian movement was one movement, whether the believers were Jews, proselytes, Samaritans, Gentiles, or former followers of John the Baptist. Especially was it necessary to show how Jewish and Gentile believers were related to each other in the Church. Thirdly, there was need for setting Paul's experiences in his missionary labors, and especially in his arrest and imprisonment, in the right light. Was he a traitor to his people and an apostate from the law, an impostor, that was deserving all the opposition and persecution that he received? And finally, there was the need for showing that God bore witness with the apostles, "both by signs and wonders, and by manifold powers, and by gifts of the Holy Spirit, according to his own will" (Heb. 2:4), thus authenticating the whole Christian movement and connecting it with the work of the risen and ascended Christ. The Book of Acts meets the challenge of this complex situation, as we shall show under *Purpose and Plan.*

Those who hold that Acts is dependent upon Josephus naturally date the book late in the nineties or early in the second century. McGiffert puts it into the reign of Domitian, i. e., 81-96;[52] Jülicher dates it ca. 100-105;[53] Schmiedel thinks it was written between 105-130.[54] Peake holds that even if Luke is dependent upon Josephus he may yet have written the book; he consequently suggests ca. 97 or 98 as the date of Acts.[55]

51. *St. Paul the Traveler,* pp. 23-28; *The Church in the Roman Empire,* pp. 151-168.
52. *The Apostolic Age,* p. 437 f.
53. *Einleitung in d. Neue Test.,* p. 262.
54. *Encyclopaedia Biblica.*
55. *A Critical Intro. to the New Test.,* p. 135.

But we have already shown that Luke is not dependent upon Josephus and so we may date the book much earlier. Kirsopp Lake's contention that "the weakening of the eschatological element, and the interest in the Church, as an institution in a world which is not immediately to disappear, point away from the very early date advocated by Harnack and others,"[56] is ill-founded in the light of such references as 1:10, 11; 3:19-21; 15:16-18; 17:6, 7, 18, 30, 31; 23:6-8; 24:14, 15. This objection to the early dating of this book is more than off-set by the many conspicuous accounts of the supernatural manifestations of the Holy Spirit in the early Church. The book was written at a time when these manifestations were still occurring and were still regarded as significant. We regard the abrupt close of the book as an indication of the date of the book. The most natural explanation of the phenomenon is that there was nothing further to report at the time. Since Paul came to Rome in A. D. 59 and had been in that city for two years when Acts closes, we confidently date the book at A. D. 61.

4. **Purpose and Plan.** In Acts occasion and purpose run into each other, i. e., the situation in the Church gives rise to the purpose of the book. The need for authoritative information concerning the activity of the leaders in the Church is supplied by the narratives that represent Peter and John as co-operating in the work and Peter and James as approving of Paul and his Gospel. The need for proof that the Christian movement is one movement is met by the accounts of how the Holy Spirit was given to Samaria by the ministry of Peter and John, to Cornelius and his household by Peter alone, and to the twelve former disciples of John the Baptist by the ministry of Paul. Paul had been approved by the Jerusalem Council, and thus mutual recognition and Christian fellowship were established among all the classes that entered the Church, and believers were, indeed, "all baptized into one body" (1 Cor. 12:13). The need for representing Paul's experience in his missionary labors and his arrest and imprisonment in the right light is supplied by the various visions that were vouchsafed to Paul, assuring us that God approved of his work and that his opponents were fighting against God and Christ. And the need

---

56. *Dict. of Apost. Church*, art., "Acts of the Apostles," I, 21.

for showing the divine approval of the whole Christian movement is met by the accounts of the miraculous manifestations in connection with the ministry of the apostolic Church. Thus the challenge of the situation was embraced and the need supplied by this book.

But we may approach the study of Luke's purpose in yet another way. It is clear that he sought to show what the ascended Christ continued "both to do and to teach" through the instrumentality of the Holy Spirit after He had returned to heaven. If this can be done, the believer in the deity of Christ will be quite convinced of the supernatural character of Christianity. To accomplish this purpose Luke begins by declaring that Christ had given commandment to the apostles and instruction concerning the kingdom of God after His resurrection and before His ascension. He continues by telling us that Christ had instructed the apostles to wait for the enduement of the Spirit before proceeding to their world task of evangelization. And he concludes by relating how Christ turned the attention of the apostles away from the idea that the earthly kingdom would be immediately set up to the great present-day task of evangelizing the world.

Having thus connected the program of the Church with the Lord's instructions and commission, Luke proceeds to trace the development of Christianity under the leadership of the Holy Spirit. He shows how the vacancy in the apostolate was supplied by prayer and the casting of the lot; how the Holy Spirit came upon the waiting apostles and instituted a great revival in Jerusalem; how the apostles were delivered in the persecutions in Jerusalem; how the believers for a time had all things in common; how God punished those who lied to the Holy Spirit; how the officers needed to attend to the temporal needs of the new Church were divinely selected; how Stephen boldly faced death and saw Christ standing at the right hand of God; how the Holy Spirit fell upon the Samaritan believers; how the persecuting Paul was brought to the feet of Jesus on the way to Damascus; how the door of faith was opened to the Gentiles in the house of Cornelius; how the Lord delivered Peter from prison; how the Gospel was carried to Asia Minor, Graeco-Macedonia, and Italy by Paul and his co-laborers; and how the freedom of the Gentiles was secured by the Jerusalem Council and the labors of the apostles. We may present most of these facts in tabular form, thus:

(1) The Commission of the Apostles from Christ, 1:1-11.
(2) The Equipment of the Disciples for their Task, 1:12-2:47.
(3) The Development of the Work in Jerusalem, 3:1-8:1a.
(4) The Extension of the Gospel to Judaea, Samaria, and the Surrounding Country, 8:1b-40.
(5) The Conversion and Early Ministry of Paul, 9:1-31.
(6) The Progress of the Gospel to the Gentiles, 9:31-11:30.
(7) The Persecutions by the Civil Government, ch. 12.
(8) The First Missionary Tour of Paul, chs. 13,14.
(9) The Victory for Gentile Freedom at the Jerusalem Council, 15:1-35.
(10) The Second Missionary Tour of Paul, 15:36-18:22.
(11) The Third Missionary Tour of Paul, 18:23-21:16.
(12) The Arrest and Trial of Paul in Jerusalem, 21:17-23:30.
(13) The Imprisonment of Paul in Caesarea, 23:31-26:32.
(14) The Voyage of Paul to Rome, 27:1-28:15.
(15) The Imprisonment of Paul in Rome, 28:16-31.

5. **Points and Peculiarities.** There are a number of striking features about the Book of Acts. We may note the following:

(1) It is a great missionary book. It recounts the founding of the Church on the Day of Pentecost, and the spread of Christianity from Jerusalem to Judaea, Samaria, Syria, Asia Minor, Macedonia, Greece, and Rome. Acts is the inspired history of the first thirty years of the Church's growth.

(2) Acts is also the inspired account of the Advent, Mission, and Operations of the Holy Spirit. It records the Pentecostal coming of the Spirit (ch. 2), the refilling of the apostles with the Spirit (4:23-31), the sin of lying against the Spirit (5:1-11), the reception of the Spirit by the Samaritans (8:14-17), the guidance of Philip by the Spirit (8:29), the reception of the Spirit by Cornelius and his household (10:44-48), the call of Barnabas and Saul by the Spirit (13:1-4), the guidance of the Spirit at the Jerusalem Council (15:28), the guidance

of Paul in his work by the Spirit (16:6, 7), the reception of the Spirit by the Ephesian disciples (19:1-6), the predictions by the Spirit of the fortunes of Paul (20:22, 23; 21:11), the appointment of bishops by the Spirit (20:28), and the claim of inspiration for Isa. 6:9, 10. Acts has rightly been called "The Acts of the Holy Spirit."

(3) In chs. 1-12 Peter is prominent; in chs. 13-28 Paul is preëminent. Chs. 1-7 center around Jerusalem; chs. 8-12, around Judaea and Samaria; chs. 13-28 describe the progress of the Gospel from Syrian Antioch to Rome.

(4) There are twenty-four addresses or excerpts from addresses in Acts, as follows: Nine by Peter (1:16-22; 2:14b-36; 3:15b-26; 4:8b-12; 5:29b-32; 8:20-25; 10:34b-43; 11:5-17; 15:7-11); nine also by Paul (13:16b-41; 14:15-17; 17:22b-31; 20:18b-35; 22:1-21; 24:10b-21; 26:2-23; 27:21-26; 28:17-20); and one each by Gamaliel (5:35b-39), Stephen (7:2-52), James (15:15b-21), Demetrius (19:25b-27), the town clerk (19:35b-40), and Festus (25:24-27).

(5) Acts records five visits of Paul to Jerusalem. The first is mentioned in 9:26-30; cf. Gal. 1:18, 19; the second in 11:28-30; the third in 15:1-29; cf. Gal. 2:1-10; the fourth in 18:21, 22; and the fifth in 21:15-23:30.

(6) The Book of Acts furnishes the background for ten of Paul's Epistles: For 1 Thessalonians, 2 Thessalonians, 1 Corinthians, 2 Corinthians, Galatians, Romans, Colossians, Philemon, Ephesians, and Philippians.

(7) Although Acts treats only two persons, Peter and Paul, as chief characters, it mentions a number of persons of second rank, as John, James, Stephen, Philip, Barnabas, James, and Apollos, and a larger number of personages of a third degree of importance, as Joseph, Barsabbas, Matthias, the Mother of our Lord, our Lord's brethren, the five deacons (in addition to Stephen and Philip), Mark, Silas, Judas Barsabbas, Timothy, Aquila and Priscilla, Erastus, Gaius, Aristarchus, Sopater, Secundus, Tychicus, and Trophimus. It also mentions a number of outstanding Roman officials, as Sergius Paulus, Gallio, Claudius Lysias, Felix, Festus, Herod Agrippa I and II, and Julius.

Chapter VIII

THE PAULINE EPISTLES

The First Group

THE two Epistles to the Thessalonians form the first group
of Paul's extant letters. They are among the earliest writings of the New Testament. Zahn thinks that Galatians is even
earlier than these Epistles;[1] but we agree with Ramsay in placing them first.[2] These two Epistles were not merely written to
the same Church, the second soon after the first, but they also
deal with much the same subject-matter. In both the doctrine
of the second advent is prominent, and so they have been
called the eschatological epistles of Paul. Practically all the
other teachings and exhortations are in some way related to
this central theme.

1. THE FIRST EPISTLE TO THE THESSALONIANS

The First Epistle to the Thessalonians is important because
it is so early, because it has so much to say about the Second
Coming of Christ, and because it gives us such a clear picture
of Paul's ministry and of the surroundings of an early Christian Church. It has been comparatively free from attack and is
today accepted by practically all New Testament scholars. But
there are some who have doubts on the subject, and so we turn
to examine the evidence for its genuineness.

1. **Attestation and Authorship.** The external evidence for
this Epistle is not as strong nor as early as we might wish; but
yet it is adequate. It is not clear whether the *Didache* used
4:16, 17 (cf. ch. xvi). Ignatius may possibly allude to 2:4 in
his *Epistle to the Romans* (ch. ii) and to 5:17 in his *Epistle to
the Ephesians* (ch. x); and the *Shepherd of Hermas* may al-

---

1. *Op. cit.,* I, 152-255.
2. *Pauline and Other Studies,* p. 365.

lude to 5:13, 14, in *Visions* (III. ix. 10). Marcion accepted it into his Canon, and it is found in the Old Syriac and the Old Latin versions. The Muratorian Canon places it sixth in the list of Paul's Epistles. Irenaeus is the first to refer to it by name, in *Against Heresies* (V. vi. 1). Tertullian also quotes it as by "the apostle," in *On the Resurrection of the Flesh* (ch. xxiv). Clement of Alexandria is apparently the first to ascribe it to Paul, in *Instructor* (I. v). After this the references to the Epistle are frequent.

As for the internal evidence we have first of all the claims of the Epistle itself. Twice the writer calls himself Paul (1:1; 2:18). It is interesting to note that in neither of the Thessalonian Epistles nor in Philippians does Paul add his title "apostle." Milligan thinks this is due to the special friendship between him and the Macedonian Churches and because his authority was never seriously questioned in these regions.[3] The historical allusions fit into and agree with the events in Paul's life as set forth in Acts: cf. 1 Thess. 2:2 with Acts 16:22, 23; 1 Thess. 3:4 with Acts 17:5; 1 Thess. 2:17 with Acts 18:5. Gloag says: "The character of Paul is impressed on this Epistle: his anxiety about his converts (3:1, 2); his earnest desire for their spiritual good (3:8-11); his almost womanly tenderness (2:7); his joy when he hears from Timothy of the steadfastness of their faith (3:6, 7); and his sympathy with them in their distress (4:13, 18)."[4]

Paul was born at Tarsus in Cilicia (Acts 21:39; 22:3). He was a Roman citizen by birth (22:28). He may have attended the famed university at Tarsus; we know that he studied at the feet of Gamaliel (22:3). He advanced more than others of his age in Judaism (Gal. 1:14) and became a leader in the persecution of the Christians (Acts 7:58; 8:1-3; 9:1). But he was saved on the way to Damascus (9:1-19). He immediately began to preach Christ (9:20-25). He spent some time in Arabia (Gal. 1:17), briefly visited Jerusalem (Gal. 1:18; Acts 9:26-29), and then went to Syria and Cilicia (Gal. 1:21; Acts 9:30). Some time later Barnabas got him from Tarsus and brought him to Antioch in Syria (Acts

---

3. *St. Paul's Epistle to the Thessalonians*, p. 3.
4. *Intro. to the Pauline Epistles*, p. 81.

11:25,26). When a famine broke out the Church at Antioch sent relief to the brethren in Judæa by Barnabas and Saul (11:27-30; 12:25).

After a time of ministry at Antioch Barnabas and Paul were separated unto the work of God (13:1-3). Together they make the first missionary journey, which was to Cyprus and Asia Minor (13:4-14:28). A difference about the necessity of circumcision for Gentile believers having arisen, the brethren sent Paul and Barnabas to Jerusalem with this question (15:1-35). Since Paul and Barnabas could not agree about taking Mark with them, they separated; Paul chose Silas as his new partner and together they made the second missionary journey. This took in Asia Minor, Macedonia, and Greece (15:36-18:23a). On the journey both Timothy and Luke joined them. Paul made his third journey to the same regions (18:23b-21:26). When he came back to Jerusalem this time he was arrested, tried before the Sanhedrin (21:27-23:30), sent to Cæsarea, and imprisoned there for two years (23:31-26:32). Then he was sent to Rome where he also was imprisoned for two years (chs. 27,28). He was released for a time, we believe, and visited some of the former scenes of his labor and probably also Spain (cf. Rom. 15:24). He was arrested a second time and imprisoned at Rome, where he was tried and executed (2 Tim. 4:6-8).

2. **Background and Destination.** On Paul's second missionary journey he and Silas were asked to leave Philippi; but Luke apparently did not go with them, for we have neither the "we" nor the "us" again until we get to Acts 20:5,6, where he rejoins Paul on his third journey (Acts 16:39,40). Timothy seems to have remained with Luke. For three Sabbaths Paul reasoned in the synagogue in Thessalonica (Acts 17:2); but he must have remained in the city much longer to achieve the results that we find in First Thessalonians (1:2,3,9,10). He preached the necessity of the sufferings and the resurrection of Christ, and must have said something also about Jesus as King (Acts 17:3,7). When some Jews, many devout Greeks, and not a few chief women fell in with Paul, the unbelieving Jews stirred up a crowd and made an uproar, seeking for the missionaries at the home of one Jason. Not finding them, they

brought Jason before the authorities, who made him give security for the peace of the city. When the brethren heard this, they immediately sent Paul and Silas by night to Berea (17:4-10).

From the above statements it would appear as if there were but three classes in the Church at Thessalonica: Some Jews, a great multitude of devout Greeks, and not a few of the chief women. But the Epistle seems to indicate that the mass of the Church consisted of converts from pure heathenism. To achieve this fruit Paul must have remained in the city much longer than three weeks. Ramsay thinks, on the basis of A and D, that there are four classes in the Church, the fourth one being the mass of Gentiles that seem so prominent in the Epistle.[5] Perhaps he is right. This is the Church of the Thessalonians to which the Epistle is addressed (1:1).

3. **Occasion and Date.** At Berea Paul and Silas again began their work in the synagogue (Acts 17:10). But when many of the Jews there believed, and not a few honorable women and men likewise, the Jews of Thessalonica came down to Berea and stirred up a strife there also (17:11-13). Then the brethren sent away Paul to the sea. Silas and Timothy, the latter having apparently come to Berea direct from Philippi without stopping at Thessalonica, remain behind at Berea (17:14). The brethren continued on with Paul all the way to Athens; and when they returned Paul requested them to instruct Silas and Timothy to come to him at once (17:15). Silas and Timothy apparently did so, coming to Paul while he was still at Athens. But he must shortly have sent both of them back, Timothy to Thessalonica (1 Thess. 3:1-3), and Silas probably to Philippi; for Paul was left behind at Athens, and they both returned to him at Corinth (Acts 18:5). It is clear that if Timothy did not go to Thessalonica, the safety of Jason might not be endangered if he now came to the city. Before Silas and Timothy returned to Paul, he had to work with his hands at tent-making (18:3); but after that he "held himself to the Word" (18:5, correct Greek text). It appears as if they had brought a gift for Paul from Macedonia (2 Cor.

5. *St. Paul the Traveler*, p. 235.

11:9), perhaps from Philippi, as that Church had twice before ministered to him at Thessalonica (Phil. 4:15 f.).

But Timothy had brought disquieting news from Thessalonica. Paul had preached in that city that there is another King, Jesus (Acts 17:7); and many had understood him to teach that Christ must immediately return. Therefore they had given up their work (cf. 1 Thess. 2:9; 4:11; 2 Thess. 3:8, 10-12) and conducted themselves in a disorderly fashion (1 Thess. 5:14; 2 Thess. 3:6,7,11). Others grieved over the death of loved ones, fearing they might have missed something since they did not live until the Coming of Christ (1 Thess. 4:13,18). Timothy also reported that the persecutions were still raging, — both the Gentiles and the Jews, the latter more than the former, harassing and tormenting the believers (2:17-3:10). He furthermore reported that the believers were loyal to the truth and anxious for Paul's return (3:6-8). This greatly cheered the Apostle's heart (3:7-13). But Timothy also reported that there was some opposition to him (as appears from Paul's defense of his ministry among them in ch. 2). This seems to have come from unfriendly outsiders and not from within the Church. Timothy appears, finally, to have reported that some were misusing their spiritual gifts and others were tempted to return to heathen impurities, — sexual impurity being their peculiar temptation (4:1-8; 5:19-21).

This situation leads Paul to write them a letter, our 1 Thessalonians. The internal evidence shows that the Epistle was written shortly after Paul's visit to Thessalonica: (1) The reports of the conversion of the Thessalonians were still spreading throughout Macedonia and Achaia (1:8,9) and Paul was still hoping to return to them soon (2:17); (2) the Apostle had already preached in Achaia (1:7,8), more specifically in Athens (3:1), which indicates that he was no longer in Berea; (3) Timothy (and Silas) had just (*arti*) returned to him from Macedonia (3:6), which was soon after Paul got to Corinth (Acts 18:5). It is, therefore, evident that the Epistle was written from Corinth, soon after Paul had visited Thessalonica.

At Corinth Paul was brought before the proconsul Gallio (Acts 18:12). This helps us to determine the date of 1 Thessalonians fairly closely, since according to an inscription at Delphi, Gallio was proconsul of Achaia in A. D. 52. The normal length of a proconsulate was one year, but sometimes it was two years; thus he might have been proconsul as early as 50 or as late as 54. But Deissmann has shown rather conclusively that he must have entered upon the proconsulship in the summer (about July 1st) of A. D. 51 and have served only one year (i. e., 51-52).[6] It appears from the context that the coming of Gallio induced the Jews to bring Paul to trial and that he, therefore, was before Gallio early in his proconsulship. Now the normal meaning of Acts 18:12 is that Paul had already been in Corinth eighteen months *before* he was brought before Gallio. If that is the case, then Paul must have come to Corinth early in 50 and have left the city in the late summer of 51. First Thessalonians was undoubtedly written during this period, and we must, therefore, date the Epistle at 50 or 51.

4. **Purpose and Plan.** Naturally the situation at Thessalonnica determined in a large measure the purpose of his letter. Thus Paul wrote to commend them for their faith; to defend himself against the charges of the enemies; to strengthen the bonds between himself and the Thessalonian Church; to exhort them to moral purity, brotherly love, and diligent application to their daily work; to correct their erroneous views of the Lord's return; and to encourage them to watchfulness, considerateness, and the fulfillment of their religious duties. We may present his plan in the form of an analysis of the Epistle, as follows:

Salutation, 1:1.

A. Reminiscence and Commendation, 1-3.

(1) The Thanksgiving for the Thessalonians, 1:2-4.

(2) The Proofs of their Election, 1:5-8.

(3) The Report Concerning the Thessalonians, 1:9,10.

(4) The Character of Paul's Ministry at Thessalonica, 2:1-12.

(5) The Response of the Thessalonians, 2:13-16.

(6) The Apostle's Subsequent Relations with the Thessalonians, 2:17-3:8.

---

6. *Paul*, pp. 280, 281.

(7) The Apostle's Renewed Thanksgiving and Prayer, 3:9-13.

B. Exhortation and Doctrine, 4,5.

(1) The Lessons in Christian Morals, 4:1-12.

(2) The Dead in Christ and the Coming of the Lord, 4:13-18.

(3) The Day of the Lord and the Need of Watchfulness, 5:1-11.

(4) The Duties of Church and Private Life, 5:12-22.

(5) The Prayer for Sanctification, 5:23,24.
Conclusion, 5:25-28.

----

2. THE SECOND EPISTLE TO THE THESSALONIANS

The Second Epistle to the Thessalonians has much in common with the First Epistle, but there are also some differences. It is important, first of all, like 1 Thessalonians, because of its teachings on the Lord's return; then because of its predictions concerning the man of lawlessness; and finally because of its instructions concerning the treatment of the idle and disorderly. Its authenticity and integrity have, however, been questioned on literary and doctrinal grounds, and so we again turn to an investigation of the evidence.

1. **Attestation and Authorship.** We note at the outset that the external evidence is both fuller and earlier than that for the First Epistle. There is a possible reference to 2:3,4,8 in *Didache* (ch. xvi) and to 3:8,10 in *Didache* (ch. xii). Ignatius may allude to 3:5 in his *Epistle to the Romans* (ch. x), but that is not certain. Polycarp seems to refer to 3:15 in his *Epistle to the Philippians* (ch. xi). Justin Martyr refers to 2:3,4 in his *Dialogue with Trypho* (ch. cx). There is a possible reference to 2:3,4 in the *Epistle of Vienne and Lyons* (see Euseb. *H. E.,* V.i). Irenæus is the first to mention it by name and to ascribe it to Paul, when speaking of 2:8,9, in *Against Heresies* (III. vii.2). Tertullian quotes 2:1-7 as by the "apostle," manifestly Paul, as seen by the context, *On the Resurrection of the Flesh* (ch. xxiv). Clement of Alexandria definitely refers to 3:1,2, in *Stromata* (V.iii). The Epistle is in the Muratorian Canon, the Old Syriac, the Old Latin, and in Marcion's Canon. The

external attestation, coming from all sections of the Christian Church, is then full and satisfactory. But does the internal evidence support the external?

We believe that it does. Note that the writer twice refers to himself as Paul (1:1; 3:17). The *hapax legomena* are very few and both vocabulary and style are in the main genuinely Pauline. No one can deny to Paul the right to use the same word in several senses in his writings, nor to use synonyms now and then. There is no real discrepancy between Paul's reasons for self-support in the two Epistles (1 Thess. 2:9 and 2 Thess. 3:8), as some have supposed, nor between his views of the Second Coming of Christ. We shall deal more fully with the latter objection in the following paragraph. Schmidt (in 1801) was the first to raise objections to 2 Thessalonians, on the ground of the similarities and differences as compared with Paul's acknowledged Epistles. He was followed by De Wette (but he later fully recognized it), Kern, Baur, and Hilgenfeld. More recent objectors have pointed out the closeness of the resemblances of the two Epistles and have concluded therefore that a forger produced the Second one. So Weizsäcker, Holtzmann, and Wrede. But Milligan points out that the parallelism of the two does not extend to more than one-third of their whole contents, and that the parallelisms in language are not always found in corresponding sections.[7] The fact that the Second Epistle is more official and severe may be accounted for by a change in the mood of the same writer and in the circumstances of those to whom he writes. The view of Ewald and West that the character of the eschatological teaching in the two requires us to place 2 Thessalonians before 1 Thessalonians in point of time, has received little recognition. Paul's reference to his past relations with the Thessalonians is more natural in his first letter, and his warning against spurious epistles, in his second (1 Thess. 2:17-3:6; 2 Thess. 2:1,2; 3:17).

Let us look briefly at the objection that the views of the second coming in the two are inconsistent. We must remember that on the basis of the Old Testament the believers would be inclined to think that the Day of the Lord was to precede the

---

7. *Op. cit.*, p. lxxxiii.

coming of the Lord. But the New Testament distinguishes two phases of His coming: His coming to raise the dead in Christ, to change the living believers, and to catch both up to meet Him in the air. This phase of Christ's advent is most fully brought out in 1 Thessalonians (see esp. 4:13-18). And His coming with His saints to judge the ungodly and destroy the man of lawlessness. This is touched on in 1 Thess. 3:13; 5:1-6, but is more graphically set forth in 2 Thess. 1:7-10; 2:1-12. The latter, with its accompanying judgments, is the ushering in of the Old Testament Day of the Lord. Apparently because of the severity of their persecutions (1:4-7) the Thessalonians had begun to wonder whether they had failed to qualify for the rapture and whether the Day of the Lord was now present (2:2, correct text). Therefore Paul exhorts them to steadfastness regarding "the coming of the Lord Jesus Christ and our gathering together unto him" (2:1,2), and informs them that certain things must happen before the Day of the Lord can come (2:3-12). At any rate, the First Epistle does not exclude the coming of the man of lawlessness, and the Second does not require protracted delay in Christ's coming for His saints. There is therefore nothing to throw suspicion on the genuineness of 2 Thessalonians.

2. **Background and Destination.** For the history of the founding of the Church and the classes of people in it, see under 1 Thessalonians. It does not seem as if either Paul or any of his helpers had returned to Thessalonica since the sending of the First Epistle. But the new teaching concerning the Day of the Lord, discussed above, had been brought to them and had caused great confusion. It appears to have originated in some imaginary revelation of the Spirit, a forged letter purporting to come from Paul (Coneybeare and Howson), or in oral and written reports from the region where Paul was ministering (Zahn). It seems, moreover, that the attack upon Paul and his associates had died down, and that the confidence of the Church in them was fully restored.

3. **Occasion and Date.** News from Thessalonica of increasing persecution against the Church (1:4,5), of the misinterpretation of Paul's teaching as to the Lord's return and the Day of the Lord (2:1-12), and of the idleness and dreamy

expectation of some of them (3:6-12), led Paul to address this second letter to them. The news probably came to Paul through the bearer of the First Epistle, and was not simply a rumor that spread at Corinth.

Zahn[8] and Milligan[9] agree that the interval between the two Epistles was a matter of a few months. But McNeile[10] thinks it equally possible that the Epistle might have been written "at any time in the four years or so between Timothy's arrival at Corinth and the mention of him at Ephesus." Coneybeare and Howson, however, give good reasons for adopting the former view. They argue thus: "(1) The state of the Thessalonian Church described in both Epistles is almost exactly the same. (a) The same excitement prevails concerning the expected advent of our Lord, only in a greater degree. (b) The same party continued fanatically to neglect their ordinary employments. Compare 2 Thess. 3:6-14 with 1 Thess. 4:10-12 and 1 Thess. 2:9. (2) Silas and Timothy were still with St. Paul. 2 Thess. 1:1. It should be observed that Timotheus was next with St. Paul at Ephesus; and that, before then, Silas disappears from the history."[11] We hold, then, that Paul wrote 2 Thessalonians while he was still at Corinth, not many months after he had written the First Epistle, early in A. D. 51.

4. **Purpose and Plan.** The following seem to be the purpose of the Epistle: (1) To comfort the Thessalonians in their persecutions (1:4-10); (2) to point out the fact that though the *Parousia* and our gathering unto Christ are imminent (2:1), the Day of the Lord will not come until *the* apostasy has set in and the "man of lawlessness" has been revealed (2:2-10); (3) to exhort his readers to steadfastness and adherence to the things he had taught them, whether by word of mouth or by an Epistle from him (2:13-3:5); (4) to admonish the disorderly and idle to a quiet and orderly walk (3:6-15); and (5) to give them a token whereby they may distinguish his Epistles from those of forgers (3:17). We should remember that Paul had already when he was with them instructed the Thessalonians about the signs that are to

8. *Intro. to the New Test.*, I, 232 f.
9. *St. Paul's Epistles to the Thessalonians*, p. xxxix.
10. *An Intro. to the Study of the New Testament*, p. 113.
11. *The Life and Epistles of St. Paul*, p. 352.

precede the Day of the Lord (2:5); and we may say with Alford, that in 2:3 we should supply the words "that day shall not come,"[12] rather than "the Parousia of the Lord will not take place," with Milligan.[13] An analysis of the Epistle will enable us to see Paul's plan in outline form.

Salutation, 1:1,2.

A. Consolation and Doctrine, 1, 2.

    (1) Thanksgiving for the Thessalonians, 1:3,4.

    (2) Encouragement in View of Christ's Return, 1:5-10.

    (3) Prayer for the Thessalonians, 1:11,12.

    (4) Events Preceding the Day of the Lord, 2:1-12.

    (5) Renewed Thanksgiving and Practical Exhortation, 2:13-15.

    (6) Renewed Prayer for the Thessalonians, 2:16,17.

B. Exhortation and Practice, 3.

    (1) Request for the Prayers of the Thessalonians, 1,2.

    (2) Confidence in their Progress, 3-5.

    (3) Charge to Discipline the Disorderly, 6-12.

    (4) Exhortations to the Loyal Members of the Church, 13-15.

    Conclusion, 16-18.

12. *Greek Testament, in loc.*
13. *Op. cit.*, p. 98.

Chapter IX

THE PAULINE EPISTLES
The Second Group

THE four Epistles in this group, 1 Corinthians, 2 Corinthians, Galatians, and Romans, are undoubtedly the greatest of Paul's Epistles. In saying this we do not mean to imply that some of his Epistles are unimportant, for that is not the case; but these four were written when the Apostle was at the height of his career and deal with some of the most stupendous themes that can engage the human mind. They are important doctrinally, for they discuss more thoroughly than any other books in the New Testament the doctrines of sin, law, works, redemption, faith, justification, adoption, sanctification, the Holy Spirit, the resurrection, Israel, etc. They are also important from the practical standpoint, for they contain regulations concerning church discipline, the behavior of women in the assembly, the observance of the Lord's Supper, the exercise of spiritual gifts, liberty and forbearance, stewardship, marriage and separation, the believer's relation to the world and the state. Since they are also accepted as genuine by all but the most radical critics who deny that Paul wrote anything, we should eagerly study and practically digest their contents.

---

1. THE FIRST EPISTLE TO THE CORINTHIANS

This Epistle gives us the best picture of the life and problems of a primitive local church. It shows us that already factions, moral laxity, want of reverence, abuses of spiritual gifts, and various doctrinal oppositions had come into the Church. The Epistle gives us Paul's inspired instructions as to the method of dealing with these and other problems. Besides this, 1 Corinthians gives us the most exhaustive discussion of the questions of marriage and separation (ch. 7), the most noble characterization of love (ch. 13), and the most thorough treatment of the doctrine of the resurrection (ch. 15) found in the Word of God. Let us then proceed to a study of the Epistle and the problems that are connected therewith.

1. **Attestation and Authorship.** The external evidence is abundant and continuous from the first century onward. Clement of Rome speaks of it as "the Epistle of the blessed Apostle Paul," in his *Epistle to the Corinthians* (ch. xlvii). There may be an allusion to 3:1,16, in the *Epistle of Barnabas* (ch. iv). The *Didache* (ch. x) says: "If any one is holy, let him come; if any one is not so, let him repent, Maranatha. Amen"; cf. 1 Cor. 16:22. There are many echoes of the thought and the language of 1 Corinthians in Ignatius. Polycarp quotes 6:2 as by Paul, in his *Epistle to the Philippians* (ch. xi). Hermas, in the *Fourth Commandment* (ch. iv), seems to contain a reminiscence of 7:39,40. Justin Martyr quotes from 1 Cor. 11:19, in his *Dialogue with Trypho* (ch. xxxv), and Athenagoras quotes a part of 15:54 as "in the language of the apostle," in his work on *The Resurrection of the Dead* (ch. xviii). Robertson and Plummer say that there are more than 60 quotations from 1 Corinthians in the writings of Irenæus; more than 130 in those of Clement of Alexandria; and more than 400 in those of Tertullian, counting the verses separately.[1] It stands at the head of Paul's Epistles in the Muratorian Canon and after Galatians in Marcion's *Apostolicon*. It was in the Old Syriac, if not from the first then at least soon after the translation appeared; it was also in the Old Latin. The external attestation is therefore full and adequate.

The internal evidence supports the external. The writer calls himself Paul a number of times (1:1; 16:21; cf. also 1:12-17; 3:4, 6, 22). There are so many coincidences with the Book of Acts and with Paul's other writings that it is impossible to believe that they are inventions or mere chance contacts. The Epistle has the ring of genuineness from beginning to end. The mention of the five hundred who had seen Christ after His resurrection, with the explanation that many of them were still alive when the Epistle was written, would be a "bad joke"

---

1 *Comm. on* 1 *Corinthians,* p. xviii.

(Godet), if it was written by a forger in the second century. Furthermore, the contents of the Epistle harmonizes with what we know of Corinth in Paul's time. Knowling says: "Few, if any, books of the New Testament come to us with better credentials than 1 Corinthians."[2] The view of the radical critics, headed by Bruno Bauer, is therefore absolutely untenable.

2. **Background and Destination.** The story of the founding of the Church at Corinth is recorded in Acts 18:1-18. Paul came to Corinth from Athens. He made his home with Aquila and Priscilla, lately come from Italy, and with them engaged in tentmaking. On the Sabbaths he preached to Jews and Greeks in the synagogue. But when Silas and Timothy came to him from Macedonia, he "held himself" (middle voice) to the Word. Probably Silas had brought a gift from Philippi (2 Cor. 11:9), so that he was henceforth free to preach the Gospel. However when the Jews opposed themselves and blasphemed, Paul withdrew to the house of Titus Justus, adjoining the synagogue, and continued his ministry there. Crispus, the ruler of the synagogue, believed with all his house, and so also did many others of the Corinthians. The Lord appeared to Paul in a vision by night and assured him that He had much people in the city. After eighteen months the Jews brought Paul before Gallio, who had apparently but recently become proconsul. But Gallio refused to interfere in a matter that he regarded merely as "questions about words and names and your own law," and drove them away. The Greeks then laid hold on Sosthenes, who had succeeded Crispus, and beat him. He had doubtlessly taken a prominent part in the proceedings against Paul;[3] but Gallio cared for none of these things. After this Paul continued yet "many days" at Corinth, and then left for Syria, having shorn his head in Cenchrea because of a vow he had taken upon himself.

From the account in Acts it would appear as if Paul had little fruit among the Jews and that nearly all of his converts were Gentiles. Most of these came from the humbler ranks, although there appear to have been some of the nobler class

2. *The Testimony of St. Paul to Christ,* p. 51.
3. Ramsay, *St. Paul the Traveler,* p. 259.

also (1:26-31). Marked social and economic differences existed among them (7:20-24; 11:21-34); some of them had even been steeped in pagan vices (6:9-11). Yet as Greeks they prided themselves on their intellectualism, although in their case it had degenerated into a crude and shallow type (1:17; 2:1-5). As Greeks they were also given to a factious spirit. To these characteristics of the people we should add the fact that Corinth was at this time the commercial and political capital of Achaia. This brought to the city great wealth, but also gross immorality.

3. **Occasion and Date.** Leaving Cenchrea with Aquila and Priscilla, Paul stopped briefly at Ephesus. He left the two in that city and hastened on to Cæsarea, Jerusalem, and Syrian Antioch (Acts 18:19-23). During this time Apollos, an Alexandrian Jew, came to Ephesus and preached boldly, knowing only the baptism of John (Acts 18:24-26a). Priscilla and Aquila took him unto them and led him into the fuller truth of the Gospel. Then he decided to go to Corinth, and when the brethren heard of his plans they wrote a letter of recommendation for him to the disciples in Achaia (Acts 18:26b,27a). He was very successful at Corinth (Acts 18:27b,28) and a party gathered around him (1 Cor. 1:12). This among a people that sought after wisdom and was naturally of a factious disposition was the cause of further trouble. Apollos saw the situation aright and withdrew to Ephesus (1 Cor. 16:12). But Paul, having gone through the region of Galatia and Phrygia and the "upper country," returned to Ephesus before Apollos got back (Acts 18:23; 19:1). Various things occurred in the Apostle's relations with Corinth during his stay at Ephesus that led to the writing of First Corinthians.

(1) For some reason or other Paul wrote a letter to Corinth that is now lost (1 Cor. 5:9). In this letter he charged them not to keep company with fornicators; he probably also exhorted them to take part in the collection for the saints (2 Cor. 8:6,10; 9:1,2), and told them about his plans regarding his return to Corinth (2 Cor. 1:15,16). The verb "wrote" (*egrapsa*) cannot be an epistolary aorist, referring to the letter then being written, for he has said nothing about these things in this Epistle thus far which needs explanation; and

1 Cor. 5:9-13 is a correction of a misapprehension of a former letter. Moffatt's suggestion that 2 Cor. 6:14-7:1 is probably a fragment of this lost letter[4] does not have many supporters.

(2) Bad news came to Paul through the household of Chloe (1:11) and Apollos (16:12). Zahn thinks the Apostle deals with this report in chs. 1-4; 5:1-8; possibly in 6:1-11; and probably also in ch. 15.[5]

(3) Paul sent Timothy and Erastus to Macedonia (Acts 19:22) and Timothy to Corinth also (1 Cor. 4:17). This takes place before he writes our 1 Corinthians, for Timothy is not associated with Paul in the opening of 1 Corinthians. Paul does not seem to have been quite sure whether Timothy would actually reach Corinth (16:10), and Lightfoot thinks[6] that Luke probably knew that he did not get that far, since he mentions only Macedonia as the destination of both (Acts 19:22).

(4) A letter from Corinth reached Paul, brought apparently by Stephanas, Fortunatus, and Achaicus (16:17; cf. 15-18). Zahn thinks that if 7:1 may be taken to refer to this letter (and it certainly may), then the similar formulas at 7:25; 8:1; 12:1; 16:1; and 16:12 warrant the assumption that chs. 7-10, 12, 14, 16:1-12 are replies to that letter. He suggests that ch. 11 may be partly due to oral and partly to written reports.[7]

(5) Paul wrote our 1 Corinthians, which he assumes will reach Corinth before Timothy gets to the city (16:10). Plummer thinks that it was sent by Titus and "the brother" (2 Cor. 12:18), someone well known to the Corinthians, and that Titus on the occasion of this visit organized the collection (1 Cor. 16:1; 2 Cor. 8:6).[8] When Titus had fulfilled his mission he returned to Paul at Ephesus.

The Epistle is thus occasioned by the reports of serious evils at Corinth, by the letter from Corinth submitting various questions to Paul for solution, and by Paul's own anxious concern for the Corinthian Church. We have already noted Zahn's opinion as to the parts that have to do with the oral reports and

4. *Intro. to the Literature of the New Testament*, p. 109.
5. *Intro. to the New Testament*, I, 261.
6. *Biblical Essays*, p. 276.
7. *Op. cit.*, I, 260 f.
8. *Op. cit.*, p. xviii.

the letter respectively; but it is not possible to be quite sure as to this.

The Apostle himself tells us that the Epistle was written from Ephesus (16:8,9, cf. vs. 19). The subscription in the Textus Receptus and the Authorized Version, saying that the Epistle was written from Philippi, is probably due to a mis-interpretation of 16:5. It must have been written in the latter half of Paul's three-year ministry in that city (Acts 20:31; cf. 19:8,10,21,22). We may, therefore, date it in the spring of A. D. 54 or 55.

4. **Purpose and Plan.** The Apostle's purpose is clearly per-ceived from the contents of the Epistle. He writes (1) to rebuke the party spirit and to give a true conception of the relation between the Christian worker and his work (chs. 1-4); (2) to enjoin the disciplining of the person guilty of incest (ch. 5); (3) to reprove the Church for not trying the griev-ances between its members, but going to law before the heathen about them (ch. 6); (4) to answer their questions concerning marriage and divorce (ch. 7); (5) and concerning the eating of food offered to idols (chs. 8-10); (6) to correct the dis-orders that had arisen in the behavior of the women (ch. 11); (7) and in the exercise of spiritual gifts (chs. 12-14); (8) to refute those who denied the resurrection of the dead (ch. 15); (9) to urge their participation in the collection for the poor saints (16:1-4); (10) to inform them of his plans regarding the future (16:5-9); and (11) to commend certain of his fellow-workers to them (16:10-18).

An analysis of the Epistle will again enable us to see Paul's plan in outline form.

Introduction, 1:1-9.

A. The Rebuke of the Party Spirit, 1:10-4:21.

B. The Problems of Sexual Morality, chs. 5-7.

(1) Discipline of the Incestuous Person, 5:1-13.

(2) (Parenthetical: Evils of Litigation before Heathen Tribunals, 6:1-11.)

(3) Fornication in the Light of the Sacredness of the Body, 6:12-20.

(4) Marriage and Divorce, ch. 7.

C. The Subject of Food Offered to Idols, 8:1-11:1.

    (1) Some General Principles, ch. 8.

    (2) The Law of Forbearance, ch. 9.

    (3) The Admonition from the History of Israel, 10:1-13.

    (4) The Prohibition of Idolatry and Idolatrous Practices, 10:14-22.

    (5) The Use and Abuse of Christian Liberty, 10:23-11:1.

D. The Disorders Connected with Public Worship, 11:2-14:40.

    (1) The Veiling of Women in Public Worship, 11:2-16.

    (2) The Disorders Connected with the Lord's Supper, 11:17-34.

    (3) The Regulations Concerning Spiritual Gifts, 12-14.

E. The Doctrine of the Resurrection of the Dead, ch. 15.

F. The Immediate Practical Concerns of Paul, 16:1-18.
    Conclusion, 16:19-24.

---

2. THE SECOND EPISTLE TO THE CORINTHIANS

The Second Epistle to the Corinthians is the most autobiographical of all Paul's Epistles. Findlay calls it "Paul's *Apologia Pro Vita Sua*." He points out that it is neither doctrinal nor practical in the strict sense of the terms, but "intensely personal, made up of explanation, defense, protestation, appeal, reproach, invective, threatening, with a vein of subduing pathos, blended with the most subtle irony, running through the whole."[9] Although the genuineness of the various parts of the Epistle has been generally recognized, the unity of the Epistle has been repeatedly questioned. It is necessary, therefore, to discuss this latter subject more particularly.

1. **Attestation and Authorship.** Both the external and the internal evidence for the genuineness of this Epistle are so strong that we really need not dwell on these points, and many recent commentaries refrain from producing the evidence. But we may profit by mentioning at least a part of it. The external evidence is not quite so early as that for 1 Corinthians,

---

9. *The Epistles of Paul the Apostle*, p. 111.

for Clement of Rome never quotes 2 Corinthians. This can only mean that by A. D. 96 the Epistle had not yet reached Rome. But Polycarp quotes 4:14 in his *Epistle to the Philippians* (ch. ii) and 8:21 (*ibid.*, ch. vi). The letter to Diognetus uses language resembling that of 6:8-10 (ch. v). Athenagoras seems to allude to 5:10 in *The Resurrection of the Dead* (ch. xviii) and Theophilus of Antioch to 1:21.[10] Tertullian cites 11:14 in his *Treatise on the Soul* (ch. lvii), *et passim* on other passages. Clement of Alexandria comments on 11:3 in *Stromata* (III.xiv), *et passim* on other passages. Irenæus frequently quotes from this Epistle, as 2:15,16 in *Against Heresies* (IV.xxviii), etc. The Epistle is mentioned in the Muratorian Canon and occupies third place in Marcion's *Apostolicon*. It is found in both the Old Syriac and the Old Latin along with the first Epistle. From the year 175 onward the attestation is abundant.

The internal evidence too is very strong. The writer twice calls himself Paul (1:1; 10:1). Bernard says: "It is unmistakably Pauline, in the tone and character of its teaching, no less than in its style and vocabulary."[11] The naturalness and vividness of it, as well as the character of its details (not particularly interesting to outsiders), form a strong proof of its genuineness. Plummer says: "It is a strange criticism that can see in all this the imagination of an anonymous inventor."[12] Since this "strange criticism" is confined to the ultra-radical school we need not stop to refute it.

2. **Background and Destination.** In spite of Paul's denunciation of factions in 1 Corinthians, the party-spirit continued to divide the Corinthian Church. Indeed, the Jewish party gained in strength and challenged the authority of Paul. Anti-Pauline teachers, apparently from Palestine, came to Corinth and organized the opposition to Paul. They represented themselves as peculiarly "Christ's" (10:7) and as "apostles of Christ" (11:13). There seems to have appeared a ring-leader of the opposition that was especially obnoxious to Paul (10:7-11; cf. 2:5-11), and it may well be that the Christ-party had

10. *To Autolycus* I.xii.
11. *Expos. Greek Test.*, III,30.
12. *Comm. on Second Corinthians*, p. xiii.

united with the Cephas-party under his leadership against the Apostle. When news of this situation reached Paul at Ephesus he paid a short visit to Corinth to meet it, but failed in the attempt (2:1; 12:14,21; 13:1,2). It appears that the ring-leader greatly insulted the Apostle (2:5-8; 7:12). Thereupon Paul returned to Ephesus. Some place this visit before 1 Corinthians, but it seems to accord better with all the facts to place it between First and Second Corinthians. It is against this background that the Second Epistle to the Corinthians is written.

3. **Occasion and Date.** Paul was deeply stirred by the developments at Corinth. He could not let matters rest as they were, and so soon after his return to Ephesus he wrote the Church a severe letter, sending it to them by Titus (2:3,4,9; 7:8-12). Some have held that our First Corinthians is that letter, but surely that Epistle did not originate in any such grief as that of which he here speaks, nor can he well have regretted writing anything that is found in that Epistle. Plummer thinks that the greater part of this letter is preserved in chs. 10-13,[13] but Bernard has rather successfully disproved this theory and shown that the Epistle is a unity.[14] Apparently this letter was aimed directly at the Judaistic party and its ring-leader. The bearer, Titus, was probably also instructed to promote the interests of the collection at Corinth.

Paul eagerly awaited the return of Titus and his report concerning the effect of his last letter. But since serious difficulties arose at Ephesus, he left that city ahead of his schedule (Acts 20:1). Paul stopped at Troas and found an open door for the Gospel in that city. However, since he did not find Titus, he hastened on to Macedonia in order to meet him the sooner and to get his report (2:12,13). In Macedonia the two met. Titus gave his report, which was on the whole most encouraging (7:6-16). The majority had been won back to Paul and had administered severe punishment to the offender (2:5-11); but there still was a rebellious minority (chs. 10-13). It is this combination of rejoicing at the repentance of the majority, together with his great concern about the collection,

---

13. *Op. cit.,* p. xviii.
14. *Expos. Greek Test.,* III,21-27.

and grief at the continued opposition of a minority that occasioned the Second Epistle to the Corinthians.

It is evident that the Epistle was written from Macedonia (2:13; 7:5-7; 8:1; 9:2-4). The subscription of the Epistle in manuscript B² and in the Peshitta, Harkleian Syriac, and Coptic versions, saying that the city was Philippi, is certainly early and may be correct. It was apparently written shortly after 1 Corinthians. Seven or eight months would suffice for all the events between the two Epistles to take place. We may, therefore, date it late in A. D. 54 or 55.

4. **Purpose and Plan.** Paul writes 2 Corinthians in order (1) to set forth the purpose of his sufferings in Asia (1:3-11); (2) to justify himself in the changing of his plans with reference to his returning to Corinth (1:12-2:4); (3) to give instructions as to the treatment of the offender (2:5-11); (4) to express his joy at the good news from Corinth (2:12,13); (5) to represent the Gospel and its ministry as superior to the law and its ministry (2:14-6:10); (6) to appeal for separation and for reconciliation with him (6:11-7:16); (7) to urge the Corinthians to bring the collection to a speedy and satisfactory conclusion (chs. 8 and 9); and (8) to establish his authority as an apostle (10-1-13:10).

Before attempting to set forth the contents of the Epistle in outline form we must briefly discuss the integrity of the Epistle. We have indicated our belief that 1 Corinthians can hardly be the severe letter of which Paul speaks and which he at one time regretted to have written (2:3,4,9; 7:8-12). In this we venture to differ from such scholars as Alford, Conybeare and Howson, and Zahn, who hold the opposite view. We have also indicated our belief in the unity of 2 Corinthians and our rejection of the view of Plummer (which is also the view of K. Lake, Moffat, D. Smith, and others) that a considerable part of this letter is preserved in 2 Cor. 10-13. We believe, instead, with such scholars as Godet, Olshausen, and Sanday that the severe letter is wholly lost. If 1 Cor. 5:9 may be taken to refer to a lost letter of Paul, then why may there not have been another letter of his which God in His providence did not see fit to preserve? May we ask, Could Paul have rightly regretted composing and sending a letter that he had written by inspiration?

Whatever may be the facts concerning the existence or non-existence of the severe letter, we have no doubts as to the unity of 2 Corinthians. Plummer admits that he has no support whatever from the Greek manuscripts, ancient versions, or patristic writings for his view and that it rests entirely upon internal evidence. He accordingly bases his opinion on various internal characteristics, such as (1) the change of tone in chs. 10:1-13:10, from the tender language of rejoicing at their reconciliation to him in chs. 1-9 to bold language of reproach, self-vindication, and warning in chs. 10-13; (2) certain supposed logical inconsistencies in ch. 1-9 as compared with chs. 10-13, dealing first with the more pleasing and then with the less pleasing subjects of his letter; (3) certain supposed references in chs. 1-9 to things in chs. 10-13, implying that the former were written after the latter, particularly in 1:23 to 13:2 and in 2:3 to 13:10; and (4) the assumed improbability that the statement "the parts beyond you" (10:16) would be used with reference to Rome and Spain if written in Macedonia, but not if written at Ephesus.[15]

The writer feels, with many others, that these arguments are far from conclusive, whether taken singly or together. The first one is perhaps the strongest of them; but it, too, can be explained, in harmony with the external evidence, as at least not disproving the unity of the Epistle. The difference in tone between chs. 1-9 and 10-13 may just as well be due to the fact that in the first case he addresses the majority who had become reconciled to him, and in the second he rebukes the minority who were still opposed to him. There is a similar change of tone in Demosthenes' oration "On the Crown." At first he speaks in a calm, deliberate tone, but after a while he turns to fierce and bitter invective. Does that mean that we have two orations pieced together? Alford suggests that on the principle of these critics 1 Corinthians might be divided into at least eight different epistles, marked off by the various changes of

---

15. See his *Comm. on the Second Epistle of St. Paul to the Corinthians*, pp. xxvii-xxxvi, for a defense of this view.

subject.[16] The remaining characteristics of 2 Corinthians, as pointed out by Plummer, can even more readily be explained in line with the conception of the unity of the Epistle. We need not undertake to demonstrate this here. Suffice it to repeat that there are no good grounds for questioning the integrity of the Epistle.

We may now set forth the plan of the Epistle in outline form:

---

16. *Greek Testament*, II,58.

(3) The Reasons for His Self-Commendation, 11:1-15.
(4) The Apostle Contrasted with the False Teachers, 11:16-33.
(5) The Apostle's Visions and Revelations, 12-1-10.
(6) The Apostle's Credentials, 12:11-18. .
(7) The Warnings Against Evil and Exhortations to Holiness, 12:19-13:10.

Conclusion, 13:11-14.

3. THE EPISTLE TO THE GALATIANS

The Epistle to the Galatians was the battle cry of the Reformation. Luther considered it in a peculiar sense his Epistle. It is a powerful polemic against the Judaizers who were trying to undermine Paul's work in Galatia and the Church's Magna Charta of freedom. Paul would have preferred to hasten to the scene of trouble at once, but found it impossible to do so at the time (Gal. 4:19,20). Since the situation was serious and demanded prompt attention, he immediately wrote this impassioned and indignant protest. Because of its intensely doctrinal character the Epistle has not been a general favorite; it was all but lost sight of from the fifth century to the Reformation. In more recent times it has served as a bulwark against that radical criticism which would deny the genuineness of all the Pauline Epistles.

1. **Attestation and Authorship.** Findlay says: "No breath of suspicion as to the authorship, integrity, or apostolic authority of the Epistle to the Galatians has reached us from ancient times."[17] Lightfoot says: "Its every sentence so completely reflects the life and character of the Apostle of the Gentiles that its genuineness has not been seriously questioned."[18] It is, therefore, not necessary to produce extensive proof of its early existence or Pauline authorship. Some few samples of this kind may, however, be introduced.

Clement of Rome may allude to 3:1 in his *Epistle to the Corinthians* (ch. ii). Polycarp used the language of 6:7 in his *Epistle to the Philippians* (ch. v), of 4:26 (ch. iii). and of

---

17. *Inter. Stand. Bible Encycl., s. v.,* "The Epistle to the Galatians."
18. *St. Paul's Epistle to the Galatians,* p. 57.

4:18 (ch. vi). Barnabas seems to allude to 6:6 in the *Epistle of Barnabas* (ch. xix). Hermas may allude vaguely to 3:26, 27.[19] Ignatius seems to allude to 1:1 in his *Epistle to the Philadelphians* (ch. 1). The *Epistle to Diognetus* speaks of "observing months and days," as in Gal. 4:10 (ch. iv). Marcion is the first to refer to it by name; he appears to have placed Galatians first in his *Apostolicon* (cf. Tertullian, *Against Marcion*, V.ii). Justin Martyr quotes Deut. 27:26 with 21:23 and interprets these Scriptures as in Gal. 3:10-13.[20] Origen says the only sentence which Celsus quotes from Paul is Gal. 6:14.[21] Both the Ophites and the Valentinians appear to have used the Epistle. In the second century it became popular. Irenæus, Tertullian, and Clement of Alexandria repeatedly quote it and ascribe it to Paul. It is found in the Old Syriac and the Old Latin, and the Muratorian Canon places it second among Paul's Epistles.

The internal evidence is likewise strong. Twice the writer calls himself Paul (1:1; 5:2). It contains numerous historical references which are all capable of being harmonized with the Acts. Lightfoot says: "As an exhibition of the working of the Apostle's mind, it lies far beyond the reach of a forger in an age singularly unskilled in the analysis and representation of the finer shades of character."[22] He asks us, What purpose could a forger have had in writing this Epistle? A Gnostic writer would have avoided representing Paul as showing deference to the original Apostles; an Ebionite would have shrunk from any seeming depreciation of the Jewish customs and leaders; and a Harmonizer of the supposed Pauline and Petrine factions would have avoided intimating that there was any conflict between them.[23] Even the Tübingen school accepted Galatians along with 1 and 2 Corinthians and Romans as genuine. Bruno Bauer (1809-1882) was the first to relegate it along with the other three to the close of the second century. He was followed by Pierson, Naber, Loman, and Van Manen. Shaw[24] gives a good reply to Van Manen's seven reasons

19. *Similitude* IX.xiii.
20. *Dialogue Against Trypho*, chs. xcv, xcvi.
21. *Against Celsus*, V.lxiv.
22. *Op. cit.*, p. 57.
23. *Op. cit.*, p. 58.
24. *The Pauline Epistles*, pp. 70-84.

against the Pauline authorship of the Epistle. It is clear, also, that the special themes of Galatians — Paul's apostleship and the question of circumcision for Gentile Christians — were burning issues in the fifties and sixties, but they had become dead issues by the end of the second century. We see, then, how strong is the evidence for the Pauline authorship of the Epistle.

2. **Background and Destination.** The term "Galatia" originated with the immigration into Asia of a large body of Gauls from Europe, c. 278-277 B. C. After 232 B. C. their boundaries were fixed and their state became known as Galatia. This situation continued until B. C. 25, when the expansion of Galatia began. King Amyntas (B. C. 36-25) was the last independent ruler of old Galatia; but in addition to old Galatia, he had also parts of Phrygia, Pisidia, Lycaonia, and Isauria. However, in B. C. 25 he bequeathed his kingdom to Rome, and it became a Roman province. To this province were added Paphlagonia in B. C. 6, a part of Pontus in B. C. 2, and Pontus Polemoniacus in A. D. 64. During the first century after Christ the term "Galatia" was used in two different senses: (1) geographically, of Old Galatia in the northern part of the central plateau of Asia Minor, where the Gauls lived, and (2) politically, of the Roman province of Galatia as it varied in extent. Some prefer the terms "ethnographical" and "provincial" Galatia to those we have given. The question is, In what sense did Luke and Paul use the term? and to what people did Paul write the Epistle to the Galatians?

Now all scholars agree that Paul was in the province of Galatia when he, on his first journey, visited Antioch, Iconium, Lystra, and Derbe. Sir William M. Ramsay has proved this conclusively and no one today disputes the assertion. But not all agree that Paul also visited North Galatia. Yet it seems clear that after he and his party had passed through South Galatia, they were "forbidden" to preach in Asia, and that they then "went through the region of Phrygia and Galatia" (Acts 16:6). This can only mean that they entered North Galatia also. They probably made some disciples in North Galatia at that time, for on his third missionary tour Paul "went through the region of Galatia, and Phrygia, in order, establishing the disciples" (Acts 18:23). Note that Luke does not say "churches." From this it is clear that in the only two instances in which Luke uses the term "Galatian" he uses it in the old territorial sense. He never uses the noun "Galatia."

Paul, however, always uses the provincial names of the districts that were under Roman domination, never the territorial, except as the two were identical in significance. Thus he speaks of Achaia, Macedonia, Illyricum, Dalmatia, Judæa (in the Roman sense of all Palestine), Arabia, and Asia as provinces. Is it likely that he would speak of Galatia in any other sense? He uses the word only three times: 1 Cor. 16:1; Gal. 1:2; and 2 Tim. 4:10. Peter surely uses the term "Galatia" in the political sense, since he employs it in a list with four others, all of which designate provinces.

Furthermore, would it not be strange for Luke to tell us so much about the founding of the Churches in South Galatia (Acts 13:14-14:23) and for Paul to say practically nothing about them? Does it not seem strange, on the other hand, to think that Paul would write so weighty a letter as the Epistle to the Galatians to Churches whose founding is practically passed over in silence by Luke? This would be the case if the Epistle is addressed to North Galatia. Would it not be strange also for the Judaizers from Palestine to pass by the most important cities of Iconium and Antioch in South Galatia, where there were a good many Jews and, no doubt, some Jewish Christians, and go to the remoter Galatian country to do their mischievous work?

But it has been said that even if we grant the force of the above arguments, we cannot suppose that Paul would call the people of Antioch, Iconium, Lystra, and Derbe "Galatians" (Gal. 3:1). To this we reply, that both Luke and Paul speak of all the inhabitants of a city or district without making ethnographical distinctions, as between Jews, Greeks, Romans, etc. Observe this in their use of the terms Alexandrians (Acts 18:24), Asians (Acts 20:4), Corinthians (2 Cor. 6:11), Macedonians (Acts 19:29; 2 Cor. 9:2,4), Philippians (Phil. 4:15), Pontians (Acts 18:2), and Romans (Acts 2:10), in the Greek text. Why should Gal. 3:1 be an exception?

It has also been objected that Paul's reference to his illness (Gal. 4:13) makes it impossible to identify the visit of which he speaks with that of which Luke writes in Acts 13:14-14:23. But since it seems not to have interfered with Paul's preaching, Luke evidently did not regard it important enough to mention. Those who hold the North Galatian theory can produce no better solution to the problem on their view. It has finally been objected that if Paul addresses the Epistle to South Galatia, then he should have mentioned his visit to them in 1:21. But Paul is concerned, in Galatians, to show his relations with Jerusalem and the original Apostles, and not to give a complete account of his work. Indeed, Gal. 2:5 seems to indicate that he had already visited them before the Jerusalem Council.

We hold, then, that the Epistle to the Galatians is primarily addressed to the Churches in South Galatia. At Pisidian Antioch Paul preached a remarkable sermon on the goodness of God in Jewish history, shown supremely in the gift of a Savior (Acts 13:16-41). The immediate effect of the sermon was good; but when many Gentiles believed, the Jews rose up and cast Paul and Barnabas out of the city (vss. 42-52). They went to Iconium, where many believed, both of the Jews and the Gentiles. The messengers did "signs and wonders" at this place. When finally the Gentiles and the Jews with their rulers sought to kill them, they fled to Lystra (Acts 14:1-6). At Lystra Paul healed a man that was lame from birth. As a result of this the people called Barnabas Zeus and Paul, Hermes and tried to offer sacrifices to them (14:11-18). But when some Jews came to Lystra from Antioch and Iconium and stirred up the multitude, they stoned Paul and left him for dead (14:19,20a). But he rose up and returned to the city. On the following day he and Barnabas went to Derbe (14:20b). They preached the Gospel in that city and made many disciples (14:21a). Then they returned to Lystra, Iconium, and Antioch, confirming the souls of the disciples and appointing elders in every church (14:21b-23). It is to these Churches that the Epistle is primarily addressed.

3. **Occasion and Date.** As we have seen, Paul, together with Barnabas, had founded these Churches on his first missionary journey (Acts 13:14-14:23). He visited them again.

accompanied by Silas, on his second tour. At Lystra he added Timothy to his party. We are also told that the visitors delivered to these Churches the decrees that had been issued at Jerusalem. The result was that the Churches were strengthened in the faith and increased in number daily (Acts 16:1-5). Probably thinking that the cause of Gentile freedom from the law was now established on a firm basis, the missionary party entered a larger field of service. They visited North Galatia, Macedonia, and Greece before retracing their steps to Jerusalem and Syrian Antioch (Acts 16:6-18:22). Luke had joined the missionaries at Troas and had accompanied them as far as Philippi (Acts 16:10-40). From Corinth Paul had written the two Epistles to Thessalonica.

Impelled to further missionary endeavor, Paul set out on his third journey, going through the region of Galatia and Phrygia, the "upper country" (Acts 18:23; 19:1), and taking up a three-year residence in Ephesus (Acts 18:23-19:41; 20:31). From Ephesus he wrote several letters to the Church at Corinth, among them our 1 Corinthians, and apparently made a short visit to that Church. Serious trouble having arisen at Ephesus, Paul hastened on to Macedonia, where he met Titus (7:6), and wrote 2 Corinthians (Acts 19:41-20:2a). He appears not to have remained long in Macedonia, but soon to have gone on to Greece, where he spent three months (20:2b, 3). During his protracted absence from South Galatia certain Jewish teachers from Palestine came to this region and violently opposed Paul and his teaching. They denied his authority as an Apostle and repudiated his doctrine of grace. The situation became very serious and Paul, unable to return to South Galatia at once (Gal. 4:19,20), wrote the Epistle to the Galatians.

We cannot tell how soon these Judaizers came to Galatia after Paul had last visited them, nor how long it took for Paul to learn of the defection in those Churches. But it was after the Jerusalem Council, where the fight for Gentile freedom was apparently won (Gal. 2:5), for Paul had already twice visited them (Gal. 4:13-16). Ramsay, holding that both of Luke's references to Galatia are to South Galatia, thinks that Paul wrote the Epistle before starting on his third visit to them. But there seems no good reason why he could not have proceeded on to Galatia at once, if he was at Antioch when the news reached him; furthermore, if the situation was thus grave it seems impossible to think that Luke would mention the third visit, shortly afterward, in but one verse (Acts 18:23). Zahn, however, believes that Paul wrote it from Corinth on his second journey, considering it Paul's earliest Epistle.[25]

The writer feels, however, that there is real force in Lightfoot's contention that Paul followed a certain doctrinal and stylistic pattern in his writings and that because of the similarity of 1 Corinthians, 2 Corinthians, Galatians, and Romans in this respect, these Epistles must have been written close together. The author further thinks that the developments in Galatia may not have started immediately after Paul last visited this region, and that the news may not have reached Paul before he got to Macedonia or Greece on his third journey. In view of these considerations he would regard the Epistle as written from Macedonia or Greece, about A. D. 55 or 56.

4. **Purpose and Plan.** Since in Galatia Paul's authority had been denied and his Gospel repudiated, he undertakes to meet this situation in the Epistle. He proceeds (1) to base salvation on the twofold work of Christ (1:1-5); (2) to assert the authenticity and divine origin of his Gospel (1:6-24); (3) to prove his official recognition by the Apostles and leaders at Jerusalem (2:1-10); (4) to show his consistency, even in dealing with Peter (2:11-21); (5) to defend the doctrine of justification by faith (chs. 3,4); (6) to establish the Galatians in the life of liberty (5:1-15); (7) to teach his readers the methods of victory and spiritual growth (5:16-26); (8) to exhort them to forbearance and brotherly sympathy (6:1-5); (9) to urge them to give liberally (6:6-10); and (10) to warn them against the Judaizers (6:11-18). We may again represent these ideas in the form of an outline:

Introduction, 1:1-5

A. The Personal Vindication, 1:6-2:21.
   (1) The Occasion Thereof, 1:6, 7.
   (2) The Authenticity of His Gospel, 1:8-10.

25. *Intro. to the New Test.*, I, 196.

(3) The Divine Origin of His Gospel, 1:11-24.

(4) The Official Endorsement of His Gospel, 2:1-10.

(5) The Consistency of His Conduct, 2:11-21.

B. The Doctrinal Justification, chs. 3, 4.

(1) The Inconsistency of the Galatians, 3:1-5.

(2) The Example of Abraham, 3:6-9.

(3) The Deliverance from the Law by Christ, 3:10-14.

(4) The Purpose of the Law, 3:15-18.

'(5) The Relation of the Law to the Promise, 3:19-22.

(6) The Superiority of the Condition under Faith Compared with that Under Law, 3:23-4:11.

(7) The Relation Between Paul and the Galatians, 4:12-20.

(8) The Relation Between the Two Covenants, 4:21-31.

C. The Practical Application, 5:1-6:10.

(1) The Admonition to the Right Use of Freedom, 5:1-15.

(2) The Methods of Victory and Spiritual Growth, 5:16-26.

(3) The Exhortation to Forbearance and Brotherly Sympathy, 6:1-5.

(4) The Argument for Liberality, 6:6-10.

(5) The Warning Against the Judaizers, 6:11-16.

Conclusion, 6:17,18.

---

4. THE EPISTLE TO THE ROMANS

This is in every sense the greatest of the Epistles of Paul, if not the greatest book in the New Testament. Shaw says: "Great intellects, like those of Augustine and Luther and Calvin, have discussed it only to discover depths beyond their depths."[26] Godet exclaims: "O St. Paul, had thy one work been to compose an Epistle to the Romans, that alone should have rendered thee dear to every sound reason."[27] The greatness of the Epistle is seen in the importance of its subject matter, the comprehensiveness of its grasp, the acuteness of its reasoning, the breadth of its outlook, and the vigor of its style. It has been generally accepted as a genuine Epistle of Paul, but in re-

---

26. *The Pauline Epistles*, p. 205.
27. *Comm. on St. Paul's Epistle to the Romans*, p. x.

cent years some questions concerning its integrity have been raised. Let us now turn to a study of this great Epistle.

1. **Attestation and Authorship.** There are many quotations and reminiscences of this Epistle in Clement of Rome,[28] in the Epistles of Ignatius,[29] in the writings of Justin Martyr,[30] in the Epistle of Polycarp,[31] and in Hippolytus' *Refutation of All Heresies.*[32] Sanday and Headlam think that there are vari ous indications that the author of *The Testament of the Twelve Patriarchs* "was closely acquainted with the Epistle to the Romans."[33] This work was probably composed before A. D. 150. Marcion is the first to ascribe Romans to Paul. It is found in the Muratorian Canon, the Old Latin, and the Old Syriac. From Irenaeus onward the references to Romans are full and complete in all the Church writers; it is uniformly recognized as by Paul and as canonical.

The internal evidence again supports the external. The writer calls himself Paul (1:1) and describes himself in such a way as can only mean Paul (11:13; 15:15-20). The breadth of its outlook, the character of its teaching, the connection with the other acknowledged Pauline writings, all point to Paul as the author of this Epistle. Evanson (1792), an Englishman, seems to have been the first to deny its genuineness. He was followed in this by Bruno Bauer and by certain other radical Dutch and Swiss theologians. They rejected it on the ground that the Book of Acts knows of no such church as that at Rome and that Paul could not have known so many people by name in a city that he had not as yet visited. But these objections have been repeatedly refuted and cannot be regarded as nullifying the strong evidence for the genuineness of the Epistle. It is today, on all hands, accepted as a genuine work of the Apostle Paul.

2. **Background and Destination.** It is clear that Paul had not been in Rome at the time when he wrote the Epistle and that he did not found the work in that city. But it is not per-

---

28. *Epistle to the Corinthians,* chs. xxxii, xxxiii, xxxv, etc.
29. *To the Smyrnaeans,* ch. i; *To the Ephesians,* chs. xviii, xix; *To the Magnesians,* ch. v; *To the Trallians,* ch. ix, etc.
30. *Dial. with Trypho,* chs. xxiii, xxvii, xliv, etc.
31. *To the Philippians,* chs. iii, iv, vi, x.
32. V.ii, VI.xxx, VII.xiii, IX.vii, etc.
33. *Comm. on the Epistle to the Romans,* p. lxxxiii.

fectly clear as to who had founded it. Three theories have been advanced: That the Apostle Peter founded it and served as its bishop for twenty-five years; that it was founded by the "sojourners from Rome, both Jews and proselytes" on their return from Jerusalem after the great events of the Day of Pentecost (Acts 2:10); and that it was founded by various Christians who had taken up their residence in Rome, many of them being Paul's converts. Let us examine each of these more closely.

Several early writers are cited in support of the first theory. Clement of Rome (c. 97) represents Peter and Paul as having been recently martyred; but he does not indicate the place at which they were killed.[34] It is assumed, however, by those who hold this view that this was in Rome. Eusebius[35] has preserved a statement from Dionysius of Corinth which associates Peter and Paul in the "planting" of the Church at Rome as they had done at Corinth. Irenaeus[36] says the Church was "founded and organized at Rome by the two most glorious Apostles, Peter and Paul," and that "the blessed Apostles having founded and built the Church committed into the hands of Linus the office of the episcopate." Tertullian[37] and Caius[38] declare definitely that both Peter and Paul were martyred at Rome. It appears also that by A. D. 200 the Roman Church believed itself in possession of the remains of both these Apostles, and by 225 that Peter had been a bishop of that Church for twenty-five years.

It is today generally admitted that Peter visited Rome and that he suffered martyrdom in that city; but outside of the Roman Catholic Church there are few that admit a twenty-five year residence in that city. At the time of the Jerusalem Council (c. 49) Peter was still settled in Jerusalem. It is highly improbable that he had been to Rome before the time of Paul's Epistle to the Romans. How could Paul have failed to send greetings to Peter if he was the bishop of the Church? How could Paul even have purposed to visit the Church if Peter had founded it, in the light of his expressed determination not

---

34. *Epistle to the Corinthians*, ch. v.
35. *H. E.*, II.xxv.8.
36. *Against Heresies*, III.iii.2,3.
37. *Scorpiace*, ch. xv.
38. In Eus. *H. E.*, II.xxv.6,7.

to build on another man's foundation (Rom. 15:20)? It is hardly less improbable that Peter got to Rome between the writing of Romans and the Prison Epistles, that is, between A. D. 56 and 62. The legend of a twenty-five year episcopate at Rome may well have grown up out of the supposed command of Christ that the Apostles were to remain twelve years at Jerusalem and the traditional date of the martyrdom of Peter, A.D. 67. We believe, however, with the majority of scholars, that Peter came to Rome some time after the year A. D. 62, and also that he suffered martyrdom in that city; but we do not believe that he founded the Church of Rome. For a good discussion of this subject, see the chapter, "The Last Twenty-five Years of Peter's Life," in Kretzmann's *The New Testament in the Light of a Believer's Research.*

The second theory seems inadequate to the manifest developments in Rome. To be sure, there were "sojourners from Rome, both Jews and proselytes," at the great Pentecost at Jerusalem (Acts 2:10), and some of these may have returned believers. But it would require a considerable time of study before such new converts would be in a position to begin a work in their home city, and there would scarcely be time for that in connection with a visit to Jerusalem. Furthermore, we do not read of any other instance where the visitors to the Jerusalem Pentecost returned and opened a new work. Without altogether denying that individual Jews returning from Jerusalem may have done something in an isolated way for the spread of Christianity at Rome, we must ascribe the founding of the Church at Rome to another instrumentality.

It is well known that Rome was the center of attraction for the whole world in the days of the Apostles. The craving for position, wealth, and pleasure drew multitudes to that city. Among the adventurers would be some Christians, and undoubtedly many of these would be Paul's own converts. The three cities, Antioch, Corinth, and Ephesus, at which he had spent the longest time, were just the three, along with Alexandria, that kept up the most active intercourse with Rome. The long list of names in Rom. 16 indicates how many of the Apostle's acquaintances had removed to Rome. Paul greets no fewer than twenty-four by name in vss. 3-15; and in addition he greets "the church" in the house of Prisca and Aquila, the "households" of Aristobulus and Narcissus, "the brethren" associated with a group of five, and "all the saints" associated with another group. There were probably also other Christians at Rome which are not definitely included in this list; but we undoubtedly have here a fair picture of the Church at the time when Paul wrote the Epistle to the Romans.

It seems as if at the time of the Epistle there was no centralized organization, but rather as if there were various small groups of believers. Five such groups seem discernible in the chapter (vss. 5, 10, 11, 14, 15). Note that Paul does not address the Epistle to "the Church at Rome" (cf. 1 Cor. 1:1; 2 Cor. 1:1; Gal. 1:2; 1 Thess. 1:1; 2 Thess. 1:1), but simply to "all that are in Rome, beloved of God, called to be saints" (1:7). The apparent ignorance regarding the Christian movement on the part of the delegates who called on Paul at Rome may be due to the fact that the believers in that city had not yet come into definite conflict with the synagogue (Acts 28:22). At any rate, we believe that the origin of Christianity in Rome must be sought primarily in the work of the converts that came to the city from various parts of the empire.

Baur introduced the theory that the Epistle is primarily addressed to Jewish Christians, basing his view on chs. 9-11. It is true, Paul deals with the Jewish questions of the Law, redemption, and righteousness in Romans. It is true also that he speaks of Abraham as "our forefather according to the flesh" (4:1); of the former state under the Law in contrast with the later state of freedom; and of the need of submission to the government, etc. (chs. 13, 14). But Paul also, in writing to the Gentile Corinthians, spoke of the Israelites as "our fathers" (1 Cor. 10:1); in this very Epistle to the Romans of the Gentiles as also being under law (2:14-16); and chs. 13 and 14 may have been needed by Gentiles as well as by Jews.

There were undoubtedly a good many Jewish believers at Rome, but they cannot have been in the majority. The majority were manifestly Gentile converts. Paul numbers the Church at Rome among the Gentile Churches (1:5-7); he includes them among the Greeks and barbarians to whom he is obligated to preach (1:13-15); he definitely addresses them as Gentiles (11:13); and he implies that the Romans are among the Gentiles whom he, as a priest, is offering up to God (15:14-16). The fact that in ch. 16 over one-half of the names are either Latin or Greek also suggests the predominance of Gentiles over Jews in the Church at Rome.

We have thus far assumed that the Epistle, as we have it today, was sent to Rome; but there are some who hold that chs. 15 and 16 were not a part of the original Epistle. Marcion seems to have omitted these chapters, and some recent scholars believe that though written by Paul, ch. 16, at least vss. 1-20, belongs to a letter written to Ephesus. It is considered unlikely that Paul would know so many people by name in a church that he had not yet visited; it is also said that the Epistle has four endings: one at 15:33, another at 16:20, another at 16:24, and still another at 16:25-27. Let us consider these matters and also the fact of the omission of the words *en Rōmēi* at 1:7 and 15 in manuscript G.

Marcion almost certainly omitted the whole of chs. 15,16, probably on the ground that in 15:8 Christ is represented as "a minister of the circumcision." At any rate, that is the ground on which F. C. Baur in recent times rejected them. But 15:1-13 is closely connected with ch. 14, and 15:14-33 is in harmony with the Apostle's plans stated elsewhere (Acts 19:21; 24:17; 1 Cor. 16:1-4; 2 Cor. 8 and 9). Furthermore, the personal touches, the boldness combined with delicacy, and the deep emotions which occasionally come to the surface are all characteristic of Paul's style of writing. Besides, although we have some 300 manuscripts of Romans, not one of them, so far as it is uninjured, fails to give the Epistle complete, as we have it today, with the one exception of the final doxology. There are few today who deny the genuineness of these chapters, and still fewer who hold that ch. 15 was not in the original Epistle to the Romans.

There are some, however, who hold that ch. 16 was not a part of the original Epistle; more particularly they hold that vss. 1-20 were a part of a letter commending Phœbe to the Church at Ephesus. It is suggested that since Paul had labored for three years in Ephesus he would know many people by name in that city. This would remove the difficulty about his knowing so many people at Rome. Confirmation of this view is thought to be found in the fact that Paul sends greetings to Prisca and Aquila (16:3-5) whom we last met at Ephesus (Acts 18:18,19), and in the mention of Epænetus as the "firstfruits of Asia" (16:5b). But Aquila and Priscilla apparently traveled a good deal (see Acts 18:2,18,19), and it is not unlikely that business interests, possibly also Paul's suggestion that they precede him to the imperial city, led them to go to Rome. It is not said that Epænetus resided in Asia at the time of the Epistle, merely that he was the first convert in Asia. Sanday and Headlam have shown that a large number of the names that occur in ch. 16 have been found in the inscriptions in Rome. This does not mean that these very persons have been identified, but it does show that these names were common at Rome. It seems altogether likely, therefore, that ch. 16 was a part of the original Epistle to the Romans.

The claim that there are four endings to the Epistle as we have it cannot be substantiated. The formula in 15:33 is not anywhere else Paul's manner of concluding an Epistle, but finds illustration in the body of his writings (cf. vs. 5 and 9:5) The Textus Receptus has an ending in 16:24, but the verse is not supported by manuscript evidence and is not found in our present critical texts. In 16:20 we have one of Paul's customary endings; but the Apostle does not always stop when he intimates that he is closing (cf. Phil. 3:1; 4:8). It appears that after he had written this verse he remembered that several others had wanted to add their greetings. So he adds vss. 21-23 as a kind of postscript and expresses these greetings. He also adds a concluding doxology in which he sums up the main thoughts of the Epistle (vss. 25-27).

Lightfoot holds that Paul himself at a somewhat later period prepared the Epistle for wider circulation by striking out the words *en Rōmēi* in 1:7 and 15, by omitting chs. 15 and 16, and by adding the doxology of 16:25-27 at the end of ch. 14. He holds that it was later placed after 16:24. But while this might explain the fact that this doxology does not always appear at the end of the present Epistle, we agree with Sanday and Headlam that it seems unreasonable that Paul would himself break off his Epistle at the end of ch. 14.[39] The reasons for this are given above. We hold, then, to the unity and genuineness of the entire Epistle.

3. **Occasion and Date.** What occasioned the Epistle is nowhere definitely stated; but from the contents and the whole situation we may make out this point with reasonable certainty. It appears to have been occasioned by Paul's interest in the Church at Rome and his purpose to visit it in the near future (Acts 19:21; Rom. 1:13; 15:22-24,28,29); by his feeling that a Church which had sprung up without any authoritative leadership needed a thorough grounding in the fundamental doctrines of the faith; by his fears that Judaizing influences might reach Rome also and destroy the work of God in that place; and finally, by the opportunity presented by the going of Phœbe to Rome to send a letter to the saints in that city (Rom. 16:1,2). All these things seem to have combined to give us the greatest Epistle from the Apostle Paul.

The Epistle was written at Corinth during his three months' stay in Greece (Acts 20:2,3). This appears from the following facts: Paul was going to Jerusalem with the collection at the time of writing (Rom. 15:25-27). He frequently stresses this collection in the earlier letters to Corinth (1 Cor. 16:1-4; 2 Cor. 8 and 9), showing that these letters were written at about the same time. Romans is later than 2 Corinthians, for he is now on the verge of departing for Jerusalem (15:25). He wrote 2 Corinthians from Macedonia; from Macedonia he went to Greece. He refers to Cenchreæ (16:1), the seaport of Corinth, as near by. He is entertained by Gaius (16:23), and he had baptized a Gaius at Corinth (1 Cor. 1:14). Erastus, too, seems to have lived at Corinth (Rom. 16:23; 2 Tim. 4:20). We conclude, therefore, that the Epistle to the Romans was written from Corinth, shortly after the writing of 2 Corinthians, or A. D. 56.

4. **Purpose and Plan.** Judging from the contents of the Epistle, the Apostle's purpose seems to be (1) to teach the believers at Rome the fundamental doctrines of salvation and so to fortify them against the error of the Judaizers (chs. 1-8);

---

39. *Op. cit.*, p. xcv.

(2) to explain the unbelief of Israel and to indicate its extent and duration (chs. 9-11) ; (3) to urge his readers to enter experimentally into the full Christian life (ch. 12) ; (4) to admonish them to be subject to the higher powers and to have love one to another (ch. 13) ; (5) to enjoin them to exercise forbearance toward the weak (14:1-15:13) ; (6) to reveal to them his purposes and plans (15:14-33) ; (7) to commend Phœbe to the Church at Rome (16:1-4) ; and (8) to send his greetings to many former associates and friends (16:5-27). We may present these ideas in outline form:

Introduction, 1:1-15.

A. The Doctrinal Exposition, 1:16-8:39.
    The Theme, 1:16,17.
  (1) The Doctrine of Justification, 1:18-5:11.
  (2) The Doctrine of Sanctification, 5:12-8:39.

B. The Dispensational Harmonization, 9-11.
  (1) The Tragedy of Israel's Rejection, 9:1-5.
  (2) The Justice of Israel's Rejection, 9:6-29.
  (3) The Cause of Israel's Rejection, 9:30-10:21.
  (4) The Extent of Israel's Rejection, 11:1-10.
  (5) The Duration of Israel's Rejection, 11:11-32.

  Doxology, 11:33-36.

C. The Practical Application, 12:1-15:13.

  (1) The Believer in Relation to God, 12:1,2.
  (2) The Believer in Relation to His Gifts, 12:3-8.
  (3) The Believer in Relation to His Fellow-Believers, 12:9-16.
  (4) The Believer in Relation to Men in General, 12:17-21.
  (5) The Believer in Relation to the State, 13:1-14.
  (6) The Believer in Relation to the Weak Brother, 14:1-15:13.

  Conclusion, 15:14-16:27.

Chapter X

THE PAULINE EPISTLES
The Third Group

THE third group consists of the Epistles of the First Roman Imprisonment. They are Colossians, Philemon, Ephesians, and Philippians. They were written at about the same time. Tychicus delivered Colossians (4:7-9) and Ephesians (6:21, 22); Onesimus accompanied Tychicus to Colosse (4:9) and delivered the letter to Philemon (Philemon 10-17). The eight persons who are mentioned in Colossians, Philemon, and Ephesians (Timothy, Luke, Aristarchus, Epaphras, Tychicus, Demas, Mark, and Jesus Justus) may well have been with Paul at the time. In all four Epistles the subject matter is quite similar, and in all four Paul's condition is much the same. He is in prison in behalf of the Gentiles (Col. 1:24; 4:3; Eph. 3:1,13; Philemon 1,9-13,23; Phil. 1:7; 2:17).

But since he was imprisoned several different times, we wonder where he was in captivity at this time. Cæsarea, Ephesus, and Rome have been suggested. But Cæsarea is out of the question, for the Book of Acts knows of no such preaching ministry at Cæsarea as he had in this imprisonment (Col. 4:2-4; Eph. 6:18-20; Phil. 1:12-18). Furthermore, it seems impossible that he should write from Cæsarea and omit all reference to Philip the Evangelist who lived in this city (Acts 21:8), for instance in Col. 4:10,11. And it is extremely improbable that a runaway slave would seek refuge in a Palestinian city like Cæsarea. Ephesus, too, is unlikely. Paul met with great opposition in Ephesus (Acts 19:23-20:1), but there is no indication that he was imprisoned in that city. It is unlikely, also, that the Philippians would send Paul a gift at Ephesus, where he had so many friends (cf. Phil. 4:10,18). It is true, Onesimus would much more likely seek refuge in a city like Ephesus than in one like Cæsarea; but he might even more likely have sought it in a large city like Rome. We hold that Paul wrote all four Epistles from his Roman imprisonment (Acts 28:30,31). This accounts best for his mention of Cæsar's household (Phil. 4:22) and the prætorian guard (Phil. 1:13), for the story about Onesimus, for the gift from Philippi, for his and his co-laborer's activity in preaching during his imprisonment, and for his silence about Philip the Evangelist.

The question of the exact time when these books were written will be taken up in connection with the separate study of each Epistle. It is here assumed that they were written in the order: Colossians, Philemon, Ephesians, and Philippians.

---

1. THE EPISTLE TO THE COLOSSIANS

Colossians, like Romans, was written to a Church which Paul had not yet visited (1:4,7,8; 2:1). It is a strong polemic against the Judaic-Gnostic heresy that had sprung up in the Lycus valley. With its teaching of ceremonialism and emanations this heresy reduced Christianity to a legal system and Christ to the position of a lesser God. Paul rose to the occasion with his doctrine of the person and work of Christ. Colossians and Ephesians are related to each other in thought: Colossians sets forth the dignity of Christ, the Head of the Church, and Ephesians presents the sublimity of the Church, the Body of Christ. Let us turn to a more detailed study of the former Epistle.

1. **Attestation and Authorship.** The external attestation to Colossians is all that can be desired. Ignatius may refer to 1:23 in his *Epistle to the Ephesians* (ch. x). *The Epistle of Barnabas* seems to refer to 1:16 (ch. xii). Justin Martyr uses the expression "the firstborn of all creation" several times;[1] and Theophilus of Antioch does so once.[2] Irenæus says that Paul, in the Epistle to the Colossians, says: "Luke, the beloved physician, greets."[3] This statement is found in Col. 4:14. Clement of Alexandria quotes 1:28 in *Stromata* (I.i), as by Paul. He

---

1. *Dial. with Trypho*, chs. lxxxiv, lxxxv, cxxxviii.
2. *To Autolycus*, II.xxii.
3. *Against Heresies*, III.xiv.1.

also quotes 3:12,14,15 in *Stromata* (IV. vii) and 4:2-4 in *Stromata* (V.x). Tertullian quotes 2:8 in *Prescription Against Heretics* (ch. vii) and 2:12,13 in *Resurrection of the Flesh* (ch. xxiii). Origen quotes 2:18,19 as in Colossians and by Paul in *Against Celsus* (V.viii)). It was in Marcion's Canon, in the Old Latin, and the Old Syriac, and is recognized in the Muratorian Fragment.

The internal evidence also is satisfactory. Three times the writer calls himself Paul (1:1,23; 4:18). The general conception of the person and work of Christ in the Epistle and the practical exhortations based on it, are genuinely Pauline. The Epistle to Philemon is today generally regarded as genuine, and the manner in which the details in Colossians and Philemon fit together argues for the genuineness of Colossians also. Five of the persons mentioned in Col. 4:10-14 are also mentioned in Philemon 23,24, — all but Jesus Justus. In Col. 4:17 he asks the Colossian Church to admonish Archippus to "take heed to the ministry" which he has received. In Philemon 2 he calls him "our fellowsoldier." The fact that in the former reference he introduces him immediately after his reference to "the Church of the Laodiceans" makes it seem probable that he was the pastor of that Church. This linking of Colossians with Philemon argues for the genuineness of the Epistle now before us.

The objections to this view can be answered satisfactorily. The one first raised by Mayerhoff (1838) on the ground of the vocabulary, style, and thought, later taken over by Baur, Hilgenfeld, Pfleiderer, and others, has been well answered by Abbott. It is alleged that Paul's favorite terms, *righteous, revelation, prove, obedience, salvation, fellowship, law,* and *believe,* as well as certain Pauline particles, are wanting. But Abbott shows that these phenomena are not without a parallel in other Epistles of similar length.[4] Salmon says: "I cannot subscribe to the doctrine that a man writing a new composition must not, on pain of losing his identity, employ any word that he has not used in a former one."[5]

The two objections based on the contents of the Epistle can

4. *Comm. on the Epistles to the Ephesians and to the Colossians,* p. lii ff.
5. *Intro. to the New Testament,* p. 398.

also be met. The first relates to the Christology of the Epistle. The character of its view of the person and work of our Lord, it is said, is too much like the Logos doctrine of John (Col. 1:13-23; John 1:1-18). But if we accept the Epistle to the Philippians, we have already accepted a more definite statement of the pre-existence, deity, and incarnation of Christ (Phil. 2:5-9) than we have in Colossians. Why should not two writers have the same view of Christ in the early Church? The second objection relates to the type of error attacked in Colossians. But we must remember that this Epistle does not deal with the fully developed Gnosticism of the second century, but merely with its incipient form. Moffatt points out that recent research has served to show that such an error as this may well have prevailed during the first century.[6] It is clear, therefore, that no valid objections to the genuineness of this Epistle have been established.

2. **Background and Destination.** Paul had never been to Colossæ. He had turned northward from South Galatia on his second journey (Acts 16:6) and had come by "the upper country" (Acts 19:1) to Ephesus on his third journey, and not by the main road that led through the Lycus valley. So he had missed Colossæ on both trips. But he yet considered the Churches in the Lycus valley, the ones at Colossæ, Laodicea, and Hierapolis, his parish. During his three-year ministry at Ephesus "all they that dwelt in Asia heard the word of the Lord, both Jews and Greeks" (Acts 19:10, cf. vs. 26). Probably both Epaphras and Philemon had been saved under Paul's ministry at Ephesus (Philemon 19,23). At any rate, Paul sent Epaphras to preach to them (Col. 1:7, A. S. V.), and he probably evangelised all three of the above cities (Col. 4:12,13). Thus Paul was greatly concerned about them, as also for the believers at Laodicea (Col. 2:1), for whom the Epistle to the Colossians was also intended (Col. 4:16).

Colossæ had had a notable history, but with certain changes in the main road the traffic and trade went more and more to the rival cities, Laodicea and Hierapolis. At this time it was apparently merely a country village. It was 10 miles southeast of Laodicea, and Hierapolis was 6 miles north of Laodicea.

---

6. *Intro. to the Literature of the New Testament*, p. 153.

The people were mostly native Phrygians and Greek colonists. There were also a considerable number of Jews in that section of the country. Antiochus the Great (B. C. 223-187) had transplanted two thousand families of Jews from Mesopotamia and Babylon to the provinces of Phrygia and Lydia,[7] and many lived in this region at this time. It is to this people that the Epistle to the Colossians was written.

3. **Occasion and Date.** During the more than two years of Paul's absence from the province of Asia, an insidious error had crept into the Colossian Church. It appears that a type of Judaistic Christians had come to Colossæ and had introduced a teaching that had three elements in it: A distinctly Jewish element, as is seen in Paul's reference to circumcision, the ordinances that are against us, meats and drinks, feast days, new moons, and sabbaths (Col. 2:11-16); an ascetic element, as seen in his reference to ordinances, "handle not, nor taste, nor touch" (Col. 2:20-23); and a speculative element, as is seen in the warning against "philosophy and vain deceit" (Col. 2:8). This latter probably refers to the denial of the full deity of Christ (2:9; cf. 1:19) and the worship of intermediary beings (2:18,19) by the errorists. Although the first element is distinctly Jewish and the second and third elements are as definitely Gnostic, the combination was given a kind of Christian coloring by the false teachers. In Galatia the error consisted of a mixture of law and grace; in Colossæ, of a Judaic-Gnostic perversion of the Gospel.

Apparently Epaphras and his fellow-workers were unable to cope with this situation, and so Epaphras went to Rome to consult Paul about it (1:7,8). Moffatt thinks we may perhaps read between the lines that the Colossians had expected or did expect a visit from Paul (2:1 f.); and also, that since he is imprisoned at the moment and cannot come in person, he writes this letter.[8] He sends it by Tychicus and Onesimus (4:7-9), since Epaphras, apparently, cannot come to them at once (4:12; Philemon 23). Paul himself "greatly" strives for them, and is concerned that they attain to "the full assurance

---

7. Josephus, *Ant.* XII.iii.4.
8. *Intro. to the Lit. of the New Testament*, p. 151.

of understanding, that they may know the mystery of God, even Christ" (2:1,2).

Although the four Prison Epistles were written at about the same time, we seem to have reason for thinking that Colossians and Philemon were written first. Epaphras had brought distressing news from Colossæ, and Paul had long wanted to send Onesimus back to his master, Philemon. These two facts induced Paul to write Colossians and Philemon, perhaps in this order, and to send them by Tychicus and Onesimus. And in connection with their going to Asia he improved the opportunity to write and send by Tychicus an Epistle of a more general character, the Epistle to the Ephesians. Later on he wrote the Epistle to the Philippians. We may, therefore, date the Epistle to the Colossians at about the middle of Paul's two-year imprisonment at Rome, say about A. D. 60.

4. **Purpose and Plan.** Paul meets these errors, "not by indignant controversy, for as yet they were only undeveloped; nor by personal authority, for these Christians were not his converts; but by the noblest of all forms of controversy, which is the pure presentation of counter truths."[9] After giving thanks for their attainments and praying for their progress (1:1-12), he sets forth the supremacy of Christ over all principalities and powers (1:13-19), the completeness of the redemption provided by Him (1:20-23), and his own sufferings and labors in the proclamation of this message (1:24-2:3); he warns the Colossians against the "philosophy and vain deceit" of the false teachers that had come to Colossæ, who ignored the provision of full deliverance from sin and from legal prescription made in Christ (2:4-15); he admonishes them, accordingly, not to submit to ritual prescriptions nor to turn to the worship of inferior beings (2:16-19), but to recognize the fact, that in dying and rising with Christ they had died to the old life and to earthly ordinances, and had risen to a new life and to heavenly principles (2:20-3:4); he exhorts them to apply this death and resurrection in a practical way in their personal lives (3:5-17) and in the various special relationships of life (3:18-4:6); he explains the mission of Tychicus

---

9. Godet, *Studies on the Epistles*, p. 185, quoted by Hayes in *Paul and His Epistles*, p. 358.

and Onesimus (4:7-9), sends greetings (4:10-17), and closes with a benediction (4:18). These thoughts may be represented in outline form.

Introduction, 1:1-12.

A. The Doctrinal Section, 1:13-2:3.
　(1) The Nature of Redemption, 1:13, 14.
　(2) The Person of Christ, 1:15-19.
　(3) The Work of Christ, 1:20-23.
　(4) The Apostle's Share in Carrying Out this Work of Christ, 1:24-2:3.

B. The Polemical Section, 2:4-3:4.
　(1) The Warning Against False Philosophy, 2:4-8.
　(2) The Person and Work of Christ, 2:9-15.
　(3) The Obligations Resulting Therefrom, 2:16-3:4.

C. The Practical Section, 3:5-4:6.
　(1) The Application of this Death and Resurrection in Personal Life, 3:5-17.
　(2) The Application of this Death and Resurrection in the Domestic Life, 3:18-4:1.
　(3) The Application of this Death and Resurrection in Relation to the World, 4:2-6.

D. The Personal Section, 4:7-17.
　(1) The Mission of Tychicus and Onesimus, 7-9.
　(2) The Salutations from His Associates, 10-14.
　(3) The Apostle's Own Salutations, 15.
　(4) The Message to Laodicea, 16, 17.
　Conclusion, 4:18.

---

2. THE EPISTLE TO PHILEMON

The Epistle to Philemon gives us an insight into early social and domestic life. Slavery was one of the curses of the ancient world. Angus says: "The Greek and the Roman saw no more wrong in having slaves than we see in having domestic servants."[10] Le Maistre thinks there were 60,000,000 slaves in the Roman Empire. However that may be, even some of the early

---

10. *The Environment of Early Christianity,* p. 38.

Christians had slaves. This is evident from the regulations which Paul lays down in this regard (1 Cor. 7:20-24; Col. 3:22-4:1; Eph. 6:5-9). Philemon was such a Christian slave-owner, and Onesimus, a Phrygian, was such a slave. In those days a slave was absolutely at the mercy of his master; for the smallest offense he might be scourged, mutilated, crucified, or thrown to the wild beasts. The Epistle does not deal with the problem of slavery, but it yet exemplifies, in the tactfulness and teaching of Paul, the Christian way of dealing with a grievous social evil that cannot be eradicated at the time.

1. **Attestation and Authorship.** Since the Epistle is very short and of a personal nature, we cannot expect many notices of it in the early literature. There are, however, proofs of its early existence and acceptance as genuine. Ignatius seems to allude to vs. 20 in *Ephesians* (ch. ii) and in *Magnesians* (ch. xii). Tertullian knew it.[11] Origen quotes vs. 14 and ascribes the Epistle to Paul;[12] he also alludes to vss. 7 and 9 in his *Commentary on Matthew* (sections 72 and 66). Eusebius includes Philemon among the *homologoumena*. The Epistle is in Marcion's Canon and is recognized in the Muratorian Fragment. It is also in the Old Latin and the Old Syriac.

The writer calls himself Paul three times (vss. 1,9,19), and the thought, sentiment, and expression are thoroughly Pauline. The Epistle is closely linked with Colossians (Col. 4:10-17; Philemon 2,23,24), and the proof of the genuineness of the one helps to establish also that of the other. In the 4th and 5th centuries it was attacked as unworthy of Paul's mind and as of no value for edification; but Jerome, Chrysostom, and others, answered these charges. In more recent times Baur and others have attacked it on purely subjective grounds. Peake says that, although the genuineness of Philemon has been disputed, "it is now amply recognized on all hands."[13]

2. **Background and Destination.** It appears that Philemon, a wealthy slave-owner, had been converted under Paul's ministry (vs. 19), perhaps on a visit to Ephesus during the Apostle's three-year ministry in that city. Onesimus was one of his

---

11. *Against Marcion*, V. xxi.
12. *Homily* XIX.
13. *A Critical Introduction to the New Testament*, p. 47.

slaves and, being a Phrygian, "he was a slave of the lowest order."[14] Not having any rights in the eyes of the law, Onesimus had come to the conclusion that he also had no responsibilities. He did not only run away from his master, but apparently stole some money or jewelry or both from Philemon as he left (vs. 18). He made his way to Rome, for nowhere could a fugitive find a safer refuge than in the imperial city.

We know nothing about Philemon except what is found in the letter addressed to him. But the Epistle is not a "strictly private letter," as Lightfoot holds,[15] for Paul very definitely includes Apphia, Archippus, and the Church in Philemon's house, along with Philemon, in the address (vss. 1,2). Was Paul not asking unusual favors of Philemon and would he not need the help of others in impressing Philemon with the justice of his appeals? Archippus was probably the pastor or leader of the group that met in Philemon's house. Lightfoot holds that he was Philemon's son,[16] but this is not certain. In any case, Paul seems to appeal to him and the whole Church, as well as to Apphia, who may have been the wife of Philemon, to help him in bringing about a reconciliation between Onesimus and Philemon.

In Col. 4:17 Paul requests the Colossian Church to exhort Archippus to fulfil his ministry. From the fact that he is mentioned immediately after Paul's reference to Laodicea, it has been inferred that he was the pastor of the Church at Laodicea.[16a] This is probable; but this raises the question whether Philemon did not also live in Laodicea. Practically all writers[17] hold that he resided at Colossæ.

There is, however, something to be said in favor of Laodicea. Goodspeed says, Col. 4:17 implies that Archippus lived at Laodicea. He adds: "If Archippus is in Laodicea, then Philemon and Apphia are also, and so is the church that meets in

---

14. David Smith, *Life and Letters of St. Paul*, p. 545.
15. *St. Paul's Epistles to the Colossians and to Philemon*, p. 303.
16. *Op. cit.*, p. 308.   16a. Lightfoot, *op. cit.*, p. 309.
17. Lightfoot, *op. cit.*, p. 304; Alford, *Greek Testament*, III, 113; Conybeare and Howson, *Life and Epistles of St. Paul*, p. 748; Shaw, *Pauline Epistles*, p. 299; Zahn, *Intro. to the New Testament*, I, 446; Smith, *Life and Letters of St. Paul*, p. 546; Moffatt, *Intro. to the Literature of the New Testament*, p. 162; Hayes, *Paul and His Epistles*, p. 333; Peake, *A Critical Intro. to the New Test.*, p. 48; Oesterly, *Expos. Greek Test.*, IV, 206; Lake and Lake, *An Intro. to the New Test.*, p. 150; and Robertson, *Word Pictures*, IV, 464.

Philemon's house."[18] On the basis of these assumptions he concludes that "the letter to Philemon was a letter to Laodicea," and therefore the letter "from Laodicea" that Paul wanted the Colossian Church also to read (Col. 4:16). He thinks that the reason why the letter did not continue to bear the name of Laodicea is due to the disfavor into which the Laodicean Church soon fell.[19] This theory was strongly advocated by Wiesler a little earlier, but has never gained wide acceptance. Certainly the so-called *Epistle to the Laodiceans* which has come down to us in Latin (apparently as a translation from a Greek original), is a forgery. While we thus grant that Philemon may have resided at Laodicea, we doubt that the Epistle to Philemon is the Epistle Paul alludes to in Col. 4:16. More will be said about this in connection with our study of Ephesians.

3. **Occasion and Date.** The run-away slave Onesimus would soon find himself in need in Rome. We do not know just how he was brought under the influence of Paul, but we know that he was (vs. 10). Perhaps one of Paul's co-laborers may have encountered him in the city and have conducted him to Paul. Smith thinks Tychicus may have done this. He was an Asian and may have visited Philemon in his home; if so, he may have recognized Onesimus in Rome.[20] Or Onesimus may have heard of Paul's preaching back home or since he came to Rome. At any rate, he came into contact with Paul, and Paul led him to Christ (vs. 10).

At once Onesimus (the name means "profitable") turned to waiting on Paul as a true son. He would gladly have kept him in Rome, that in Philemon's place he might minister to him; but he did not feel free to do so without Philemon's consent (vss. 13, 14). Furthermore, as Lightfoot remarks, there was need for Onesimus to return to his master; he "had repented, but he had not made restitution."[21] Paul felt that Onesimus must return, and Onesimus probably felt the same way about it. But to send him back was to place him at the mercy of his master. The Roman law practically imposed no limits to the power of a master over his slave. When, then, Tychicus was

---

18. *An Intro. to the New Test.*, p. 112.
19. *Op. cit.*, p. 117.
20. *Life and Letters of St. Paul*, p. 546.
21. *Op. cit.*, p. 314.

dispatched to Asia with the Epistles to the Ephesians and to the Colossians, Onesimus was sent with him. Tychicus would plead with Philemon for the penitent slave. But Paul thought it necessary to write a brief note of personal entreaty and to send it with Onesimus. This is the occasion for the Epistle to Philemon.

Since this Epistle is so closely connected with the Epistle to the Colossians and since the two were sent at the same time, we naturally date the present Epistle the same as the Epistle to the Colossians, viz., at A.D. 60.

4. **Purpose and Plan.** Paul's main purpose is to effect a reconciliation between Philemon and Onesimus. And with what delicate tact he pleads the cause of Onesimus! After an affectionate salutation to Philemon, to Apphia, who probably was his wife, to Archippus, who may have been his son, and to the Church which met in his house (vss. 1-3), he gives thanks for Philemon's faith toward the Lord Jesus and his love, shown in charitable deeds toward the saints (vss. 4-7). He then presents a series of arguments why Philemon should forgive Onesimus and receive him back, and gives some hints that Philemon might want to set him free (vss. 8-21). These arguments are his authority, his age, his imprisonment, his relations to Onesimus, his relations to Philemon, his offer to pay whatever Onesimus may owe Philemon, and his hope that Philemon will rejoice his heart. He ends with a statement concerning his prospects and plans (vs. 22), and sends greetings from his fellow-workers (vss. 23, 24). These thoughts may be grouped under the following heads, thus:

> Salutation, 1-3.
> (1) The Thanksgiving for Philemon, 4-7.
> (2) The Entreaty for Onesimus, 8-21.
> (3) The Apostle's Personal Affairs, 22-24.
> Benediction, 25.

Of the effect of this appeal we have no certain knowledge. But as Lightfoot says: "It is reasonable to suppose, however, that Philemon would not belie the Apostle's hopes; that he would receive the slave as a brother; that he would even go beyond the express terms of the Apostle's petition, and emancipate the penitent" (*op. cit.*, p. 315 f.).

3. THE EPISTLE TO THE EPHESIANS

Although Ephesians and Colossians have many similarities, they also have some differences. From the standpoint of subject-matter Colossians sets forth the dignity of Christ, the Head of the Church, and Ephesians the sublimity of the Church, the Body of Christ. From the standpoint of style Colossians is largely controversial, while Ephesians is calm and almost entirely free from controversial elements. Moorehead says: "We pass into the stillness and hush of the sanctuary when we turn to Ephesians. Here prevails the atmosphere of repose, of meditation, of worship and peace."[22] Among Paul's Epistles there is none more sublime and profound, none greater than Ephesians. Yet, as Salmond points out, there have been students, "who with an almost incredible lack of insight have considered it an insipid production or a tedious and unskilful compilation."[23] Several problems face us as we approach the study of this Epistle, and we now turn to them.

1. **Attestation and Authorship.** Lewis says: "None of the epistles which are ascribed to St. Paul have a stronger chain of evidence to their early and continued use than that which we know as the Epistle to the Ephesians."[24] Clement of Rome uses language resembling 1:18 in his *Epistle to the Corinthians* (ch. xxxvi) and 4:4-6 in the same Epistle (ch. xlvi). Ignatius uses a phrase recalling 3:3,4,9 in his *Epistle to the Ephesians* (ch. xii). In his *Epistle to Polycarp* (ch. v) he uses the language of 5:25. Polycarp refers to 4:26 in his *Epistle to the Philippians* (ch. xii). Hermas uses 4:30 in his *Commandment* Tenth (chs. i and ii). Clement of Alexandria quotes from 5:21-25 in *Stromata* (IV.viii). He calls it "the Epistle to the Ephesians" (*ib.*). Clement also uses 4:13-15 in the *Instructor* (I.v). Tertullian says: "We have it on the true tradition of the Church, that the epistle was sent to the Ephesians, not to the Laodiceans."[25] He says that it was Marcion that called it the "Epistle to the Laodiceans" (*ib.*). Irenæus quotes 5:30 in his work *Against Heresies* (V.ii.3). Hippolytus tells us that the Epistle was used by the Ophites, Basilides, and Valentinus.

---

22. *Outline Studies in Acts and the Epistles*, p. 214.
23. *Expositor's Greek Testament*, III, 208.
24. "The Epistle to the Ephesians," in *Inter. Stand. Bible Ency.*, II, 956.
25. *Against Marcion*, V. xvii.

Marcion had it in his Canon and the Muratorian Fragment of the Canon recognizes it.

The internal evidence, too, is strong. The writer twice calls himself Paul (1:1; 3:1). The Epistle is written after the usual Pauline pattern, beginning with greetings and thanksgiving, leading on to a doctrinal discussion, and concluding with practical exhortations and personal matters. The language, too, is Pauline. Nearly every sentence has verbal echoes of what Paul has said elsewhere. Especially close is its resemblance to Colossians in this respect. Lewis says: "Out of 155 verses in Ephesians 78 are found in Colossians in varying degrees of identity."[26] This is, no doubt, due to the fact that Paul had just written the Epistle to the Colossians and the ideas of that Epistle were still in his mind. 1 Peter, Hebrews, and the Apocalypse seem to show acquaintance with Ephesians. Abbott lists the similarities in these Epistles.[27] This would indicate that Ephesians is earlier than 1 Peter, Hebrews and the Apocalypse.

The genuineness of the Epistle has, however, been questioned. Schleiermacher (1768-1834) seems to have been the first to cast doubt upon it. He suggested that Tychicus wrote it. De Wette called it a "verbose amplification" of the Epistle to the Colossians and regarded its style as definitely inferior to that of Paul. But such men as Chrysostom, Erasmus, and Coleridge had a very different opinion of its style. Coleridge called it "the divinest composition of man." Lünemann and Meyer answered De Wette. Baur and his followers thought to find Gnostic and Montanist language and ideas in both Colossians and Ephesians and so they rejected both Epistles. In recent times Moffatt, Goodspeed, and Dibelius deny the Pauline authorship of this Epistle.

Several objections are brought forward. It is said that Ephesians has 42 words that are peculiar to it. But, in reality, that is no more than is found in the recognized Epistles of Paul. It is objected that synonyms are used instead of Paul's

---

26. "The Epistle to the Ephesians," *Inter. Stand. Bible Ency.*, p. 956.
27. *The Epistles to the Ephesians and to the Colossians*, pp. xxiii-xxix.

usual words, and that more words are used in a new sense. Strange criticism, that detects a forger when the same words are used and also when synonyms are employed! The terms *mystery, stewardship* (dispensation), and *possession* are said to be used in a new sense in this Epistle. But this is doubtful. Besides, is a man always obliged to use a word in the same sense unless he does not care about losing his identity? It is held that the reference to "the holy apostles and prophets" (3:5; cf. 2:20; 4:11) indicates that the writer belonged to the second generation, when these were put on a high plane. But this cannot be, for the writer includes himself among "the holy ones (saints)" (3:8). The absence of personal greetings in the last chapter is due to the encyclical character of the Epistle (see the next section). The reference to *the* Church, rather than to some local church or churches, is likewise in harmony with the destination of the letter. This conception of the Church is, however, older than the Epistle to the Ephesians (see Matt. 16:18; Acts 20:28; 1 Cor. 12:28; 15:9; Gal. 1:13; Col. 1:18,24).

The similarities in the Epistle to the Ephesians and in 1 Peter do not disprove the Pauline authorship of Ephesians. If there is any dependence between the two writers, it is more likely that Peter borrowed from Paul than that Paul borrowed from Peter. The similarities between Ephesians, Hebrews, and the Apocalypse are only such as may be expected in writers that have a common doctrinal view-point. Basic doctrinal ideas are apt to be expressed in the same language by all of them.[28] From all this we conclude that there are no insurmountable obstacles to the traditional view of the Pauline authorship of this Epistle.

2. **Background and Destination.** Paul laid the foundation of the Church at Ephesus on his return trip from his second missionary journey; but he remained there only a short time on that occasion (Acts 18:19-21). Apparently Priscilla and Aquila carried on the work during his absence (Acts 18:20-19:1). When he returned to Ephesus on his third missionary tour, he spent three years in that city (Acts 19:1-20:1). He

---

28. For a fuller discussion of these and other objections to the genuineness of this *Epistle,* see Abbott's *Epistles to the Ephesians and to the Colossians* (pp. ix-xxiii).

now won twelve disciples of John the Baptist to Christ and preached three months in the synagogue (Acts 19:1-8). When the opposition to his message became keen, he withdrew to the school of Tyrannus, where he preached for two years more (19:9,10a). During this time the word of the Lord went out to all Asia (vs. 10b). Paul wrought special miracles here and induced many to give up their magical arts (vss. 11-19). But when Demetrius and his craftsmen set the city on an uproar, which involved two of Paul's companions, Gaius and Aristarchus, and even the town-clerk could scarcely quiet the mob, Paul left Ephesus for Macedonia (19:23-20:1). On his return from Greece by way of Macedonia he met the elders of Ephesus at Miletus and gave them one of the most touching charges of which we have any record (20:17-38). It appears that later on, at least for a time, Timothy was stationed at Ephesus (1 Tim. 1:3). At some time or other Onesiphorus ministered at Ephesus (2 Tim. 1:18). Finally John the Apostle removed to this city and made it his headquarters. It appears that although there were both Jews and Gentiles in the Church at Ephesus, the Gentiles were by far in the majority.

But was the Epistle written to the Church at Ephesus? The early Church seems to have believed that it was. The Muratorian Canon, Irenæus,[29] Tertullian,[30] Clement of Alexandria,[31] and Origen[32] speak of it as the Epistle to the Ephesians. In addition to this is the fact that all the manuscripts, both uncial and minuscule, with the exception of three, have the words *en Ephesōi* in 1:1. Then also all the ancient versions reproduce this phrase in the translations. All this seems to make a very strong case for the traditional view.

Does this, however, establish it? We fear not. Look at the other side of the evidence. The three Greek manuscripts that do not have the words are Aleph, B, and 67². The first two are our most important uncials and the last is a good minuscule. Lightfoot maintains that whenever these three are found together, they almost always represent the original text. In

---

29. *Against Heresies*, V. ii. 3.
30. *Against Marcion*, V. xvii.

31. *Stromata*, IV. viii.
32. *Against Celsus*, III. xx.

addition to this Basil the Great (c. 329-379) testifies that these words are not found in any of the ancient manuscripts.[33] Some think that Origen, more than a century earlier, intimates the same thing.[34] It is likely, also, that Tertullian did not have the phrase in his copy, for he does not charge Marcion with falsifying the text, but with supplying a new title. And although all versions have it, none of those which have come down to us are as old as Aleph and B.

The internal evidence strongly supports Aleph, B, and 67[2]. It would be strange indeed for Paul to say to the Church at Ephesus that he knew of their conversion only by report (1:15; 4:21), since he had spent three years with them (Acts 20:17, 31). It would be equally strange for him to say that this church knew him only by hearsay (3:2) and that they must judge by what he had written as to whether or not God had given him a revelation of the truth (3:2-4). It would also seem strange that he should send no greetings to a church that knew him so intimately. As Findlay says: "Not once does he address his hearers as 'brethren' or 'beloved'; 'my brethren' in Eph. 6:10 is an insertion of the copyists. There is not a single word of familiarity or endearment in the whole letter. The benediction at the end (6:23,24) is given in the third person, not in the second as everywhere else."[35]

If this is the situation, how then shall we explain the presence of the words *en Ephesōi* in so many of the documents and the opinion of the early Church that the Epistle was addressed to the Church at Ephesus? We suggest the following explanation of these phenomena: Paul wrote this Epistle as a circular letter to the province of Asia. Perhaps he left a blank space after the words "which are" in the first verse, which was to be filled in with the name of the church to which it was to be delivered, either by the bearer or by someone else, or which was inserted by the church in the copy which it made of the original. On this theory nearly all of the manuscripts and versions that have come down to us were made from the copy possessed by the Church at Ephesus. Or perhaps the first verse originally read: "to the saints who are also faithful," without a

33. *Against Eunom.,* ii. 19.
34. See Cramer's *Catena, in loc.*
35. *The Epistles of Paul,* p. 180.

blank space for the name of the church. We regard this as the more probable theory. Since the Epistle was meant for Ephesus and her daughter churches, and since it was undoubtedly distributed from Ephesus, it soon came to be known as the Epistle to the Ephesians. By and by the phrase *en Ephesōi* got into one document and from that document into practically all the manuscripts and versions that have come down to us. Aleph and B here, as practically always, represent the earlier form of the text.

The theory seems to explain the textual problem and to account for the more formal and impersonal character of the Epistle. It also enables us to understand how Marcion could speak of it as the Epistle to the Laodiceans. It was our Epistle to the Ephesians without any name, which he found at Laodicea or obtained from Laodicea. Furthermore, if the original document did not contain the name of any specific church, Paul could refer to it as "the Epistle from Laodicea" (Col. 4:16). Indeed, this theory seems best to explain all the phenomena. We hold, therefore, that the Epistle to the Ephesians was originally written as an encyclical to the churches of the province Asia, which were composed chiefly of Gentiles, but included also some Jews.

3. **Occasion and Date.** Indirectly Paul considered himself the spiritual father of all the Churches in the province Asia (Acts 19:10; Col. 2:1), and they looked to him for doctrinal and practical instruction. This is seen from the fact that when a Judaic-Gnostic heresy sprang up at Colossæ Epaphras came from that city to Rome to obtain Paul's advice and help in dealing with the problem. We have already seen how Paul rose to the occasion in writing the Epistle to the Colossians and arranging for its safe transmission.

But Paul had had much opportunity for reflection in prison and he had increasingly seen the need for a fuller statement of God's program for the universe. He now also realized the danger to the other churches in the province Asia from the heresy that had gained such a foothold at Colossæ. Inasmuch as Tychicus and Onesimus had already been deputed to bear the Epistle to the Colossians and the Epistle to Philemon to Asia, and inasmuch as the various churches of that area had much the same need, he decided to write an encyclical letter and send it along with Tychicus (Eph. 6:21,22). Thus he came to write the Epistle to the Ephesians. Paul had already before this encouraged the circulation of his Epistles among the churches. He addresses 2 Corinthians to "the church of God which is at Corinth, with all the saints that are in the whole of Achaia" (1:1), and he says to the Colossians: "And when this epistle hath been read among you, cause that it be read also in the church of the Laodiceans; and that ye also read the epistle from Laodicea" (Col. 4:16).

The fact that Paul was in bonds (3:1; 4:1; 6:20), that Tychicus is represented as the bearer of this Epistle (6:21,22), as also of the Epistles to the Colossians and to Philemon (Col. 4:7-9), and that the doctrinal content of these three Epistles is much the same, suggests that they were written at the same time. We, therefore, date this Epistle the same as the Epistle to the Colossians, namely A. D. 60.

4. **Purpose and Plan.** Goodspeed holds, as does also Jülich-er, that the purpose of Ephesians was "to serve as an intro-duction to a collection of Pauline letters."[36] He does not accept the Epistle as genuine, but holds that someone collected the Epistles of Paul at Ephesus and that this collector composed Ephesians as an introduction to the collection. He thinks that Marcion transposed Ephesians from the first place in this collection to the fifth place in his collection and Galatians from the fifth place in the original collection to the first place in his.[37] But our proof of the Pauline authorship of this Epistle makes Goodspeed's theory that the Epistle is a forgery untenable. It was written by Paul himself, whatever may be the facts as to the place that was assigned to it in the earlier collection of the Apostle's writings.

Paul's real object in the writing of this Epistle is to set forth God's purpose of summing up all things in Christ, the things in the heavens, and the things upon the earth (1:9,10). That is, Christ is predestined to be the center and administrator of all. More particularly he thinks of the Church and the part which it is to play in the carrying out of this program. After

36. *An Intro. to the New Test.*, p. 222.
37. *Op. cit.*, pp. 222-226.

the salutation (1:1,2), he sets forth the believer's blessings in Christ (1:3-14), prays for them to come to an understanding of their dignity and privileges (1:15-23), explains what they have already experienced (2:1-10), extols the new relation of the Gentiles to the Jews in Christ (2:11-22), glories in the revelation and proclamation of this union of the two in the body of Christ (3:1-9), indicates the meaning of the Church to the principalities in the heavenlies (3:10-13), and prays that they may live up to their opportunities (3:14-21).

Then he admonishes his readers to unity in life and doctrine (4:1-6), sets forth the nature and purpose of Christ's gifts to the Church (4:7-16), exhorts his readers to forsake the old life and turn to the new (4:17-5:21), applies these principles to the relations between husbands and wives (5:22-33), children and parents (6:1-4), servants and masters (6:5-9), exhorts his readers to put on the whole armor of God and do battle for Christ (6:10-20), explains the mission of Tychicus (6:21,22), and pronounces a benediction (6:23,24). These thoughts may again be represented in outline form.

Salutation, 1:1, 2.

A. The Doctrinal Section, 1:3-3:21.
(1) The Believer's Blessings in Christ, 1:3-14.
(2) The Prayer for Illumination, 1:15-23.
(3) The Power of God Manifested in our Salvation, 2:1-10.
(4) The Unification of Jew and Gentile in Christ, 2:11-22.
(5) The Revelation and Proclamation of this Union of Jew and Gentile, 3:1-9.
(6) The Meaning of the Church to the Principalities in the Heavenlies, 3:10-13.
(7) The Prayer for the Realization of all this in his Readers, 3:14-21.

B. The Practical Section, 4:1-6:20.
(1) Admonitions to Unity in Life and Doctrine, 4:1-6.
(2) Instructions Concerning the Nature and Purpose of Christ's Gifts to the Church, 4:7-16.
(3) Exhortations to Forsake the Old Life and Turn to the New, 4:17-5:21.

(4) Application of these Principles to Various Special Rela
tionships, 5:22-6:9.

(5) Admonitions to Put on the Whole Armor of God, 6:10-20.

(6) Explanation of the Mission of Tychicus, 6:21, 22

Benediction, 6:23, 24.

---

4. THE EPISTLE TO THE PHILIPPIANS

The Epistle to the Philippians is a letter, rather than a
treatise, and it is a letter full of tender affection and unfeigned
joy. It is addressed to the first church that Paul founded in
Europe. This church was in a sense his best-loved church, for
it entered more sympathetically into his sufferings and needs
than any other church. The Church at Thessalonica also held
a large place in Paul's affections, but the ties between him and
the Philippian Church were even closer than that. He more
highly commends the Philippian Church and utters no mis-
givings as to their loyalty to him. He looks upon the members
of this church as his personal friends and writes to them with
a feeling of great joy. Let us turn to the study of this gracious
letter.

1. **Attestation and Authorship.** The genuineness of this
Epistle is now generally recognized, but some express doubts
as to its unity. The external evidence for it is strong. Ignatius
alludes to 4:13 in his *Epistle to the Smyrneans* (ch. iv) and to
3:15 in the same *Epistle* (ch. xi). Clement of Rome seems to
use 1:27 in his *Epistle to Corinth* (ch. xxi) and 4:15 in the
same *Epistle* (ch. xlvii). *The Epistle of Diognetus* seems to
allude to 3:20 (ch. v). Polycarp admonishes the Philippians
to study carefully the letters that Paul had written to them.[38]
He has echoes of 2:17 and 4:10 in this *Epistle* (ch. i), of 2:10
and 3:21 (ch. ii), and of 2:16 (ch. ix), etc. *The Epistle of the
Churches of Vienne and Lyons* makes unequivocal use of the
language of Philippians.[39] Irenæus cites 4:18 in his work
Against Heresies (IV.xviii.4), ascribing the statement to Paul
in his Epistle to the Philippians. Clement of Alexandria and
Tertullian frequently cite it. It was in Marcion's Canon, in the

---

38. *Epistle to the Philippians,* ch. iii.
39. Eusebius, *H. E.,* V. ii.

Muratorian Canon, and in the Old Latin and the Old Syriac versions.

The internal evidence is equally convincing. The writer calls himself Paul (1:1). The historical details, the language and style, and the tone of the letter, all point to Paul as the author. Kennedy says: "Perhaps no Pauline epistle bears more conclusively the stamp of authenticity. There is an artlessness, a delicacy of feeling, a frank outpouring of the heart which could not be simulated."[40] McGiffert says: "There is nothing in the epistle which need cause doubt as to its genuineness."[41]

Yet Baur and some others have cast doubt upon it. Four reasons for this have been brought forward: (1) Traces of imitation in the Epistle, (2) ecclesiastical anachronisms, (3) echoes of Gnostic ideas, and (4) doctrinal differences from the recognized Epistles of Paul. But the language of the Epistle is not only genuinely Pauline, but has a warmth, frankness, and artlessness about it that could not be imitated. The reference to "bishops and deacons" (1:1) is not strange in the light of the fact that Paul appointed "elders" in the Churches of Galatia on his first tour (Acts 14:21-23). Besides, Paul had used the term "bishops" of the Ephesian elders at Miletus some time before this (Acts 20:28); and he may have used the word "deacon" in the sense of Rom. 12:7. Why should anyone have difficulty with Paul's conception of Christ in Phil. 2:5-11 if he accepts Col. 1:13-19 as a genuinely Pauline statement? And the alleged doctrinal differences between Philippians and the other Pauline Epistles are purely imaginary.

More recently the unity of the Epistle has been questioned. It is said that it consists of two letters, one (1:1-3:1; 4:21-23) being addressed to the Church in general, the other (3:2-4:20), to the more prominent members of it. Some find the division between the two letters in another place. All these critics agree that Paul can hardly have turned abruptly from a grateful and admonitory tone in 1:1-3:1, to a sharp combative one at 3:2 ff. From this point on he speaks out boldly against the Judaizers, as in Galatians, and laments that they are libertines as well as false teachers. Those who would thus partition the Epistle

---

40. *Expos. Greek Test.*, III, 407.
41. *Apostolic Age*, p. 393.

yet hold that Paul wrote both these letters to the Philippians
and that they were later joined together. A little color is lent
to this view by the fact that Polycarp reminds the Philippians
of the "letters" which Paul wrote them.[42] But Polycarp may
have used the plural for the one letter, or Paul may have
written another letter to the Philippians that is now lost, or
Polycarp may have included the Epistles to the Thessalonians
in his statement as being also to the Philippians. If, as we
believe, Paul could change his language abruptly in writing
2 Cor. 10-13, we see no reason why he could not do so also in
writing to the Philippians.

2. **Background and Destination.** Paul had founded the
Philippian Church on his second missionary journey (Acts
16:9-40). A vision that he had at Troas induced him, with
Silas, Timothy, and Luke (who joined the party at Troas),
to cross over into Europe and to make his way to the city of
Philippi. There was apparently no synagogue in the city, for
on the Sabbath he and his party had to resort to the river-side
for prayer. Lydia, a seller of purple from the city of Thyatira,
a worshipper, was converted and baptized with her household.
One day Paul cast out a spirit of divination from a slave-girl.
This caused her masters to seize on Paul and Silas and drag
them to the rulers, who had them beaten and cast into the
inner prison. But God miraculously delivered them that night
and used them to the conversion of the jailor and his house.
The next morning the magistrates led them out of prison, and
after Paul and Silas had seen Lydia and the brethren, they left
the city. Luke, however, remained at Philippi, as is evident
from the fact that from this point onward he uses the third
person in speaking of the party. However, on Paul's return
trip to Macedonia on the third journey he rejoined the party
(Acts 20:5,6). Timothy probably also tarried at Philippi a
while longer.

Since there was apparently no synagogue at Philippi we may
conclude that Judaism had not gained a firm foothold in that
city. The people seemingly looked upon the Jews with con-
tempt (Acts 16:20). The first converts consisted of Lydia, a

---

42. *Epistle to the Philippians,* ch. iii.

proselyte, and her household, the slave-girl whom Paul delivered from an evil spirit, and the jailor, no doubt a pure heathen, and his household. There were also other "brethren" in the church at this place (Acts 16:40). Two other women members are mentioned in the Epistle (4:2). We may conclude that the membership consisted almost exclusively of Gentiles. If there were any Jewish Christians in the Church, they had not yet made themselves obnoxious by stressing the principles of Judaism. There appears to have been much unity in the Church and undivided loyalty to Paul. Twice it had sent a contribution while he was at Thessalonica (Phil. 4:15,16). This was a privilege Paul would not grant the Corinthian Church (2 Cor. 11:7-12). It appears as if Philippi also sent him a gift at Corinth (Acts 18:5; 2 Cor. 11:8,9). This is the Church to which the Epistle before us is directed.

3. **Occasion and Date.** In Paul's day letters were written to people at a distance when opportunity presented itself to forward them to their destination. Epaphroditus was about to return to Philippi (2:28). He had brought Paul a gift and possibly also a letter from the Philippian Church (4:10-14,17, 18). Notice some possible intimations that Paul is replying to a letter at 1:12; 1:19; 1:25 f.; 2:26; 3:2; 4:10-13. But whether or not he had recently received a letter from them, we know that he had received a generous gift from them. Since Epaphroditus was about to go back to Philippi, Paul embraced the opportunity to send with him this warm expression of gratitude and fervent admonition to steadfastness and humility.

Lightfoot and some others put Philippians next to Romans, because of the similarity of thought in the two Epistles. They consequently hold that it is the earliest of the epistles of the first Roman Imprisonment. But several things militate against this view. In the first place, the similarity between the two epistles is not very great, — not nearly as great as that between Galatians and Romans on the one hand or as that between Colossians and Ephesians on the other hand. There are, besides, some marked resemblances between it and Colossians. Certainly, this argument does not have much weight in this case.

In the second place, the Epistle was manifestly written from Rome, as is indicated by 1:13; 4:22, not from Cæsarea. Note the differences in Paul's situation in the two imprisonments (Phil. 1:19-29; Acts 23:23-26:32). And it must have been written near the end of the two whole years in Rome (Acts 28:30,31). Considerable preaching had already been done in that city since Paul's arrival (1:12-18). Furthermore, his case is on the verge of a final decision (1:12,13,23-26). This could not have been the case in the early months of his imprisonment in that city. Then also, considerable time was needed for the events to transpire that lie between the Apostle's arrival at Rome and the writing of the Epistle. (1) News of Paul's arrival had to travel to Philippi; (2) Epaphroditus had to come from Philippi; (3) the news of his illness at Rome had to get back to Philippi; and (4) the news of their concern for Epaphroditus had to get back to Rome. Lightfoot's theory does not allow sufficient time for all these things to transpire. And finally, Luke and Aristarchus went to Rome with Paul (Acts 27:1,2). They both send greetings to the Colossian Church (Col. 4:10,14); but neither of them does so to the Philippian Church. This must mean that they were no longer with Paul when he wrote Philippians; for it would be very strange for Luke not to send greetings to a church that knew him so well, if he had been with Paul at that time.

We hold, then, that Philippians is the last of the four so-called Prison Epistles. If the first three of these epistles were written in A. D. 60, Philippians must have been written toward the close of the year 61. This is also the view of Turner[43] and of Kennedy.[44]

4. **Purpose and Plan.** As has already been said, Paul wrote this Epistle primarily to express his gratitude for the gift which the Philippians had sent him and to admonish them to steadfastness and humility. But there are also other purposes discernible. We gather the following from the contents of the Epistle: He wrote (1) to express his appreciation of their fellowship, confidence in their progress, and ambition for them (1:3-11); (2) to report on his circumstances, hopes, and fears (1:12-26); (3) to exhort them to unity, humility, and consis-

---

43. "Chronology of the New Test.," Hastings' *Bible Dictionary.*
44. *Expos. Greek Test.*, III, 406 f.

tency (1:27-2:18); (4) to inform them of his purpose to send Timothy and Epaphroditus to them (2:19-30); (5) to warn them against the Judaizers (3:1-14) and against antinomianism (3:15-4:1); (6) to appeal for the reconciliation of Euodia and Syntyche (4:2,3); (7) to admonish them to joyfulness, prayerfulness, and the pursuit of all that is good (4:4-9); (8) to express his gratitude for their recent gift (4:10-20); and (9) to send greetings (4:21-23).

It is difficult to arrange these ideas in outline form. This is, no doubt, due to the fact that Philippians is so definitely a letter. We may, however, suggest the following outline.

Salutation, 1:1,2.

A. The Thanksgiving and Prayer, 1:3-11.
  (1) Fellowship, 3-5.
  (2) Confidence, 6-8.
  (3) Ambition, 9-11.

B. The Apostle's Personal Circumstances, 1:12-26.
  (1) The Progress of the Gospel in Rome, 12-14.
  (2) The Rivalry and Zeal among the Preachers, 15-18.
  (3) His own Hopes and Fears, 19-26.

C. The Exhortation to Fulfil Various Duties, 1:27-2:18.
  (1) To Unity, 1:27-2:4.
  (2) To Humility, 2:5-11.
  (3) To Consistency, 2:12-18.

D. The Apostle's Plan for the Future, 2:19-30.
  (1) To Send Timothy Soon, 19-24.
  (2) To Send Epaphroditus At Once, 25-30.

E. The Warnings Against Judaism and Antinomianism, 3:1-4:1.
  (1) Against Judaism, 3:1-14.
  (2) Against Antinomianism, 3:15-4:1.

F. The Appeal for the Reconciliation of Euodia and Syntyche. 4:2,3.

G. The Exhortations to Follow His Example, 4:4-9.
  (1) In Rejoicing, 4.
  (2) In Prayerfulness, 5-7.
  (3) In the Pursuit of All Good, 8,9.

H. The Acknowledgement of the Gift They Had Sent, 4:10-20.
  Salutation and Benediction, 4:21-23.

Chapter XI

THE PAULINE EPISTLES
The Fourth Group

THE Fourth Group of the Pauline Epistles, 1 Timothy, Titus, and 2 Timothy, is also known as the Pastoral Epistles. Regarded as mere personal letters, they were at first separated from the epistles to the Churches and classed with Philemon. But soon it was seen that they had a bearing on Church life, while Philemon was strictly private. It was in the 18th century that they were first called "Pastoral Epistles," and this title has been generally applied to them since that time. Lock says: "This title well describes them, though in rather different degrees: 1 Timothy is entirely pastoral and perhaps intended to be of universal application; Titus is mainly pastoral, but also a letter of commendation and a letter of recall; 2 Timothy is mainly personal, a letter of recall, and only incidentally pastoral; yet all may be for many purposes treated as a unity."[1]

We may do this particularly in regard to their *attestation and authorship*. Since they are so closely connected in thought and style they are usually either all accepted or all rejected. With few exceptions, they were accepted as genuine by all, Christians and non-Christians, until Schmidt in 1804 denied the genuineness of 1 Timothy. The exceptions are Marcion,[2] who denied the Pauline authorship of all three, and Tatian,[3] who denied that of the two Timothys only. Tertullian, Clement of Alexandria, and Jerome, assert that this was due to their dislike of the teachings of these books (see below). Schleiermacher followed Schmidt in rejecting 1 Timothy; but it was soon seen that the same arguments which Schleiermacher had used against 1 Timothy would also apply against the other two.

---

1. *Comm. on the Pastoral Epistles*, p. xiii.
2. Tertullian, *Against Marcion*, V. xxi.
3. Jerome, *Prologue to Titus*.

Accordingly, first Eichhorn and then others rejected all three. Let us examine the external evidence more in detail. Falconer says: "While the witness of the earliest non-canonical writers is not so strong for the Pastorals as for Romans and Corinthians, it compares favorably with that for Galatians and Philippians, and is much better than that for 1 and 2 Thessalonians. The fact that they were addressed not to churches but to private persons may account for the silence."[4]

Clement of Rome, in his *Epistle to the Corinthians,* alludes to Tit. 3:1 (ch. ii), to Tit. 2:10 (ch. xxvi), and to 2 Tim. 1:3 (ch. xlv). Ignatius has a likely reference to 1 Tim. 6:1,2,[5] to 2 Tim. 2:4,[6] and to Tit. 1:14; 3:9.[7] Polycarp uses the language of 1 Tim. 6:7,10,[8] and of 2 Tim. 4:10.[9] Knowling says: "Harnack lays stress upon the fact that Polycarp not only knows the Pastoral Epistles himself, but presupposes that his readers know them; and whilst in some cases he thinks that it may be urged that Polycarp may be merely referring to some commonplace saying, or to some common basis in his special appeal to his converts, yet in ch. v of Polycarp's Epistle, 2 Tim. 2:12 is too plainly cited to admit of any such explanation."[10]

The Epistle of Barnabas seems to allude to 2 Tim. 4:1 (ch. vii) and to 1 Tim. 3:16 (ch. xii). *The Epistle to Diognetus* has a possible reminiscence of Tit. 3:4 (ch. ix) and of 1 Tim. 3:16 (ch. xi). Justin Martyr seems to use a phrase from Tit. 3:4[11] and another from 2 Tim. 4:1.[12] Athenagoras speaks of a "light unapproachable," reminding us of 1 Tim. 6:16,[13] and alludes to 1 Tim. 2:2.[14] Theophilus uses a phrase from Tit. 3:5[15] and another from 1 Tim. 2:2.[16]

Clement of Alexandria quotes 1 Tim. 6:20,21 as by "the apostle," and adds: "Convicted by this utterance, the heretics reject the Epistles to Timothy."[17] He refers to 1 Tim. 4:1,3 in connection with his rebuke of those who despise marriage,

4. *Dict. of the Apostolic Church, s. v.,* "The Pastoral Epistles," II, 592.
5. *Epistle to Polycarp,* ch. iv.
6. *Ib.,* ch. vi.
7. *Magnesians,* ch. viii.
8. *Epistle to the Philippians,* ch. iv.
9. *Ib.,* ch. ix.
10. *The Testimony of St. Paul to Christ,* p. 126.
11. *Dial. with Trypho,* ch. xlvii.
12. *Ib.,* ch. cxviii.
13. *A Plea for the Christians,* ch. xvi.
14. *Ib.,* ch. xxxvii.
15. *To Autolycus,* II. xvi.
16. *Ib.,* III. xiv.
17. *Stromata,* II. xi.

declaring this to be the statement of Paul.[18] Tertullian cites 1 Tim. 6:20; 2 Tim. 1:14; 1 Tim. 1:18; 6:13, and says these are the statements of Paul.[19] He also quotes Tit. 3:10,11, and says these are the words of Paul addressed to Titus.[20] Irenæus begins his Preface with Paul's statement in 1 Tim. 1:4.[21] He also cites 1 Tim. 6:20,[22] and many other passages from the Pastorals. These books were in the Muratorian Canon, the Old Latin and the Old Syriac. White says: "They are included in all manuscripts, versions, and lists of the Pauline Epistles without exception, and in the same order (i. e., 1 Tim., 2 Tim., Tit.)"[23] From that time on they were received by all until the time of Schmidt (1804).

The internal evidence sustains the external evidence. In each of these Epistles the writer calls himself Paul (1 Tim. 1:1; 2 Tim. 1:1; Tit. 1:1). Harrison denies their genuineness, but, like so many, thinks the author was "not consciously deceiving anybody," and that his readers probably knew that the epistles were forgeries.[24] But with Simpson: "We cherish a loftier estimate of the ethical standard of primitive Christianity than that. . . . Such sanctimonious knaveries are the antipole of the code of veracity taught by Christ and His apostles, with its drastic disavowal of all jesuitical artifices."[25] But let us look at the proof of their genuineness.

In the Epistles of Timothy there are a good many personal references. Who but Paul could call himself an "insolent" person (1 Tim. 1:13), or the "chief" of sinners (1 Tim. 1:15)? The writer has the Pauline sense of the divine calling and appointment (1 Tim. 2:7; 2 Tim. 1:11); he displays the same Pauline conception of the dependence of character on doctrine as is found in the recognized Epistles of Paul; he uses the same practical wisdom as is seen in them. Timothy is represented as young, timid, physically weak, in need of self-discipline and encouragement. 2 Timothy has twenty-three personal

---

18. *Ib.*, III. vi.
19. *On Prescription Against Heretics*, ch. xxv.
20. *Ib.*, ch. vi.
21. Preface to *Against Heresies*, Book I.
22. *Ib.*, II. xiv. 7.
23. *Expos. Greek Testament*, IV, 76.
24. *The Problem of the Pastoral Epistles*, p. 12.
25. "The Authenticity and Authorship of the Pastoral Epistles," *The Evangelical Quarterly*, Vol. XII, No. 4 (Oct. 15, 1940), p. 295.

allusions. A *falsarius* would be careful not to compromise himself by too many specific particulars and the mentions of too many persons by name. The writer preserves the Pauline combination of affection and authority in the Timothean letters. In Titus we have the same display of affection and authority. The writer uses the term "Savior" six times in Titus; this also is a Pauline trait. The quotation from Epimenides (Tit. 1:12) is in the manner of Paul's style. The doctrinal viewpoint is also distinctly Pauline. He has the same conception of grace, redemption through the death of Christ, the purpose of the law, the Scriptures, the need of practical godliness, the universality of Christ's provision against sin, etc., as we find in the well recognized Epistles of Paul. His stress upon church organization and discipline is also genuinely Pauline.

But various objections to the genuineness of these Epistles have been brought forward in recent times. They are all based on internal evidence and broadly fall into three classes: Chronological, linguistic, and ecclesiastical. Let us look at these more carefully.

(1) The Chronological Objections. It is assumed that Paul was imprisoned at Rome but once, and that therefore, since the Pastorals cannot be fitted into the period of the Acts, these Epistles are not genuine. But the third group of Paul's Epistles distinctly favors the supposition that Paul was released after the two years (Acts 28:30, 31). Compare Philemon 22 and Phil. 1:25 with the tone of 2 Tim. 4:6-8. Recall also Paul's purpose to visit Spain (Rom. 15:24, 28). Zahn asks: "How could Paul say that he had finished his course if he had remained continuously in Rome, where he is now about to be executed! If Paul wrote both Rom. 15 and 2 Tim. 4, then from 2 Tim. 4:7 it may be certainly concluded that Paul regained his liberty as he expected when he wrote Philippians, and visited, among other places, Spain."[26]

These internal evidences are corroborated by tradition. Clement of Rome says of Paul: "After preaching both in the east and west, he gained the illustrious reputation due to his faith, having taught righteousness to the whole world, and come to

---

26. *Intro. to the New Test.*, II, 10.

the extreme limit of the west, and suffered martyrdom under the prefects."[27] Ramsay, Mayor, and Zahn confidently infer from Clement's statements that Paul paid a visit to Spain. That presupposes his acquittal, which was not unlikely before A. D. 64. The Muratorian Canon also refers to Paul's visit to Spain. It says: "Luke compiled for 'most excellent Theophilus' what things were done in detail in his presence, as he plainly shows by omitting both the death of Peter and also the departure of Paul from the city, when he departed for Spain." And, finally, Eusebius expressed the belief of the early Church. He says: "Paul is said, after having defended himself to have set forth again upon the ministry of preaching, and to have entered the same city a second time, and to have there ended his life by martyrdom. Whilst then a prisoner, he wrote the Second Epistle to Timothy, in which he both mentions his first defence, and his impending death."[28] There is no contrary tradition; nor is it easy to see what could have been gained by the invention of this one.

But Moffatt and others have sought to identify Clement's "limit of the west" with Rome. Yet Rome was not on the circumference of the Empire, but at its center. It is difficult to believe that Clement, a native of Rome, writing from Rome, would speak of the imperial city as the West or the "limit of the west." From all these things we gather that Paul was set free after some two years of imprisonment and that he engaged in further missionary activity. During this time he visited not only the churches he had founded, but also paid a visit to Spain. During this time also he wrote 1 Timothy and Titus; and from his second imprisonment at Rome he wrote 2 Timothy.

(2) Linguistic Objections. The linguistic peculiarities of the Pastorals is considered one of the strongest evidences against the genuineness of these Epistles. Harrison says there are 175 *hapax legomena* in the Pastorals: 1 Timothy has 96, 2 Timothy 60, and Titus 43.[29] This is about twice as many as in any other of Paul's Epistles. We have no intention to minimize

---

27. *Epistle to the Corinthians*, ch. v.
28. *H. E.*, II. xxii.
29. *The Problem of the Pastoral Epistles*, p. 20.

the problem presented by this phenomenon, but believe there is a rational and satisfactory solution to it.

White calls attention to the fact that though the early Greek critics commented on the "un-Pauline" style of Hebrews, they did not do the same on the supposed "un-Pauline" style of the Pastorals.[30] He also says: "Antecedently, we should not expect that an author's favorite expressions would be distributed over the pages of his book like the spots on a wall-paper pattern."[31] We would ask, Would a plagiarist deviate so far from his models? For all admit that the writer was a devout admirer of Paul who sank his own personality in the greater personality of Paul.[32]

But, to deal with the problem more directly, the phenomenon presented by the vocabulary has again and again been shown to be no clue to the authorship of a literary composition. Shaw refers to the studies of Workman and Masson to substantiate this point. Workman, writing for the *Expository Times* (VII, 418), says that the number of unusual words in an author may vary as 3 to 1, and shows that "the proportion in Shakespeare varies from 3.4 to 10.4 per page."[33] Masson claims that "in *L'Allegro* Milton shows only 10 per cent. of non-Saxon words; in *Il Penseroso,* he shows 17 per cent.; and in *Paradise Lost,* in Book VI, 20 per cent., and in other places even 30" (*ib.*) We would not insist that Shakespeare's shorter writings must have a certain percentage of the words of any one of his plays; how much less can we insist that the Pastoral Epistles, which cover only about seventeen pages out of a total of 128 for all of Paul's Epistles in the writer's Westcott and Hort's New Testament, must have a certain percentage of the words in the rest of his Epistles. Style and vocabulary are primarily functions of the topic handled. In the Pastorals Paul deals with things pertaining to church organization and certain heretical tendencies. He needs new terms to express these ideas. It is safe to say, that in spite of the unusual terms, the old staple ones are also in evidence. This writers like Moffatt, Peake, and Deissmann admit, although they ascribe it to fragmentary

---

30. *Op. cit.,* p. 63.
31. *Ib.,* p. 68.
32. See Moffatt, *op. cit.,* p. 414.
33. *The Pauline Epistles,* p. 438.

notes that had come down from Paul and pure imitation. But we have shown that this hypothesis is superfluous. It is also to be remembered that Paul is now an old man, not so much in years as in mind. He had lived such a strenuous life and had suffered so much, that he shows it in his tamer style and simpler syntax. Thus, we believe, the linguistic factors, while presenting somewhat of a problem, do not prove the spuriousness of the Pastoral Epistles.

(3) Ecclesiastical Objections. It is said that the Pastorals imply too advanced a stage of Church organization for Paul's day. But already on his first missionary journey Paul ordained elders in every city (Acts 14:23); in Ephesians he speaks of the appointment of "pastors and teachers" (4:11); and in Philippians he addresses the Church, "with the bishops and deacons" (1:1). Nor are Timothy and Titus invested with episcopal powers of appointment. The organizations are simple; the terms "presbyters" and "bishops" are used interchangeably (Tit. 1:5, 7). There is not a vestige of second century sacerdotalism in evidence in any of these Epistles.

Some have said that the Pastorals have a lower theology than the known Pauline theology. Moffatt, for instance, says: "No possible change of circumstances or rise of fresh problems could have made Paul thus indifferent to such cardinal truths of his gospel as the fatherhood of God, the believing man's union with Jesus Christ, the power and witness of the Spirit, the spiritual resurrection from the death of sin, the freedom from the law, and reconciliation."[34] But Simpson replies: "These criticisms are altogether wide of the mark. For doctrinal edification lies outside the immediate scope of the Pastorals; they comprise executive counsels blended with ethical. . . . Besides, the allegation contravenes the facts. Occupied as he is with practicalities rather than principles, he does not wholly drop his old battle-cries."[35]

Some also insist that the Pastorals deal with the Gnostic doctrine of a later date. But the difference between the references to Gnostic speculation in Colossians and the Pastorals is not great. Certainly 1 Tim. 6:20, 21 is not a polemic against Mar-

34. *Op. cit.*, p. 412.
35. *Op. cit.*, p. 301.

cion, as some would like to think. The term *gnosis* has come down from Aristotle and is merely filled with a new content by the errorists of Paul's day. The Apostle is still merely alluding to incipient Gnosticism, which Simpson characterizes as "an intellectual caste, professing an esoteric philosophy of religion, one of whose main tenets was the evil of matter."[36]

We hold, then, that both the external and the internal evidence sustains the traditional view that the Pastorals are genuine Epistles of Paul. We proceed now to note certain facts that are peculiar to each of the three.

---

1. THE FIRST EPISTLE TO TIMOTHY

This Epistle is undoubtedly first among the Pastorals in point of time, in spite of the theory of McGiffert, Moffatt, McNeile and others, that the order is 2 Timothy, Titus, and 1 Timothy. McNeile justifies his opinion thus: "Since 1 Timothy is the richest in doctrinal and ecclesiastical matter, and 2 Timothy contains least of these but apparently most of St. Paul's own work, it is probable that the order of writing was 2 Timothy, Titus, 1 Timothy."[37] But since we accept all three as genuine Epistles of Paul, and since the Apostle was manifestly at liberty and somewhere in the East at the time when he wrote this Epistle, whereas he was again in prison when he wrote 2 Timothy, we find ample proof that this Epistle was written first. 1 Timothy is the most truly "pastoral" of the three; it was probably intended to be of universal application. The personal and local elements are strongly marked, although some sections are also very general. Let us note several things regarding this Epistle.

1. **Background and Addressee.** Paul was tried and acquitted. The flimsy charges against him (Acts 25:14-27; 26:30-32) did not convince even a Nero of the Apostle's guilt. Certain expressed purposes of Paul in the Prison Epistles (Phil. 2:23, 24; Philemon 22) and certain references to men and places in the Pastorals (to be noted) enable us to deter-

---

36. *Op. cit.,* p. 300.
37. *Intro. to the Study of the New Test.,* p. 187.

mine his movements and activities after his release with some feeling of certainty.

From Rome he probably went to Brundisium, crossed the Adriatic, either to Apollonia or to Dyrrachium, and then took the Egnatian Road to Macedonia and Philippi. He probably did not stay long at Philippi at this time, but hastened on to Ephesus and from this as a center he visited Laodicea, Colossae, and other cities in this neighborhood. After spending the biggest part of a year in the East, he probably set out for Spain. There was constant intercourse between the East and Massilia (the modern Marseilles), and so he would have no difficulty in reaching the "limit of the west." It is thought that he remained about two years in Spain. During this time, probably, Timothy took up the work at Ephesus. It appears, however, as if somewhere on Paul's way back from Spain to Macedonia Timothy asked Paul to allow him to leave Ephesus and to travel with him once more. But this Paul did not allow (1 Tim. 1:3). Some time after this the Apostle wrote 1 Timothy to his faithful co-worker.

Timothy, converted under Paul's ministry (1 Tim. 1:2, 18) on his first missionary journey (Acts 14:6-23), became the Apostle's assistant on the second journey (Acts 16:1-3) after his ordination to the ministry (1 Tim. 4:14; 2 Tim. 1:6). He was with Paul at Troas, Philippi, Berea, and Athens. From the last place he made a trip to Thessalonica and returned to Paul at Corinth (Acts 18:5). Then we lose sight of him for about five years (Plummer). He reappears at Ephesus, on Paul's third journey, and is sent by the Apostle with Erastus to Macedonia (Acts 19:22). Paul hoped he would get to Corinth also, but it is not certain whether Timothy ever reached that city (1 Cor. 4:17; 16:10). He is with Paul again in Macedonia when Paul writes 2 Corinthians (2 Cor. 1:1, 19), and must have accompanied him to Corinth, for he sends greetings when Paul writes Romans (Rom. 16:21). He returned with Paul to Macedonia and to Asia, at least as far as Troas (Acts 20:3-6). Then we again lose sight of him for the two years of Paul's Caesarean imprisonment. We next find him at Rome, joining Paul in sending greetings to Colossae, Philemon, and Philippi. From Rome he, undoubtedly, made the trip to Philippi of which Paul speaks (Phil. 2:19-23), after which he again disappears from the record. We may, however, assume that he was with Paul in some of his further ministries in various eastern cities; but it is not likely that he accompanied the Apostle to Spain. Some time during Paul's visit to Spain he probably took up the work at Ephesus. While still at this place he received what we call The First Epistle to Timothy.

Zahn[38] notes that Timothy's position cannot be described as that of a bishop, for that was an office for life and confined to the local Church. Timothy was, instead, Paul's temporary representative in his apostolic capacity at Ephesus and the other Churches of Asia, as he had earlier been at Thessalonica (1 Thess. 3:1-8) and Philippi (Phil. 2:19-23). Zahn thinks also at Corinth (1 Cor. 4:17; 16:10), but to us it is a question whether he ever reached Corinth. Yet in spite of these facts, by the time of Eusebius[39] the notion that Timothy was the first bishop of Ephesus had firmly established itself.

2. **Occasion and Date.** Paul had warned the elders of Ephesus at Miletus, saying, "Grievous wolves shall enter in among you, not sparing the flock; and from among your own selves shall men arise, speaking perverse things, to draw the disciples after them" (Acts 20:29, 30). Perhaps sooner than he had expected this prophecy had been fulfilled (1 Tim. 5:15). By this time Hellenic philosophy was blended with Oriental theosophy, and Jewish superstition and Persian speculation combined with the great thirst for wisdom in Asia Minor. Hymenaeus, Alexander, and Philetus from the very bosom of the Ephesian Church (1 Tim. 1:19, 20; 2 Tim. 2:17; 4:14, 15) were sowing the seeds of error. Conybeare and Howson describe the error thus: "The outward forms of superstition were ready for the vulgar multitude; the interpretation was confined to the aristocracy of knowledge, the self-styled Gnostics (1 Tim. 6:20); and we see the tendencies at work among the latter, when we learn that, like their prototypes at Corinth, they denied the future resurrection of the dead, and taught that the only true resurrection was that which took place when the

---

38. *Op cit.*, II, 34, 35, 41.
39. *H. E.*, III. iv. vi.

soul awoke from the death of ignorance to the life of knowledge."[40]

Paul was prevented by other duties from returning to Ephesus at the time; perhaps his physical condition also made it necessary for him to slow up somewhat in his work. He promised, however, that he would come soon. But fearing that he might be delayed longer than he expected, he wrote to encourage Timothy in his most difficult task and instructed him how to carry on until he did come (1 Tim. 3:14 f.; 4:13). It appears, as Zahn points out,[41] that Timothy "was endeavoring to escape from the duty enjoined upon him." He seems to have excused himself on the ground of his youth (1 Tim. 4:12), poor health (5:23), and a certain distaste for the task (4:15, 16). These things furnish the occasion for this Epistle.

It is difficult to say how long it was after his release that Paul wrote this Epistle. But since the three Pastorals have an affinity of language, similarity of thought, and likeness of error to combat they must all have been written at about the same time. If Paul was released in 61, and if we allow one year for his travels and work in the East and two years for his work in Spain, we get 64 or 65. This, then, is the date we would suggest for 1 Timothy.

3. **Purpose and Plan.** Paul seems to have had four main purposes in writing to Timothy: To encourage him to oppose the false teachers (1:3-7, 18-20; 6:3-5, 20, 21); to furnish him with these written credentials of his authorization by Paul (1:3, 4); to instruct him as to the manner in which men ought to conduct themselves in the Church (3:14, 15); and to exhort him to be diligent in the performance of all his ministerial duties (4:6-6:2). A fuller idea of Paul's purpose and plan in 1 Timothy may be gathered from the following outline of the Epistle.

Salutation, 1:1, 2.

(1) The Injunctions to Rebuke the False Teachers, 1:3-20.
(2) The Regulations for the Church, 2:1-3:13.
(3) The Central Truth of the Christian Life, 3:14-16.

---

40. *Life and Epistles of St. Paul*, p. 809.
41. *Op. cit.*, II, 29.

(4) The Warnings Against Apostasy and a False Asceticism, 4:1-5.
(5) The Prescriptions for Ministerial Conduct, Private and Public, 4:6-6:2.
(6) The Contrast Between the False and the True Teacher, 6:3-19.
(7) The Final Appeal to Faithfulness, 6:20, 21.

---

2. THE EPISTLE TO TITUS

The Epistle to Titus is somewhat simpler than the First Epistle to Timothy and deals less with the problems of organization. Although there is a good deal that is personal in this Epistle, there is more that is official. There are also two notable doctrinal pasages in Titus: 2:11-14 and 3:3-7. None of the fathers of the first two centuries were capable of writing passages like these. Farrar well asks: "Will anyone produce from Clement, or Hermas, or Justin Martyr, or Ignatius, or Polycarp, or Irenaeus—will anyone even produce from Tertullian, or Chrysostom, or Basil, or Gregory of Nyssa—any single passage comparable for terseness, insight, or mastery to either of these?"[42] Let us turn to the study of this letter to Titus.

1. **Background and Addressee.** Probably soon after Paul had written 1 Timothy he made a trip to Crete (Tit. 1:5). The Apostle's ship had touched on the island of Crete on his voyage to Rome, but contrary to his advice the vessel did not stop long at this place (Acts 27:7-13, 21). He probably had done no preaching in the island at that time. Christianity may have been introduced to Crete by the visitors to the first Christian Pentecost (Acts 2:11); but of this we cannot be sure. At any rate, Paul did not found the church in Crete on the present occasion, although he may have reorganized it. The whole tenor of the Epistle shows that it had been established long ago. Titus accompanied the Apostle to the island and remained in charge of the work there when Paul left (Tit. 1:5).

Titus is not mentioned by name in the Book of Acts. He was a Greek (Gal. 2:1-3), converted under Paul's ministry

---

42. Quoted by Hayes, in his *Paul and His Epistles*, p. 478, from Farrar, *Life of Paul*, pp. 662, 663, note.

(Tit. 1:4) from pure heathenism. He apparently lived in Syrian Antioch; at any rate, it seems as if Paul and Barnabas took him along to Jerusalem from this place (Acts 15:2). Some think that since Paul refers to him in the Epistle to the Galatians, he must have been well known to the Galatians; but that to us is not certain. For some five or six years after the Jerusalem Council there is no mention of him in the records. At the end of this time he, together with an unnamed "brother" (2 Cor. 12:18), seems to have borne our 1 Corinthians to its destination and to have organized the collection in Corinth Some time after this Paul seems to have sent him with a severe letter to Corinth (2 Cor. 2:3, 4, 9; 7:8-12). Paul eagerly awaited Titus' report as to the effect of this letter, and when, on his brief stop at Troas he did not find him there, he hastened on to Macedonia (2 Cor. 2:12, 13), where the two met and where Titus gave his report (2 Cor. 7:5-16). Then Paul wrote our 2 Corinthians and sent Titus and two brethren with it to Corinth (2 Cor. 8:16-24).

From this time on, i. e., A. D. 54 or 55, we hear nothing of Titus until after Paul's release in 61; indeed, it is not until after Paul had written 1 Timothy, in 64 or 65, that he again comes to our notice. At this time we find him on this missionary journey with Paul to the island of Crete. Paul had to leave the work in an unfinished state, and so he asked Titus to remain and organize and direct the work in the island (Tit. 1:5), as we have already said (above). But the Apostle does not want him to remain permanently in Crete; he says he will send Artemas or Tychicus to the island to take over the work, and that when one or the other of these arrives, Titus is to come to him to Nicopolis, for there he wants to winter (Tit. 3:12). We do not know whether this plan was carried out or not; but we do know that Titus was again with Paul in his second Roman imprisonment. This we gather from the fact that he went to Dalmatia from Rome, not as a deserter, but as a representative and helper of Paul (2 Tim. 4:10).

Titus, like Timothy, was not a bishop of Crete, but merely a representative of the Apostle for the time being, although Eusebius calls him "bishop of Crete."[43] He was, however, one

---

43. *H. E.*, III. iv, vi.

of Paul's very dear and most trusted friends; he calls him "my partner and my fellow-worker to you-ward" (2 Cor. 8:23). He had, apparently, a stronger personality than Timothy; witness the work he accomplished in Corinth.

2. **Occasion and Date.** Three things seem to have led the Apostle to write this Epistle: The condition of the work in Crete, Titus' need of instruction and encouragement, and the going of Zenas and Apollos to the island. Paul had begun to organize the work in the island, but was obliged to leave before the task was completed. The appearing of many false teachers, chiefly of the circumcision, stressing Jewish fables and the commandments of men, wasting their time on foolish questions, genealogies and strifes about the law, called for someone to take a strong stand for the truth. Apart from this, Titus had a more difficult task than Timothy. The latter was left in Ephesus where the work was already well organized; he was merely to organize it in the other cities of Asia. But Titus was to do the primary organizing of the work, and there seem to have been believers in every city of the island (Tit. 1:5). He, therefore, needed careful instructions to guide him in the work assigned to him and encouragement to meet the opposition of the false teachers. When, then, Zenas and Apollos planned a journey which would take them through Crete, Paul sent his faithful representative this short letter of instruction and encouragement by them (Tit. 3:13).

We do not know from what place Paul wrote this Epistle,— Macedonia, Ephesus, Nicopolis, and Corinth have been suggested. If Apollos had at this time carried out his intention to return to Corinth (1 Cor. 16:12) and Paul had also come to this city at this time, the two would, of course, meet. It would, in that case, be easy to see how Paul could send the Epistle by Zenas and Apollos. But, of course, Paul and Apollos may also have been together in some other city at this time. Inasmuch as the thought and style of this Epistle is more like 1 Timothy than 2 Timothy, we hold that it was written soon after 1 Timothy. We may, therefore, date it A. D. 65.

3. **Purpose and Plan.** Paul's purpose here is much the same as in 1 Timothy. After a somewhat extended salutation (1:1-4), he (1) urges Titus to complete the organization of the work

in Crete (1:5), (2) instructs him as to the qualifications required of elders (1:6-9), (3) insists that a strong stand be taken against the false teachers (1:10-16), (4) informs Titus how to deal with the various classes in domestic relations (2:1-10), (5) explains how such a life is made possible (2:11-15), (6) encourages the teaching of good citizenship (3:1, 2), (7) indicates why believers should live like that (3:3-8), (8) warns Titus against false teachings and teachers (3:9-11), (9) speaks of his plans for the future (3:12-14), and (10) sends greetings (3:15). We may again arrange these thoughts in outline form, thus:

Salutation, 1:1-4.

(1) The Problems of Church Organization, 1:5-9.

(2) The Character of the Cretan Heresies, 1:10-16.

(3) The Regulations Concerning Domestic Relations, 2:1-10.

(4) The Provisions for the True Christian Life, 2:11-15.

(5) The Teaching Concerning Christian Citizenship, 3:1, 2.

(6) The Reasons for Living a Godly Life, 3:3-8.

(7) The Method of Dealing with Heretics, 3:9-11.
Conclusion, 3:12-15.

---

3. THE SECOND EPISTLE TO TIMOTHY

This is undoubtedly the last of Paul's Epistles that have come down to us. It is mainly personal, only incidentally pastoral, and less doctrinal than the other two Pastoral Epistles. It is generally conceded that 2 Timothy contains most of Paul's own work by those who deny the genuineness of the Pastorals. It is an Epistle of mingled gloom and glory. The Apostle rejoices at the prospect of soon seeing the Lord Whom he so dearly loved and so earnestly served, but he is affected by the ignominy of his present condition and immediate prospects. Much more, however, is he depressed by the sense of loneliness,— his friends have forsaken him, some for worthy reasons, some for unworthy. In addition to this, he feels the serious times that await the Church in the future. Let us note the details concerning the Epistle.

1. **Background and Addressee.** Paul undoubtedly carried out his plans and proceeded to Nicopolis (Tit. 3:12). But since there are eight places that bore that name, we cannot be sure which one is meant. The prevailing opinion is that Paul went to the famous city in Epirus by that name. If this is the place, then he probably chose it for the purpose of the further evangelization of Dalmatia and Illyricum. But by this time the Neronic persecution of the Christians was in full swing, and Paul, deeming it unwise to remain any longer within easy reach of Rome, appears to have fled from Nicopolis across Macedonia to Troas. Here he was entertained by Carpus. Circumstances seem to have made it necessary for him to leave Troas suddenly; for he left his cloak, some books, and the parchments of the Old Testament Scriptures with Carpus (2 Tim. 4:13). It is impossible to reproduce with certainty the Apostle's movements during this period; all that we can do is to suggest a plausible course of events. The one thing we know is that he was now arrested and hurried to Rome for trial.

The Apostle's condition was now very different from what it was during the first Roman imprisonment. Then he was accused by the Jews of heresy and sedition; now he is persecuted by Rome and treated as a malefactor. Then he preached to all who came to him in his own hired house and a number of his associates carried on missionary activity in the city and surrounding district; now his friends can see him only with difficulty and none stood by him in court. Then he looked forward to acquittal; now he looks forward to death. It is out of this background that Paul writes 2 Timothy.

Timothy had apparently left Ephesus by this time, for Paul writes that he has sent Tychicus to that city (4:12). He seems to have been engaged in evangelistic work, either in Macedonia or in the province Asia, at the time. Troas was apparently on the way to Rome (4:13), and the fact that Paul warns Timothy against Alexander the coppersmith (4:14, 15) and sends greetings to Onesiphorus (4:19), both of whom lived at Ephesus (1 Tim. 1:20; 2 Tim. 1:16-18), seems to indicate that Paul expected him to pass through Ephesus also. If Paul's request for Timothy to come before winter implied, among other things, that he would travel by sea, then we may assume that

Timothy was somewhere in Macedonia when he received Paul's letter. But he may also have been somewhere in the province Asia and have traveled northward through Troas and Macedonia, on his way to Rome. More than this we cannot say about Timothy's whereabouts at this time.

2. **Occasion and Date.** Three things seem to have led Paul to write this Epistle: His concern for Timothy as he was confronted by the false teachers of his day; his desire for fellowship with his most trusted and faithful co-worker; and his need of the cloak, books, and parchments which he had left at Troas. Timothy was fearful and hesitant and needed now and then to be reminded of his responsibility and to have his courage re-inforced. Paul felt that he must once more admonish him to give himself wholly to his task, particularly since the false teachers were multiplying (4:3, 4). They were deceiving the people (3:13), perhaps with magical charms, as the word seems to indicate, and tickling the ears of the people with their "fables" (4:4). Some were even teaching that the resurrection was past already (2:18). Timothy must be urged to stand against these false teachers.

The other two things are of a more private nature. Paul felt lonesome. In Asia all had turned against him (1:15). This probably means merely that at the time of his arrest no one did anything to help him. How careful he is to note the one exception: Onesiphorus of Ephesus had sought him out at Rome (1:16-18)! Of those in Rome, no one stood by him in court, but all forsook him; he prays that it be not laid to their charge (4:16-18). Indeed, at the time only Luke was with him (4:9-11). He is lonely and wants to share his feelings with some one who understands. And then Paul needed his cloak in the cold damp dungeon at Rome, as also the books and the parchments (4:13). These are the things that led Paul to write this Epistle.

Paul seems to have been executed shortly before Nero's death, i. e., before June 8, A. D. 68. It is clear that 2 Timothy was written shortly before Paul's execution. We may, therefore, date this Epistle in the early autumn of 67 or the spring of 68.

3. **Purpose and Plan.** Paul undertook to relate his own experiences and expectations and to encourage and instruct Timothy. After the salutation (1:1-3), he (1) appeals for brave adherence to the Gospel (1:3-18) and for steadfastness and endurance in the work (2:1-13), (2) gives instructions concerning Timothy's personal and ministerial conduct (2:14-26), (3) warns concerning the grievous times that are coming(3:1-9), (4) urges Timothy to follow his example (3:10-13), (5) encourages him on the ground of his early training (3:14-17), (6) appeals for faithful preaching of the Word in the light of the coming apostasy and his approaching martyrdom (4:1-8), (7) expresses his longing for fellowship (4:9-18), and sends greetings (4:19-22). We may arrange these thoughts in outline form, thus:

Salutation, 1:1-3.

(1) The Appeal for Faithfulness and Endurance, 1:4-2:13.
(2) The Instructions Concerning Private and Ministerial Conduct, 2:14-26.
(3) The Warnings Concerning the Future, 3:1-9.
(4) The Reminder of Paul's Example and of Timothy's Early Training, 3:10-17.
(5) The Exhortation to Biblical Preaching in the Light of the Future, 4:1-8.
(6) The Intimations of the Apostle's Loneliness, 4:9-18.
Conclusion, 4:19-22.

Chapter XII

THE GENERAL EPISTLES
The First Group

THE seven Epistles written by James, Peter, John, and Jude
have been known as the Catholic Epistles at least as far
back at the time of Origen. The term was used in the sense of
general or universal, to distinguish them from the Pauline
Epistles which were addressed to individual churches or persons. The Second and Third Epistles of John seem to be an
exception to this rule; but they were, no doubt, included among
the Catholic Epistles as properly belonging to 1 John and as of
value to the general reader.[1] All of these, save 1 Peter and 1
John, were referred to as the *antilegomena* by Origen and
Eusebius. We shall note proof of their early existence and recognition as genuine. They were written over a period of some
forty years and have little in common, save their catholic character. In general we may say that James and 1 Peter are predominantly ethical, 2 Peter and Jude, eschatological, and the
Epistles of John, Christological and ethical. Let us turn to the
study of the individual Epistles.

---

1. THE EPISTLE OF JAMES

There is no more Jewish book in the New Testament than
the Epistle of James, not even excluding Matthew, Hebrews,
and the Apocalypse. Hayes says: "If we eliminate two or three
passages containing references to Christ, the whole epistle might
find its place just as properly in the Canon of the Old Testament as in that of the New Testament, as far as its substance
of doctrine and contents is concerned. That could not be said
of any other book in the New Testament."[2] Some have even

1. See under *The Canon of the New Testament*, above.
2. "The Epistle of James," in *Inter. Stand. Bible Ency.*

thought that it was written by a non-Christian Jew, and that it was later adapted to Christian use by the insertion of the two phrases that contain the name of Christ (1:1 and 2:1). The fact of the matter is that the Christianity of the Epistle is seen, not so much in its subject-matter, as in its spirit. It is an inter pretation of the Old Testament law and the Sermon on the Mount in the light of the Christian Gospel. Let us note the facts and problems that are connected with this Epistle.

1. **Attestation and Authorship.** It was not until the Third Council of Carthage (A. D. 397) that the Epistle of James came to be generally recognized as canonical. Eusebius classed it among the *antilegomena,* as we have seen, but yet quotes James 4:11 as Scripture.[3] The Muratorian Canon omits it. But the Epistle was probably more widely known in the first three centuries than has been supposed. The Old Syriac Version early included it. Westcott is confident of Hermas' use of James. He says: "The *Shepherd* bears the same relation to the Epistle of St. James as the Epistle of Barnabas to that to the Hebrews. The idea of a Christian Law lies at the bottom of them both: but according to St. James it is a law of liberty, centering in man's deliverance from corruption within and ceremonial without; while Hermas rather looks for its essence in the rites of the outward Church. Both St. James and Hermas insist on the necessity of works; but the one regards them as the practical expression of a personal faith, while the other finds in them an intrinsic value and recognizes the possibility of supererogatory virtue."[4] Some of the more striking resemblances of Hermas and James are: *Vision* III. ix and James 5:1-4; *Commandment* XII. v and James 4:7. There are many more remote resemblances.

More remote resemblances we find also in other early writings. Clement of Rome may allude to 3:16 in his *Epistle to the Corinthians* (ch. iii), to 4:2 (*ib.*), to 5:10 (ch. v), to 4:16 (ch. xxi), to 3:13 (ch. xxxviii). The *Epistle of Barnabas* has language resembling 1:21 (ch. i), 3:1 (ch. i), 2:5 (ch. xvi). James is frequently alluded to in the *Testaments of the Twelve Patriarchs.* Ignatius has phrases like those in 1:4 in his *Epis-*

3. *Comm. in Psalm.*
4. *On the Canon of the New Testament,* p. 180.

tle to the Smyrneans (ch. xi) and his *Epistle to Polycarp* (chs. i, ii). Polycarp may allude to 1:18, 25 in his *Epistle to the Philippians* (ch. iii), and to 1:26; 3:2 (*ib.*, ch. v). But none of these show certain dependence upon James. For a full study of the quotations and allusions in the early writings see Mayor *The Epistle of St. James*, pp. xlviii-lxviii.

Yet Origen recognized James as Scripture,[5] as did also Cyril of Jerusalem, Gregory of Nazianzus, Athanasius, Jerome, and Augustine. It thus appears that while the Epistle was long questioned at Rome and Carthage, the Church at Jerusalem and probably the Syrian churches from a very early period acknowledged it. And it is included in the catalogues of accepted books that have come down to us from Asia Minor and Egypt. Mayor says: "The difference is easily explained from the fact that the Epistle was probably written at Jerusalem and addressed to the Jews of the Eastern Dispersion; it did not profess to be written by an Apostle or to be addressed to Gentile churches, and it seemed to contradict the teaching of the great Apostle to the Gentiles."[6]

The internal evidence is stronger than the external. The Epistle harmonizes with what we know of this James from Josephus (*Ant.* XX. ix), from the Book of Acts (15:13-21; 21:17-25), and from Galatians (1:19; 2:9, 10), and with the known circumstances of the Jewish Christians in the Dispersion. The supposed opposition to Paul is purely imaginary; for when the Epistle is put into its rightful place chronologically the "opposition" completely disappears. There is no adequate reason for a forgery; for the Epistle is without much doctrinal content and a forger would far more likely have chosen the name of an outstanding Apostle than that of the more obscure name of James, the Lord's brother. A comparison with the Epistle of Clement of Rome, the Epistle of Barnabas, and the Shepherd of Hermas will convince any one of the enormous superiority of the Epistle of James to all of these.

We have already intimated that the author is James the Lord's brother; but is that really true? The New Testament mentions at least four who bore the name of James: (1) The

---

5. *Hom. in Jos.* vii. 1.
6. *Op. cit.*, p. li.

son of Zebedee (Matt. 4:21), (2) the son of Alphaeus (Matt 10:3), probably the same as the Little or the Less (Mark 15:40; John 19:25), (3) the father of Judas the Apostle, not Iscariot (Luke 6:16), and (4) the Lord's brother (Matt. 13: 55; Gal. 1:19). Which of these is the author of the Epistle? The father of Judas can be dismissed at once as being entirely unknown, except for this relation to the Apostle Judas. The son of Alphaeus, too, is not likely to be the author. He is al-most unknown, except for the mention in the lists of Apostles. The son of Zebedee is more conspicuous in the Gospels, but he, too, does not seem to have been prominent. He is usually re-ferred to as the son of Zebedee or is associated with his broth-er John. The last two were Apostles; but the author of the Epistle merely calls himself "James, a servant of God and of the Lord Jesus Christ" (1:1). The hesitation of some to accept the Epistle would be strange, if it had been reputed to be of Apostolic authorship. Furthermore, James the son of Zebedee was martyred under Herod Agrippa I, not later than the spring of A. D. 44; and that an apostle would write an encyclical let-ter before this date is so unlikely that it does not need to be con-sidered. We take it, then, that the author of this Epistle was James the Lord's brother.

This James was really the Lord's half-brother: the two had the same mother, but not the same father (Matt. 13:55; Mark 6:3). He was probably among those who sought an interview with Jesus somewhere in Galilee (Matt. 12:46); he probably also went with Jesus to Capernaum (John 2:12), and later joined in the attempt to persuade Him to go to Judaea for the Feast of Tabernacles (John 7:3). He himself went up to the Feast, but he was an unbeliever at that time (John 7:5, 10). After the crucifixion he apparently remained with his mother in Jerusalem. We are told that after the resurrection Christ ap-peared to James also (1 Cor. 15:7). This may have led him to believe in Jesus, for he is next seen among the Lord's brethren, waiting for the coming of the Holy Spirit (Acts 1:14). He may have taken part in the selection of Matthias to take the place of Judas (Acts 1:15-25).

About A. D. 35 or 36 this James was still in Jerusalem and had a visit from Paul when the latter returned from his three

years' stay in Damascus and Arabia (Gal. 1:18, 19; cf. Acts
9:26). By the time that Peter was imprisoned in Jerusalem,
i. e., about A. D. 44, James seems to have been a leader in Jerusalem (Acts 12:17). He apparently presided at the Jerusalem
Council (Acts 15:13, 19; Gal. 2:1, 9, 10). Eusebius says:
"Clement in the sixth book of his Hypotyposes writes thus:
'For they say that Peter and James and John after the ascension of our Savior, as if also preferred by our Lord, strove not
after honor, but chose James the Just bishop of Jerusalem'."[7]
But we cannot be certain that this is a true tradition.

Later some Jews, professing Christians, came to Antioch in
Syria in the interests of a Judaistic Gospel; they represented
themselves as coming "from James" (Gal. 2:12). This does
not, however, mean that James had sent them, or even that he
approved of their mission. The only other time that he is mentioned in the New Testament is in connection with Paul's return to him at Jerusalem when he presented the Gentile offering (Acts 21:18-25). Josephus tells us that James was stoned
by order of Ananus the high priest,[8] but Eusebius says that
he was thrust down from the pinnacle of the temple and then
beaten to death with a club.[9] Hegesippus combines all these
three things in his account. Hayes says: "There would seem
to have been a widespread conviction among both the Christians and the Jews that the afflictions which fell upon the holy
city and the chosen people in the following years were in part
a visitation because of the great crime of the murder of this
just man."[10] It is easy to see how a man like this would write
an Epistle so Jewish and so insistent on practical morality.

2. **Background and Destination.** At various times in the
history of Israel some or all of the tribes were transplanted to
other countries by their heathen captors. In addition to this
many Jews in pursuit of commerce sought homes in foreign
lands. In the Book of Acts there is scarcely a place mentioned
that does not have at least one synagogue. Josephus makes
Strabo say: "Now these Jews are already gotten into all cities,
and it is hard to find a place in the habitable earth that hath

---

7. *H. E.*, II. i.
8. *Ant.*, XX. ix.
9. *H. E.*, II. xxiii.
10. "The Epistle of James," in the *Inter. Stand. Bible Ency.*

not admitted this tribe of men, and is not possessed by it."[11] It is interesting that there were present on the day of Pentecost: "Parthians and Medes and Elamites, and the dwellers in Mesopotamia, in Judaea and Cappadocia, in Pontus and Asia, in Phrygia and Pamphylia, in Egypt and the parts of Libya about Cyrene, and sojourners from Rome, both Jews and proselytes. Cretans and Arabians" (Acts 2:9-11). And those who disputed with Stephen in the synagogue are said to have been freedmen of Cyrene, Alexandria, Cilicia, and Asia (Acts 6:9).

Now some of these, no doubt, carried the Gospel back to their home country. In addition to this we know that the Glad Tidings were early brought to Damascus (Acts 9:2, 10, 14, 19, 25), Cyprus (Acts 4:36, 37; 11:19), Antioch (Acts 11:19, 20), Phoenicia (Acts 11:19), and, it may be, Babylon (1 Pet. 5:13), by Christian missionaries. It may, therefore, be assumed that the Word was preached in many other countries also. Surely, the Apostles did many things to spread the message outside of the few that are related in the Acts. James probably intended his Epistle for all the Christian Jews wherever they were, and yet he may have aimed particularly at the Eastern Dispersion. This is Mayor's view, who shows that Peter, who addresses the Diaspora in Asia Minor, probably did so because the believers in that section would be less likely to know the Epistle of James. Here we must let the matter rest.

3. **Occasion and Date.** The Epistle seems to have been occasioned by the outward experiences, spiritual state, and doctrinal misconceptions of the Jewish Christians in the Dispersion These Christians were surrounded by various kinds of trials, such as persecutions from their own countrymen, unjust treatment by the rich, and physical afflictions. Their spiritual state was low. They took the wrong attitude toward God and His gifts; they indulged in unbridled speech; strifes and factions were among them; and they had a worldly spirit. They also labored under great doctrinal misconceptions. Many acted as if knowing the truth was sufficient and as if faith without works met all the requirements. These conditions among his

---

11. *Ant.,* XIV. vii.

fellow Jewish believers led the strict and righteous James to write this Epistle.

The prevailing view today favors an early date. There is no reference to the fall of Jerusalem in the Epistle, which means that it must have been written before that event occurred or a considerable time after it. If James wrote the Epistle, then we must date it before A. D. 62 or 63, for according to Josephus[12] that was the time when he was killed. The internal evidence points to a date still earlier than this. First, the Church order and discipline of the Epistle are very simple. There is no mention of "bishop" or "deacon"; the leaders are called "teachers" and "elders." There was apparently no very close organization, for various members of the congregation put themselves forward as teachers. The believers still met in the "synagogue," one, of course, in which the Christians had control. All this points to a very early period in the history of the Church.

Secondly, the doctrinal character of the Epistle points in the same direction. The question of the admission of the Gentiles seems not yet to have come to the fore. This indicates that the Epistle must have been written before the Jerusalem Council (A.D. 48 or 49), for that was the great question at that meeting. There is no contradiction between James and Paul, but surely James would have avoided the *apparent* contradiction between himself and the Apostle to the Gentiles (cf. James 2:14-26; Gal. 3:6-14; Rom. 3:19, 20, 28; 4:1-5), if he had written after the Jerusalem Council over which he presided (Acts 15:13-21; Gal. 2:7-10). There is, in fact, a total silence in the Epistle with regard to the non-Jewish world and to men in the Church of Gentile birth. Instead, there is a Judaic tone throughout. Notice the emphasis on the Law. True, it is the "royal law" and the "law of liberty," but it is yet the Law. In accord with this is James' emphasis on works. But Paul and James do not contradict each other; for Paul believes in works in their rightful place just as much as James (see Rom. 2:6-10; 2 Cor. 9:8; Eph. 2:10; 2 Thess. 2:17; 1 Tim. 6:18; Titus 3:8); and James believes in saving faith just as well as Paul

---

12. *Ant.*, XX. ix. 1.

(see 2:1, 5, 22-24). Notice also his emphasis on faith in connection with prayer (1:3, 6; 5:15).

On the other hand, there are indications in the Epistle that his readers had been Christians for some time. They are not recent converts; they are established in a certain type of service and worship. The Epistle must have been written after the stoning of Stephen, when the persecutions that followed led to a more energetic evangelizing of the areas outside of Palestine. Perhaps it is safe to say that James was written somewhere between A.D. 45 and 48.

4. Purpose and Plan. The author undertakes to meet the needs of his fellow Jewish Christians in the Dispersion. After a brief salutation (1:1), (1) he admonishes his readers to take a right attitude towards trials and temptations (1:2-18) and (2) exhorts them to receive the Word properly (1:19-27); (3) he forbids them to show partiality to others (2:1-13); (4) he demonstrates to them the insufficiency of faith without works (2:14-26); (5) he warns them against the sins of the tongue (3:1-12); (6) he sets forth the nature of true and false wisdom (3:13-18); (7) he rebukes them for quarrelsomeness, worldliness, and pride (4:1-10); (8) he instructs them to be considerate toward their brethren (4:11, 12); (9) he upbraids them for their attitude and conduct in their business life (4:13-5:6); (10) he exhorts them to patient endurance of the ills of life (5:7-12); (11) he tells them what to do in times of affliction (5:13-18); and (12) he points out the importance of restoring an erring brother (5:19, 20).

James wants each of his readers to become a "perfect man" (3:2). Bearing this ideal in mind, we may outline the Epistle as follows:

Salutation, 1:1

(1) In His Attitude Toward Trials and Temptations, 1:2-18
(2) In His Reception of the Word, 1:19-27.
(3) In His Impartiality Towards Others, 2:1-13.
(4) In His Credentials of Faith, 2:14-26.
(5) In His Use of the Tongue, 3:1-12.
(6) In His Attitude Toward True Wisdom, 3:13-18.

(7) In His Amiableness, Unworldliness, and Humility, 4:
1-10.

(8) In His Considerateness of His Fellows, 4:11, 12.

(9) In His Business Affairs, 4:13-5:6.

(10) In His Patience and Endurance, 5:7-12.

(11) In His Conduct in Affliction, 5:13-18.

(12) In His Effort in Behalf of an Erring Brother, 5:19,20.

***

2. THE FIRST EPISTLE OF PETER

The First Epistle of Peter is the Epistle of hope in the midst of suffering. Some seven words for suffering occur in it. The Apostle represents suffering as in the will of God (4:19); he reminds his readers of the sufferings of Christ (1:11; 2:21, 23; 5:1) and holds Him up as an example to the believers in this respect (2:21; 4:1, 2). He admonishes them to expect suffering (4:12) and not to be troubled by it (3:14), but to bear it patiently (2:23; 3:9), yea, even to rejoice in suffering (4:13), knowing that their brethren elsewhere suffer the same things (5:9). He points out the value of sufferings (1:6, 7; 2:19, 20; 3:14; 4:14) and warns against suffering as an evil doer (2:20; 4:15). The Epistle is thus predominantly practical and not doctrinal. Let us study it more in detail.

1. **Attestation and Authorship.** This Epistle was universally recognized as a work of the Apostle Peter in the early Church. Eusebius placed it among the *homologoumena,* and no book has earlier or stronger attestation than 1 Peter. 2 Pet. 3:1 is the earliest acknowledgement of the First Epistle; for even those who deny the genuineness of that Epistle admit that it is a very early book. There are possible allusions to 1 Peter in the *Epistle of Barnabas,* Clement's *Epistle to the Corinthians,* and the *Testaments of the Twelve Patriarchs.*[13] Hermas alludes to 1:7 in *Vision* (IV. iii), to 4:15 in *Similitudes* (IX. xxviii). Polycarp quotes 1:8; 3:9; 2:11 in his *Epistle to the Philippians* (chs. i, ii, v, respectively), and other refer-

---

13. See Bigg, *A Critical and Exegetical Commentary on the Epistles of St. Peter and St. Jude,* pp. 7-9.

ences; but he nowhere mentions the author by name. Theophilus of Antioch seems to allude to 4:3 in *To Autolycus* (II. xxxiv). Irenæus is the first to quote it by name.[14] Tertullian quotes 2:20 in *Scorpiace* (ch. xii) and 4:8 (*ib.*, ch. vi). He uses language closely resembling 3:1-6 in *On Prayer* (ch. xx). Clement of Alexandria quotes freely from every chapter of the Epistle; for example, 2:11 f. in *Stromata* (III. xi) and 2:1-3 in *Instructor* (I. vi). The Epistle was in the Old Syriac, the Old Latin, and the Old Egyptian versions. Marcion rejected it, and it is not in the Muratorian Fragment; but it is found in all the catalogues of the New Testament given by Westcott in Appendix D of his book on the Canon.

The internal evidence sustains the external. Once the writer calls himself Peter (1:1). He is well acquainted with the life of Christ and with Christ's teachings. The words "gird yourselves with humility" (5:5) seem to allude to Christ's girding Himself with a towel when he washed the disciples' feet (John 13:3-5). The admonition to "feed the flock of God" (5:2) recalls Christ's word to Peter, "Feed my lambs," "tend my sheep," and "feed my sheep" (John 21:15-17). Perhaps there are reminiscences of the Lord's saying also in Peter's "If ye are reproached for the name of Christ, blessed are ye" (4:14), "casting all your anxiety upon him" (5:7), "be sober, be watchful" (5:8), etc. He claims to have been "a witness of the sufferings of Christ" (5:1); notice the force of his words in 3:18; 4:1 in view of this fact. He lingers over the Person of Christ in His sufferings (2:19-24) and admonishes his readers to remember that they are partakers of the sufferings of Christ (4:13). We may also point out the similarity of Peter's speeches in Acts and his words in the Epistle (*e. g.,* Acts 10:34 and 1 Peter 1:17; Acts 2:32-36; 10:40, 41 and 1 Peter 1:21; Acts 4:10, 11 and 1 Peter 2:7, 8, etc.). We shall see presently that there is nothing in the Epistle that is impossible in the last days of Peter's life. We find in the Epistle the same recognition of the equality of Gentile and Jewish Christians that we have in Acts. There can be no doubt, therefore, that the Epistle was written by the Apostle Peter.

---

14. *Against Heresies,* IV. ix. 2; IV. xvi. 5; V. vii. 2.

Let us briefly sketch the life of the author. Peter, also called Simon or Simeon (Acts 15:14; 2 Pet. 1:1), was born at Bethsaida (John 1:44). His father's name was Jonas (Matt. 16:17) or John (John 1:42), with whom he and his brother Andrew carried on the trade of fishermen at Capernaum, and where he afterward resided (Matt. 8:14) with his wife's mother (1 Cor. 9:5). He was brought to Christ by Andrew, and Jesus gave him the name Cephas (John 1:40-42). This was his first call; it was a call to discipleship. He had two other calls: one to constant companionship with Christ (Matt. 4:19; Luke 5:10) and another to apostleship (Matt. 10:2; Mark 3:14-16). His ardor, earnestness, and courage marked him from the first as the leader of the disciples. His name always appears first in the lists of the apostles (Matt. 10:2· Mark 3:16; Luke 6:14; Acts 1:13) and of the three in the inner circle. His life may be studied in two parts: Before and after Pentecost.

During the former period Jesus healed his mother-in-law (Matt. 8:14 ff.), gave him a great draught of fishes(Luke 5:1-11), and called him as an apostle (Matt. 10:2). When Jesus came to the disciples walking on the sea, Peter attempted likewise to walk on the sea (Matt. 14:28); he made two great confessions of Christ (John 6:68, 69; Matt. 16:13-17), witnessed the raising of Jairus' daughter (Mark 5:37) and the Transfiguration (Matt. 17:1-5), and benefitted by the miracle of the tribute money (Matt. 17:24). At the last Supper he at first objected when Christ wanted to wash his feet (John 13:1-10). He boasted of his devotion to Christ (Luke 22:31-33), but Christ predicted that he would deny Him thrice (Matt. 26:31-35). He was one of the three that were allowed to follow Christ into Gethsemane (Matt. 26:36-46); he drew the sword and cut off the ear of the high priest's servant (John 18:10-12). At the trial of Christ he denied him thrice; but he also repented genuinely (Matt. 26:56-75). He ran with John to the tomb (John 20:1-10); the angel directed the women to tell his disciples "and Peter" (Mark 16:7); the Lord appeared to him (Luke 24:34; 1 Cor. 15:5); and he was fully restored and recommissioned (John 21:15-19). No doubt he saw the

Lord ascend (Acts 1:9, 10). After that he presided at the choice of Matthias (Acts 1:15-26).

At the first Christian Pentecost he preached the sermon (2:14-41). In company with John he healed a man who was lame from birth (Acts 3:1-10); he preached another sermon (3:11-26); he and John were arrested, tried, and released (4:1-22). He dealt with Ananias and Sapphira (Acts 5:1-11), was arrested with the other apostles and miraculously released, tried, beaten, and dismissed (5:12-41). He was sent to communicate the Holy Spirit to the believers in Samaria (Acts 8:14-25). Back in Jerusalem, Paul paid him a brief visit (Gal. 1:18). After this he journeyed in various parts of Judæa and Samaria. He healed Aeneas at Lydda and raised Dorcas at Joppa; he saw a vision and preached to the conversion of Cornelius and his household at Cæsarea (Acts. 9:32-10:48). Returning to Jerusalem, he gave an account of his mission to Cornelius (Acts 11:1-18). He was imprisoned by Herod Agrippa I, but was miraculously released (Acts 12:1-17a); then he went to "another place" (12:17b). He was present at the Jerusalem Council and took a leading part in it (Acts 15:1-21; Gal. 2:6-10). When he came to Antioch a little later he withdrew his fellowship from the Gentile Christians and was rebuked by Paul (Gal. 2:11-15). Little more is known of him authentically, except that he traveled extensively, being often accompanied by his wife (1 Cor. 9:5). He may have paid a visit to Asia Minor, especially to the provinces Pontus, Cappadocia, and Bithynia, which Paul did not visit; and he probably made a longer visit to Babylon on the Euphrates. According to tradition he finally went to Rome (but this cannot have been before A. D. 65), where he died a martyr's death in 67 or 68.

2. **Background and Destination.** The Epistle is addressed to "the elect who are sojourners of the Dispersion in Pontus, Galatia, Cappadocia, Asia, and Bithynia" (1:1). The word "elect" as well as the whole contents of the Epistle indicates that the readers were Christians. But what does the term "sojourners of the Dispersion" mean? James writes to "the twelve tribes which are of the Dispersion" (James 1:1), and these are manifestly Jewish Christians outside Palestine,

perhaps of the Eastern Dispersion (see under James); but Peter does not address his readers as "the twelve tribes." It seems clear that he does not have in mind exclusively or even primarily Jewish Christians, for he calls the former state of his readers, "the time of your ignorance" (1:14), and reminds them "of him who called you out of darkness into his marvelous light: who in time past were no people, but now are the people of God: who had not obtained mercy, but now have obtained mercy" (2:9,10). He also says to them, that "the time past may suffice to have wrought the desire of the Gentiles, and to have walked in lasciviousness, lusts," etc. (4:3-5). In other words, his readers were chiefly Gentile Christians.

In what sense then were they "sojourners of the Dispersion"? In the sense that they were strangers and sojourners on earth (2:11; cf. Heb. 11:13-16; 13:14). In other words, he looks upon the Christians as dispersed among the heathen. Salmon thinks this statement may also have a literal meaning, referring to "the members of the Roman Church whom Nero's persecution had dispersed to seek safety in the provinces, Asia Minor being by no means an unlikely place for them to flee to."[15] This is possible; but even so we believe that Peter primarily thought of the believers as "sojourners and pilgrims" on the earth.

In what sense are Pontus, Galatia, Cappadocia, Asia, and Bithynia to be understood? Zahn points out that not one of the old geographical names is mentioned which is not also the name of a Roman province; which indicates that the Epistle is intended for all of Asia Minor. Cilicia alone is omitted, which is probably due to the fact that it was separated from the rest of Asia Minor by the Taurus mountains, and was so closely allied with the Church in Syrian Antioch as to be considered under the supervision of that Church. The Book of Acts, the Epistles to the Galatians, Colossians, and Ephesians show that Paul and his assistants had founded the churches in Galatia and Asia. The churches in Pontus, Cappadocia, and Bithynia had not been founded by Paul, at least not directly by him, for there are no indications that he had ever visited these provinces; but they may have been founded by Paul's converts in

---

15. *Intro. to the New Testament*, p. 466.

Galatia and Asia. We have seen that Peter traveled extensively after the Jerusalem Council, and it is barely possible that he may have visited these three provinces. But there are no indications that he founded any of the churches in these areas.

We take it, then, that the believers addressed were predominantly Gentiles. They had been saved and established on the teaching of Paul and been organized according to his methods (cf. Acts 14:21-23). If anyone still feels that the Epistle is addressed to the Jewish Christians in these provinces, a view that arose with Origen, let him read Zahn's refutation of this conception.[16]

3. **Occasion and Date.** We can learn the state of these churches only from the Epistle itself. We observe that they were under "elders" (5:1; cf. Acts 20:17-35). Some sort of persecution was in progress (3:17; 4:12-19); but there is no hint of martyrdoms, imprisonments, confiscations, or demands of emperor worship. The persecutions were rather in the nature of slanderous and calumnious attacks upon them as Christians (4:14,15). They seem to have been ridiculed for withdrawing from the licentious shows and amusements of the heathen (4:4,5); they may even have been accused of disloyalty to the state (2:13-17). There may also have been certain tendencies in the churches that caused Peter to write, as the tendency to fall in with the heathen way of living (2:11,12,16; 4:1-5) and a greedy and domineering spirit among the elders (5:2,3).

The Epistle shows acquaintance not only with the earlier Epistles, such as James, 1 Thessalonians, and Romans, but also with Colossians, Ephesians, and Philippians (cf. Col. 3:22 with 1 Pet. 2:18; Eph. 1:1-3 with 1 Pet. 1:1-3; Eph. 5:22-24 with 1 Pet. 3:1-6; Phil. 4:19, 20 with 1 Pet. 5:10,11). It must therefore have been written after the Prison Epistles were written. Some hold that Peter was martyred in the persecution of A. D. 64; that would allow a margin of only two or three years. But Robertson says: "The *Chronicon* of Eusebius (Armenian version) puts the martyrdom of Peter under Nero the thirteenth year of Nero's reign (A.D. 67-68), the probable year also when Paul was beheaded by Nero's orders, though

---

16. *Intro. to the New Testament*, II, 136-145.

apparently before Paul's death."[17] The Neronic persecutions may, quite conceivably, have emboldened the provinces in Asia Minor to malign and persecute the Christians in their borders also. We would therefore date this Epistle A.D. 65.

We incline to the view that "Babylon" (5:13) refers to the city on the Euphrates (so Erasmus, Calvin, Hort, Gregory, Alford, Mayor, and Moorehead), although the majority of writers hold that it is a symbolical reference to Rome. That Peter was in Rome seems evident from the testimony of Ignatius (?), Papias, First Clement, Hegesippus, Clement of Alexandria, Origen, Dionysius of Carthage, Tertullian, and Jerome: but there is no historical proof that he got there before Paul's release from prison in Rome. He may have reached the imperial city any time after 62, although he more probably did not get there until after 64. So even if "Babylon" is taken to mean Rome, the Epistle can still have been written in 65. But there is no evidence that this term was ever applied to Rome until after the writing of the Apocalypse. It is true, there is no corroborative historical evidence that Peter made a journey to Babylon, but neither is there anything to disprove it. We have been reminded that Caligula (died 41) persecuted the Jews at Babylon, that as a result many migrated to the rising Seleucia (about 40 miles distant), and that five years later a plague further diminished their number. But during the twenty years following they may well have returned to their homes and increased. There is a problem as to the order in which the provinces are mentioned. Perhaps it is due simply to some personal acquaintance Peter had with the separate provinces. If it was meant to indicate the order in which Silvanus would deliver the Epistle, then the possibility of its Babylonian origin has a slight advantage over the Roman. Alford's reason for accepting the view that the reference is to literal Babylon commends itself to us. He thinks that "we are not to find an allegorical meaning in a proper name thus simply used in the midst of simple and matter-of-fact sayings."[18]

4. **Purpose and Plan.** It is highly probably that Silvanus was not only the bearer of the Epistle, but also Peter's amanuensis

---

17. *Epochs in the Life of Simon Peter*, p. 319.
18. *Greek Testament*, IV, 129.

(5:12), and that he corrected Peter's dictation. The one "in Babylon, elect together with you" (5:13), is probably some well-known woman in that city, or perhaps Peter's wife; it can hardly be taken as a figurative representation of the Church. Peter wrote to encourage the believers in their present trial to admonish them to live the life befitting so great a salvation, and to magnify the grace of God in their salvation. Stated in his own language, he had written them, "exhorting, and testifying that this is the true grace of God" (5:12). The "grace of God" speaks of the salvation that Paul had preached to the churches in Asia Minor, and that Peter also proclaimed. The believers needed to be assured that they were fundamentally right. He exhorts them to make full use of this grace in their daily lives. We may represent the plan of the Epistle in outline form.

Salutation, 1:1, 2

(1) The Certainty of the Future Inheritance, 1:3-12.
(2) A Befitting Personal Life, 1:13-2:10.
(3) A Befitting Social and Domestic Life, 2:11-3:12.
(4) A Befitting Faith and Conduct in the Midst of Persecution, 3:13-4:6.
(5) A Befitting Conduct and Attitude in the Light of the End, 4:7-19.
(6) A Befitting Relationship Between the Elders and the Congregation, 5:1-11.

Conclusion, 5:12-14.

---

3. THE SECOND EPISTLE OF PETER

In 1 Peter the emphasis falls on *suffering,* in 2 Peter, on *false teachers and false teachings;* consequently the former Epistle is one of *consolation,* the latter, of *warning.* Peter's antidote to false teaching is true spiritual knowledge. The word *know* and its cognates occurs sixteen times in the Greek text.[19] In six of these references Peter uses an intensified form of the word.[20] This word means additional knowledge, full

---

19. 1:2, 3, 5, 6, 8, 12, 14, 16, 20; 2:9, 20, 21 twice; 3:3, 17, 18.
20. 1:2, 3, 8; 2:20, 21 twice.

knowledge. Peter speaks of a knowledge that rests on facts and is communicated to the believer by the Holy Spirit. The grace and peace which he invokes upon his readers are to issue in "the knowledge of God and of Jesus our Lord; seeing that his divine power hath granted unto us all things that pertain unto life and godliness, through the knowledge of him" (1:2,3). Let us study carefully this most practical and timely Epistle.

1. **Attestation and Authorship.** Moorehead says: "The Second Epistle of Peter comes to us with less historical support of its genuineness than any other book of the New Testament."[21] There are points of resemblance between 2 Peter and a number of the writings between A. D. 90 and 130, as in the *Shepherd of Hermas, First Clement, Second Clement,* and the *Didache,* and it may have been known to Clement of Alexandria.[22] Irenæus knew 1 Peter, but it is not certain that he knew 2 Peter. But the Churches of Vienne and Lyons, with which Irenæus was closely connected, seem to have known it.[23] The apocryphal Apocalypse of Peter seems to quote from it. Zahn says: "There is no evidence that before the time of Origen, 2 Peter was accepted anywhere in the Church as a writing of the same rank as 1 Peter."[24] For Origen's opinion see Eusebius.[25] It is not mentioned in the Muratorian Fragment, nor is it found in either the Old Syriac or the Old Latin versions. Eusebius included it among the *antilegomena,* but only under those disputed and not under those actually spurious. He says that "the many," apparently the majority, accepted it, as he himself probably did. We ought not to wonder too much at this paucity of external attestation. The Epistle is very brief, is not addressed to any specific person or Church, and contains little that is new. It may be that for these reasons it was long neglected by the Christian public. Zahn thinks that we have an early attestation of it in the Epistle of Jude and that we really need no other.[26]

The internal evidence is stronger than the external. The writer calls himself Simon Peter (1:1). Neither the charge

---

21. "The Second Epistle of Peter," in *The Inter. Stand. Bible Ency.,* IV. 2355.
22. Euseb., *H. E.,* VI. xiv. 1.
23. Euseb., *H. E.,* V. i. 36, 45, 55.
24. *Op. cit.,* II, 263.
25. *H. E.,* VI. xxv. 8.
26. *Op. cit.,* II, 265.

that the writer's name is a later interpolation nor that it was falsely used by a forger in the first place, can be proved. The former is always a convenient device with those who approach any book with prejudice; and although there were forgeries in early times, yet, as Dods says, "There is no Christian document *of value* written by a forger who uses the name of an apostle."[27] Lumby says: "It is almost inconceivable that a forger, writing to warn against false teachers, writing in the interest of truth, should have thus deliberately assumed a name and experience to which he had no claim."[28] Bigg shows that the dependence of Peter upon the so-called Apocalypse of Peter is improbable; that, instead, the Apocalypse of Peter is dependent upon the inspired Second Epistle of Peter.[29] The differences in style and vocabulary between 1 and 2 Peter have been brought forward against the genuineness of the latter. As for the former it is enough to assume that for 1 Peter the Apostle used Silvanus (5:12) or some one else as his amanuensis, and that for 2 Peter he either had another amanuensis or wrote the Epistle with his own hand. While there are some differences in vocabulary between the two Epistles, Dods[30] and Zahn[31] show that there are also some very remarkable similarities. We sincerely ask, Would a forger risk detection by neglecting closer attention to the style and language of 1 Peter?

Bigg wonders what motive for pseudonymous composition could be found in 2 Peter. The Epistle is not unorthodox; it is not a romance; it contains no anachronisms, at least none that are indisputable; and it tells nothing new about Peter. This is not true of the Gospel of Peter or the Apocalypse of Peter, which are both spurious. If 2 Peter is a forgery, then we have here a forgery without an object, without any of the ordinary marks of forgery, and without any resemblance to undoubted forgeries.[32] The autobiographical allusions are true to the facts, as the reference to the Transfiguration (1:16-18) and to Christ's prediction of the martyrdom of Peter (1:12-14). We must remember that this statement was written

27. Quoted from *S. B. D.*, by Moorehead, in *The Inter. Stand. Bible Ency.*, p. 2356.
28. *Expositor's Bible*, VI, 675.
29. *Op. cit.*, p. 207 f.
30. *An Intro. to the New Testament*, pp. 210, 211.
31. *Op. cit.*, II, 289 f.
32. Bigg, *op. cit.*, p. 242.

before the Gospel by John that predicts it (John 21:18, 19). Furthermore, Noah is spoken of as a preacher of righteousness (2:5), and this is probably also the meaning in 1 Pet. 3:18-20). The reference to Paul's Epistles (3:15,16) does not imply that they had already been collected or even that they had already all been written; it merely includes all such as Peter had come to know. The errorists are much like those against whom Paul warns in his Epistles. Their doctrines are "fables" (1:16; 1 Tim. 1:4; 4:7); they are actuated by covetousness (2:3; 1 Tim. 6:5; Tit. 1:11); they promise their votaries liberty (2:19; 1 Cor. 10:29; Gal. 5:13); they are false brethren that have come into the Church (2:1; Gal. 2:4). Surely, 2 Peter does not deal with a more advanced stage of the error than Paul. Finally, the Christian earnestness, apostolic tone, and autobiographical allusions make it impossible to believe that the Epistle is spurious. We, therefore, accept it as a genuine work of the Apostle Peter.

2. **Background and Destination.** Zahn holds that 2 Peter was written before 1 Peter and that to a large group of Churches who owed their Christianity to the preaching of Peter and the other disciples of Jesus. He thinks that the believers in these Churches were chiefly Jewish Christians and that they lived in Palestine and the regions adjoining, except those north and northwest of Syrian Antioch. He makes much of the fact that Peter here uses his Hebrew name Simon (Simeon, in some manuscripts) (1:1), and argues that 3:15 implies not only that Paul had written to the same people as he addresses, but also on the same subject as he discusses in ch. 3. And since none of the extant Epistles of Paul fulfil this requirement, he holds that the reference is to an Epistle of Paul that is now lost.[33] But with due respect for Zahn's scholarship, we believe that in this instance his reasoning is a bit far-fetched. There were Jewish Christians in all of the Churches in Asia Minor, and the use of the name "Simon" does not indicate that a large proportion of them were such. Furthermore, whether or not the Epistle of Paul to which Peter refers in 2 Pet. 3:15 is extant, there is no ground for insisting that Peter meant to

33. *Op. cit.*, II, 206-269.

say it dealt with the same subject as that which he discusses in that chapter.

Some would say that the letter Peter refers to is Hebrews; but Bigg holds that it is highly improbable that Paul wrote to Jewish Christians as such.[34] When Peter refers to his readers as those who "have obtained a like precious faith with us" (1:1), he most naturally distinguishes them as Gentiles from himself and other Jewish Christians as Jews. Besides, it seems clear that he refers to 1 Peter, when he speaks of 2 Peter as "the second Epistle" that he has written to the same people (3:1). Zahn is obliged to make this reference speak of an Epistle of Peter that is lost, which seems a needless hypothesis. We take it, then, that the readers addressed in this Epistle are at least included among those addressed in 1 Peter. Peter may have reference to Paul's Epistles to the Galatians, Colossians, and Ephesians in 3:15. He distinguishes between the things Paul wrote to them (3:15) and the rest of his Epistles (3:16). The Epistle does not intimate, as Zahn holds, that Peter had an official relation to the people he addresses. All the facts can be reconciled with the view that 2 Peter is written to the same people as 1 Peter.

3. **Occasion and Date.** An incipient Gnosticism had crept in among the believers, with its intellectual and antinomian characteristics (ch. 2). It was primarily antinomian, with its immoral tendency. It was already active in some places (2:11, 12,17,18,20; 3:5,16), and Peter foresaw that it would soon be more generally operative (2:1,2; 3:3). Paul had dealt with this error in his Epistle to the Colossians, but it was still active. Although, as we have said, Peter did not have an official relation to the people he addresses, he may yet have visited them during the time of Paul's imprisonment at Rome. He, along with others, had made known unto them "the power and coming of our Lord Jesus Christ" (1:16) and he feels some responsibility for them (1:1-14, *et passim*). This, then, led to the writing of this Epistle.

2 Peter is earlier than Jude, for the latter quotes from the former. Jude quotes from tradition (some say from the

---

34. *Op. cit.,* p. 246 f.

apocryphal Books of the Assumption of Moses and of Enoch) ; Peter scarcely quotes at all. So Jude is more likely to cite 2 Pet. 2:1-3:3 than Peter, Jude 4-16. In 2 Peter the false teachers are in some measure still future (2:1,2,3,12) ; in Jude they are already present (vss. 4,8,10-13,16). More particularly, Jude seems definitely to allude to 2 Pet. 3:1-3 in vss. 17, 18 of his Epistle. He says: "But ye, beloved, remember ye the words which have been spoken before by the apostles of our Lord Jesus Christ; that they said to you, In the last time there shall be mockers, walking after their own ungodly lusts." This noun for mockers (*empaiktēs*) is found only in this reference and in 2 Pet. 3:3, although the verb occurs a number of times in the Synoptic Gospels. Peter was an apostle and he had spoken of the coming of such mockers. Paul was another apostle who had said things to the same effect (1 Tim. 4:1-3; 2 Tim. 3:1-5; Acts 20:29,30). Jude could thus correctly speak of the Apostles as having predicted the coming of these men. We hold, then, that 2 Peter was written shortly after 1 Peter and before Jude. The years 66 or 67 A. D. would seem to fulfill all the requirements, and we would, therefore, assign to it this date.

4. **Purpose and Plan.** From the contents of the Epistle we draw the conclusion that Peter wrote to stir up his readers to growth in Christian character (1:5-15; 3:18), to encourage them to a patient expectation of the Lord's return (3:1-14), and to warn them against "being carried away with the error of the wicked" (3:17), *i. e.,* with the heresies which he rebukes. He wants them to grow in "the grace and knowledge of our Lord and Savior Jesus Christ." This means in the *realm* of both. They had been introduced into the realm of grace and into the realm of knowledge by the Holy Spirit and the testimony of the apostles and prophets (1:16, 19-21). This knowledge of Christ is the knowledge of "the right way" (2:15) and "the way of righteousness" (2:21). Accordingly Noah is represented as "a preacher of righteousness" (2:5) and Lot as "righteous Lot" (2:7). The two are introduced by way of contrast to the "unrighteous" (2:9) and to "wrong-doing" (2:13,15).

We may represent the plan of this Epistle in outline form.

Introduction, 1:1-4

(1) The Exhortations to Develop the Christian Graces, 1:5-11.
(2) The Ground for Peter's Authority to Exhort and to Teach, 1:12-21.
(3) The Warnings Against False Teachers, ch. 2.
(4) The Admonitions in the Light of the Certainty and Imminence of the Lord's Return, ch. 3.

---

4. THE EPISTLE OF JUDE

Jude, like 2 Peter, deals primarily with the false teachers that had crept in among the believers (Jude 4-16; 2 Pet. 2:1-3:3). They and their propaganda imperiled the soundness of doctrine and the purity of morals in the Christian Church. Jude uses the language of tender affection when addressing the Christians (vss. 1-3, 17-25), but even stronger language than 2 Peter when speaking of the false teachers and their teachings. He does not, however, so much refute them as denounce and threaten them. Both 2 Peter and Jude deal with conditions to some extent already present in their day; but both are probably also to be regarded as predictions of the conditions that are to prevail in the last time. From this standpoint they are fitting introductions to the Apocalypse. Let us now turn to a study of the Epistle of Jude.

1. Attestation and Authorship. Hermas has much to say about "defiling the flesh" in *Similitudes* (V.vii); cf. Jude vs. 8. Polycarp speaks of "building you up in that faith which has been given you" in *Epistle to the Philippians* (ch. iii), which seems to allude to Jude 3, 20. There is a possible allusion to Jude 6 in Athenagoras' *Plea for the Christians* (ch. xxiv). Theophilus of Antioch speaks of the planets as a type of fallen man, which figure occurs only in Jude.[35] The Epistle is not in the Old Syriac, but the Muratorian Fragment recognizes it. Tertullian says: "To these considerations is added the fact that Enoch possesses a testimony in the Apostle Jude."[36] Eusebius says, Clement of Alexandria in the *Hypotyposes* "has made abbreviated narratives of the whole testimony of Scripture;

---

35. Not in the Book of Enoch (*To Autolycus* II, xv); cf. Jude vs. 13.
36. *On the Apparel of Women*, I. iii.

and has not passed over the disputed books, — I mean Jude and the rest of the Catholic Epistles and Barnabas, and what is called the Revelation of Peter."[37] He cites vss. 5, 6 in the *Instructor* (III.viii) as by Jude and vss. 8-17 in *Stromata* (III.ii). Eusebius puts Jude among the *antilegomena,* although not among those which he considered spurious, but only among those which were disputed. Jude thus has stronger external attestation than 2 Peter. This is remarkable considering its brevity, its polemic character, its alleged reference to apocryphal literature, and its non-apostolic authorship.

The internal evidence is in accord with the external. The writer calls himself "Jude, a servant of Jesus Christ, and brother of James" (vs. 1). James was the brother of Jesus (as we have shown under The Epistle of James), therefore Jude was also a brother of Jesus. The Gospel record shows that Jesus had a brother by that name (Matt. 13:55; Mark 6:3). He is, therefore, not to be identified with any of the other six Judes or Judases mentioned in the New Testament: (1) Judas the ancestor of Jesus (Luke 3:30), (2) Judas the Galilean (Acts 5:37), (3) Judas Iscariot (Mark 3:19), (4) the Judas with whom Paul lodged in Damascus (Acts 9:11), (5) Judas Barsabbas (Acts 15:22), and (6) Judas the son (or brother) of James (Luke 6:16; Acts 1:13; John 14:22), an Apostle, and commonly identified with Lebbæus or Thaddæus. We have seen (above) that Tertullian identified him with the Apostle Jude; but the writer does not only refrain from calling himself an Apostle, but distinguishes himself from the Apostles (vs. 17). The fact that he distinguishes himself from other Judes by reference to his brother rather than his father, is due to the fact that his brother had achieved great prominence among his readers. Both James and Jude indicate that they were not apostles by the omission of the apostolic title.

We know practically nothing about the life of this Jude. He was apparently one of the younger brothers of Jesus (Matt. 13:55; Mark 6:3). With the rest of the brothers he seems to have disbelieved in Jesus before the resurrection (John 7:3-8);

---

37. *H. E.,* VI. xiv.

but he was apparently convinced of the deity of Jesus by that event and is found with the other brothers and Mary in the upper room after the ascension (Acts 1:14). He was married and apparently traveled a good deal, taking his wife with him on his travels (1 Cor. 9:5). He probably confined his ministry to Israel, carrying out the general agreement of the Jerusalem Council (Gal. 2:9). Hegesippus tells us that near the end of Domitian's reign (c. A.D. 95), two grandsons of Jude, farmers, were brought before the emperor on the charge that they were descendants of David and were Christians. When Domitian learned that they were poor and saw their horny hands, he dismissed them as harmless Jews.[38] It really does seem as if a forger would have selected the name of some more outstanding personage if he wanted to gain prestige for his Epistle.

Clement of Alexandria, Tertullian, Jerome, Augustine, and the Church Fathers generally held that Jude quotes from several apocryphal books. It was on this ground that they long rejected it. It was held that at vs. 9 the writer quotes from the Assumption of Moses and at vs. 14 f. from the Book of Enoch. Philippi vigorously denied this, saying that Jude merely wrote from oral tradition, and this is possible. The fragment of the Assumption of Moses that has come down to us is broken off before the burial of Moses is reached, and we really cannot tell what followed in the part that is missing. There is a great similarity between Enoch 1:9; 5:4 and Jude 14 f. Moorehead admits the possibility of a quotation in both instances. With regard to the Book of Enoch in particular he says: "Granting such quotation, that fact does not warrant us to affirm that he indorses the book. Paul cites from three Greek poets: from Aratus (Acts 17:28), from Menander,[39] and from Epimenides (Tit. 1:12). Does anyone imagine that Paul indorses all that these poets wrote? To the quotation from Epimenides the apostle adds, 'This testimony is true' (Tit. 1:13), but no one imagines he means to say the whole poem is true. So Jude cites a passage from a non-canonical book, not because he accepts the whole book as true, but this particular prediction he receives

---

38. Eusebius, *H. E.*, III. xix f.; xxxii. 5 f.
39. I Cor. 15:33; see Earle, *Euripedes*, 'Medea,' Intro., 30, where this is attributed to Euripedes.

as from God."[40] This seems to us to be a satisfactory solution to the problem.

2. Background and Destination. It is impossible to determine with certainty the locality for which the Epistle was intended. Palestine, Asia Minor, and Alexandria have been suggested, but the letter offers no real clue as to its destination. Jude merely says: "To them that are called, beloved in God the Father, and kept for Jesus Christ" (vs. 1). He admonishes them to build themselves up in their most holy faith (vs. 20). The persons addressed were Christians, then; but they apparently embraced all Christians, whether Jews or Gentiles, whether inside or outside Palestine. The contents are such as would chiefly interest Jewish Christians, and the Epistle may have been intended primarily for those in Palestine and adjoining countries; but the address does not limit the message to them. All Christians are before the writer's mind. The evils are those opposed in 2 Peter, and it does not seem as if both would write to the same people, especially not if Jude is somewhat dependent upon 2 Peter. It seems more likely that Jude was meant for the same people as those for whom the author's brother James wrote his Epistle.

3. Occasion and Date. Very distressing news had reached Jude as to the state into which some Christians were drifting. Perhaps in his journeys as an evangelist he had learned of the serious condition of these people. He had planned to write them a doctrinal treatise on the common salvation, but found it necessary to write about the false teachers and their teachings (vs. 3). These teachers had stealthily crept in among the believers (vs. 4) and were, generally speaking, abusers of the grace of God and deniers of the Lord Jesus Christ (vs. 4). They were sexual perverts (vs. 1), haughty railers (vss. 8,9), ignorant calumniators (vs. 10), potential murderers (vs. 11), greedy imposters (vs. 11), defiers of Church authorities (vs. 12), blemishes (perhaps, rather than "rocks") at the love-feasts (vs. 12), self-appointed leaders (vs. 12), empty pretenders (vs. 12), wild and aimless wanderers (vs. 13), murmurers, complainers, pleasure seekers, boasters, selfih (vs. 16), schismatics and sensualists (vs. 19). What an array of wickedness!

---

40. "The Epistle of Jude," in the *Inter. Stand. Bible Ency.*, p. 1771.

The knowledge of the presence of these wicked persons among the believers led Jude to write this Epistle.

It is difficult to determine the exact date. If it is true that Jude was written after 2 Peter, then it cannot be earlier than 66 or 67. Jude may have been ten years younger than Jesus, since he appears to have been one of the youngest of the sons (see above). The Epistle can therefore be put at 75 or 80 without making Jude a very old man. It is possible that some years intervened between the conditions described in 2 Peter and those in Jude, and we would therefore, with Zahn,[41] date the latter at A. D. 75.

4. **Purpose and Plan.** As in the other Epistles, the need determines the purpose of the writer. Jude is much concerned about "the faith which was once for all delivered unto the saints" (vs. 3). By "the faith" he does not mean mere trust or mental assent to a doctrine, but that body of doctrine, both dogmatic and practical, which has been committed to the Church by divine authority and is fixed and unalterable. He exhorts his readers to "contend earnestly" for that faith, particularly now that certain false brethren have crept in among them (vss. 3,4). He reminds them that judgment had fallen upon sinners in the past (vss. 5-7), denounces the false teachers who had come in among them (vss. 8-13), cites Enoch and the Apostles to show that the ungodly will be judged (vss. 14-19), exhorts his readers to spiritual growth and soul-winning (vss. 20-23), and pronounces the doxology (vss. 24, 25). We may again arrange these materials in outline form, as follows:

Salutation, 1, 2.

(1) The General Admonition to Contend for the Faith, 3, 4.
(2) The Historical Proof that God Judges the Wicked, 5-7.
(3) The Stern Denunciation of the False Teachers and their Teachings, 8-13.
(4) The Authoritative Assurances that God Will Judge the Wicked, 14-19.
(5) The Earnest Admonition to Spiritual Growth and Soul-Winning, 20-23.

The Doxology, 24, 25.

---

41. *Op. cit.*, II, 255.

Chapter XIII

HEBREWS AND THE GENERAL EPISTLES
The Second Group

1. THE EPISTLE TO THE HEBREWS

THE Epistle to the Hebrews is not one of the General Epistles, but is here introduced somewhat arbitrarily as a summarization of the transition from the old system to the new. From the standpoint of doctrinal contribution and literary excellence it is without a peer among the books of the New Testament. It shows that the change from the Levitical to the Christian system was prefigured and predicted in the Old Testament, particularly the change to a new priesthood, a new covenant, a new sacrifice, and a new sanctuary. March says: "It is the earliest exposition of the Christian tradition by one who had all the instincts of a scholar and a philosopher."[1] Classified from the standpoint of literature, Rees says: "Hebrews begins like an essay, proceeds like a sermon, and ends as a letter."[2] Deissmann, who, in our judgment, exaggerates the difference between "letters" and "epistles," considers Hebrews "as most unmistakably of all an epistle."[3] Let us turn to the study of this charming and most important book.

1. **Attestation and Authorship.** The external evidence clearly and abundantly attests the early existence of this Epistle, but does not contribute very much to the solution of the problem of its authorship. Clement of Rome quotes Hebrews copiously. He uses the language of 11:37 in his *Epistle to the Corinthians* (ch. xvii) and of 1:3,4 in the same work (ch. xxxvi). Westcott thinks that the way in which he uses its language (e. g., in chs. ix, xii, xl) indicates that he had the

---

1. "The Epistle to the Hebrews," in *Dict. of the Apost. Church,* I, 541 f.
2. "The Epistle to the Hebrews," in *Inter. Stand. Bible Ency.,* II, 1355.
3 *Bible Studies,* p. 49.

text before him.[4] Polycarp calls Jesus Christ "our everlasting high priest," in his *Epistle to the Philippians* (ch. xii), which title is peculiar to Hebrews. Justin Martyr speaks of a "new law and a new covenant," as in 8:7 f., in *Dialogue with Trypho* (ch. xxxiv, cf. lxvii), and of those "who no longer were purified by the blood of goats and of sheep, or by the ashes of an heifer," etc., as in 9:13,14, in the same work (ch. xiii). Dionysius of Alexandria quotes it as an Epistle of Paul.[5] Theophilus of Antioch may allude to 12:9, in *To Autolycus* (II.xxv). But Marcion does not recognize it, nor does the Muratorian Fragment.

According to Eusebius,[6] Clement of Alexandria held that Paul wrote the Epistle in Hebrew and that Luke translated it. He speaks of Paul as "writing to the Hebrews," so and so (*Stromata* VI,xiii). Eusebius also makes Pantænus of Alexandria say that Paul, as "a work of supererogation," wrote to the Hebrews (*ib.*). Origen repeatedly cites it as by Paul.[7] Eusebius quotes Origen as saying: "The thoughts are the thoughts of the apostle, but the language and its composition that of one who recalled from memory and, as it were, made notes of what was said by the master." Origen admits that "men of old time have handed it down as Paul's. But who wrote the Epistle God only knows certainly."[8] Eusebius himself held that it was originally written in Hebrew and that Clement of Rome had translated it; he sometimes placed it among the *homologoumena*[9] and sometimes among the *antilegomena*.[10] Athanasius included it among the fourteen Epistles of Paul. Tertullian knew the Epistle, but considered it to have been written by Barnabas.[11] Cyprian does not quote from it; Irenæus and Hippolytus were acquainted with it, but held that it was not by Paul.[12] From Athanasius onward the Greek writers universally ascribed it to Paul. Jerome and Augustine adopted the opinion of the East, and after that the authority of the Epistle was established.

---

4. *The Epistle to the Hebrews*, p. lxii.
5. Euseb., *H. E.*, VI. xli.
6. *H. E.*, VI. xiv.
7. *De Orat.*, XXVII, and in his *Comm. on John and Romans*.
8. *H. E.*, VI. xxv.
9. *H. E.*, III. xxv.
10. *H. E.*, VI. xiii.
11. *On Modesty*, ch. xx.
12. Euseb., *H. E.*, V. xxvi.

The internal evidence as to its authorship is rather indefinite. Some things in the Epistle seem to point to Paul as the author. Among these is the reference to Timothy (13:23), Paul's long-time associate (but see below); the affinities in language and thought between Hebrews and the recognized Pauline Epistles (e.g., Heb. 1:4 and Phil. 2:9; Heb. 2:2 and Gal. 3:19; Heb. 2:10 and Rom. 11:36; Heb. 7:18 and Rom. 8:3; Heb. 7:27 and Eph. 5:2; Heb. 8:13 and 2 Cor. 3:11; Heb. 10:33 and 1 Cor. 4:9; Heb. 11:13 and Eph. 2:19; Heb. 12:22 and Gal. 4:25,26); and the centrality of the person and work of Christ, as in the other Pauline Epistles. It is, however, possible that the affinities in language and thought are mere indications of the fact that all Christian teachers in those days used much the same language in their preaching, or a proof that the writer of Hebrews had so absorbed the terminology of Paul that he spontaneously used a good deal of it. And as for the centrality of the person and work of Christ in Hebrews and the known Pauline Epistles, that, too, is not a certain indication of Pauline authorship. Surely, many of the leaders in those early days had the same doctrinal grasp of these truths as Paul had (John, for instance), although Paul has left us more in writing than any of the others.

We believe, however, that no argument against the Pauline authorship can be established on the ground that in the Pauline Epistles the emphasis is on the death, resurrection, and presence of Christ among His people and in Hebrews it is on the high-priestly work of Christ in heaven (as Rees tries to do, *op cit.*); for Paul is not absolutely silent with regard to Christ's present work in heaven (*e.g.,* Rom. 5:9,10; 8:34), nor is Hebrews with regard to the death and exaltation of Christ (e. g., Heb. 2:9; 9:24-28; 10:11-14). Paul was a man of profound insight, and he may well have decided to devote one Epistle to an enlargement on certain truths that he had mentioned only incidentally in his other letters. Nor can an argument be based on the absence of a discussion of the doctrine of justification by faith in Hebrews, for the writer recognizes the importance of the doctrine in salvation (10:38; 11:7) and has much to say about faith as the condition to acceptance with God (ch. 11). Nor is yet the Pauline authorship disproved by the fact, as Rees puts it, that "for Paul the Old Testament is law, and stands in antithesis to the New Testament, but in Hebrews the Old Testament is covenant, and is the 'shadow' of the New Covenant" (*op. cit.*); for although from one standpoint Paul regards the law as a rudimentary system of religion (Gal. 4:3,9), — Hebrews does so too (7:16,18), — from another he regards it as "holy, righteous, and good" (Rom. 7:12) and "glorious" (2 Cor. 3:7-11). The fact is, that in the Pauline Epistles the law is viewed in its ethical aspects and in Hebrews, in its ceremonial, and there is no contradiction between these two view-points.

There are other things in the Epistle that make the Pauline authorship questionable. (1) The writer of Hebrews does not mention his name, whereas Paul always does so in the recognized Pauline Epistles. But the explanation of Clement of Alexandria, that to avoid prejudice against the Epistle he omitted it, may be correct.[13] The translation, "my bonds," at 10:34, according to the A. V., has been rightly changed to "them that were in bonds," in the A. S. V. (2) The statement in Heb. 2:3 seems to make the author dependent upon those who heard the Lord, whereas Paul declares his absolute independence of man in his message (Gal. 1:11-24); but, of course, the writer may want to use the plural "us" in order to identify himself more fully with his readers. This is, however, not a very good explanation of the phenomenon. (3) The writer to the Hebrews uses the Septuagint throughout (except, possibly at 10:30, where he appears to use Rom. 12:19), whereas Paul uses both the Hebrew and the Septuagint. Some think this fact indicates that the writer was an Alexandrian, for at Alexandria the Septuagint was the popular Bible. (4) The statement about Timothy's release seems to fit in best with the idea that this faithful servant came to Rome at Paul's suggestion (2 Tim. 4:9,21), and was put into prison; but, since he had not been a conspicuous leader thus far, he was released, possibly after Paul's death. There is no other indication that Timothy was ever imprisoned; but, of course, the argument from silence never settles a question conclusively. And (5) the style and vocabulary of Hebrews is against the Pauline authorship. Only

---

13. Euseb., *H. E.*, VI. xiv.

the student of the Greek Testament can appreciate this situation fully. It is a difference that is not easily explained by the change of subject-matter or the variation of moods in a writer.[14]

We do not deem the above considerations absolutely sufficient to disprove the Pauline authorship of Hebrews, but wonder if they do not point in that direction. There is, of course, no doubt of its divine inspiration and indispensability in the Christian Canon. With regard to this point we would say with Westcott: "If we hold that the judgment of the Spirit makes itself felt through the consciousness of the Christian Society, no Book of the Bible is more completely recognized by universal consent as giving a divine view of the facts of the Gospel, full of lessons for all time, than the Epistle to the Hebrews."[15] Various opinions as to the identity of the author have been expressed by those who hold that Paul cannot have written it; but none of them is more than a guess. Peake is for Priscilla; Harnack for Priscilla and Aquila; Erasmus was for Clement of Rome; Clement of Alexandria for Paul and Luke; Eusebiu. for Paul and Clement of Rome; Calvin and Delitzsch for Luke; Tertullian, B. Weiss, Zahn, Godet, Salmon, Gregory for Barnabas; and Luther, Alford, Moulton, Farrar, and A. T. Robertson for Apollos. But we are obliged to say with Origen, "Who wrote the Epistle God only knows certainly."[16]

2. **Background and Destination.** Manuscripts Aleph, A, and B, have the title *Pros Hebraious,* but place the Epistle before the Pastorals. This title must have been given to it very early; Moffatt thinks during the early part of the second century, though erroneously.[17] This was afterwards enlarged to "the Epistle to the Hebrews" and finally to "the Epistle to the Hebrews of Paul the Apostle." The original title was, no doubt, rightly given to the book. The author "assumes an exclusively Jewish point of view in the minds of his readers as his major premise."[18] Westcott says: "The arguments and reflections in their whole form and spirit, even more than in

14. See Alford for a careful analysis of this factor, in his *Greek Testament,* IV, 41.
15. *The Epistle to the Hebrews,* p. lxxi.
16. Euseb., *H. E.,* VI. xxv.
17. *Intro. to the Lit. of the New Testament,* p. 448.
18. Rees, *op. cit.,* p. 1359.

special details, are addressed to 'Hebrews,' men, that is, whose hearts were filled with the thoughts, the hopes, the consolations, of the Old Covenant."[19]

This view is sustained by the fact that there is no reference to Gentiles or Gentile controversies in the Epistle. Nothing is said about circumcision, abstinence from things sacrificed to idols, or the equality of Jew and Gentile in the Church. Instead, Abraham, not Adam, is singled out for help from God (2:16); this, combined with the prominence given to him in the seventh chapter, esp. in 7:4, and in 11:11,12, makes it natural to think that the writer had those in mind who were physical descendants from Abraham. The characteristics of the readers in the Epistle are in accord with this view. They had heard the Gospel from the immediate disciples of Christ (2:3) and had witnessed not only "signs and wonders" and "manifold powers," but also "various gifts of the Holy Spirit" (2:4). They had been made "partakers of Christ" and needed only to hold fast the beginning of confidence firm unto the end" (3:14). They had engaged in the ministry to the saints (6:10); they had in former days, perhaps in connection with the persecution that broke out when Stephen was stoned, endured suffering and persecution, although not unto blood, and had shown compassion toward those who were imprisoned (10:32-34; 12:4). They had been believers for some time: their leaders had already died (13:7) and they themselves should be teachers by this time (5:12). They had a good understanding of "the first principles of Christ" (6:1), but they had become "dull of hearing" (5:11) and "sluggish" in their conduct (6:12). The writer fears that some of them are in danger of apostasy (6:4-8). Their besetting sin was unbelief (3:12). All this fits in with the view that the persons addressed are Jewish Christians.

But we still ask, Was the Epistle addressed to the Hebrew Christians as such, or to those in a particular locality? Undoubtedly the latter; for the various things said about them could not be true of all Hebrew Christians in the same way (*e. g.*, 2:3,4; 10:32-34; 13:7,19,23). Those in Palestine, Alex-

---

19. *Op. cit.*, p. xxviii.

andria, Syria (especially at Antioch), Asia Minor, Greece,
North Africa, and Italy (especially at Rome) have all been suggested by someone. The internal evidence seems to point most
distinctly to Jerusalem and its neighborhood. All held that the
temple at Jerusalem was the true center of worship; the one at
Leontopolis in Egypt never had the same influence as the one
in Jerusalem. The only other suggested destination that needs
consideration is Rome. It is held that on the basis of the
subject-matter, the greeting from those "of Italy" (13:24),
and the many quotations in *First Clement,* the people addressed
lived in Rome. Marsh holds that they were most likely Jewish
Christians at Rome.[20]   Others hold that they were Gentile
Christians in that city.[21] But the subject-matter fits Jewish
Christians much better than Gentile, and the greeting may
equally well have been sent by Christians which the writer had
met in various places in Italy. As for the quotations in *First
Clement,* they cannot prove the Roman destination in view of
the absence of all other evidence in Rome that the Epistle was
known there and in view of the long time it took before the
Epistle was recognized by the Church there. We hold, then,
that Hebrews was sent to Jewish Christians in Jerusalem and
its surrounding country.

3. **Occasion and Date.** Considerable time had already elapsed
since Christ was here on earth. The early expectation of His
speedy return had begun to wane. Persecution and loss of their
possessions had tested the believers' patience. Their close connection with the temple, with its splendors and venerable ritual,
made the severance from Judaism a most grievous thing to
those who had been in it from youth. The growing difficulties
with Rome increasingly placed the Christians, who knew that
Jesus had predicted the destruction of Jerusalem, in an em-
barassing position. Many were beginning to wonder whether
they had been carried away by an unfounded enthusiasm;
whether the dangers of the nation did not demand a return to a
patriotic support of the temple and its service. Consequently
they had become "dull of hearing," "sluggish" in conduct, weak

20. *Dict. of the Apost. Church,* I, 538.
21. Moffatt, Goodspeed, McNeile.

in faith, and near apostates. There were probably also some moral failures among them that needed correcting. All these led to the writing of the Epistle.

It seems clear that the temple was still standing and that its service was still being continued. Notice the repeated use of the present tense in this connection.[22] It seems evident, also, that the readers had been Christians for a long time, that they had already suffered persecution and the plundering of their goods, that they were again face to face with persecution, and at least some of their first leaders had already died. And if we are right in surmising that the imprisonment and release of Timothy followed on his complying with Paul's request for him to come to Rome (2 Tim. 4:9-13,21), then the Epistle was probably written after Paul's death. We would, therefore, assign it to A. D. 67-69.

4. **Purpose and Plan.** The principal aims of the writer are to establish the supremacy of Christ and Christianity (1:1-10:18) and then, as required by the acceptance of that truth, to warn the readers against apostasy (6:4-8; 10:26-31; 12:14-19), to encourage them to renewed effort (6:1,9-12; 10:19-39; 12:12-17), and to exhort them to make a complete break with Judaism (12:18-13:17). More in detail: After giving a summary view of his main subject (1:1-4), the writer sets forth the superiority of Christ to angels (1:5-2:18) and to Moses and Joshua, the founders of the Old Economy (3:1-4:2); he exhorts his readers to enter into the rest provided (4:3-16); he expounds the nature and scope of Christ's High-Priesthood, representing it as after the order of Melchisedec, but functioning in the manner of the Levitical high-priesthood (chs. 5-7); he contrasts the sanctuary and service under the old covenant with those under the new (chs. 8 and 9) and legal sacrifices with the sacrifice of Christ (10:1-18); he admonishes his readers to be faithful to the new covenant, in view of the dangers of apostasy, their former endurance, the achievements of faith on the part of the ancients and of Christ, the proofs of sonship, and the greater privileges of the Christian dispensation (10:19-12:29); he concludes with exhortations to prac-

---

22. E. g., 8:4, 13; 9:4, 5, 9; 10:1, 8, 11; 13:10, 11.

tice the Christian principles and to separate from Judaism (ch. 13). We may again represent the writer's plan in outline form.

Introduction, 1:1-4.

A. The Superiority of the Son to Angels, 1:5-2:18.
   (1) The Proofs from the Old Testament, 1:5-14.
   (2) The Obligation Resulting Therefrom, 2:1-4.
   (3) The Reasonableness of the Humiliation of Christ, 2:5-18.

B. The Superiority of the Son to Moses and Joshua, chs. 3 and 4.
   (1) The Superiority of Christ to Moses, 3:1-6.
   (2) The Failure of Israel under Moses and Joshua, 3:7-4:2.
   (3) The Proofs that the Rest is Still Available, 4:3-10.
   (4) The Need of Striving to Enter this Rest, 4:11-13.
   (5) The Triumph of Christ, our High Priest, an Incentive to Drawing Near, 4:14-16.

C. The Nature and Scope of Christ's High-Priesthood, chs. 5-7.
   (1) The Qualifications of Christ as High-Priest, 5:1-10.
   (2) The Need of Effort to an Understanding of Spiritual Truth, 5:11-6:20.
   (3) The High-Priesthood of Christ Prefigured by Melchisedec, 7:1-25.
   (4) The High-Priesthood of Christ Contrasted with the Levitical, 7:26-28.

D. The Ministry of Christ as High-Priest, 8:1-10:18.
   (1) The Circumstances of His High-Priestly Ministry, ch. 8.
   (2) The Sanctuary and Service under the Two Covenants, ch. 9.
   (3) The Contrast between the Levitical Sacrifices and the Sacrifice of Christ, 10:1-18.

E. The Application of these Truths to the Readers, 10:19-12:29.
   (1) The Exhortations to Faithfulness to the New Covenant, 10:19-39.
   (2) The Encouragement by the Achievements of Others, 11:1-12:4.
   (3) The Consolation by the Fact of Sonship, 12:5-13.

(4) The Warning Against Failure and Apostasy, 12:14-17.
(5) The Enforcement by the Greater Position of the Christian, 12:18-29.

Conclusion: Social and Religious Duties; Personal Instructions, ch. 13.

---

2. THE FIRST EPISTLE OF JOHN

In the writings of Paul the doctrine of justification is prominent; in those of John, the doctrine of regeneration. Paul conceives of the natural man as out of favor with God; John, as outside the family of God. But though there is this difference of emphasis in the two Apostles, neither of them limits himself to the one doctrine: Paul also believes in the doctrine of regeneration and John, in that of justification. Ironside says: "The writings of the Apostle John have always had a peculiar charm for the people of the Lord, and I suppose, if for no other reason, for this, that they are particularly addressed to the family of God as such."[23] Although the First Epistle is chiefly didactic and controversial, the personal note is not entirely absent. Yet there are no proper names (except that of our Lord), nor historical or geographical allusions in it. The writer deals with the errors which he combats from the high standpoint of a personal relationship to and fellowship with God, and not from that of a theoretical polemicist. We do well to study this rich Epistle in detail.

1. **Attestation and Authorship.** The Epistle has early and strong external attestation. Polycarp has an almost verbal reproduction of 4:2, 3 in his *Epistle to the Philippians* (ch. vii). Papias is described by Irenæus as a "hearer of John and a companion of Polycarp"; he is said by Eusebius to have "used some testimonies from John's former Epistle."[24] The *Epistle to Diognetus* seems to allude to the ideas in 4:19 (ch. x). The Muratorian Fragment recognizes two Epistles of John, but does not name them; undoubtedly 1 John was one of them. It was in the Old Syriac. There are linguistic resemblances to it in the *Epistle of the Churches of Vienne and Lyons*. Irenæus quotes 4:1, 2, although not exactly as we have these verses in

23. *Addresses on the Epistles of John*, p. 7.
24. *H. E.*, III. xxxix.

our text, and 5:1 almost verbally.[25] He says, "John the disciple of the Lord" testifies in his Epistle, and then quotes 2:18, 19 somewhat loosely.[26] Clement of Alexandria says, "John . . . in his larger Epistle" teaches in these words, and then quotes almost verbally 5:16, 17;[27] he also introduces his quotation from 1:6, 7 with the words, "John says in his Epistle."[28] He quotes the Epistle frequently. Tertullian gives the substance of 4:1-3 and assigns it to the "Apostle John" in *Against Marcion* (V. xvi) ; he quotes 1:1 as by John, in *Ad Praxeas* (ch. xv) ; he combines the ideas in 2:22; 4:2, 3; 5:1, in the same work (ch. xxviii). He, too, frequently quotes from 1 John. Cyprian, Origen, and Dionysius of Alexandria all quote it, but it is not necessary to list the examples. Eusebius placed it among the *homologoumena*. After his day it was generally received.

The author represents himself as an eye-witness of Christ (1:1-4; 4:14). The plural is not used in a collective sense of himself and the Church in general,—the words are too studiously chosen for that,—but in the collective sense of himself and the other personal followers of Christ while He was here on earth. The ancient and unbroken testimony which ascribes the Epistle to the Apostle John also supports this view. The writer seems to stand in relation to his readers as teacher and taught (cf. 1:2, 3). This theory accounts for the absence of the writer's name and other details about himself: they were superfluous, his thoughts, language, and emphasis were too well known to be mistaken.

Furthermore, we have shown above that the Apostle John wrote the Fourth Gospel. There is practical unanimity of opinion that the one who wrote the Gospel wrote also the Epistle. The fact that a few words occur in the one and not in the other does not affect the question of authorship, in view of the long list of words that occurs in both. Notice a part of that list: Word, light, eternal life, love, new commandment, abide, lay down one's life, take away sins, works of the devil, over-

---

25. *Against Heresies,* III. xvi. 8.
26. *Ib.,* III. xvi. 5.
27. *Stromata* II. xv.
28. *Stromata* III. iv.

come the world, murderer, pass from death unto life, Paraclete, water and blood, Savior of the world, begotten of God, joy fulfilled, bear witness. What if the words "propitiation," "anointing," and "parousia" do not occur in both? Does an author have to use his entire vocabulary every time he writes for fear of not being recognized as the author? Both books have the same Hebraistic style, make the same use of parallelism, and have the same simplicity of sentence construction. We, therefore, hold that 1 John as well as the Fourth Gospel were written by the Apostle John.

2. **Background and Destination.** Little need or can be said on this point, for there is little indication, either externally or internally, as to the people to whom the Epistle was sent. We do not believe, however, that it was sent to the Parthians (Augustine), or to the Jewish Christians in Palestine (Benson), or to the Church at Corinth (Lightfoot). It was apparently not written to any particular local Church, but to a group of Churches. Alford thinks the warning against idols (5 21), combined with the fact that there is little reference to the Old Testament in the Epistle, indicates that the readers were mostly Gentiles.[29] This may be true; but whether or not this is the case, the writer knows their circumstances and had some special reason for interest in them.

Irenæus twice in the same section represents John as residing in Ephesus during the latter days of his life. In the first place he calls him "the disciple of the Lord," and in the second he refers to him in the following way: "Then, again, the Church in Ephesus, founded by Paul, and having John remaining among them permanently until the time of Trajan, is a true witness of the tradition of the apostles."[30] It seem as if John had taken over, not only the Church of Ephesus, but also all the Churches of the surrounding country, as the Churches of Smyrna, Pergamos, Thyatira, Sardis, Philadelphia, and Laodicea (Rev. 2 and 3). John would visit the neighboring districts of the Gentiles, appoint overseers, and organize new Churches. What is more natural than to suppose that the First Epistle is directed to these believers?

29. *Greek Testament*, IV, 167.
30. *Against Heresies*, III, iii. 4.

3. **Occasion and Date.** The Epistle was apparently called forth by the error that had crept in among the believers in these regions and by their need for instruction and warning. Irenæus tells us about these things. He says: "John, the disciple of the Lord, preaches this faith, and seeks, by the proclamation of the Gospel, to remove that error which by Cerinthus had been disseminated among men, and a long time previously by those termed Nicolaitans, who are an offset of that 'knowledge' falsely so called, that he might confound them."[31] Historically, he represents the Nicolaitans as being earlier, at least they were earlier in this region. He identifies them with Nicolaus (Acts 6:5) and says: "They lived lives of unrestrained indulgence. The character of these men is very plainly pointed out in the Apocalypse of John as teaching that it is a matter of indifference to practice adultery, and to eat things sacrificed to idols."[32] He represents Cerinthus as having been educated in Egypt, and as holding that the world was made by a lesser God, that Jesus was born of Mary and Joseph, that at baptism the Christ descended upon Him, that then He proclaimed the unknown Father and performed miracles, and that the Christ departed from Him before He died and rose again.[33] Thus the error seems to have involved a claim to superior knowledge by all; on the part of some also the denial of the reality of the body of Jesus; on the part of others, of the permanent indwelling of Christ in Jesus; and, at least on the part of some, the open practice of licentiousness.

The internal evidence indicates that some of the errorists had withdrawn from the Church (2:18, 19). The believers knew the truth (2:21), but they tended to love the world and the things of the world (2:15-17) and to remain indifferent toward their needy brethren (3:15-18). This was because they were untrue to their light (2:24-27) and had not entered into the full assurance of salvation (5:13). They were hated by the world (3:13) and needed to know the true character of the world (5:19). Moved by these facts John wrote this Epistle.

---

31. *Against Heresies* III. xi. 1.
32. *Ib.*, I. xxvi. 3.
33. *Ib.*, I. xxvi. 1.

At the earliest, we cannot think that John got to Ephesus until after Paul's last visit to that region, say after 66 or 67; more likely he did not get there until after the fall of Jerusalem in A. D. 70. This tragic event dispersed the Church, and a colony of believers came to Asia Minor. According to tradition, the Apostles John, Philip, and Andrew were among them. We have noted Irenæus' claim that John lived until the time of Trajan (98-117) (see above). The Epistle must have been written a considerable time after the destruction of Jerusalem. The question arises, Was it earlier than the Gospel? Hug thought so; he regarded it as an introduction to the Gospel. But the Gospel does not need an introduction and the Epistle supplies none. Again and again the Epistle assumes an acquaintance on the part of its readers with the facts of the Gospel narrative. The Epistle is a kind of moral and practical application of the Gospel. The time between the writing of the two cannot have been long. We would date it the same as the Gospel, A. D. 85-90, but place it a little later than the Gospel.

4. Purpose and Plan. John wrote to meet the doctrinal and practical needs of his readers. More specifically, he seems to have had four great purposes: (1) to enhance his own joy (1:4, thus the best text), (2) to keep them from sin (2:1), (3) to lead them into an assurance of salvation (5:13; cf. 2:12), and (4) to warn them against error (2:26). Still more in detail, he (1) affirms the reality of the incarnation (1:1-4), (2) discusses the practical aspects of the sin question (1:5-2:6), (3) stresses the new commandment of love of the brethren (2:7-11), (4) exhorts all classes to separate from the world (2:12-17), (5) warns his readers against heretical teaching (2:18-29), (6) admonishes them to live in the light of what they are and what they shall be (3:1-12), (7) supplies various tests of salvation (3:13-24), (8) shows how to distinguish between the spirit of truth and the spirit of error (4:1-6), (9) entreats his readers to practice brotherly love (4:7-21), (10) sets forth the logical outworking of faith in Christ (5:1-12), (11) assures his readers of their eternal salvation and encourages them to make full proof thereof (5:13-17). and (12) summarizes the things that the believer really knows (5:18-21). We may present these ideas in outline form, as follows:

(1) The Reality of the Incarnation, 1:1-4.
(2) The Practical Aspects of the Sin Question, 1:5-2:6
(3) The New Commandment of Love of the Brethren, 2:7-11.
(4) The Exhortations to Separation from the World, 2:12-17.
(5) The Warning Against Heretical Teaching, 2:18-29
(6) The Admonition to Live Consistently, 3:1-12.
(7) The Tests of Salvation, 3:13-24.
(8) The Distinctions Between the Spirit of Truth and the Spirit of Error, 4:1-6.
(9) The Entreaty to Practice Brotherly Love, 4:7-21.
(10) The Logical Outworking of Faith in Christ, 5:1-12.
(11) The Assurance of Salvation and the Outworking Thereof, 5:13-17.
(12) The Things which the Believer Really Knows, 5:18-21.

---

3. THE SECOND EPISTLE OF JOHN

This brief Epistle is a note from "the elder unto the elect lady and her children" (vs. 1). Since it is so short and of a private character, it was not circulated as early or as widely as 1 John. Consequently we do not find many early quotations of or definite allusions to it. Eusebius classed it with the *antilegomena,* though merely with the disputed and not with the spurious. Irenæus quotes vss. 10, 11 somewhat loosely[34] and vss. 7 and 8 almost verbally, although he seems to think he is quoting from the First Epistle.[35] This may be due to the fact that, as we have shown under the Canon, some early writers sometimes included 2 and 3 John in 1 John, and sometimes spoke of John's three Epistles as two, as seems to be the case in the Muratorian Fragment. Origen did not accept the Epistle, or at least had doubts regarding it. According to Jamieson, Fausset, and Brown, Clement of Alexandria says in his *Adumbrations* (p. 1011) : "John's Second Epistle which was written to the virgins is the simplest; but it was written to a certain Babylonian named the Elect lady."[36] Dionysius of Alexandria says

---

34. *Against Heresies* I. xvi. 3.
35. *Ib.,* III. xvi. 8.
36. *Crit. and Explan. Comm. on the Bible,* p. 538.

John does not name himself in his Epistles, "not even in the Second and Third Epistles, although they are short Epistles, but simply calls himself the presbyter."[37] Cyprian introduces a quotation from vs. 10 as being written by "John the Apostle."[38]

Objection has been raised on the ground that the writer calls himself an "elder" instead of an "apostle" (vs. 1); but if Peter could call himself an "apostle" (1 Pet. 1:1) and also a "fellow-elder" (5:1), why could not John speak of himself as an "elder"? We should also remember that Papias used the term "elder" of apostles.[39] The Greek word *presbuteros* (vs. 1) also means "advanced in years," "aged," and it is possible that the writer used it in that sense (it is so used in Acts 2:17). We need not here discuss the question whether John the Presbyter is a different person than John the Apostle (see under the Gospel of John, above). The style and vocabulary of 2 John are so much like that in the Gospel that the one who wrote the latter must also have written the former. Besides, there is no conceivable ground for forgery in this case; surely, a forger would have represented the writer as an apostle, and not as an elder. We hold, then, that this Epistle, too, was written by the Apostle John.

Five views have been advanced as to the meaning of the terms "the elect lady and her children" (vs. 1). Jerome said, the whole Church; Lightfoot, Brooke, and Zahn say some local Church whose location we cannot now determine; Wordsworth thinks it is the Church in Babylon, holding that we have a hint of this usage in 1 Pet. 5:13. But the statement in 1 Peter is more naturally understood to refer to some influential woman in Babylon, perhaps Peter's wife; and it seems very unlikely that in so short an Epistle the Apostle would use allegorical language without any hint that he is using it. It is much more likely that he wrote it to some influential lady somewhere in his circuit of Churches. The address in vs. 5 and the salutation in vs. 13 more naturally refer to an individual than a Church.

---

37. Euseb., *H. E.*, VII. xxv.
38. *De Haereticis Baptizandis.*
39. Euseb., *H. E.*, III. xxxix.

But here again there is difference of opinion. Law holds that the word translated "elect" should be regarded as a proper noun and that the Epistle is addressed to the "Lady Electa." But this term is not known to have been a personal name. Alford, Kerr, and D. Smith hold that the word translated "lady" is a proper noun and that the Epistle is addressed to the "elect Kyria." Bengel held that the Greek word *kuria* (vs. 1) answers to the Hebrew Martha, and that she and her family had settled in Asia Minor in one of the cities under John's care. Research has shown that Kyria was sometimes used as a proper name; but that this Epistle is addressed to one by that name, more particularly to Martha, is a mere fancy. We take it, then, that 2 John is a personal note, sent by the Apostle John to an "elect lady and her children" whose names we do not know, but who lived somewhere in the circuit of Churches over which the Apostle had the oversight.

The "elect lady" was a person of influence and esteemed by all (vss. 1, 2). It may be that like Nympha[40] in Laodicea (Col. 4:15), she had a church meet in her house. It appears also from vs. 10 that she had hospitably entertained itinerant preachers who had visited the community. John had met some of the children of this lady and had been well impressed with their devotion to the truth. He also knew how persistent the false teachers were in this area. These things led him to write the Epistle. There was probably no great interval between the writing of 1 John and 2 John; so we may assign the date A. D. 85-90 to this Epistle also.

The Apostle wrote to express his appreciation of the loyalty of this "lady and her children" (vss. 1-4), to entreat the "lady" to walk in love and to keep the Lord's commandments (5, 6), to warn her against the deceivers that were abroad (7-11), to inform her of his plan to visit her soon (12), and to convey the greeting of the children of her sister (13). Special attention is called to the hospitality that John prohibits (vss. 10, 11).

---

4. THE THIRD EPISTLE OF JOHN

The Third Epistle of John is the shortest book in the New Testament: in Greek, it is about a line shorter than 2 John.

---

40. West. and Hort and Nestle text.

The external evidence for this Epistle has already been mentioned in connection with our study of 2 John (see above). Origen classed it with the *antilegomena* and Eusebius did so also. But Clement of Alexandria and Dionysius of Alexandria seem both to have accepted it. The former wrote a commentary on all Catholic Epistles except James, 2 Peter, and 3 John, but apparently accepted all the books we have in our New Testament. Neither 2 nor 3 John are in the Old Syriac; the Muratorian Fragment, as we have seen, is indefinite. Cyril of Jerusalem (c. 349) accepted all of the Catholic Epistles; and they were all endorsed by the Third Council of Carthage (397). The internal evidence is of the same nature as that for 2 John: the ideas, vocabulary, and style all point to the Apostle John as the author. The term "elder" (vs. 1) unites it closely with the Second Epistle (vs. 1).

The letter is addressed to "Gaius the beloved" (vs. 1). But we do not know whether it is Gaius of Macedonia, a companion of Paul on his third journey (Acts 19:29), Gaius of Derbe (Acts 20:4), Gaius of Corinth, Paul's host when in that city (Rom. 16:23; 1 Cor. 1:14), or some other Gaius. The name was very common, and he may well have been some other Gaius. The *Constitutions of the Holy Apostles* says that a certain Gaius had been ordained as "bishop" of Pergamos by the Apostle John (VII, xlvi). But this work is after all from about the middle of the fourth century and is not reliable. Whoever he may be, he was apparently a prominent member of some Church in Asia Minor under the Apostle's supervision, if not its bishop or presbyter.

Trouble had arisen in the Church of which Gaius was a member or the leader. Itinerating preachers, seemingly sent by John, had visited the Church; but Diotrephes, apparently an influential layman, had spoken against the Apostle, had refused to recognize the messengers of the Gospel, and had opposed those who received them. No reason for his attitude and conduct is given, except that he wanted to have the pre-eminence. It was probably not doctrinal, although, since there were various schisms in the Church in those days, Diotrephes may have preferred Paul to John. There is, however, no proof for this. This distressing situation in the Church led John to write this letter.

It, too, was apparently written soon after 1 John, and so we give it the same date, A. D. 85-90.

John wrote the Epistle to express his love for Gaius (vs. 1), to assure him of his prayers for his prosperity and health (2), to tell him of his joy at his stand for the truth (3, 4), to commend him for having received the visiting preachers (5, 6a), to encourage him to do it again when they return (6b-8), to inform him that he may come and deal with the domineering Diotrephes (9, 10), to commend Demetrius, who was probably the bearer of this Epistle (11, 12), and to inform him that he hopes shortly to visit him and talk things over with him face to face (13, 14). Thus we have in this Epistle an intimate glimpse into some aspects of church life in Asia Minor toward the close of the first century.

Chapter XIV

THE APOCALYPSE

THIS book purports to be "the Revelation of Jesus Christ" (1:1). With due respect for the scholarship that differs with us, we take this to be an objective genitive, "the Revelation of the Person and Work of Christ." It would seem that of the twelve times that the word "revelation" (*apokalupsis*) occurs with a genitive, outside the present reference, only two could be subjective genitives (2 Cor. 12:1; Gal. 1:12), "the Revelation from Jesus Christ"; all the others are objective genitives (Luke 2:32; Rom. 2:5; 8:19; 16:25; 1 Cor. 1:7; 2 Thess. 1:7; 1 Pet. 1:7, 13; 4:13). When we add to this the fact that 2 Cor. 12:1 and Gal. 1:12 may also be intended to be objective genitives, the position we have taken for Rev. 1:1 becomes very strong. It would seem that in the earliest times the book received the title, "Apocalypse of John," to distinguish it from the many other "apocalypses" in circulation. In the fourth century this title was expanded to include the words "the Divine."

The book belongs to the type of literature that is known as "apocalyptic." In this kind of writing the predictive element is prominent, the symbols are often arbitrary (*e. g.,* the beast with seven heads and ten horns), and the visions become the vehicle of the message. The symbols are usually left unexplained. The Book of Revelation is related to the same type of prophecies in Daniel, Ezekiel, and Zechariah, as also to the prophetic teaching of Jesus Himself. The present-day attempt to put it on the same plane as the Book of Enoch, the Apocalypse of Baruch, the Assumption of Moses, the Ascension of Isaiah, and other apocalyptic books, is not only unwarranted on the ground of the contents of the books, but irreverent.

These other books are but the conceptions of men; this is a divine revelation given to John.

1. **Attestation and Authorship.** The external attestation for this book is as strong as one might wish. There are possible traces of its use in Barnabas, Ignatius, the Teaching of the Twelve Apostles, and the Testaments of the Twelve Patriarchs; but they are not very clear. Justin Martyr says that John, one of the Apostles of Christ, prophesied "that those who believed in our Christ would dwell a thousand years in Jerusalem."[1] Irenæus says, "John also, the Lord's disciple, ... says in the Apocalypse," and then quotes 1:12-16; 5:6; 19:11-17 almost verbally, in *Against Heresies* (IV. xx. 11). In the same work (V. xxvi.1) he does the same for 17:12-14. Indeed, he quotes from nearly every chapter in the book. In the same work (V. xxx. 3) he says that John saw the Apocalypse "towards the end of Domitian's reign." Tertullian says, "the Apostle John" beheld the city come down out of heaven, referring to 21:10-23, in *Against Marcion* (III. xxv.). He refers to 1:16 in the same work (III. xiv) and to 2:14 in *Prescription Against Heresies* (ch. xxxiii). In *Scorpiace* (ch. xii), he quotes from a number of the seven letters in chs. 2 and 3 and summarizes the blessings promised to the overcomers. He quotes from every chapter in the book, with the possible exception of chs. 9, 13, and 15. Hippolytus, disciple of Irenæus, in *Treatise on Christ and Antichrist* (sections 36-42), quotes chs. 17 and 18 almost word for word and assigns them to "John, apostle and disciple of the Lord."

To the same effect is the testimony of the eastern writers. Clement of Alexandria tells of the return of "the Apostle John" to Ephesus from the isle of Patmos, in *Who Is The Rich Man That Shall Be Saved?* (XLII). He speaks of those worthy to sit upon the twenty-four thrones, as in 4:4; 11:16, in *Stromata* (VI. xiii), and quotes 6:9, 11, with a slight change, in *Instructor* (II. xi). Origen says, in *De Principiis* (I. ii. 10), "Listen to the manner in which John speaks in the Apocalypse," and then quotes from 1:8. In the same work (IV. i. 25) he refers to the statement in 14:6, "an everlasting Gospel," and says that it is "employed by John in the Apocalypse." In his

---

1. *Dialogue with Trypho*, ch. lxxxi.

work *Against Celsus* he refers to the seven thunders in 10:4 and the eating of the book in 10:9 (VI. vi), and to the prayers of the saints in 8:3, 4 (VIII. xvii). In his *Comm. on Matthew*, from which Eusebius has preserved a fragment,[2] he declares that tradition identifies the John who was banished to the isle of Patmos with the son of Zebedee.

Victorinus writes the earliest commentary on the Apocalypse that has come down to us. He refers the statement about the seven thunders in 10:3, 4, to John the Apostle, in this *Commentary* (*in loc.*) The Muratorian Fragment says: "Among Apocalypses, we receive only those of John and Peter, though some of our friends do not wish this (the apocalypse of Peter?) to be read in the Church." Alford says, Ephraim Syrus, the greatest Father in the Syrian church, repeatedly cites the Apocalypse as canonical and as by John. He thinks this is all the more remarkable inasmuch as neither the Old Syriac, the Philoxenian Syriac, nor the Harkleian Syraic had it.[3] After this there are many other early witnesses to the Apostolic authorship of this book.

Not until the time of the Alogoi was there any difference of opinion on this point. This small sect was opposed to the book on doctrinal grounds and ascribed it to Cerinthus, the Gnostic. But their teaching was so manifestly absurd that it did not get any foothold in the Church. Dionysius of Alexandria, however, laid the foundations for the modern views as to the authorship of the Apocalypse. He approached the book with a strong anti-chiliastic bias, compared its language with that of the Gospel and the Epistles, and ascribed it to another John. Sometimes he seems to hint that this is John Mark, and then again he opposes this idea. At any rate, he held that the Apostle did not write it.[4] Eusebius is indefinite, sometimes appearing to regard it as Apostolic, and at other times, as not.[5] Many hold that John the Presbyter wrote the book; but we know absolutely nothing about him for certain, not even whether he is a person distinct from the Apostle. Ancient tradition uniformly

---

2. *H. E.*, VI. xxv.
3. *Greek Testament*, IV, 202.

4. Euseb., *H. E.*, VII. xxv.
5. *H. E.*, III. xxiv and xxxix.

recognizes John the Apostle, and neither John Mark nor John the Presbyter, as the author of this book. The Reformers Luther, Zwingli, and Erasmus rejected it as non-apostolic; but in the light of this array of external testimony their opinion cannot carry any weight. Calvin does not discuss the question.

Four times the writer calls himself John (1:1, 4, 9; 22:8). He does not call himself an apostle, but merely a "servant" of Christ (1:1) and a "brother and partaker with you in the tribulation and kingdom and patience which are in Jesus" (1:9). These statements have been used against the apostolic authorship of the book. It has even been suggested that in speaking of the names of the twelve apostles on the foundations of the walls of the New Jerusalem (21:14), he definitely distinguishes himself from the apostles. But to one who believes that the Apostle John wrote the Fourth Gospel, the humility of the writer of the Apocalypse serves to identify him with the Apostle. Paul calls himself an apostle (Eph. 1:1) and also refers to the apostles in the third person in the same Epistle (2:20; 3:5). This John was in exile on the isle of Patmos (1:9), and the Fathers declare that it was John the Apostle who was banished to the isle. Clement of Alexandria says that the Apostle John returned from this island;[6] Eusebius says that he returned after the death of Domitian;[7] and Irenæus says that he remained in Ephesus after his return until the times of Trajan.[8] This would seem to settle the question on historical grounds.

But from the time of Dionysius of Alexandria onward objection to the apostolic authorship of the book has been raised on linguistic grounds. The arguments are based on the barbarisms and solecisms in the Apocalypse, the differences in vocabulary between it and the other Johannine writings, the Hebraistic style in the book, etc. But the barbarisms and solecisms have been greatly exaggerated. The solecisms are largely forms of *anacoluthon* (1:5; 2:17; 3:12), attempts on part of the writer to emphasize certain words and phrases (1:4; 3:3; 9:5; 14:14,—with the latter compare 1:15; 9:7), and con-

---

6. *Who Is the Rich Man*, etc., XLII.
7. *H. E.*, III. xx.
8. *Against Heresies*, III. iii. 4.

structions according to sense rather than grammar (4:1; 9:13, 11:15; 13:14). If he breaks the rule in one place, he observes it in another. Although there are differences in vocabulary between the Apocalypse and the other writings of John, there are also significant similarities (*e. g.*, the Word, he who overcomes, water of life, show, little lamb, etc.) The Hebraistic style is only what we might expect in a book that makes such large use of Old Testament imagery.

There are, however, grammatical irregularities that some think are more difficult to explain. But the difference in subject-matter in the Apocalypse accounts for the difference in vocabulary. Again, in the Apocalypse the seer is carried from vision to vision and appears to have written immediately the things which he saw (cf. 10:4), whereas in his other writings the author calmly collected and arranged his materials. And again, John may have written the Apocalypse without an amanuensis and have had one for his other writings. Anyone that is at all familiar with the vernacular *Koinē* Greek finds nothing peculiar in the Apocalypse in this respect. As a matter of fact, many of the irregularities in grammar in this book are also found in the writers of classical Greek; and the greater frequency of their occurrence in the Apocalypse is due to the nature of the subject and the circumstances. We take it, then, as fully proved that the Apostle John wrote the Apocalypse.

2. **Background and Destination.** John came to Ephesus in the year 69 or 70. He appears to have taken charge of a number of churches in Asia. Ephesus, Smyrna, Pergamos, Thyatira, Sardis, Philadelphia, and Laodicea appear to have been in this circuit. No doubt Ephesus was his headquarters; but as time allowed and need arose the Apostle would visit other cities, appoint leaders in the Churches, and help to set in order the things wanting. According to Eusebius,[9] he was imprisoned in the isle of Patmos in the fifteenth year of Domitian, and according to him also[10] he returned in the beginning of the reign of Nerva. Clement of Alexandria agrees with this date and tells about John's activity after his return. He says: "For

---

9. *H. E.*, III. xviii.
10. *H. E.*, III, xx.

when, on the tyrant's death, he returned to Ephesus from the
isle of Patmos, he went away, being invited, to the contiguous
territories of the nations, here to appoint bishops, there to set
in order whole churches, there to ordain such as were marked
out by the Spirit." He then tells an interesting story of a
youth whom the Apostle committed to the bishop in a certain
city, who baptized him. This youth fell in with bad company
and was led far away from the truth, until he ended up as the
head of a band of robbers. When John returned to this city,
he enquired after the young man; and when he was told that
he had backslidden, he asked for a horse and sought him out
and brought him back to the truth.[11]

The Apocalypse is, no doubt, first of all intended for the
seven churches of Asia mentioned several times (1:4, 10, 11;
chs. 2 and 3). But it was undoubtedly also intended for the
neighboring churches and beyond them for the whole Church.
Colossæ and Hierapolis had been destroyed by an earthquake
since the days of Paul, and we do not know their state of
restoration at this time. It would seem that copies were early
made and sent to the near-by places. There were other churches
in Asia. Ignatius writes to the Magnesians and the Trallians.
There was undoubtedly also a church at Troas, and perhaps another at Miletus. The fact that only seven of the Asian
Churches are addressed seems to indicate that the Holy Spirit
is thinking symbolically of the whole Church. Everyone, therefore, who reads, hears, and keeps the things written in this
book, has the promise of divine blessing (1:3).

3. **Occasion and Date.** John tells us that he wrote this book
at the direct command of the Lord, apparently Christ Himself
(1:10-13). This is the only instance in the New Testament in
which a writer gives this as his reason for writing. No doubt
behind the Lord's command lay the needs of the Churches in
a day of fierce persecution and of the Church of all time since
then. It is just possible that the "angels" of the Churches are
the ministers of the congregations. If that is so, then these
"messengers" (the real meaning of the Greek *aggeloi*) may
have visited John in his banishment and have informed him of

---

11. *Who is the Rich Man*, etc., XLII.

the condition of their parishes. In that case, their report would be another occasion for the Apocalypse.

Westcott, Lightfoot, Hort, Salmon, and others, hold that the book was written about 68 or 69. Generally speaking, two reasons are given for the earlier date: the character of the Greek and the teaching concerning the seven heads on the beast in chs. 13 and 17. Since the Apocalypse is inferior to the Gospel and the Epistles in its linguistic qualities, some hold that the Apocalypse was written first, when John did not know his Greek very well, and that the other books were written later, when he had learned a good deal more Greek. But we have already explained the linguistic differences as due to change of subject-matter and circumstances, differences of amanuensis, etc. And since five of the kings were already fallen, one was, one was to come and continue for a short time, and after that the eighth was to appear, some take this to refer to the emperors of Rome. Those who begin the count with Julius Cæsar, date the book in the reign of Nero (Moses Stuart); those who begin with Augustus, in the reign of Galba (Ewald); or, if Galba, Otho, and Vitellius, who had only about a year between them, are counted as usurpers, then in the reign of Vespasian (Eichhorn, Bleek).

The claim that it was written in the time of Nero is supported by the mystical number, six hundred and sixty-six (13:18). It is said that if we omit the *yodh* in the Hebrew words *Kaisar Neron,* we get the number 666. But the defective writing of *Kaisar,* i. e., without the *yodh,* is rather unusual, as is also the final "n" in *Neron.* Without going into the meaning of this number, we would say that this solution is inadequate. The theory involves the belief that after Nero there would be a short reign by a seventh emperor, and that after that Nero would return and be an eighth, with whom the end would come. All this was to happen in three and one-half years. History has, of course, long ago disproved this theory. Nero did not return; Jerusalem was destroyed and not exalted; Rome did not perish; and the three and one-half years did not bring the end. Yet in spite of all these failures, the Church everywhere received the book as inspired. This indicates that the early date is incorrect.

The majority of recent expositors (*e. g.,* Alford, Swete, Milligan, Orr, Moffatt, Zahn) hold that the book was written in A. D. 95 or 96. They base their view on the testimonies of Irenæus (above), Clement of Alexandria (above), Eusebius (above), and others, that the banishment to Patmos and the receiving of the Visions was in the latter time of the reign of Domitian. Since he was emperor from A. D. 81-96, the Apocalypse may be dated 95 or 96. This view also accords with the fact that the persecution under Domitian, unlike that under Nero, was due to the refusal of the Christians to worship the emperor; cf. 1:9 and a possible anticipatory fulfillment in 13:9, 10, 12. The Greek words translated "on the Lord's day" (1:10) can only mean Sunday.[12] Ignatius says to the *Magnesians* (ch. ix) : "No longer observing the Sabbath, but living in the observance of the Lord's Day." Eusebius says,[13] Melito of Sardis wrote a treatise "Concerning the Lord's Day." Swete says before the end of the second century this term was generally used for Sunday. Alford says, there is not a single indication that this Greek phrase was ever used for the prophetic Day of the Lord.[14]

4. **Approach and Interpretation.** It makes all the difference how one approaches any book that he studies; this is peculiarly true of one's approach to the study of the Apocalypse. The so-called "literary" approach, for instance, which dissects the book and finds in it nothing but sources, interpolations, redactions, etc., robs it of all significance, except that of a literary curiosity, if not monstrosity. Very different is that approach which recognizes the Apocalypse as a divinely inspired book, written at the command of God by the Apostle John during the last days of his life. The one who thus approaches it will regard the book as a welcome gift from God which brings to him an unfolding of the redemptive purposes of God. This is what the book claims to be (1:1-3; 22:6, 7). But even among those who accept it as a divine revelation there are great differences of opinion as to the way in which it should be interpreted. Let us turn to a brief examination of the four best known methods of interpretation.

---

12. *Didache,* ch. 14; cf. Deissmann, *Bible Studies,* p. 219.
13. *H. E.,* IV. xxiii.
14. *Greek Test.,* IV, 554.

(1) *The Spiritual Method.* The earlier form of this method originated in the allegorical teaching of the Alexandrian Fathers, Clement and Origen. Approaching the book with a strong anti-chiliastic bias, they allegorized everything they could not understand and also much that they could. In their day the belief in a millennial kingdom on earth, to follow the second advent of Christ, was widely diffused; but the Alexandrians were not in sympathy with this belief and held that it was a sign of maturity to proceed from the literal interpretation to the spiritual. The results of this method were, however, very unsatisfactory; for everyone interpreted the symbols and figures in his own way, and so the book conveyed no definite message to the Church. Jerome and Augustine adopted this method with certain modifications.

The modern form of this method looks upon the Apocalypse as dealing with the conflict between the Church and the forces of evil through the whole Christian dispensation,—not as giving us a divine forecast of specific events, but as indicating great principles which are in conflict. Milligan says: "These successive waves of judgment are obviously successive in thought rather than time."[15] To this writer the book becomes, "not a history of either early or mediæval or last events written of before they happened, but a spring of elevating encouragement and holy joy to Christians in every age."[16] Now while we agree that the Apocalypse affords encouragement to tried saints in all periods of the Church's history, we, nevertheless, feel that the advocates of this view do not go far enough. It seems to us that they too largely overlook the fact that the book claims to be a prophecy (1:3; 10:11; 22:7, 10, 18, 19) and that it points immediately to the second advent (1:7; 3:11; 16:15; 19:7; 22:7, 12, 20).

(2) *The Praeterist Method.* This theory holds that practically all of the book has already been fulfilled. The older Praeterist view, of which Moses Stuart of Andover is a representative, held that chs. 6-11 were fulfilled in "the humiliation and prostration of the Jewish persecuting enemies of the

---

15. *Lectures on the Apocalypse*, p. 148.
16. *Ibid.*, p. 155.

Church,"[17] and ch. 13-19, mainly in the reign of Nero.[18] All
the rest, Stuart held, is merely vaguely intimated, except that
chs. 21, 22 are definitely future. The modern Praeterist view
originated with the Jesuit Alcasar (d. 1613). He held that
chs. 4-11 refer to the conflict of the Church with Judaism, and
chs. 12-19, with paganism, while chs. 20-22 speak of her present triumph and power. Grotius of the Netherlands and Ham-
mond of Great Britain have held much the same views. The
fanciful meaning that is given to the symbols by this system is
enough to discredit it, to say nothing of the indications that
chs. 4-19 deal with a relatively short period of time in connection with the second coming of Christ.

(3) *The Continuous-Historical Method.* This method holds
that the book covers the whole history of the Church from the
time of John to the end of the world. Berengaud (9th cent.)
seems first to have suggested this approach, although he carried the history of the book back to the creation of the universe. It was not until the twelfth century that the method was
popularized. At that time Joachim, a Roman Catholic, advocated it. There are some indications that Anselm also espoused
this view. Strange to say, however, the methods of Joachim
led some of the Reformers to adopt this view and to identify
the Pope or the Papacy with the Antichrist. Wycliffe, Luther,
Joseph Mede, Sir Isaac Newton, Wm. Whiston, Elliott, Vi-
tringa, Bengel, and Barnes are considered supporters of this
method of interpretation. A year-day theory is generally associated with this interpretation. Alford accepts the view in part,
but expresses his disgust with some of the historical interpreters who wrest "the text to make it suit a preconceived
scheme."[19]

But it seems to us that there are many objections to this approach. In the first place, we say with Milligan: "Could it be
a part of the Divine plan to make the understanding of a revelation so earnestly commended to us dependent on an acquaintance with the ecclesiastical and political history of the world
for many hundred years? The very supposition is absurd. It
is inconsistent with the first promise of the book, 'Blessed is

17. *Comm. on the Apocalypse,* p. 531.
18. *Ibid.,* p. 699 f.
19. *Op. cit.,* IV, 248 f.

he that readeth, and they that hear the words of the prophecy'."[20] Milligan would not agree with our interpretation of
the book either, but we believe that he is right in this statement. In the second place we wish to say that many of the
figures and symbols will not bear the interpretation put upon
them by this theory (as that the first four trumpets predict the
overthrow of the Roman empire; the first two woe trumpets,
the overthrow of the Saracens and the Turks; and that the
beast, ch. 13, and the scarlet woman, ch. 17, are both the
Papacy). Furthermore, we feel that the theory has difficulties
with the details of the book. Holding, as it does, that much of
the book has already been fulfilled, it finds in the prophecy allusions to Ignatius, Justin, Polycarp, Irenæus, Cyprian, Alaric,
Genseric, Attila, etc.[21] Finally, we regard the hopeless differences among the historical interpreters as a strong proof that
they are on the wrong track.

(4) *The Futuristic Method.* This view maintains that the
book relates mainly to things which are yet to come; more
particularly, that from chs. 4-22 practically all is still future.
It connects these chapters with the second coming of Christ
and the millennium. The beast is an empire that is yet to arise
and that will be headed by a great monster; the scarlet-colored
woman is the false ecclesiasticism of the last days. It is impossible to cite the early Church in favor of this view; but it
seems to us they must have held it. They believed in the imminence of the Lord's return; they believed in an earthly millennium; and they believed that there would be a period of
tribulation that would introduce the kingdom. It is clear that
Justin Martyr, Irenæus, Hippolytus, Tertullian, and apparently
Victorinus, held the literal view of the kingdom. They were
chiliasts.

It is true that this view was lost to the Church for a long time;
but in the sixteenth century it was revived by Ribera. Many
notable men have supported it, *e. g.,* Maitland, Todd, Isaac
Williams, etc. Zahn represents himself as holding "a futuris-

---

20. *Op. cit.,* p. 131.
21. See Elliott's *Horae Apocalypticae* with chart, as an example.

tic view."[22] In what respect he is a futurist may be gathered from his interpretation of the seven-sealed book. He says: "Just as in Germany before the introduction of money-orders, everyone knew that a letter sealed with five seals contained money, so the most simple member of the Asiatic churches knew that a *biblion* made fast with seven seals was a *testament*. When the testator dies the testament is brought forward, and, when possible, opened in the presence of the seven witnesses who sealed it; i. e., unsealed, read aloud, and executed. . . . So also here, the document fastened with seven seals is an easily understood symbol of the promise and assurance by God to His Church of the future *basileia*. . . . The returning Christ will open the testament of God and execute it."[23]

5. **Purpose and Plan.** The purpose of the book is by the Holy Spirit Himself declared to be, "to show unto his servants the things which must shortly come to pass" (1:1). There ought not to be any difficulty about the clause, "which must shortly come to pass." God does not reckon time as we do (2 Pet. 3:8); besides, the New Testament constantly represents the coming of the Lord as near at hand (1 Thess. 4:16, 17; Phil. 4:5; James 5:8, 9; 1 Pet. 4:7). It asks us to watch and look for Him at any time (Mark 13:33-37; 1 Thess. 1:10; Rom. 13:11, 12; Tit. 2:13; Heb. 9:28). This clause, therefore, does not necessarily mean that the fulfillment will actually begin at once, but merely that we are to look for it to begin at any time in the future. Involved in this general purpose are such immediate aims as the purification, encouragement, and fortification of the seven churches, and beyond them the whole Church; and the establishment of God's people in the belief of the ultimate triumph of Christ and His cause.

As was pointed out at the beginning of this chapter, this book is "the Revelation of the Person and Work of Christ." The verb *gave* (*edōken*) is a Hebraism and meants *granted*. It is not to be supposed that Jesus even in His glorified state did not know the events of the future until the Father made them known to Him. He knew them immediately and completely.

22. *Op. cit.*, III, 436.
23. *Op. cit.*, III, 394 f.

The thought is rather that God granted Him this wonderful revelation of Himself in connection with the outworking of His future purposes. Regarding this as the probable meaning of the opening words of the book, we would analyze it as follows:

Introduction, 1:1-11.

A. The Self-Revelation of Christ, 1:12-20.

    (1) The Place of Christ, 12, 13.
    (2) The Characteristics of Christ, 13-16.
    (3) The Message of Christ, 17-20.

B. Christ and the Church, chs. 2 and 3.

    (1) The Church in Ephesus, 2:1-7.
    (2) The Church in Smyrna, 2:8-11.
    (3) The Church in Pergamum, 2:12-17.
    (4) The Church in Thyatira, 2:18-29.
    (5) The Church in Sardis, 3:1-6.
    (6) The Church in Philadelphia, 3:7-13.
    (7) The Church in Laodicea, 3:14-22.

C. Christ and the Great Tribulation, chs. 4-19.

    (1) The Preparations in Heaven, chs. 4 and 5.
    (2) The Opening of Six Seals, ch. 6.
    (3) The First Parenthesis, ch. 7.
    (4) The Opening of the Seventh Seal, 8:1.
    (5) The Sounding of Six Trumpets, 8:2-9:21.
    (6) The Second Parenthesis, 10:1-11:14.
    (7) The Sounding of the Seventh Trumpet, 11:15-18.
    (8) The Third Parenthesis, 11:19-14:20.
    (9) The Pouring Out of the Seven Bowls of Wrath, chs. 15 and 16.
    (10) The Judgment of Babylon, chs. 17 and 18.
    (11) The Marriage Supper of the Lamb, 19:1-10.
    (12) The Public Appearing of Christ and His Own, 19:11-21

D. Christ and the Millennial Reign, ch. 20.

    (1) The Binding of Satan, 1-3.
    (2) The Millennial Reign, 4-6.

(3) The Loosing and Final Doom of Satan, 7-10.

(4) The Judgment of the Great White Throne, 11-15.

E. Christ and the Eternal State, 21:1-22:5.

(1) The New Realms: The New Heaven, the New Earth, the New Jerusalem, 21:1,2.

(2) The Blessedness of the New Realm, 21:3-6a.

(3) The Invitation to the New Realm, 21:6b, 7.

(4) The Portion of those Excluded from the New Realm, 21:8.

(5) The Description of the New Jerusalem, 21:9-22:5. Conclusion, 22:6-21.

THE END

BIBLIOGRAPHY

BIBLIOGRAPHY

This list of books is not intended to be exhaustive, but representative. Those works whose position is thoroughly or generally conservative are indicated by an asterisk (*).

Introductions to the New Testament

*Cartledge, Samuel A., *A Conservative Introduction to the New Testament*. 2d ed.
Deissmann, Adolf, *The New Testament in the Light of Modern Research*.
Dibelius, Martin, *A Fresh Approach to the New Testament and Early Christian Literature*.
*Godet, F. L., *An Introduction to the New Testament*. 2 vols.
Goodspeed, Edgar J., *An Introduction to the New Testament*.
Jülicher, Adolf, *An Introduction to the New Testament*.
*Knowling, R. J., "Criticism," *A Dictionary of Christ and the Gospels*.
*Knowling, R. J., *Literary Criticism of the New Testament*.
Lake, Kirsopp, and Lake, Silva, *An Introduction to the New Testament*.
*M'Clymont, J. A., *New Testament Criticism; Its History and Results*.
*M'Clymont, J. A., *The New Testament and Its Writers*.
Mc Neile, A. H., *An Introduction to the Study of the New Testament*.
Moffatt, James, *An Introduction to the Literature of the New Testament*.
Peake, Arthur S., *A Critical Introduction to the New Testament*.
*Salmon, George, *A Historical Introduction to the Study of the Books of the New Testament*.
*Zahn, Theodor, *Introduction to the New Testament*. 3 vols.

Canon and Text of the New Testament

*Burgon and Miller, *The Traditional Text of the Holy Gospels*.
*Gaussen, L., *The Canon of the Holy Scriptures*.
Goodspeed, Edgar J., *The Formation of the New Testament*.
Gregory, Caspar Rene, *Canon and Text of the New Testament*.
*Gregory, *Textkritik des Neuen Testaments*.
Kenyon, Frederic, *Our Bible and the Ancient Manuscripts*.
*Riggs, James S., "The Canon of the New Testament," *Inter. Stand. Bible Encyclopaedia*.
*Robertson, Archibald T., *An Introduction to the Textual Criticism of the New Testament*.
*Robertson, Archibald T., *Studies in the Text of the New Testament*.
*Sitterly, Charles F., "Text and Manuscripts of the New Testament," *Inter. Stand. Bible Encyclopaedia*.
Soden, H. von, *Die Schriften des Neuen Testaments in ihrer ältesten erreichbaren Textgestalt*.
Souter, Alexander, *The Text and Canon of the New Testament*.
*Westcott, B. F., *A General Survey of the History of the Canon of the New Testament*.

BIBLIOGRAPHY—Continued

*Westcott and Hort, *An Introduction to the Greek New Testament.*
*Zahn, Theodor, "The Canon of the New Testament," *The New Schaff-Herzog Encyclopedia of Religious Knowledge,* II, 393-400.

Revelation and Inspiration

*Elliott, Charles, *A Treatise on the Inspiration of the Holy Scriptures.*
*Gaussen, L., *Theopneustia: The Plenary Inspiration of the Holy Scriptures.*
*Hodge, Charles, *Systematic Theology,* I, 151-188.
Orr, James, *Revelation and Inspiration.*
*Shedd, W. G. T., *Dogmatic Theology,* I, 61-110.
*Warfield, B. B., "Inspiration," *Inter. Stand. Bible Encyclopaedia.*
*Warfield, B. B., *Revelation and Inspiration.*

SPECIAL STUDIES AND COMMENTARIES

General Commentaries and Essays

Not all the contributions to these sets are equally acceptable from the conservative standpoint, but no attempt is here made to indicate the differences. Some of the more satisfactory expositions will be found listed under the commentaries on the individual books.

Alford, Henry, *The Greek Testament.* 4 vols.

Bengel, John A., *Gnomon of the New Testament.* 3 vols.

Briggs, Driver, and Plummer (eds.), *The International Critical Commentary* (on the New Testament).

Lightfoot, J. B., *Biblical Essays.*

Lock, Walter (ed.), *The Westminster Commentaries* (on the New Testament).

Meyer, H. A. W. (ed.), *Critical and Exegetical Commentary on the New Testament.*

Nicoll, W. Robertson (ed.), *The Expositor's Bible* (on the New Testament).

Nicoll, W. Robertson, *The Expositor's Greek Testament.* 5 vols.

Orr, James (ed.), Kyle, M. G. (revision editor), *The International Standard Bible Encyclopaedia.* 5 vols.

Parry, R. St. John (ed.), *The Cambridge Bible for Schools and Colleges* (on the New Testament).

Perowne, J. J. S. (ed.), Parry, R. St. John (later editor), *The Cambridge Greek Testament.*

Robertson, Archibald T., *Word Pictures in the New Testament.* 6 vols.

Vincent, Marvin R., *Word Studies in the New Testament.* 4 vols.

Zahn, Theodor (ed.), *Kommentar zum Neuen Testament.* 18 vols.

The Four Gospels

Burton, E. D., *A Short Introduction to the Gospels.* Revised by H. R. Willoughby.

*Chapman, Dom John, *Matthew, Mark, and Luke.*

BIBLIOGRAPHY—Continued

Dibelius, Martin, *From Tradition to Gospel.*
Filson, F. V., *Origins of the Gospels.*
*Gloag, Paton J., *Introduction to the Synoptic Gospels.*
Harnack, Adolf, *The Date of the Acts and of the Synoptic Gospels.*
Hawkins, John, *Horae Synopticae.*
*Hayes, D. A., *The Synoptic Gospels and the Book of Acts.*
*Iverach, James, "The Synoptic Gospels," *Inter. Stand. Bible Encyclopaedia.*
Redlich, E. Basil, *Form Criticism: Its Value and Limitations.*
Ropes, James H., *The Synoptic Gospels.*
Scott, Ernest F., *The Validity of the Gospel Record.*
Smith, Harold, *Ante-Nicene Exegesis of the Gospels.* 5 vols.
Stanton, V. H., *The Gospels as Historical Documents.* 3 vols.
Torrey, C. C., *Our Translated Gospels.*
*Westcott, B. F., *Introduction to the Study of the Gospels.*

*Broadus, John A., *A Commentary on the Gospel of Matthew.*
*Chadwick, G. A., "The Gospel According to St. Mark," *Expositor's Bible.*
Creed, J. M., *The Gospel According to St. Luke.*
*Farmer, J. H., "The Gospel of Mark," *Inter. Stand. Bible Encyclopaedia.*
*Godet, F. L., *A Commentary on the Gospel of St. Luke.*
Harnack, Adolf, *Luke the Physician.*
*Plummer, Alfred, *An Exegetical Commentary on the Gospel According to St. Matthew.*
*Plummer, Alfred, *The Gospel According to St. Mark* (Cambridge Greek Testament).
*Plummer, Alfred, *A Critical and Exegetical Commentary on the Gospel of St. Luke* (International Critical Commentary).
*Robertson, Archibald T., *Studies in Mark's Gospel.*
*Robertson, Archibald T., "The Gospel of Luke," *Inter. Stand. Bible Encyclopedia.*
*Robertson, Archibald T., *Luke the Historian in the Light of Research.*
*Schodde, G. H., "The Gospel of Matthew," *Inter. Stand. Bible Encyclopaedia.*
Swete, H. B., *The Gospel According to St. Mark.*

*Abbott, Peabody, and Lightfoot, *The Fourth Gospel: Evidences External and Internal for Its Johannean Authorship.*
Burney, C. F., *The Aramaic Origin of the Fourth Gospel.*
*Chapman, Dom John, *John the Presbyter and the Fourth Gospel.*
Colwell, E. C., *The Greek of the Fourth Gospel.*
*Godet, F. L., *A Commentary on the Gospel of St. John.*
Hoskyns, Edwyn C., *The Fourth Gospel.* 2 vols.
*Hovey, Alvah, *A Commentary on the Gospel of John.*
Howard, W. F., *The Fourth Gospel in Recent Criticism and Interpretation.*
*Iverach, James, "The Gospel of John," Inter. Stand. Bible Encyclopaedia.
*Plummer, Alfred, *The Gospel According to St. John* (Cambridge Greek Testament).

BIBLIOGRAPHY—Continued

*Sanday, William, *The Criticism of the Fourth Gospel.*
*Westcott, B. F., *The Gospel According to St. John.* 2 vols.

The Book of Acts

Foakes-Jackson, F. J., and Lake, K. (eds.), *The Beginnings of Christianity.* 5 vols.
*Hackett, Horatio B., *A Commentary on the Original Text of the Acts of the Apostles.*
Harnack, Adolf, *The Acts of the Apostles.*
*Knowling, R. J., "The Acts of the Apostles," *Expositor's Greek Testament.*
*Rackham, R. B., *The Acts of the Apostles* (Westminster Commentaries)
Ramsay, Wm. M., *St. Paul the Traveler and the Roman Citizen.*
*Stifler, J. M., *The Acts of the Apostles.*
*Stokes, G. T., "The Acts of the Apostles," *Expositor's Bible.*

The Pauline Epistles

*Findlay, George G., *The Epistles of Paul the Apostle.*
*Hayes, D. A., *Paul and His Epistles.*
Lake, Kirsopp, *The Earlier Epistles of Paul.*
*Machen, J. Gresham, *The Origin of Paul's Religion.*
Sabatier, A., *The Apostle Paul: A Sketch of the Development of His Doctrine.*
*Shaw, R. D., *The Pauline Epistles.*
Smith, David, *Life and Letters of St. Paul.*

Barth, Karl, *The Epistle to the Romans.*
*Denney, James, "St. Paul's Epistle to the Romans," *Expositor's Greek Testament.*
*Godet, F. L., *A Commentary on St. Paul's Epistle to the Romans.*
*Hodge, Charles, *An Exposition of the First Epistle to the Corinthians.*
*Moule, H. C. G., "The Epistle to the Romans," *Expositor's Bible.*
*Philippi, Friedrich Adolph, *Commentar über den Brief Pauli an die Römer.*
*Sanday and Headlam, *A Critical and Exegetical Commentary on the Epistle to the Romans* (Inter. Crit. Commentary).
*Shedd, W. G. T., *A Critical and Doctrinal Commentary upon the Epistle of St. Paul to the Romans.*

*Ellicott, Charles J., *A Critical and Grammatical Commentary on St. Paul's First Epistle to the Corinthians.*
*Godet, F. L., *A Commentary on St. Paul's First Epistle to the Corinthians.*
*Hodge, Charles, *An Exposition of the First Epistle to the Corinthians.*
*Robertson and Plummer, *A Critical and Exegetical Commentary on the First Epistle of St. Paul to the Corinthians* (Inter. Crit. Commentary).
*Bernard, J. S., "The Second Epistle to the Corinthians," *Expositor's Greek Testament.*

BIBLIOGRAPHY—Continued

*Denney, James, "The Second Epistle to the Corinthians," *Expositor's Bible*.

*Hodge, Charles, *An Exposition of the Second Epistle to the Corinthians*.

*Plummer, Alfred, *A Critical and Exegetical Commentary on the Second Epistle of St. Paul to the Corinthians* (Inter. Crit. Commentary).

Burton, Ernest D., *A Critical and Exegetical Commentary on St. Paul's Epistle to the Galatians* (International Critical Commentary).

*Ellicott, Charles J., *A Critical and Grammatical Commentary on St. Paul's Epistle to the Galatians*.

*Lightfoot, J. B., *St. Paul's Epistle to the Galatians*.

*Luther, Martin, *Commentary on St. Paul's Epistle to the Galatians*. New edition.

*Ramsay, Wm. M., *A Historical Commentary on St. Paul's Epistle to the Galatians*.

*Abbott, T. K., *A Critical and Exegetical Commentary on the Epistles to the Ephesians and to the Colossians* (International Critical Commentary).

*Dale, R. W., *The Epistle to the Ephesians*.

Duncan, George S., *St. Paul's Ephesian Ministry*.

*Ellicott, Charles J., *A Critical and Grammatical Commentary on St. Paul's Epistles to the Philippians, Colossians, and to Philemon*.

*Hodge, Charles, *A Commentary on the Epistle to the Ephesians*.

*Lightfoot, J. B., *St. Paul's Epistle to the Philippians*.

*Lightfoot, J. B., *St. Paul's Epistles to the Colossians and to Philemon*.

*Moule, H. C. G., *Philippian Studies*.

*Nicholson, W. R., *Oneness with Christ* (Colossians).

*Robertson, Archibald T., *Paul and the Intellectuals* (Colossians).

*Salmond, S. D. F., "The Epistle to the Ephesians," *Expositor's Greek Testament*.

*Denney, James, "The Epistles to the Thessalonians," *Expositor's Bible*.

*Ellicott, Charles J., *A Critical and Grammatical Commentary on St. Paul's Epistles to the Thessalonians*.

*Findlay, George G., *The Epistles to the Thessalonians* (Cambridge Bible for Schools and Colleges).

*Milligan, George, *St. Paul's Epistles to the Thessalonians*.

*Plummer, Alfred, *A Commentary on St. Paul's First Epistle to the Thessalonians*.

*Plummer, Alfred, *A Commentary on St. Paul's Second Epistle to the Thessalonians*.

*Ellicott, Charles J., *A Critical and Grammatical Commentary on the Pastoral Epistles*.

Harrison, P. N., *The Problem of the Pastoral Epistles*.

*Hayes, D. A., "The Pastoral Epistles," *Paul and His Epistles*.

*Knowling, R. J., "The Pastoral Epistles," *The Testimony of St. Paul to Christ*. 3 ed.

337

BIBLIOGRAPHY—Continued

*Lock, Walter, *A Critical and Exegetical Commentary on the Pastoral Epistles* (International Critical Commentary).

*Plummer, Alfred, "The Pastoral Epistles," *Expositor's Bible.*

*Simpson, E. K., "The Authenticity and Authorship of the Pastoral Epistles," *The Evangelical Quarterly,* Oct. 15, 1940.

*White, N. J. D., "The Pastoral Epistles," *Expositor's Greek Testament.*

The Epistle to the Hebrews

*Anderson, Robert, *The Hebrew Epistle in the Light of the Types.*

*Delitzsch, Franz, *A Commentary on the Epistle to the Hebrews.* 2 vols.

*Griffith-Thomas, W. H., *Let Us Go On.*

*Saphir, Adolph, *The Epistle to the Hebrews.* 2 vols.

*Westcott, B. F., *The Epistle to the Hebrews.*

The General Epistles

*Dale, R. W., *The Epistle of James.*

*Knowling, R. J., *The Epistle of St. James* (Westminster Commentaries).

*Mayor, J. B., *The Epistle of St. James.*

*Plummer, Alfred, "The General Epistles of St. James and St. Jude," *Expositor's Bible.*

Rendall, G. H., *The Epistle of St. James and Judaic Christianity.*

*Bigg, Charles, *A Critical and Exegetical Commentary on the Epistles of St. Peter and St. Jude* (International Critical Commentary).

*Lumby, J. R., "The Epistles of St. Peter," *Expositor's Bible.*

Mayor, J. B., *The Epistle of St. Jude and the Second Epistle of St. Peter.*

*Plummer, Alfred, *The Second Epistle of Peter and the Epistle of Jude* (Ellicott's Commentary for English Readers).

*Warfield, B. B., "The Defense of Second Peter," *Southern Presbyterian Review,* January, 1882.

*Alexander, William, "The Epistles of St. John," *Expositor's Bible.*

*Smith, David, "The Epistles of St. John," *Expositor's Greek Testament.*

*Westcott, B. F., *The Epistles of St. John.*

The Apocalypse

*Alford, Henry, "Revelation," *The Greek Testament.*

*Hort, F. J. A., *The Apocalypse of St. John I-III.*

*Milligan, William, *Lectures on the Apocalypse.*

*Ramsay, Wm. M., *The Letters to the Seven Churches of Asia.*

*Scott, Walter, *An Exposition of the Revelation of Jesus Christ.*

*Seiss, J. A., *Lectures on the Apocalypse.* 3 vols.

*Swete, H. B., *The Apocalypse of St. John.*

*Trench, R. C., *A Commentary on the Epistles to the Seven Churches.*

INDEX

INDEX